Humanitarianism and Human Rights

This book explores the fluctuating relationship between human rights and humanitarianism. For most of their lives, human rights and humanitarianism have been distant cousins. Humanitarianism focused on situations in faraway places dealing with large-scale loss of life that demanded urgent attention while human rights advanced the cause of individual liberty and equality at home. However, the twentieth century saw the two coming much more directly into dialogue, particularly following the end of the Cold War, as both began working in war zones and post-conflict situations. Leading scholars probe how the shifting meanings of human rights and humanitarianism converge and diverge from a variety of disciplinary perspectives ranging from philosophical inquiries that consider whether and how differences are constructed at the level of ethics, obligations, and duties, to historical inquiries that attempt to locate core differences within and between historical periods, and to practice-oriented perspectives that suggest how differences are created and recreated in response to concrete problems and through different kinds of organized activities with different goals and meanings.

Michael N. Barnett is University Professor of International Affairs and Political Science at the George Washington University. He has written critically acclaimed books on global ethics, humanitarian intervention, and humanitarianism, including *Eyewitness to a Genocide: The United Nations and Rwanda* (2002) and *Empire of Humanity* (2012), and edited *Paternalism Beyond Borders* (2016).

Human Rights in History

Edited by

Stefan-Ludwig Hoffmann, University of California, Berkeley

Samuel Moyn, Yale University, Connecticut

This series showcases new scholarship exploring the backgrounds of human rights today. With an open-ended chronology and international perspective, the series seeks works attentive to the surprises and contingencies in the historical origins and legacies of human rights ideals and interventions. Books in the series will focus not only on the intellectual antecedents and foundations of human rights, but also on the incorporation of the concept by movements, nation-states, international governance, and transnational law.

A full list of titles in the series can be found at:
www.cambridge.org/human-rights-history

Humanitarianism and Human Rights

A World of Differences?

Edited by

Michael N. Barnett

George Washington University, Washington DC

CAMBRIDGE
UNIVERSITY PRESS

University Printing House, Cambridge CB2 8BS, United Kingdom

One Liberty Plaza, 20th Floor, New York, NY 10006, USA

477 Williamstown Road, Port Melbourne, VIC 3207, Australia

314–321, 3rd Floor, Plot 3, Splendor Forum, Jasola District Centre, New Delhi – 110025, India

79 Anson Road, #06–04/06, Singapore 079906

Cambridge University Press is part of the University of Cambridge.

It furthers the University's mission by disseminating knowledge in the pursuit of education, learning, and research at the highest international levels of excellence.

www.cambridge.org
Information on this title: www.cambridge.org/9781108836791
DOI: 10.1017/9781108872485

© Cambridge University Press 2020

First published 2020

A catalogue record for this publication is available from the British Library.

Library of Congress Cataloging-in-Publication Data
Names: Barnett, Michael N., 1960– editor.
Title: Humanitarianism and human rights: a world of differences? / edited by Michael N. Barnett.
Description: New York, NY: Cambridge University Press, 2020. | Series: Human rights in history | Includes bibliographical references and index.
Identifiers: LCCN 2020012055 | ISBN 9781108836791 (hardback) | ISBN 9781108872485 (epub)
Subjects: LCSH: Humanitarian intervention. | Human rights.
Classification: LCC JZ6369 .H895 2020 | DDC 341.5/84–dc23
LC record available at https://lccn.loc.gov/2020012055

ISBN 978-1-108-83679-1 Hardback
ISBN 978-1-108-81920-6 Paperback

Contents

Contributors

MICHAEL N. BARNETT is University Professor of International Affairs and Political Science at the George Washington University.

CHARLES BEITZ is the Edwards S. Sanford Professor of Politics at Princeton University.

ILANA FELDMAN is Professor of Anthropology, History, and International Affairs at the George Washington University.

JEFFREY FLYNN is Associate Professor of Philosophy at Fordham University.

STEPHEN HOPGOOD is Professor of International Relations at the School of Oriental and African Studies, University of London.

FABIAN KLOSE is Professor of International History at the University of Cologne.

BRONWYN LEEBAW is Associate Professor of Political Science at the University of California-Riverside.

ALAN LESTER is Professor of Geography at the University of Sussex.

SAMUEL MOYN is the Henry Luce Professor of Jurisprudence at the Yale Law School and Professor of History at Yale University.

AISLING SWAINE is Professor of Gender Studies at the School of Social Policy, Social Work and Social Justice at University College Dublin.

BERTRAND TAITHE is Professor of History and the Executive Director of the Humanitarian and Conflict Response Unit at the University of Manchester.

MIRIAM TICKTIN is Associate Professor of Anthropology at the New School for Social Research.

Acknowledgments

My first thanks go to those who contributed to the volume and participated in the two workshops at George Washington University. In addition to those who wrote, I want to thank the following for their commentary and contributions: Susanna Campbell, Daniel Cohen, Ruti Teitel, Kathryn Sikkink, Bill Luban, Melani Macalester, and a huge thanks and debt of gratitude to Sally Engle Merry. I also benefited from presentations given at various institutions and conferences on the topic: University of Minnesota; University of Sydney; a conference on the history of the ICRC at the University of Adelaide; a presentation at a conference on the history of humanitarianism at the Leibniz Institute of European History, Mainz; and the University of Washington. Although he declined to review the book for Cornell University Press, Roger Haydon provided some exceptional suggestions that strengthened the manuscript and made it more likely to survive the review process at Cambridge. The volume also benefited considerably from the trenchant reading by and suggestions from two anonymous reviewers, and Samuel Moyn and Stefan-Ludwig Hoffman, the editors of the series in which this book appears. Last but hardly least, Danielle Gilbert helped organize the two workshops at GWU. It is fair to say that none of this would have been possible without her, in part because I never would have organized a conference on my own.

Much like humanitarianism and human rights, all the good thoughts, hard work, and compassionate criticism would not have been possible without a donor with money. The generous donor in this case is the Office of the Provost at the George Washington University, which provides the funds for the university professorship that I am able to use for events such as the ones that made possible this volume.

Lastly, thanks to Michael Watson and Emily Sharp at Cambridge University Press for expertly shepherding the manuscript through the entire process.

Introduction
Worlds of Difference

Michael N. Barnett

For most of their lives, human rights and humanitarianism have been distant cousins. They were the offspring of the Enlightenment, Christianity, and humanity, but they soon went their separate ways. Humanitarianism focused on situations in faraway places where natural or humanly made events caused large-scale loss of life that demanded urgent attention. Human rights, on the other hand, advanced the cause of individual liberty and equality at home. Because they were doing different things in different places, they rarely encountered or took the measure of the other. World Wars I and II reduced some of the distance. After World War I, humanitarianism became attentive to refugees, who were conferred rights, and human rights became more international with the invention of international minority rights. After World War II and decolonization, each went through a growth spurt that brought them into greater proximity. Although now circulating in some of the same networks, they largely kept to themselves.

Everything changed beginning in the 1990s. The end of the Cold War produced an explosion of internal conflicts and humanitarian emergencies from the former Yugoslavia to Somalia and beyond. In these so-called "new" wars, civilians were not "collateral damage" but rather the intended targets. Millions of innocents fled conflict and sought shelter and protection where they could. Sometimes they managed to cross a border and become bona fide refugees where they received aid in internationally organized camps. But in many instances the displaced were stuck in their home country, requiring aid agencies to undertake a perilous mission of bringing relief to them. For many the temporary became the long term, and agencies had to consider questions of education, livelihoods, community organization, and even rights. Because of these and other changes on the ground and the growing ascendency of a human rights discourse, aid organizations began embracing a "rights-based" framework. Human rights ascendant included an expansion into armed conflict and the protection of the same populations that concerned humanitarians. Challenging the artificial boundary between needs and

1

rights, human rights activists insisted that victims had a right to, and not just a need for, relief, alongside other basic rights. Furthermore, relief might be adjusted to better prepare the ground for human rights.

Now that human rights and humanitarianism were occupying the same spaces and working with the same populations, they had to address their relationship. Some imagined them becoming a force multiplier, stronger together than apart, and with enhanced capacity to protect vulnerable populations. Each could learn from each other. They could develop a sequenced division-of-labor, with aid agencies saving lives and then rights activists protecting them from other harms and injecting the rule of law into states and societies. One possibly provided support for the other. The humanitarian concern for refugees and asylum seekers can open the door to human rights and justice.[1] The human rights community's concern for gender-based violence prodded more and specialized attention from the humanitarian field. Long-standing distinctions between international humanitarian law (IHL) and international human rights law (IHRL) began to erode. Traditionally IHL covered armed conflict and IHRL relations between states and their citizens, but in the 1990s, they began to converge, producing a "humanity's law."[2]

Others rejected the idea that all good things go together, and identified tensions and warned of conflicts between the two. For example:

On engaging perpetrators: Human rights activists tended to name and shame, make noise, and heckle rights-violating states to get them to cease their violations; humanitarian organizations prefer quiet diplomacy.

On the use of drones: Human rights organizations might fly drones to try and identify where atrocities were occurring and identify the names and faces of the perpetrators; humanitarian organizations might fly drones in the same area to identify the location of the victims, their needs, and survey logistical hurdles. Whereas human rights agencies have relatively little need for the cooperation of the perpetrators, aid agencies do, and "rights" drones might make the latter's operations much more difficult and dangerous because they must now try to negotiate with much more suspicious armed actors.[3]

On conditionality: Humanitarian organizations insist that there is a near "right to relief," while human rights activists judge this relief in relationship to the broader goals of human rights protection and justice.[4]

On construction of the "other": Humanitarian reason can lead from a politics of pity to the demonization of refugees, while human rights activism can foster inclusion.[5]

On the effects of the discourse of "emergency" and "crisis": Labeling something as a humanitarian emergency or crisis can displace attention from the causes, including a lack of rights.[6]

On humanitarian intervention: Human rights has tended to favor the idea of humanitarian intervention whereas humanitarian organizations have been lukewarm to cold.[7]

On international criminal justice: The International Criminal Court (ICC) requires first-hand accounts and evidence for its proceedings, and aid workers are often eyewitnesses. But if they cooperate with the ICC, or any legal process, they risk being expelled from the country, or worse. This is exactly what happened in the Sudan when the ICC indicted Sudanese president Bashir for genocide.[8] The search for justice might cost lives.

On pandemics: COVID-19 has demonstrated a series of tensions around priorities and trade-offs when balancing saving lives and protecting human rights and privacy. In order to mitigate the spread of the virus, there is considerable need for data regarding individuals' actions, whereabouts, movements, and networks. Without contact tracing and other forms of prevention and mitigation, more people are at risk and will needlessly die. Human rights and civil liberties groups are worried that these new surveillance technologies will be appropriated by states and others to violate human rights and represent a threat. Although human rights actors want to save lives, and humanitarian actors are worried about the growing use of biometric data and threats to privacy, they often prioritize lives and rights differently and are prepared to make the trade-offs between the two in different places.[9]

On protection: The concept of protection has expanded considerably since its earliest days in the beginning of the 1990s. Much of the initial attention emerged from within the humanitarian system and the need to highlight the physical threats to civilians. But over time it expanded to include human rights.[10] From one angle, the expansion from protection to prevention is a natural development. From another, a broader version of protection and the centrality of human rights law, as Taithe illustrates in this volume, potentially undermines humanitarian's notion of protection.[11]

On gender-based violence: Relief and rights organizations can adopt different approaches to violence against women in conflict in part because, as Swaine observes in this volume, they have different objectives: the former treats physical harms and psychosocial trauma, while the latter interviews victims to collect stories, information, and first-hand experiences in order to prosecute perpetrators and seek justice. But interviewing victims of sexual violence can retraumize the victims.[12]

Each community has registered wariness of the other, but my reading is that the field of humanitarianism has been more worried than the field of human rights (though in Chapter 1 Moyn makes the opposite case). Why? Humanitarianism stayed closer to home as it remained largely focused on situations of armed conflict and natural disasters, and exhibited little interest in the wider world of human rights. Human rights, on the other hand, was expanding into the known and unknown worlds, penetrating deep into humanitarian territory, and possibly altering humanitarian practices in the process.[13] For instance, humanitarian agencies have increasingly defined protection to include advocacy, almost to the point that advocacy displaces real protection; when women in refugees camps in Darfur were being raped as they searched for firewood outside the camps, aid agencies, according to one critic, spent more time calling attention to their situation than offering the remedy of bring firewood into the camps.[14] One International Committee of the Red Cross (ICRC) official fatalistically observed that the war between the two bodies of law was over, and IHL needed to consider the terms of its surrender.[15] This was not a merger but a hostile takeover. The ICRC's Hugo Slim, who once wrote sympathetically about the need for humanitarianism to embrace a rights-based framework, called on humanitarianism to maintain its identity in the face of the human rights revolution.[16]

A similar story of independence followed by debates about boundaries also occurred in the scholarly fields of human rights and humanitarianism. Human rights scholarship grew considerably beginning in the 1980s, appearing in flagship journals and creating a growing number of specialized outlets. Scholars of international law were examining the mutual influence and growing overlap between international human rights and humanitarian law.[17] Political scientists were exploring the remarkable spread of contemporary human rights, how transnational activists influenced states, and why states felt compelled to comply with the growing web of nonbinding international human rights law.[18] Historians were debating the origins and evolution of human rights, and when human rights globalized and became *international* human rights.[19] Anthropologists were exploring variations in the meanings of human rights, including how human rights was understood, redefined, vernacularized, and practiced across different societies.[20] Sociologists were examining the social movements and combination of structure, agency, and contingency that propelled human rights from infancy to maturity.[21] Some writings turned human rights on its head, seeing them not as pathways to emancipation but rather as stealth weapons of domination and reinforcing a highly unequal global order.[22] The totality of these writings and scholarly activity, both euphoric and critical, was creating a bona fide human rights field. There were more courses on human rights. Universities began establishing stand-alone human rights centers, offering minors and masters programs.

The human rights field was becoming established when the humanitarian field got its start beginning in the 1990s. Prior to then there was scattered work on the ICRC, international humanitarian law, sacrificing saviors, and the occasional history of an aid agency. Changes in the world and academics led to growing interest in the topic. As scholars picked up the pace, they shifted from angelology toward ponerology, adopting a much more critical perspective. Historians began digging through archives, finding a more complicated and profane history rooted in national, transnational, and international forces.[23] Political scientists challenged the "purity" of humanitarianism, observing how state power and financing shaped the humanitarian sector and caused aid organizations to compete in ways that shifted their energies from the survival of victims to organizational survival.[24] Anthropologists began exploring how humanitarianism's ethics of care masked the presence of power disparities between the givers and receivers.[25] Foucault and Agamben were important inspirations, as the former offered an alternative way to think about governance outside the state and the latter states of exception.[26] Under their influence, refugee camps became institutions of internment and imprisonment and aid workers prison guards. Cultural theorists began excavating the sometimes profane origins and practices of compassion.[27] Scholars began creating genealogies of IHL that excavated gendered, racial, and civilizational discourses.[28] Humanitarianism became Dr. Jekyll and Mr. Hyde.

Like the debates among practitioners in the human rights and humanitarian communities regarding the relationship between them, scholars began to probe the historical and conceptual boundaries between these two fields of study.[29] And similar to my observation that practitioners of humanitarianism were more sensitive to intrusions from human rights than the reverse, scholars of humanitarianism seemed much more concerned about protecting their turf from human rights than the reverse.[30] I participated in this search for boundaries, arguing that whereas humanitarianism was constituted by needs, sad stories, and charity, human rights emphasized rights, law, and justice.[31] In this volume Samuel Moyn criticizes my claim, rightly so, and for reasons that I knew at the time I offered them, but nevertheless wanted to help make humanitarianism an autonomous object of study. My critical error was to depart from my social constructionist position in a direction that inched toward essentialism. Specifically, although I could be interpreted as suggesting that these social constructs possess some nearly essential or enduring characteristics, my epistemological commitments and narrative of humanitarianism depended on the very opposite.

This volume explores the fluctuating relationship between human rights and humanitarianism. There are decades when they exhibited parallel play, with each doing its own thing and without much awareness of the other. There are instances when they appeared to join forces, not only collaborating but also developing something of a "we-feeling." There are contrasting illustrations, though, when their proximity generated anxiety, leading to defensive action. Over the decades, human rights and humanitarianism have resembled an air show, with moments in which they fly parallel to each other followed quickly by separation, low-flying dips, high-flying loops, and even the occasional game of chicken.

The reason for these twists and turns is because human rights and humanitarianism have no fixed meaning, are social constructions, are historically situated, and have been distant and intimate from each other over the decades. If this was ever in question, it can no longer be, as scholars continually plumb the histories of each to discover unknown and poorly understood events, trends, and configurations. New findings became conventional wisdoms only to be debunked by theoretical interventions and revisionist historical understandings. But this pliability does not imply that meaningful and enduring differences and distinctions cannot be located, a view shared by all the contributors, except for Hopgood who argues that, at best, there are fleeting differences without a distinction.

The chapters address the question of the differences and the relationship between human rights and humanitarianism from various perspectives. There are philosophical inquiries that attempt to understand whether and how differences are constructed at the level of ethics, obligations, and duties. There are historical inquiries that attempt to locate core differences within and between historical periods and witness their histories converging and diverging. There are settled and unsettled periods; the former is associated with identifiable patterns and the latter with turbulence, and the last three decades have been quite unsettled. And a major part of the reason for this period's volatility is because each is working out its identity in relationship to the other. There are practice-oriented perspectives that suggest how differences are created and recreated in response to concrete problems and through different kinds of organized activities with different goals and meanings. Many of the chapters locate differences in emotions; different kinds of suffering can trigger a range of socially organized emotional responses. The chapters wrestle with whether the differences between the two are major or minor, trivial or substantial. In many respects, the significance of these differences is in the eye of the beholder. Is there a difference or a distinction between a language and a dialectic?[32] Is there a difference or distinction between human rights and humanitarianism? It depends – on granularity, composition, and perspective. Regardless of whether one discerns differences or distinctions, the search for similarities and contrasts forces students of human rights and humanitarianism to clarify what they believe is particular and core to each, to articulate the characteristics that often form the ideal types that, in turn, become the basis for comparison, and to consider whether and how each is sacred in a world of the profane.

What Is at Stake?

This collection probes the possible boundaries and the variety of relationships that exist between human rights and humanitarianism. Because this exercise can have a clinical feel, it is paramount to recognize that humanitarianism and human rights are ethical projects that can have life and death consequences for vulnerable and marginalized populations. What are people talking about when they are talking about human rights and humanitarianism? Lives, yes. But also a spirit of humanity. Everyday practices of humanity are tied to the transcendent, and the transcendent shapes practices of humanity. These practices have worldly and heavenly aspirations. Human rights and humanitarianism represent a resistance to a world that can treat others like human waste. They follow Michel Foucault's admonition that "the misfortunes of men must never be the silent leftover of politics."[33] They are advancing not only the material needs of others, but also their own spiritual needs. Helping others but also helping themselves – it is through acts of compassion that individuals enact their humanity. To help others is to be humane, and to be indifferent inhumane.

Human rights and humanitarianism are expressions of the world that exists, the world we hope to exist, and our pragmatic calculations about how to narrow the difference between the world that is and that world that can be. These themes of global ethics are the background and foreground of human rights and humanitarianism, but each occupies a different standpoint. A major branch of global ethics regards what we owe strangers and the ethical significance of boundaries.[34] Can we, and on what basis, treat outsiders different from our compatriots and fellow citizens? What is the nature of our obligations and duties to others beyond our borders, and based on what principles? Are our obligations fulfilled by charity, or do they demand more extensive and long-lasting commitments? Do our duties focus on protection or extend toward empowerment? How do these ethics apply in specific circumstances and do they allow for recognition of difference? What is the balance between the universal and the particular? How do these philosophical judgements translate into practice in a world of sovereign states? Do our ethics become practical and bow to the world that is, or do they aspire to create a bridge to a better world?

The exchanges during the workshops for this volume occasionally became quite spirited because of the associated ethical commitments and ambitions of human rights and humanitarianism. To give a flavor of that conversation and the connections to global ethics, this section briefly reviews two foundational questions. Why act to relieve the unnecessary suffering of distant strangers? The second question moves from motives to effects as it questions whether these well-meaning interventions are reforming or reproducing an unjust global order. Human rights and humanitarianism do not have single answers to these questions, and often there is considerable overlap between them. But for argument's sake and in the spirit of ideal types, the ethics of humanitarianism and human rights cluster around different responses – with the former organized around the world as it is and the latter around a vision of the world that should be. The wager is that what is lost by simplifying and stereotyping is gained by illuminating some potentially critical points of comparison.

Why Act? Reason, Sentiment, and Humanity

The sources of altruism, compassion, and beneficence have drawn considerable scholarly attention in recent years, traversing disciplines as diverse as cultural studies, gender studies, neuroscience, sociobiology, evolutionary theory, religious studies, law, philosophy, psychology, media and communication studies, political science, geography, history, political theory, and sociology. The chapters in this volume address two critical questions. The first is whether individuals are motivated to act because of reason and rationality or because of sad stories and sentimentality, an issue considered at length in Part I. The reason and rationality approach emphasizes the rational exchange of views and the search for a better argument, learning, and interest-based motives, including forms of diffuse reciprocity and principled claims that become generalized to all members of the community.[35] It stands to reason that we have mutual obligations to each other, or it makes sense for the preservation of the species and the individual to care about neighbors and suffering strangers. Some of these appeals to reason, moreover, are intertwined with utilitarian and consequentialist ethics. Peter Singer's highly influential arguments grounds the decision to give on whether our actions will make a difference in the lives of others and enhance the world's welfare without doing appreciable harm to our own lives.[36]

But the desire and decision to act, at least according to the chapters and other research, is driven as much by emotion as by reason.[37] Compassion is often the first feeling mentioned when considering the imperative to respond to human rights violations and humanitarian emergencies. When confronted by knowledge or images of unnecessary suffering, we do not stop to ask: whether the person in need will help me if I am in a similar situation in the future, perform a utilitarian calculation in relationship to general welfare or invoke an enlightened rationality. Instead, feelings, not rationality,; dominate, and not just any feelings but feelings of compassion, which represent the "better angels of our nature." But is it the distress and despair provoked by images of distant suffering that move us to reach for our wallets? If so, is this compassion, or something else? Human rights violations often trigger outrage and anger.[38] The demand to end impunity arguably is based less on its deterrence value than on the grotesque possibility that the bastards might get away with their crimes. Humanitarianism is about feelings, but not only compassion. It can also be about pity.[39] And pity is often connected to feelings of guilt. How much of humanitarianism is tied to feelings of white, liberal, guilt? And which emotions are more likely to provide a sustained connection to others and commitment to humanity? Fury or pity?

The other big debate regards the historical development of humanitarianism and human rights. The rationality and sentimentality theses lean toward different reasons why humans do and should care about distant others, but agree that societies have varied in terms of their propensity to respond to unnecessary suffering of strangers. Compassion has always existed in human history, but has been scattershot and is often the domain of religion and religious institutions. The current wisdom is that something extraordinary began to evolve in the mid-eighteen century as cold, calculating individuals that were historically indifferent to the suffering of others became "men of feelings" that helped to build states, societies, and institutions that were organized around the relief of unnecessary suffering and the betterment of society.[40] This was the origin of humanitarian governance: "the administration of human collectivities in the name of a higher moral principle of that sees the preservation of life and the alleviation of suffering as the highest values of action."[41] How and why these feelings of compassion and care emerged and became institutionalized is a matter of controversy; the safe answer is that there were a conjunction of religious, economic, political, sociological, and cultural causes that combined structure, agency, and contingency. For many scholars, the rise of British abolitionism is Exhibit A in this historical development because a British society became mobilized to alleviate the suffering of a dark-skinned people from a different continent that most had never seen in person. In any event, as Hannah Arendt famously observed, but with some concern, there was now a "passion for compassion."[42]

The emergence of human rights and humanitarianism is bound up with the construction of "humanity." Humanity is a tricky concept. Humanity is not a fact of nature but rather has a history, and a rather recent one. It became part of the vocabulary in the 1700s because of Christianity and the Enlightenment, but its invention did not come with a set meaning. Instead, humanity has been a work in progress.[43] Central to the debate about and expansion of humanity is: Who is the human? The evolving concept of humanity was intertwined with debates about what physical and cognitive qualities an individual must possess to be counted as a human and whether all humans are truly equal. As Flynn and others in this volume underscore, distinctions have been made according to race, culture, religion, gender, and other categories of discrimination, and it is only recently in human history that those who argue in favor of forms of discrimination – and that some are more human than others – are on the defensive. Today, humanity means a belief that: all individuals are humans are equal, obligated to respect each other's dignity, and must "treat fellow humans as family."[44] But who knows what will be tomorrow. Will humanity extend to animals? Will robots be conferred human-like qualities and qualify for membership in humanity? Will they have rights and be deserving of charity?

The world is filled with suffering, but not all suffering matters, or equally, or becomes a matter of social concern.[45] Humanitarianism and human rights, in this way, operate according to a form of social triage – distributing attention and resources according to different kinds of suffering. Humanitarianism operates on the principle of need and with a bare-bones notion of humanity that is often described as "bare life." It concentrates on giving people what they need to survive, and anything above and beyond these basic needs migrates into wants. Humanitarianism does not deny that there is something beyond bare existence, but it resists going beyond the minimum. Human rights, on the other hand, includes those things that individuals require to flourish. People deserve not just food in their bellies but the dignity that comes from being treated humanely and with respect, praying (or not) as they like, speaking their minds, and living a full and fulfilling life as they define it. Because human rights imagines an extensive list of rights, there are debates regarding which of these rights are foundational and universal. But there is no doubt that it scans for a wider array of suffering than does humanitarianism.

Humanitarianism and human rights also occupy different positions regarding whether individuals are allowed to choose to act in response to suffering, a topic explored in the chapter by Beitz. Human rights tends to adopt the forceful language of obligations and operate with the claim that many rights are nonderogable. States cannot choose, for instance, whether to recognize the right of religious liberty or freedom of conscience. The language of perfect duties observes that states do not have the right to decide whether to torture or not – they cannot. They must follow this perfect duty, and if they do not then they are violating the basic human rights of others. And if rights are being violated, then we, as part of humanity, have an obligation to help stop it. Humanitarianism, on the other hand, typically accepts that individuals have discretion over whether and how to perform their (imperfect) duties. We can choose to show mercy and be charitable – or not. I get to decide whether to be a good Samaritan or a by-stander. I might feel shame as a consequence, as Leebaw observes in her chapter, but I get to decide if I prefer being ashamed to following my duties.

Palliation or Transformation?

Humanitarianism and human rights exist because we live in a cruel and unjust world that is drowning in unnecessary suffering. But they differ with regards to what kind of suffering matters and what should be done about it. One way of distinguishing the two is by contrasting humanitarianism's emphasis on palliation and human rights' concern with transformation. Humanitarianism deals with the world as it is with the hope of alleviating the suffering at the moment, whereas human rights hopes to transform the world so that suffering might become a thing of the past. Or, in more streetwise language, humanitarianism deals with symptoms and human rights with root causes.[46] Many of the chapters distinguish humanitarianism and human rights on precisely these grounds. For instance, Lester argues that a function of humanitarian governance is to improve human life within an existing political order while human rights envisions overturning the political order itself. Swaine offers a comparable contrast between how human rights and humanitarian organizations approach wartime sexual violence. Similarly, Flynn claims that humanitarianism is about unnecessary suffering and human rights about unjustifiable status hierarchies. Below I want to suggest how a humanitarianism concerned with palliation and a human rights with transformation shapes six critical differences relating to global ethics.

Ethics of Death and Life

Palliation and transformation can be linked to an ethics of death and ethics of life, respectively. A politics of death is about keeping people alive by providing them with basic needs such as water, nutrition, shelter, medical care, and other life-giving assistance. Humanitarians adopt practices of triage as they place color-coded tags on the toes of casualties to prioritize treatment. The politics of death also exists in the growing concern with "end of life" and palliative care.[47] When life cannot be saved, then humanitarianism is reduced to comforting the dying. In his classic *Memory of Solferino*, Henry Dunant wrote movingly of his overwhelming sense of helplessness watching wounded soldiers thrash in pain and slowly die a miserable and lonely death. He did what he could, holding their hands, applying compresses to their mouths and foreheads, offering deathbed prayers, and listening to their last words.[48] An ethics of death provides few reasons to go beyond a moral minimalism.

An ethics of life concerns transforming societies to promote the ability of individuals to live a flourishing life.[49] It aspires to provide individuals with the capabilities that make it possible for them to choose their best course. Unlike humanitarianism that helps, human rights promotes self-help. It is not enough to provide fish to the starving. People must be taught to fish; they should be given fishing rods, nets, and boats, and legal access to the shoreline. And people need to include women. Instead of limiting their role to fishmongers in the market, they must be incorporated into all facets of fishing and be allowed to keep their earnings.[50] An ethics of life, in this way, can lead to moral maximalism. Some human rights activists pledge a moral minimalism – they limit themselves to those rights that they believe are foundational and generative of other rights. But moral minimalism often leads to a moral maximalism, as one right leads to another and the attempt to reform and enforce laws leads to a consideration of all aspects of culture, economics, and politics.[51] Even the dead have rights.[52] Human rights has few limits, in this world and the next.

Politics: Yes or No

It is not just an ethics of death or life that divides humanitarianism and human rights – it also is their broader stance toward politics. Humanitarianism famously insists that it is apolitical because it saves lives – which is part of humanity, and not part of politics – and it has no ambition to remake the world. This stance is born not from abstract philosophy but rather pragmatism. Aid workers want access to victims, and embracing an apolitical stance creates a humanitarian space and gives assurance to political authorities that they need not fear those bearing gifts. Yet humanitarianism is very much a form of politics: a politics of refusal to treat individuals as disposable waste. Human rights, on the other hand, embraces politics. These are activists that are change agents, want to teach people about their rights, are willing to speak truth to power and compel the state to recognize individual rights, and empower individuals to lead a life of their choosing.[53]

These different stances toward politics are bound up with the famous contrast between a humanitarianism that provides charity and a human rights that aspires to deliver justice. Humanitarianism concerns giving to others in need out of the goodness of one's heart. Charity, in this way, makes limited demands on givers and has very limited aims.[54] We give what we choose to give. It does not ask why people are in need, but instead responds to these needs.[55] It does not attempt to change the unjust circumstances that led to need, but rather tries to minimize its consequences. This avoidance of justice is not accidental. In his foundational text on the Fundamental Principles of the Red Cross, the ICRC's Jean Pictet argued that charity means that one gives first and worries about the justice second, if ever. As he observed, "One cannot be at one and the same time a champion of justice and charity. One must choose . . . The ICRC has long since chosen to be a defender of charity."[56] As one Médecins Sans Frontières (MSF) official starkly put it, "We do surgery. We do medicine. We do clean water. We don't do justice."[57]

Human rights seeks justice. There is no consensus view about what justice entails, but, from the perspective of the ICRC's Jean Pictet, "Justice rewards each person according to his rights," and to judge is to "separate the good from the bad, the just from the unjust."[58] When individuals have their rights violated, they are caused an injustice and deserve justice.[59] If perpetrators go unpunished, then their impunity constitutes an act of injustice. For states and societies to come to terms with the past they must complete a process of transitional justice. Injustice occurs not only when there are human rights violations and an infringement on liberty, but also when structures of inequality and exclusion persist that reproduce inequalities and limit the ability of individuals to pursue a free and full life. Human rights wrongs, and by righting wrongs, human rights advances justice.[60]

Paternalism

But can either a humanitarianism that provides charity or a human rights that seeks justice do so in a way that does not create or reinforce existing inequalities between themselves and those who are supposed to benefit from their interventions? Not according to many of the chapters, which point to the presence of paternalism.[61] Paternalism is the ability of one actor to substitute its judgment for another actor claiming it will advance the latter's welfare, values, and interests. Importantly, the presumption is that those who act in the name of human rights and humanitarianism are genuinely concerned about the welfare of others, but knowingly and unknowingly exercise power and paternalism in the process. For instance, human rights activists are in the business of teaching people what sorts of claims they can and should make and which sorts of cultural practices are civilized and which are barbaric. Humanitarianism is about meeting the needs of others in extremis, but what is given is often not what recipients need – and while agencies have attempted to introduce mechanisms to allow the recipients to articulate their needs, there is little evidence that aid organizations listen. Interestingly, several of the chapters speculate that while both human rights and humanitarianism contain elements of paternalism, humanitarianism is the more paternalistic of the two. Why? Because its charity model suggests that the potential recipients are either incompetent or incapacitated and therefore cannot really know what they want or how to achieve it. In contrast, human rights contain a strong egalitarian ethos, desires to empower the dominated, and eliminates status inequalities and other systems of oppression.

Cosmopolitanism in a World of Sovereignty

Palliation and transformation also shape positions toward an unequal world order that generates a gush of unnecessary suffering, evident in contrasting evaluations of cosmopolitanism and the existing system of sovereign states. Both human rights and humanitarianism are intimately connected to cosmopolitanism. Closely related to humanity, cosmopolitanism is an equally contested concept.[62] Philosophically speaking, cosmopolitanism can be understood as including and imposing a way of seeing oneself in relationship to all others. Cosmopolitanism transcends particularism and nurtures a moral vision from the self to the other, and, in doing so, creates a healthy distance from one's culture and achieves a more complex and complete human experience.[63] Cosmopolitanism also demands that our choices incorporate how they affect others, which entails both negative and positive duties. It obligates us to avoid taking action that produces unnecessary and foreseeable harm. It also obligates us to try to prevent human suffering, create the possibility for human empowerment, and nurture human solidarity. There is a chasm between the world that exists and the world that cosmopolitans hope to exist, but they believe that humans have the potential to live their ideals – and that a purpose of cosmopolitan politics is to encourage individuals to live their ideals to bring this world into existence.

The cosmopolitanism associated with human rights and humanitarianism is the belief that all individuals are equal because of their humanity and that individuals are expected to treat others as equal. Humanity naturally exists, even if people need to be coaxed to acknowledge it. What prompts and coaxes such feelings? Suffering. Suffering resides at the core of the meaning and practice of human rights and humanitarianism, and both operate with the assumption that it is the recognition of our common experience of suffering that shapes conceptions of humanity. In this way, suffering dissolves differences, making "humanity visible."[64] The implication is that we only recognize the humanity of others when they are suffering or dead.

This is a cosmopolitanism of suffering. But can suffering produce a humanity founded on equality? Or, is it more likely to produce a new form of inequality based on victims and their saviors, each with their own roles to play, unequal social capacities, and norms? Victims, as Tiktin notes in her chapter, are expected to have certain characteristics, to be passive, to be grateful for what they are given, and to demonstrate little agency. Saviors, on the other hand, will often see themselves as heroic, compassionate, and good. They will treat victims as inferior, and as innocent or ignorant and unable to help themselves. Victims cannot be another more than their suffering. This simplification and distortion means that it is nearly impossible to truly know those who are being helped, resulting in a humanity that is profoundly unequal.[65] This is not a solidarity based on friendship or even civic equality, but instead is based on inequities and potentially leads, as Hannah Arendt warned, to a "politics of pity."[66] But are humanitarianism and human rights equally susceptible to this form of cosmopolitanism? Some of the chapters suggest that humanitarianism is the more vulnerable of the two, and for the same reasons that are used to explain why humanitarianism is hypothesized to be more prone to paternalism than is human rights.

Cosmopolitanism has produced a range of political projects and movements that can be measured in relationship to their acquiescence to a sovereign-states system. Some versions imagine nation-states melting into a global federation of peoples. Others visualize a state-friendly version, one that consecrates universal values but nevertheless respects state sovereignty. An even milder version resembles forms of internationalism, in which states are expected to incorporate the interests of other states, not only because of principles but also because of pragmatism. To the extent that they challenge the state's authority, and especially its core competences, then states are quite likely to take defensive action. During the nineteenth century and the rise of the nation-states, cosmopolitanism was often treated as a threat to the nation-state, a disease carried by rootless people such as the Jews that had designs on the world. In the post-World War II period, milder forms of cosmopolitanism became celebrated precisely because they were thought to be an antidote to a toxic nationalism and sustenance for an enlightened sovereignty.[67] At this moment cosmopolitanism seems to have run into strong headwinds and resemble the nineteenth-century challenges.

The cosmopolitanism of human rights and humanitarianism potentially lead to different stances toward sovereignty. Human rights has tended to treat humanity as the ultimate source of authority, transcending state sovereignty. It does not necessarily seek the destruction of the sovereign-states system, but states are expected to conform to universal ethics and human rights norms and law. Humanitarians, though, avoid directly challenging the sovereignty and authority of the state. States created the Geneva Conventions and the ICRC. ICRC is highly cognizant that its ability to act depends on the cooperation of states. When aid organizations want to help they first ask for permission and the proper permits from state officials. If they are denied, they remain on the other side of the border. And if they are invited in and then asked to leave, they go. In general, while human rights is populated by activists that often speak of a human rights revolution, humanitarians seem much quicker to accommodate themselves to state authority.

Can We Talk about Progress?

Discussions about cosmopolitanism and its promise often segue into ideas of progress. Progress is not a fashionable concept these days. It is closely associated with nineteenth-century civilizing missions, Eurocentrism, vainglorious confidence in the superiority of the West, and the general belief that the West represents the "end of history" and shows the rest of the world its future. The meaning of progress is generally in the eye of the beholder, and those with the power usually define its meaning. Those who continue to insist on the possibility of progress can often airbrush a twentieth century defined by horrific episodes of mass killing, often engineered by those who claimed to be the paragons of civilization. Currently in this moment of high anxiety, talk of progress is frequently dismissed as foolishness or Polyannishness.

Despite the baggage associated with progress, it is an idea that is never far away, either from the practices or the studies of human rights and humanitarianism. Indeed, the very notion of the idea of progress was born with the Enlightenment, and thus shares bloodlines with the concepts of human rights and humanitarianism. Ever since, the existence and definition of progress have been in dispute, but those who entertain the possibility typically divide progress into two: material and moral progress.[68] Material progress regards whether there is an improvement in human welfare and betterment, generally measured in terms of wealth and health. Moral progress concerns the depth and breadth of compassion, kindness, and acceptance, and the extension of humanity to those once considered outsiders or others. Human rights and humanitarianism differ in terms of not only how they define progress, but also whether they choose to think about it at all.

Human rights is tethered to the idea of progress.[69] Deriving from the Enlightenment tradition and the role that reason and liberty can play in the creation of a better world, human rights almost always contains a vision of the destination and the belief that society is undergoing a constant process of perfection.[70] Justice is not an afterthought but an integral part of progress. There has been an explosion of human rights law, a "human rights revolution" and a "justice cascade" that has led to a marked advance in humanity.[71] These accounts of progress have come under considerable criticism in recent years. They are accused of having a Whiggish quality as they start their version of history with the present and then work backwards, cherry picking the achievements and over-looking the inhumanity. While human rights scholars and activists insist that human rights are not imposed but rather are achieved by reason, human agreement, or an overlapping consensus, this is a charitable and convenient version of how human rights have ascended and which human rights have been legitimated. While recognizing in principle cultural diversity, the human rights community will often operate under the influence of universalism. While human rights advocates deny that they have a predetermined view about where history is headed, many confidently articulate values, principles, and laws that overlap considerably with liberalism. A full and flourishing life can often be defined in ways that emphasize the individual over the community, perhaps shredding the collective basis for what counts as good and just. There are many meanings of justice, but the human rights community has tended to lean on a carceral justice to the neglect of dis-tributive justice. While human rights scholars and activists have accepted many of these criticisms, there nevertheless remains the stead-fast belief that the world can be made into a better place, human rights is both a measure and deliverer of this progress, and human rights narra-tives operate with a vision of the "better" defined by standards set by a Western-influenced version of human rights, justice, and human flourishing.[72]

Humanitarianism offers a contrasting story of precarity and the belief that "things fall apart, again."[73] Before I elaborate, scholars of humani-tarianism have advanced that moral progress depends on the expansion of the circle of humans that are viewed as worthy of compassion.[74] Benevolence is the surest sign of a moral community, and the expansion of benevolence to incorporate those who were once considered outside that community is the surest indicator of progress. This is as good as progress gets. Within the humanitarian community, aid workers will talk about improvement defined by greater efficiency at alleviating suffering and reducing the number of corpses. Yet even here they refuse to let themselves off the hook as the field has become consumed by their short-comings and unintended consequences. Instead of recording achieve-ments they pledge to "do no harm."[75]

Humanitarians resist any notion of progress with a capital P and instead just focus on small achievements in the here and now.

Humanitarians imagine no Spielberg-esque happy ending. Many books on humanitarianism wear their misery, shortcomings, and precarity in their titles: *Hope in Hell*; *Chasing Chaos*; *Humanitarian Quest, Impossible Dreams*; *Bed for the Night*; *An Imperfect Offering*; *Mountains Beyond Mountains*; *The Big Truck Went By*; and on and on. MSF's Jean-Hervé Bradol argues that all world orders are international sacrificial orders.[76] Some sacrificial orders might be better than others to the extent that they have different levels of tolerance toward the sacrifices, but these preventable deaths are treated as acceptable sacrifices. Humanitarianism does not advocate for alternative world orders that might abolish such sacrifices but instead limits itself to the goal of reducing the number of sacrifices in the existing order. Peter Redfield's detailed account of MSF illuminates how aid workers refuse to be seduced by thoughts of hope or progress.[77] "We are not prepared for any radiant or bright future," observes MSF's Rony Brauman. "We can only focus on what we do now, in the present, with those in front of us. Our success can only be in the moment."[78] As another MSF worker reflected, "We are the world's gravediggers, finding our happiness amidst the growing numbers of massacres and battlefields."[79] Another veteran of the aid community remarked that humanitarianism is "an effort to snatch a small locus of mercy in the middle of the horrors of organized death and destruction."[80] Whereas human rights looks to the heavens, humanitarianism struggles to avoid hell.

Useful Idiots?

Do human rights and humanitarianism provide just the appearance of progress or the real thing? Are they outside the existing international order or its creature? Do their actions help to reduce inequality and injustice or reproduce it? In many respects it depends on whether we treat human rights and humanitarianism as: entities that are outside the existing order armed with their humanity-driven ethics; or creatures of the existing order whose ethics are themselves products of power and politics. Many of the chapters reference global structures such as geopolitics, liberalism, capitalism, Christianity, and civilization as the origins of the ethics and practices of humanitarianism and human rights, with the possible consequence that they are not part of the resistance but rather are part of the custodians of the existing order. In the context of criticizing reform organizations in a capitalist society, Marx and Engels offered a classic statement regarding how ethical projects can be imprinted by and help to reproduce existing orders:

A part of the bourgeoisie is desirous of redressing social grievances, in order to secure the continued existence of bourgeois society. To this section belongs economists, philanthropists, humanitarians, improvers of the condition of the working class, organisers of charity, members of societies for the prevention of cruelty to animals, temperance fanatics, hole-and-corner reformers of every imaginable kind.[81]

In their view, do-gooders are operating under false consciousness and self-soothing ideologies, oblivious to how their interventions provide comfort to an unjust order. They think that they are challenging the order, but instead they are its silent partner.

A standard critique of humanitarianism is that it addresses suffering while leaving the sources untouched, which owes partly to humanitarianism's indebtedness to the charity model. But humanitarianism can also be a way to self-medicate, to make us feel like we are doing something even if that something is not doing very much.[82] And sometimes these humanitarian "gifts" are conditional on surrendering capital and capabilities that are subsequently used for the benefits of the economic and political elite.[83] A standard critique of human rights is that it focuses on political and civil rights to the neglect of economic rights; and the morals of neoliberalism have imprinted contemporary human rights.[84] And when it does address economic rights, it often wants to help individuals gain access to markets, thus introducing new sources of dependence and exploitation.[85]

While humanitarianism and human rights cast themselves as fighting for the oppressed, the powerful are the real beneficiaries of their actions. The human rights and humanitarian communities were largely formed by educated, relatively well-off elite from the West, especially when compared with those they wanted to help outside the West. At times, and perhaps increasingly so in today's world of a globalized elite in contemporary capitalism, it is the very individuals that are partly responsible for the causes of inequality and domination that have become the agents of change. Accordingly, they will never advocate for change that potentially threatens their power and privileges. For instance, change through markets rather than through political power. And in doing so, the privileged might be more generous than ever before, but also more predatory than ever before – as they provide philanthropy with one hand but haul away truckloads of resources with the other. The powerful can feel self-satisfied and sleep well at night because they have made the system a little less miserable and forestalled the possibility of revolution.[86] This pattern existed from the very start of humanitarianism. The abolitionists were intent on freeing the slaves, but could not imagine that these primitive and Godless people should be left to their own devices. Instead of imagining them having rights and autonomy, many of the abolitionists were advocates of colonialism and missionaries who wanted to civilize the ignorant and backward heathens.

There is one other way that the discourses of humanitarianism and human rights tend to operate in a way that reinforce existing patterns of inequality: they often advocate action on behalf of others because of our moral responsibilities. We should give because of our felt connections and duties that exist because of our humanity. An alternative form of responsibility is causal responsibility, and argues that we should give because our prior actions are responsible for the suffering others, and perhaps have even indirectly benefited from those actions.[87] The dominance of moral responsibility over causal responsibility also guides the powerful to identify the sources of suffering as home-grown rather than international. But local suffering and injustices often have international roots – legacies of colonialism, globalization that generates inequalities, Western support for autocratic regimes, unfair international property rights and trade policies that disadvantage the most marginal. Contemporary conversations in the United States about how to deal migration from Central America rarely extend into a sober realization that American policies contributed to the misery that are forcing these refugees and migrants to flee their homes. Humanitarianism can contribute to the belief that all causes are local because it tends to focus on symptoms and black box the causes. Human rights advocates can sometimes unknowingly adopt language for mobilization that reinforces stereotypes and racism. For instance, calling the Congo the "rape capital" of the world might bring greater attention to the problem of sexual violence but at the cost of playing into racist images of the sexually rapacious African male.

But humanitarian and human rights organizations are not necessarily the "useful idiots" presented by Marx, Engels, and their unforgiving critics. They might be useful to those in power because they help to maintain the existing order by containing the possibility of more radical resistance, but they are hardly idiots because they are often quite aware of the compromises they are making. Compromises must be made, and not all compromises are rotten compromises. Human right organizations often choose to focus on some rights rather than others because they believe them to be necessary for other rights; voting rights, for instance, might be a prerequisite to economic justice. They also might recognize the centrality of economic rights, but nevertheless strategize and make pragmatic decisions which are most likely to gain the most traction – and in liberal societies this is often in the areas of political and civil rights. Aid organizations know that they are always in danger of being instrumentalized: they gain access to victims not because those who might be responsible for the suffering have remorse and guilt, but rather because they calculate that humanitarian action can further their goals, including a share of the aid, legitimacy, popular support, and even battlefield advantage.[88] Consequently, the choice is often not between being instrumentalized or not at all, but rather between what is acceptable and unacceptable instrumentalization in relationship to the goal of saving lives. Humanitarian organizations know that they can be a "fig leaf" for states that use aid as a substitute for costlier and more consequential action, and that there are no humanitarianism solutions to humanitarian problems. From the moment of its birth, there were those who criticized the ICRC for offering an olive branch to the excesses of war rather than advocating for pacifism and peaceful change. Its standard response is that abandoning victims of war in the utopian hope that it might produce pacificism treats the victims as necessary sacrifices.

Organization of the Volume

The volume is divided in two. Part I comprises chapters 1 to 4 and offers four historically informed analyses regarding the relationship between human rights, humanitarianism, their changing boundaries, and whether these are differences without a distinction. There is broad agreement that the two are distinct and that many of the participants have a stake in keeping them that way, though Hopgood insists that while there are differences, they are trivial. And those who agree on the existence of differences nevertheless offer alternatives views regarding the characteristics that justify the boundaries, where to draw them, when and why they have been redrawn, and who has been most involved in the process of boundary drawing. Part II probes and complicates the accepted view of many of the rationalities and emotions that are associated with each, and examines the practices that have helped to shape and define what it means to do humanitarianism and human rights. Together these chapters provide grounds for looking for boundaries between human rights and humanitarianism, but also cautions against presuming that these boundaries are stable or that the practices that are used to distinguish the two are fixed.

In Chapter 1, Samuel Moyn argues that human rights and humanitarianism have historically been distinct, have become less so, and that human rights is worse off because of it. He opens by observing that human rights and humanitarianism began their lives apart because of the former's interest in citizenship and state-society relations and the latter with life-saving relief. It is only beginning in the 1990s that human rights and humanitarianism truly began to converge. Many of those writing from a humanitarian perspective observe that human rights consumed humanitarianism, but Moyn argues that the reverse happened. Human rights used to be concerned with the conditions of citizenship and ensuring that individuals possessed rights that they could make claims on the state. But the more it became involved in situations of armed conflict and other areas of a traditional humanitarian concern, it lost sight of the standard rights concerns in favor of protection and keeping people alive. Moyn, in this respect, makes the provocative claim that an expanding human rights discourse went through a process of humanitarianization. This is an empirical and historical argument – and a highly normative one. Moyn suggests that this process of humanitarization altered the kind of cosmopolitan politics once imagined and practiced by human rights, as it became much more status quo oriented and much less concerned with issues of justice. Moyn implies, in other words, that humanitarianism has pulled human rights down to its level, hinting that human rights, at least the human rights of old, was ethically superior to humanitarianism. Neither human rights nor humanitarianism can offer much hope, but they are not quite hope-less. At least not quite.

In Chapter 2, Jeffrey Flynn grapples with the relation between human rights and humanitarianism by tracing relations of both to two forms of the "politics of humanity" that arose in eighteenth-century Western societies: a "politics of suffering" aimed at mitigating unnecessary suffering and a "politics of status" aimed at eliminating unjustifiable status hierarchies. Setting things up this way allows Flynn to identify points at which human rights focused mainly on status and humanitarianism on suffering – particularly in the eighteenth century – while also analyzing how subsequent developments have brought claims to equal status into humanitarianism and appeals to suffering into human rights practice. This boundary crossing can pose challenges to both, especially when the status egalitarian dimension of human rights confronts the hierarchical giver–recipient relationship in humanitarianism, or when appeals to suffering lead to a "humanitarianization" of human rights in which pity takes the place of genuine solidarity among equals. Flynn also poses crucial questions about how equal status gets instantiated differently within human rights and humanitarianism, and whether narratives that appeal to suffering can avoid falling into a politics of pity. The ultimate challenge he identifies for both humanitarianism and human rights is whether either can fulfill the more radical potential of a politics of suffering or a politics of status.

A common way to differentiate human rights and humanitarianism is to associate the former with justice and the latter with charity. This distinction runs deep in international law and transnational social action, but what about practice? In Chapter 3, Beitz opens by laying out his understanding of practice and how it applies to humanitarian and human rights practice. In rhetoric and presentation, human rights activists are committed to righting wrongs, while humanitarians to relieving suffering. Although these distinctions might have mapped onto practice at one point, Beitz argues they no longer do. What happened? Like others in the volume, he points to changes in armed conflict and jurisprudence. Accordingly, while those who identify with humanitarianism and human rights will often offer distinctions based on harms alleviation and injustice, they nevertheless work in both domains. And if they have converged, then what is the point of maintaining the distinction? Is there ethical significance for doing so? Beitz turns to the presence of different kinds of duties: perfect duties are those in which we have no choice but to honor, such as no torture, whereas imperfect duties allow discretion, such as helping those in need. Beitz then observes that duties of the first kind (perfect) tend to map onto demands of justice whereas duties of the second kind (imperfect) map onto beneficence. This mapping seemingly parallels common understanding of human rights and humanitarianism. But not completely, at least not today where there are shifting shades. But the continued use of human rights and humanitarianism as distinctive categories possibly reveals how we understand moral demands, how much discretion we have in avoiding these demands, the priorities we assign to them, and where to invest scarce resources. The problem, though, is that misnomers do our thinking for us.

In Chapter 4, Stephen Hopgood argues that there is no bright line that separates humanitarianism and human rights – not conceptually and not historically. They were always dancing around the same flame. There are two foundational reasons for the lack of distinction. Fundamental to both is humanism. And neither community has ever agreed on what are its core or boundaries. There are no loyalty oaths or mechanisms for excommunicating heretics. The only point of divergence, according to

Hopgood, is institutional, that is, their business models and mental and material technologies. When Hopgood addresses the future, though, he suggests that humanitarianism will have more resilience than human rights. The values, ideologies, and discourses that have sustained the humanist project are crumbling. But Hopgood suggests that the minimalist and muted practices of humanitarianism will have an advantage over the maximalist and noisy practices of human rights. Humanitarianism, Hopgood concludes, will have to carry the torch of humanism into the long, dark, night.

Looking at the nineteenth-century British Empire, in Chapter 5 Alan Lester argues that there was a relationship between human rights and humanitarianism – antagonistic. He does not contest the general claim that human rights and humanitarianism were largely independent of each other until the late twentieth century, but he does insist that government officials were more inclined to favor one over the other because it fitted their political interests. Similar to Moyn and Flynn, he locates human rights and humanitarianism in relationship to the prevailing political order. Lester argues that human rights was part of a revolutionary tradition designed to level privileges and status categories in favor of new forms of equality tied to citizenship. Humanitarianism, on the other hand, was part of a conservative politics because it was designed to ameliorate the harms caused by inequality, not remove them. Humanitarianism, in this respect, was not just a discrete intervention but rather was part of a structure of governance, which he calls humanitarian governance. But humanitarianism, and humanitarian governance, were not coherent things, but rather had different branches. Using the careers of two British colonial authorities, George Arthur and George Grey, Lester charts two different versions of humanitarianism as it related to British imperialism. George Arthur pioneered a form of colonial humanitarian governance rooted in the amelioration of slavery and designed to protect Indigenous peoples from the rapacious and exploitative practices of settler communities. Existing Indigenous communities should be protected from harm and enjoy some degree of autonomy. In other words, his understanding of humanitarianism created room for difference and diversity. But this was not equality. Instead, George Grey practiced a form of colonial humanitarian governance that imagined that the best form of protection was assimilation. Engaging in what Lester calls a form of cultural genocide, the goal was to use various governance techniques to slowly bring about the cultural extinction of local populations. In order to turn aboriginal populations into tea-drinking English, Grey intervened in all aspects of their lives.

Humanitarian intervention is a contemporary practice that seems to integrate humanitarianism and human rights. Indeed, for many scholars and practitioners humanitarian intervention is the perfect blend. It is humanitarian because it is designed to save lives that hang in the balance. But it also is often referred to as the use of force to protect the fundamental right of all individuals – the right to life. In Chapter 6, Fabian Klose asks: should we think of humanitarian intervention as part of the history of human rights or humanitarianism? Or both? And if both, how do they connect? But the story requires more historical nuance because, as Klose contends, humanitarian intervention began in the nineteenth century once there was intervention not in the defense of a particular religious community but rather the "human." It was not until the early twentieth century that humanitarian intervention became more fully lodged in the "human," and humanitarian intervention became more fully inscribed in humanitarian norms in international law. But, Klose emphasizes, humanitarian intervention did not include human rights in its modern usage. Klose surveys several eminent jurists and legal scholars to see how they linked humanitarian intervention and the emerging body of international human rights law. It was not until the late twentieth century that humanitarian intervention became more fully located in international law with a solid footing in human rights law. But, Klose observes, it would probably be more accurate to call humanitarian intervention human rights intervention beginning in the twentieth century.

In Chapter 7, Bronwyn Leebaw examines how the concept of shame is employed as a strategy by rights and humanitarian actors. Similar to other contributions, she notes the importance of emotions for understanding various aspects of each. As she explains, shame differs from other emotional responses to suffering and injustice because the feeling can be experienced as a punishment for failing to conform. But feelings of shame can originate from outside or inside. Human rights is famously associated with "name and shame" that depends on what others say, whereas the shame associated with humanitarianism comes from an inner voice. Of the two possibilities and mechanisms, shame is most powerful when it is internally generated. Humanitarians, she argues, generate shame when they appeal to how people should feel. If they do not respond in the right way to suffering, they should be ashamed. There are several potential consequences of this strategy. It can reinforce the emphasis on the needs of the giver. Moreover, Leebaw asks, why should such feelings of shame be limited to those who are close to death? Such feelings are not so easily compartmentalized. Mobilizing these images to shame people into giving can reinforce stereotypes of the "other." The human rights use of shaming tactics often begin with images of the victim. In contrast to the humanitarian image of helplessness, human rights portrays the victim as innocent because they did nothing to deserve their suffering. After noting that these two shaming strategies might conflict, Leebaw turns to the writings of W. E. B. Du Bois to move from the individual to the collective. Shame is experienced by individuals and not institutions, but as individuals become part of systems of rule they tend to shift responsibility and accountability from themselves to the institution; this move can leave them beyond shame, and even when the institutions they serve normalize and rationalize abuse that they privately see as unjust. The challenge, then, is get individuals to feel shame for supporting these taken-for-granted systems of rule that produce violence and inequalities; to recognize the system-wide pattern of abuse; and to acknowledge that they are the beneficiaries of the system. Human rights and not humanitarian discourse might be a better reality check.

In Chapter 8, Aisling Swaine examines how human rights and humanitarianism respond to conflict-related violence against women. Her chapter offers several important observations. To begin, neither field exhibited much interest in gender-based violence (GBV) prior to the mid-1990s. Human rights began to do so in the last quarter of the twentieth century, but it focused on traditional issues regarding women's status in the domestic realm. Many of the premier aid agencies, such as ICRC, were focused on keeping people alive, and while victims of rape suffered greatly, their injuries were not necessarily life-threatening. But several of the conflicts of the 1990s featured mass rape, and rape as a strategy of war, which grabbed the attention of human rights activists; humanitarian organizations lagged behind. Critically, according to Swaine, the fields differed in how they responded to GBV, with each drawing from its existing practices and strategies. Human rights organizations have treated violence against women as part of a discourse of "discrimination" that should be remedied through legal mechanisms that would prosecute perpetrators, promote the rule of law, and produce justice. Humanitarian organizations, on the other hand, have used a reproductive health lens to respond to the physical and psychosocial consequences. In short, the foundational boundaries of human rights led to a legalized response whereas that of humanitarianism led to a medicalized response. This divergence in programming also can produce a tension between the two. Health providers are most concerned with providing the right medical and psychosocial treatment whereas human rights actors often focus on collecting the evidence for legal redress. However, the kinds of interventions required for individual healing might be inconsistent with the kind of data collection required for legal accountability. Another divergence is that the human rights field sees GBV as part of broader patterns of discrimination that require a "public" remedy for "private" harms, whereas aid agencies prefer a response that is "apolitical" and, consequently, tends to erase gender. Humanitarianism and human rights also constitute the kinds of harms against women that are a matter of concern. For the former it is about violence directly caused by conflict, whereas for human rights it the violation of rights.

In Chapter 9, Miriam Ticktin examines how innocence and humanity separate and bind contemporary practices of human rights and humanitarianism. What does innocence suggest about how humanity is practiced, and practiced differently, by these movements? Humanity is often understood as an equalizing principle. All are human. Yet innocence plays a complicated role here. On the one hand, it promises equality by giving everyone the benefit of the doubt. On the other hand, in practice it inexorably constitutes hierarchies, distinguishing between deserving and undeserving. Ticktin is interested in exploring how far innocence goes to further the recognition of universality (whether as shared suffering, or as rights), and when it works instead to institute moral hierarchies. She argues that humanitarianism and human rights both work to buffer the tendency to use innocence to create moral distinctions, albeit differently so – one through the concept of life, the other through the practice of law. Nevertheless, she suggests that innocence primarily works to divide humanity, rather than to unify it as an affective, ethical, or political collectivity. Ultimately, innocence cannot escape its conceptual history as the limit of humanity and the creation of moral distinction. Given these observations, is it possible to imagine humanity without innocence?

In Chapter 10, Ilana Feldman examines how temporalities conceived by Palestinian refugees, and especially the relationship between past, present, and future, led them to blur conventional boundaries between human rights and humanitarianism. Humanitarianism tends to operate with a sense that there is an urgent present. Emergencies require immediate action to save lives, and the longer action is delayed, the more lives will be lost. Yet what happens when the emergency ends but lives are still in limbo, as is the case for millions of refugees who are warehoused in camps and linger in a legal and political no-man's-land? For them, the issue is often no longer about needs, as conceived by aid workers, but rather about rights: access to education and work, protection from political authorities, ability to assemble, religious freedom, and so on. Indeed, Feldman argues that the insistence on calling such protracted situations "emergencies" distracts from the fundamental importance of rights. The Palestinians' current condition and lingering memories also can reshape the boundaries between human rights and humanitarianism. There were wrongs committed in the past that must

be addressed and demand justice. This is traditionally a demand for
human rights, but in the case of the Palestinians it is evoked in
a humanitarian condition. The bending and blurring of human rights
and humanitarianism can create something that many observers might
consider an oxymoron: humanitarian rights.

In Chapter 11, Bertrand Taithe goes to the Cambodian-Thai border
between 1979 and 1999 to examine how humanitarian workers nego-
tiated the changing security and political challenges – and finds that they
answered those challenges in part by developing protection practices that
assimilated a rights-based approach to humanitarian relief. The initial
challenge on the border was keeping people alive. Splayed across various
camps, Cambodian survivors of the genocide and the Vietnamese invasion huddled on both sides of the border. Aid organizations began delivering life-saving relief, and this demand continued for more than
a decade. In these circumstances, they began to refer to their programs
as protection practices. But protection slowly began to incorporate
a rights dimension. These refugees were fleeing a situation in Cambodia
because of mass violations of human rights. And as refugees languished in
camps, with the threat of refoulement dangling over them, the more
important rights became for their protection. In response, aid workers
began to incorporate a rights dimension into their work. But, Taithe
argues, the incorporation of rights into humanitarianism did not necessarily lead to an emancipatory view of human rights. Instead, it led to
a paternalistic and neocolonial positioning. Rights were things that were
given, and not something claimed.

A major change occurred with the successful conclusion of the
Cambodian peace negotiations in 1992. The refugees were coming
home, and aid workers were going with them. Aid and rights agencies
now had to position themselves in relationship to this new political
environment and transitional government. Taithe argues that they
began to adopt rights discourse and align themselves with a Hun Sen
government that they had previously denounced. This was a critical
moment: international agencies were now working with the same
Cambodian leaders who had been accused of mass violations of human
rights to create the rule of law. International NGOs, in short, had been
coopted. Eventually alert to what had happened, aid organizations began
to separate themselves from the rights community. Taithe concludes that
humanitarian organizations must maintain their distance from human
rights if they are to provide protection.

The Conclusion returns to the question of the differences between
human rights and humanitarianism. There are no permanent differences
and thus there cannot be eternal distinctions. But all of the chapters,

including Hopgood's that claimed differences without a distinction, found differences between the two. And if the chapters are a good guide, these differences became more contested, unsettled, inflamed, and moved from the background to the foreground after the 1990s. The Conclusion picks up on the theme of difference in three ways. It emphasizes that these differences that appear and disappear, migrate and settle, are social constructions – but that does not make them any less real or significant. These differences are not trivial but often refer to what counts as the core of each – what it means to do human rights or humanitarianism. This emphasis on "doing" points to the importance of practices, the second point. The differences between their practices were produced by the interplay between the definition of the problem to be solved, the kinds of material and mental technologies that were viewed as the industry standard for solving them, the background knowledge that shaped implicit understanding of the contours and core aspects of each field, and the meanings these actions had for the members of the field. One of the defining features of this historical period is not only the contestation of the boundaries between the two but also the institutionalization of both fields in ways that helped to stabilize these boundaries. But whatever differences and even distinctions that might exist, they might be trivial when situated in the contemporary world-historical moment that is just as likely to see humanity as a threat as it is part of the sacred. The third and final thought, then, speculates about their possible futures given what we think we know about contemporary global trends.

Part I

Differences or Distinctions?

1   Human Rights and Humanitarianization

Samuel Moyn

In this chapter, I will offer two suggestions about the relationship of human rights and humanitarianism. First, I will contend that they have mostly traveled separate paths through modern history, whether considered in their intellectual premises, spiritual postures, or political implications. To a very great extent, in Jeffrey Flynn's terms, status was reserved for citizenship politics, while a politics of suffering operated abroad.[1] Second, the two converged in living memory. And this convergence occurred on humanitarianism's terms: the recent history of human rights is the history of their humanitarianization through internationalization.

For a long time, it seemed as if the unerring rule for humanitarianism and human rights was: never the twain shall meet. To say so, of course, is a generalization; like any generalization in human affairs, it is not an invariant natural law that one counterexample refutes, but an overall trend that prevailed and predominated. With some notable exceptions, identification with suffering almost never involved the attribution of moral rights to others. And no wonder: what has been defended in humanitarianism, past and present, is not citizenship but life. To the extent the two interacted, it was in domestic settings that could sometimes lead to status claims, which often took the forms of demands for rights. But the same did not happen for a long time in global politics; when it did, it was as part of a politics of global suffering rather than one of global status – other than in the provision of a new kind of succor in the form of a nominal rhetoric of global rights enjoyment that differed little in practice from an older imperial and transnational humanitarianism.

The separation of humanitarianism and human rights was so powerful that, even at the level of scholarly investigation, professional historiographies of humanitarianism and human rights were separately initiated – by different people at different times. For this reason, it is useful to take up the historiographies of humanitarianism and human rights alongside their histories. Writing about their trajectories is now popular; and both their

33

early development and current golden age are as revealing about the changing assumptions of the last few decades across which, once investigated separately, humanitarianism and human rights are often conceptualized together. Most of what follows therefore illustrates the long separation of humanitarianism and human rights both historically and historiographically, whatever the minor simplifications such separation has sometimes involved. I want to defend, then, the default though not universal view among historians that these are different topics and that less is gained than lost by muddying the line between them – until recently when the very temptation to muddy the line arose.

Failure to appreciate how distinct the two phenomena were in the more remote past leads directly to an even worse mistake: failure to appreciate their contingent and unprecedented intersection in our time. And more is at stake than merely a historical error: it leads to, except to the extent it is often motivated by, ethical and political error. Briefly put, I will argue that the convergence of humanitarian and human rights today is bound up with the mainstream abandonment of a more believable and effective cosmopolitan language and practice of structural justice, as morality in global affairs of all kinds generally becomes defined and shaped as a humanitarian ethics of care and succor.[2] Humanitarianism did not "swallow" human rights but did affect them in strong and unprecedented respects. Once comprising an anti-hierarchical language of egalitarian citizenship, human rights have frequently been humanitarianized, and their defenders are themselves victims of the repetitious confirmation of hierarchical relations which has been the central truth of humanitarian ethics for much longer.

Separation: Historiographical Origins

Among professional historians, there was a fascinating historiography of humanitarianism long before there really was one concerning human rights.[3] The initial driver of the literature was the search to explain the rise of transnational anti-slavery sentiment. In his classic *The Problem of Slavery in Western Culture*, David Brion Davis drew on early scholarship in literary history to assign the lion's share of credit for this development to the emergence of "the man of feeling."[4] The secularization of an originally religious impulse to heal suffering as one of the highest types of good works was perhaps the most pivotal source of change in attitudes toward human bondage after a millennia of (occasionally glum) acceptance of the practice.

Some have speculated that the deep origin of this constitutive spectatorial relation of the humanitarian imagination to the body in pain stretched back to medieval reinterpretations of the meaning of Jesus Christ on the cross – since the centrality of his suffering had to be learned – and the rise of a then-novel imperative of compassion.[5] But the new sympathetic culture of the eighteenth century let loose this identification with one man for the sake of all men – and even more commonly, women, and even sometimes even nonhuman animals. (The striking paradox is that animal protection movements originate from the rise of humanitarianism.)

In the reconstitution of this epoch-making moral departure, the very centrality of anti-slavery to the origins of the professional historiography of humanitarianism was as much an interference as an engine. Observers of the Enlightenment knew that anti-slavery was a just instance of the rise of a new culture of feeling in the eighteenth century – one with many other ramifications. Davis had relied on famed literary scholar R. S. Crane in developing his original account, and it was other literary critics who continued for a long time to do most to illuminate the relevance of feeling in the "age of reason."[6] The rise of a culture of sentiment also had philosophical dimensions, mostly taken up by students of moral philosophy (especially Scottish moral sense philosophy). A broader account awaited the cultural historian Thomas Laqueur, in one of the most historiographically influential and innovative essays of the 1980s, to demonstrate that the new novel and philosophy of feeling were part of a whole cultural revolution.[7] The "humanitarian narrative" that resulted from this departure in thinking and action presented the violation of individual bodies before a new kind of fellow-feeling spectator, and new media of the period schooled him in a new cultural program in regarding the pain of others. The last remnants of a millennial ethic of martial glory were extinguished; emulation of those who sympathized with injury triumphed.

Historians thus discovered and elaborated what Hannah Arendt and, before her, Friedrich Nietzsche had known: "It is by no means a matter of course for the spectacle of misery to move men to pity. . . . [In] the eighteenth century . . . this age old indifference was about to disappear."[8] Yet not one of the founders of the recent historiography of humanitarianism mentioned human rights in framing his topic. (Nor, for that matter, did Arendt in her acid portrait of Jacobin politics of misery or, before her, Nietzsche in his angry denunciation of the rise of sentimental philosophy.) Indeed, most of its historians, who tended to be skeptics of bourgeois and Christian morality alike, were not set on celebrating what enthusiastic psychologist Steven Pinker, later reading this literature selectively and triumphalistically in search of human progress, called "the humanitarian revolution."[9] Their goal, instead, was to try to understand the causal origins, characteristic limits, and common perversions of a new moral culture beginning in the eighteenth century.

Was humanitarianism best understood as the obverse of the invention of sadism, as Nietzschean Michel Foucault contended in passing (and as several historians followed up to explore)?[10] Was the rise of humanitarianism part of the establishment of the "hegemony" of capitalism, as Davis went on to speculate, sparking a once touchstone debate about precisely how to explain the elective affinity between the rise of new globalized commercial relations and the characteristic emotional lives of modern Western citizens?[11] Or was humanitarianism most of all, as more recent historians have begun to contend, a trademark stance of that political form called empire? More specifically, did it find its natural home among those leaders and followers of modern progressive empires who needed their own hierarchy to be "moral," taking up a deterritorialized sympathetic ethics primarily to critique the empire of benighted rivals for inflicting too much pain or (rather more rarely) stigmatizing the most egregious practices of their own empire for the sake of its improvement?[12] Such questions never disturbed a more popular consensus that humanitarianism was something to celebrate – but they were disquieting and they were utterly central to the inception of the professional historiography of the humanitarian phenomenon.

That nobody writing foundational histories of the rise of humanitarianism mentioned human rights, let alone regarded the one as the source of the other, is easy to explain. For there simply was no (or not much) of a historiography of human rights, even as that around humanitarianism accelerated. Outside history, there were arguments about Stoic and Christian origins of natural law and the rise of early modern natural rights – with their anticipation of John Rawls's rehabilitation of the concept for our time. In France, during the 1989 bicentennial of the French Revolution's outbreak, there was meditation on the ideological origins of its Declaration of the Rights of Man and Citizen. Even as a historiography of humanitarianism burgeoned in the 1970s and especially in the 1980s, however, no historiography of human rights – for example, one making the birth of the Universal Declaration of Human Rights (1948) central or focusing on claimants on its legacy since – followed. That literature required the millennial hype around human rights in the 1990s to appear – even as the interdisciplinary study of humanitarianism exploded, too, in the post-Cold War world. As if to return the favor, early histories of "human rights" did not mention humanitarianism, even when they canonized anti-slavery as an early human rights movement, before going on to give attention to the twentieth-century history of international politics.[13]

I want to defend the proposition that it was not merely a matter of contingent separate origins that these literatures did not initially intersect; it was substantively correct since they were dealing with genuinely separate phenomena. It is increasingly popular to claim that some master concept – the recent candidate is human dignity – lies in the background of both; but whether plausible or not to say so after the fact of their increasing overlap in our time, the historical truth is their separation for the longest time both conceptually and institutionally.

One proposal to the contrary, of course, came in historian Lynn Hunt's revolutionary intervention that singlehandedly refounded the historiography of human rights ten years ago now, and remains the most important work so far published in its field. But to cast a glance back at her trendsetting *Inventing Human Rights* confirms that it was far more than a counterexample in staging a historiographical intersection of human rights and humanitarianism – which nobody in either camp had done before her. It reflected our contemporary experience of the intersection of humanitarianism and human rights, anachronistically projecting it onto a past in which such intersection had not yet occurred.[14]

On Hunt's argument, a culture of humanitarianism, which she depicted in the first half of the book, led to a politics of human rights, sketched in the second half of the book, on declarations of rights in Atlantic revolutionary experiences. Historiographically speaking, Hunt simply updated Laqueur for the sake of a new historiography of human rights, drawing on the "new cultural history" they had together elaborated as fellow Berkeley professors in the 1980s but that one had applied to humanitarianism two decades before the other rehabilitated it to explain human rights. Even in Hunt's essay, of course, the two phenomena of humanitarianism and human rights are partly dissociated at the start: identification with bodily suffering thanks to new media comes first and separately. But then a tight causal linkage is suggested between the two, such that humanitarianism transforms into human rights more or less automatically.

As Hunt's many critics have pointed out, however, there are serious troubles with this scheme. The minor one, however significant within the boundaries of her book itself, is that it offers little to no argument for how humanitarianism powered the annunciation of human rights; the connection is just asserted as if *post hoc ergo propter hoc*. What really follows from Hunt's argument is how unrelated humanitarianism and human rights were in their Enlightenment co-emergence. Worse, to suggest that one sparked the other leaves a fateful rise in public salience in the appeal of natural rights and *les droits de l'homme* and their eventual relation to emancipatory political revolution unexplained (which it still is).[15] The political mobilization of the moral claim that individuals have rights on the basis of their humanity in the Atlantic revolutions was for a long time allied to the invention of citizenship among equals in a sovereign polity through their own agency – associations all radically distinct from the apolitical, deterritorialized, hierarchical, and passive implications of humanitarianism past and present.

Hunt herself insisted, furthermore, that human rights were secular. But while (following Laqueur) Hunt is absolutely correct that a new "secular" culture of humanitarianism burgeoned in the eighteenth century, its content was incubated in reformist Christian circles and has never strayed all that far from reformist Christianity's ethical maxim – even or especially among certain kinds of Protestants – to do good works. (To which one must add that its secular forms have always paled beside the constant prevalence of religious piety as the driver of the majority of forms of modern humanitarianism.)[16] Precisely to the extent "human rights" have been about secular citizenship, something else was afoot in them.[17]

But the major trouble, beyond the chronological and especially geographical boundaries of Hunt's book on the eighteenth century, is that subsequent history shows that nobody can rely on the direct or necessary transformation of humanitarian relations into human rights relations. Just to the contrary, in fact. For a long time, the human rights politics of the transatlantic eighteenth century primarily portended revolutionary nationalism and the search for post-imperial sovereignty through modern history. It was almost always a language for fellow insiders. Meanwhile, humanitarianism was multiscalar from the beginning or very early, traveling the wings of "new media" to allow local empathy to be globalized. Indeed, insofar as humanitarianism has had a politics, it is hard to avoid the impression that, long into the twentieth century (and perhaps the twenty-first), it is a global imperial politics of fellow-feeling across massive gradients of power and wealth. Even when people were brought within the circle of care locally or globally, they were not elevated to the rank of citizen equals at a national scale.

According to many observers of the past (and the present), humanitarianism characteristically humanizes empire, forestalling its overthrow. For two centuries, by contrast, the characteristic cause the slogan of human rights served was the achievement and reform of citizenship in the nation-state. Not just during but also after the Atlantic revolutions, it fitted snugly in the ideological atmosphere of the egalitarian relations of citizenship in a state and especially nation-state; humanitarianism prospered in the long-standing ambiance of diverse empires that advertised their moral superiority to one another – hence the centrality of Britain in the history of imperial humanitarianism – and maintained diverse status relations internally that were themselves unchallengeable, though they were open to humanitarian prettification.[18] One might also want to suggest that, according to the gender norms of the time, rights were associated with masculine self-assertion and humanitarianism with feminine care.

For such reasons, when I wrote *The Last Utopia: Human Rights in History* (2010), I recommended near-absolute prophylactic separation of the two.[19] Such a prophylactic separation, of course, comes with the risk of error; but, as with all historical generalizations, the question is what bigger risks one courts with messier categories or none.

Separation: The Nineteenth Century and Beyond

As Abigail Green has most compellingly argued, nineteenth-century humanitarianism, though largely a Christian project, was also often a liberal one, and thus regularly associated with the propagation of liberal norms abroad – so that there was no absolute and watertight separation between rights at home and an early history of rights abroad.[20] And fair enough, up to a point – and, on reflection, to a very limited extent. This is, of course, not to say that humanitarianism was always a liberal project. But to the extent it was, it is important to chart how much liberals pursued rights transnationally whether in a humanitarian guise or not.

Citizenship at home, as all historians of the nineteenth century know, was moving away from the centrality of claims to human rights in disputes around the nature of citizenship (and, in particular, the role of the state it securing its perquisites, notably on the long road to social citizenship). More important, the truth was that liberalism fighting oppression abroad was primarily focused on the fortunes of white male Christians, and debates about interference for their sake – almost exclusively with the Ottoman Empire – really meant helping them help themselves through revolution. As a result, to note the association of liberal politics at home with humanitarian ones abroad really suggests how far away from any recognizable commitment liberals were during the period from either a universal understanding of "humanity" or rights as the premier language to frame and pursue its entitlements.

More glaringly, of course, liberals did not pursue liberalism abroad for non-Christians or nonwhites, except insofar as liberalism justified imperial conquest and rule in the name of a "civilization" that might lead backwards people to modernity at some unspecified later time. Even when Christians agitating for better perquisites under Ottoman rule or engaging in outright nationalist revolt incited counterinsurgency to the occasional point of genocide, early liberal identification with victims of atrocity and "humanitarian intervention" on their behalf did not take place in the name of universal rights. Indeed, historians have recovered widespread appeals to "humanity" in nineteenth-century international politics, but next to none to human rights.[21] For most liberals, then, the language of human rights – to the extent used at all in the century when it stagnated even as humanitarianism exploded – was still tethered to its revolutionary origins. If foreigners had a right, it was primarily the entitlement to revolt, at least if they were the right kind (and their rulers the wrong kind) of people. Humanitarianism was largely for fellow white Christian and liberals beyond borders whose search for their own national citizenship failed, and mass victimhood resulted.

The record of the transnational plight of slaves and women in the humanitarian century tells a similar truth. When it came to slavery, rights were much more likely to be invoked when debating the entitlements of those within one's state or empire, especially by Americans before the Civil War (as well as when they argued for better outcomes for blacks after), or in France in the arguments around the end of slavery in 1848.[22] Slavery abroad was, instead, a humanitarian cause and pretext for imperial conquest and displacement – notably but not exclusively in the famous "scramble for Africa" as well as in sequels to it like the reallocation of King Leopold's Congo to Belgian superintendence and substitution for atrociously with merely outrageously brutal mismanagement. Similarly, even to the extent there was supranational liberal concern, there was not a comparable transnational liberal politics of women's rights, though there certainly was a humanitarian campaign around (once again, white Christian) women's suffering – especially when it threatened gendered virtue, as in campaigns against "white slavery" of sex trafficking.[23]

Finally, the frequently cited "humanization of the laws of war" starting in the same century forces parallel conclusions. The boom in the historiography of the laws of war occurred independently of that of either humanitarianism or human rights – not so much as a result of the end of the Cold War as thanks to the return of direct great power intervention in world affairs after the September 11 attacks; and given this belated timing, it became tempting to regard the milestones in the evolution of the law of war as coinciding with an emergent historiography of human rights. But further inspection of their trajectory through the nineteenth and even long into the twentieth century suggested other conclusions. For one thing, the early phases of the laws of war stretched very clearly back to medieval times if not long before. In modern times, given that most legalization then and now occurs because of interstate coordination, humanitarianism was an important factor in its path but not the most vital one. Indeed, the laws of war were only rebranded "international humanitarian law" in our time, and the bulk of their modern history may fit better within other explanatory frameworks.

It is certainly fair to observe that the sort of internationalism that Swiss Red Cross founder Henry Dunant called for, in his *A Memory of Solferino*, involved a classic "humanitarian narrative" (in Laqueur's phrase) featuring the spectacle of violated bodies and the evocation of pity for the sake of virtuous reform. And Florence Nightingale really existed before she became a myth. But legally speaking, the law of war was about providing aid to and later controlling forces, not investing civilian victims with rights (certainly not justiciable ones). More deeply, premature conflation mistakes that the project of humanizing warfare – initially restricted to soldiers – operated within a framework of compassionate succor and evil abatement, especially when in the twentieth century publics and their states finally began to take seriously not the plight of their own soldiers but that of foreign civilians. Long into the twentieth century, humanization of warfare was separate (eventually, intentionally kept separate) from the newfangled idea of internationalizing rights, until the two began to be connected – in the late 1960s at the very earliest.[24]

Ideologically and practically, in summary, none of transnational antislavery, humanitarian intervention, or law of war in their long-standing forms was trying to export citizenship or some internationalized functional equivalent of aspects of it, the project for which "human rights" had been invented and were largely reserved – even when (as in the unusual case of the law of war) there were novel uses of international law as a central humanitarian device. Unsurprisingly, none even rhetorically scaled human rights up from the domestic citizen experience where they remained locked up.

Intersection: The (Late) Twentieth-Century Humanitarianization of Rights

In the late twentieth century, human rights and humanitarianism drifted much more into one another's orbits – and humanitarianism proved to have the much bigger gravitational pull of the two. Humanitarianism came close to annexing and redefining human rights as they were incorporated in the familiar script of empathy in the face of the spectacle of the body in pain as viewed across gradients of wealth and power – a script that still defines humanitarianism today. Not only did this not happen all at once, but it also did not happen comprehensively. Human rights retained their power as a citizenship language, and much of humanitarianism went on as before. But relative to the past, the most striking phenomenon was their intersection, which most often took place on humanitarianism's terms.

Above all, the internationalization of rights did not occur as an expansion of the experience of territorial citizenship that had previously defined the language. It retreated to the search for a minimal baseline of protection to be secured, and astonishingly often the protection of life itself. How could it have been otherwise, when lots of people eventually committed to internationalizing the concept of human rights, while practically nobody dreamed of scaling citizenship up beyond its original limitations? No wonder, then, that the internationalization of rights transformed the language so that it both sounded and worked in an increasingly humanitarian mode. It is interesting to think about whether, in the process, humanitarianism was compelled or invited to shift away from the language and practice of benevolence across hierarchy to be infused by justice. But arguably, this transformation happened much less than the redefinition of justice itself in the image of humanitarian ethics.

Historians can quibble among themselves about when precisely this major development occurred in the twentieth century.[25] Much depends on the details of the historiography of humanitarianism as its forms and institutions expanded rapidly across the time period, a massive phenomenon that historians – after giving more attention to humanitarianism's founding centuries for a long time – are now dutifully reconstructing.[26] In my opinion, the evidence for now that a powerful intersection with human rights began to occur earlier than the 1970s and 1980s is weak. Humanitarian initiatives were reactivated right away after World War II, for sure, as histories of the sector in the period prove (with the founding of Oxfam the exemplary moment); but the annunciation of international human rights remained an essentially separate – not to mention much smaller – story. The broader history of international organization tracked this separation as a matter of institutional design. The humanitarian causes begun under the League of Nations were significantly broadened under the new United Nations, but the latter's human rights commission remained an almost entirely distinct enterprise organizationally – and for many decades, a dead end.[27]

For those who could assert them, human rights remained in the tradition of citizenship. As recently as the 1940s, the creation or renovation of egalitarian citizenship in a social direction afforded rights their predominant ambiance – weighted more heavily than ever before toward distributive and not simply political egalitarianism, in the presence of the frightening geopolitics of communism's own vision of "humanity."

In the face of the postwar spectacle of mass displacement of Jews, the biggest immediate humanitarian problem after World War II, the world responded with some care but no serious international human rights for refugees then (as Arendt complained) or later (as contemporary politics illustrates).[28] Now that people are far less sure that the international declaration of human rights in the 1940s must have been propelled by the victimological concern with Jewish suffering during World War II, with other causal settings like the rise of the social democratic welfare state and the stabilization of conservative Christian Democracy in Western Europe of far greater importance, it is easier to properly date their intersection with humanitarianism to a later time. In their initial internationalization, rights were offered essentially as a template for welfare states for those already in them, or for those who got the chance to try to build them in a still formally imperial world. Like other refugees, Palestinians were allocated to ongoing humanitarian management even as Jews who made it to the area succeeded in capturing "the right to have rights" of founding their own nation-state – wanting social(ist) citizenship most of all, like other peoples that already had citizenship or could get it.

In the law of war, the new Geneva Conventions (1949) were propounded in the shadow of the Universal Declaration but kept apart from its premises. Even experimental invocations of the law of war during the 1950s and 1960s wars of late empire did not venture to integrate human rights within evolving rules for "humane" war. Decolonization was the globalization through nationalism of citizenship, except that – since it was conducted by nonwhites – liberals were far less likely to sympathize with it than they had been in the nineteenth century. After all, it involved the breakup of their own empires rather than a "backwards" Muslim one. Anti-colonialism aimed higher than the promise of entitlement to bare life itself that it has always been the humanitarian agenda to safeguard. Anti-colonialism engaged the law of war as an instrument to its high end of a social(ist) welfare state for citizens, not mainly for the sake of the independent goal of making war humane. "Lawfare" – strategic invocation of the Geneva Conventions by subaltern actors under threat of counterinsurgent imperial violence – was born as a tool to achieve the postcolonial state. Unlike the law of war, international human rights were rarely invoked in such struggles, even instrumentally. For such reasons, the era of decolonization is the last in which a warning against the historiographical "premature conflation" of human rights and humanitarianism seems of critical importance.[29]

Like the nineteenth century, then, the two decades after 1945 were still in radical contrast with our time. Now, many think humanitarianism and human rights are close enough to strive to connect more fundamentally or even speak about in public settings (and histories of various times and places) interchangeably. What happened in the meantime? In *The Last Utopia*, I referred to "the slow amalgamation of humanitarian concern for suffering with human rights."[30] I contended, to excess I now think, that the earliest self-styled human rights movements in the 1970s were directed at stigmatizing authoritarianism and totalitarianism, and most of all political imprisonment, rather than atrocity or catastrophe or hunger that have afforded the classic occasions for humanitarian concern. Even on the brink of a later moment of combination, in the 1970s the prominent causes through which international human rights became famous were specifically not ones establishing humanitarian care as the vital emotional relation or political crucible. I think that this contrast remains true and valuable – after all, there is no gainsaying the authoritarian and totalitarian targets of the human rights revolution – but recent argument and research certainly proves that the picture is considerably messier than I originally suggested.

The details are still rather unclear, however, simply because far less research has been done on the conflationary period of the 1970s through 1990s than on the nineteenth century or 1940s when no intersection really occurred. At least as of Amnesty International's Campaign against Torture in the early 1970s, a clear humanitarian logic applied near the start, dramatizing the body in pain and eliciting transnational sympathy (indeed, if one historian is correct, a kind of "moral panic" sensationalizing the violation of female bodies in particular).[31] Amnesty's style during and beyond that campaign rejoined many strands of the history of humanitarianism, from its "bourgeois" mode of activism to its pseudo- or post-Christian accoutrements. The same is true in philosophy: the earliest serious theory of global basic rights, developed by Henry Shue in his case for worldwide entitlements to subsistence, is explicitly developed in terms of a minimalist healer's ethic of palliation in the face of implacable disease. Human rights were going to be about justice, not philanthropy, but first of all and for an indefinite period the "basic" achievement of keeping everyone alive.[32] More broadly, the explosion of post-ideological informational politics within burgeoning human rights movements of the age – going beyond lighting candles and writing letters – reactivated naming and shaming practices of nineteenth-century humanitarianism, including versions of "ethical consumption."

And new studies of the reception of humanitarian tragedies from Biafra to Cambodia indicate the rising salience of international human rights frameworks applied to atrocity and genocide roughly in the same time period.[33] If Holocaust consciousness was far more absent in the 1940s (including as a motivation for declaring human rights) than people have wanted to admit, the vagaries of the definite explosion of Holocaust memory from the 1960s through 1980s so far permit no absolute caesura to be located – as if from one day to the next the invocation of human rights suddenly conjured up to most people violent depredations abroad. For sure, the notion of human rights had never been singularly focused on the phenomenon of foreign atrocity in any prior era, but when precisely the association crystallized after the 1970s is either not yet known or a matter of a surreptitious conversion.[34] Finally, both humanitarianism and human rights were brought into proximity because the trajectory of each was profoundly inflected by crisis and reorientation of the international left between the 1960s and 1980s – which itself occurred in complex stages, not all at once.[35]

Whatever the precise chronology of the partial merger of human rights into a humanitarian ambiance, I do still think it is correct to say that, at some point, "human rights and humanitarianism [became] fused enterprises, with the former incorporating the latter and the latter justified in terms of the former."[36] They both became part of the moral cosmetology of a neoliberal epoch (which is not to say either is reducible to the neoliberalism that has done most to define the age of their intersection). True card-carriers in both professionalizing fields in the era learned and now know well how to draw distinctions. The bigger event was not this ordinary expert boundary work, however, but the historic intersection of humanitarianism and human rights in the first place.

And as human rights became not merely a language of local citizenship they sometimes remain but rather a rhetoric of global care, they accommodated to the global hierarchy that has always defined humanitarianism in theory and practice. Not always, of course. Not only alternative cosmopolitanisms to human rights were in contention for human allegiance for most of modern history, but also alternative versions of human rights that placed greater stress on local agency. But there is no denying that for several decades a human rights revolution swept the world that favored a narrow set of norms, pursued by transnational elites, funded in rich capitals, with little grassroots traction, and humanitarian concern occupying the heart of the human rights imaginary. Morality was redefined to revolve around "the secular value of life," a kind of tragic vocation in its defense, and ethical witnessing of the remainder of horror, with appeals to humanity mostly functioning as a gesture toward unavailable justice – though perhaps the moral arc of history would bend toward it someday.[37]

Conclusion: Contingent Histories versus Categorical Opposition

I close this chapter contrasting my historical account of the evolving relations of human rights and humanitarianism from separation to inter-section with stories developed elsewhere, notably in the anthropology and international relations of humanitarianism. Both have relied on strong contrasts between humanitarianism and human rights, which fail to recognize the basis of their past distinction and therefore the significance – analytically and politically – of their present conflation.

In the main synthetic account of the history of humanitarianism, based on an important periodization of the phenomenon, international relations scholar Michael Barnett offers three grounds for avoiding human rights altogether. First, he writes, the humanitarian "discourse of needs" is separate from a rights-based language of entitlements. Second, "human rights relies on legal discourses and frameworks, whereas humanitarian-ism shifts attention to moral codes and sentiments." Third, "human rights typically focuses on the long-term goal of eliminating the causes of suffering, humanitarianism on the urgent goal of keeping people alive."[38]

But the fact that a series of contingent reasons established separate imaginaries and practices cannot possibly mean that they remain distinct today. And their intersection is precisely on the terrain of humanitarian-ism and need – leaving the law and politics of international human rights equally open to the worry that they have lacked the structural imagina-tion, and often share in the sentimental interest in the immediate and spectacular, that Barnett thinks distinguishes humanitarianism.[39] In light of this reality, it is a mistake to retrospectively erect a long-term separation into a theory of permanent essences. Brutally put, for a long time it was unnecessary to distinguish international humanitarianism from interna-tional human rights: the latter did not exist. And after recent develop-ments, not one of Barnett's distinctions works, because human rights have been humanitarianized. Offered in terms of ideal-typical categories, Barnett's separation misses the lasting reasons the two were distinct in the beginning as well as the fact that they converged recently.

Similarly, anthropologists of humanitarianism skilled at contemporary and synchronic analysis frequently fail to dramatize the same transforma-tions because they do not acknowledge the extent to which human rights have themselves become humanitarianized. In the tracks of Didier Fassin's "critique of humanitarian reason," it is now common to analyze humanitarianism through the juxtaposition to human rights – as if it tracked a juxtaposition of humanitarian care with entitled justice. But what if global justice itself – in its dominant imaginative and practical forms – has become humanitarian?[40]

Thus Miriam Ticktin, in a useful recent summation of the state of the field and application of its insights to contemporary migration crisis, contends that charity and humanitarianism are not enough relative to rights-based entitlements.[41] But a historical view of the shifting relations of these categories might well conclude that – at least to a startling extent – humanitarianism has helped redefined human rights as a global response to hierarchy and the organized misery at its nether pole. As Ticktin points out, agitation for human rights can promisingly indict the limits of humanitarian compassion; but it will not do, in calling for a "political" alternative to care and pity, to surmise that human rights as we have known them in our time already provide it, even in theory. (Among other things, international human rights have not been defined as a distributively egalitarian language.)[42] Indeed, the overall truth is that they have come to share many of the defects of humanitarianism, which makes them a dubious candidate to provide a strong or viable contrast to it.

In any event, there is no way to reach any conclusion without conducting an ethnography in situ of the specific forms of both human rights activism and humanitarian care. I do not know of ethnographies that do so. I would speculate that, precisely to the extent the frame of human rights allows more appeals to justice, it makes less profound effects in the world; it does not, one might worry, provide even care to the suffering, which is at least something to reckon against the ancillary effects that humanitarian "management" of misery certainly involves. Consider, for example, the Palestinian case, as one that has been studied by separate anthropologists, each interested one of the two categories. Ilana Feldman has shown that "the humanitarian condition" many decades after Palestinians were initially allocated to it is grim. But Lori Allen has documented that their own turn to human rights since 1980 – along with an increasing number of external advocates – has not even made the difference humanitarianism does.[43]

I do not mean to imply that total conflation of human rights into humanitarianism ever occurred.[44] Rights remain available as a potentially transformative citizenship language and mobilizing for their sake sometimes brings about more just outcomes. Beth Simmons has even contended that the main if not sole significance of internationalizing human rights in our time (in treaty law, at least) has been to provide new tools of domestic citizenship in the highly specific circumstances that such tools can make such difference.[45] Before the continent entered crisis, Europeans brought about an unprecedented regionalization of citizenship through rights law, whatever its faults of substance and process. In transnational settings, rights activism has sometimes delivered improvement, or at least allowed for the allocation of stigma by global outsiders to local politics. But on balance over time, humanitarianization has been visited to a significant extent on human rights in global affairs, leaving them imaginatively and practically close to humanitarianism like never before. Their vocation, for most observers and participants in the enterprise, is a weak solidarity with the wretched of the earth – whether the latter are fighting for life itself or, in an age of triumphant global anti-poverty amidst exploding national inequality almost everywhere, claiming entitlements to the basics of a tolerable human existence.

It is not immoral in the face of continuing world hierarchy, in my view, to have an ascendant moral language of human rights to indict the illegitimacy of global misery. For its harshest critics, such weak humanitarianism helps entrench the hierarchies it merely struggles to make less flagrant and violent – or even worsens them in doing so.[46] On another detailed powerful account, the glitzy mediatization of humanitarianism (or "post-humanitarianism") is what really matters about it today.[47] I suspect that neither disturbing allegation is broadly true. No doubt, some part of humanitarianism and human rights alike functions to distract from pursuing justice and launder shame among those with a bad conscience that they are powerful where others are weak. But there is no reason to doubt the moral bona fides of humanitarianism and human rights and grant them credit for their modest effects.

From my perspective, it is not so much that the contemporary modes of identification that human rights and humanitarianism both involve almost never lead to improvement, as that even their rare successes leave the selected beneficiaries only a little better off. As long as domination is the way of the world, it is better for it to be humane than not, and it is excellent that a few at the top struggle to help those at the bottom in the name of humanitarianism and human rights, separately or (more and more often) together. But many will still find the vision of humanity of both optics morally insufficient, if their prime credential is merely that they are better to have around to define our time than no morality at all.

2   Suffering and Status

Jeffrey Flynn

Neither human rights nor humanitarianism are static constructs. Exploring the relations between them requires attention to history. The guiding idea of this chapter is that a complete story about the relation between human rights and humanitarianism must account for their connections to two powerful modern ideals: the commitment to alleviating avoidable human suffering and the commitment to eliminating unjustifiable status hierarchies. It is tempting to identify the former with humanitarianism and the latter with human rights. That way of carving things up makes some sense when referring to developments within Western societies in the eighteenth century, a century that witnessed both the rise of a sentimental mode of humanitarianism focused on alleviating suffering and the revolutionary overturning of social and political hierarchies in the name of the Rights of Man. This chapter takes that period as its starting point. But things get more complicated when moving beyond those eighteenth-century developments. One aim here is to step back and gain critical distance from preconceptions about what "human rights" or "humanitarianism" are all about by seeing various ways in which *both* have incorporated claims to equal status or relied on appeals to suffering. That is not to say that the politics of suffering or the politics of status are themselves static; each has a broader history of its own.[1] The point is to see how both have provided rich resources from which human rights and humanitarian practice have drawn. This also makes it possible to highlight how more radical versions of both the politics of equal status and the politics of suffering have gone unrealized in particular instantiations of human rights and humanitarian practice.

I am a philosopher, not a historian. Philosophers sometimes fly high above the contingencies of history when defining concepts. Historians often develop detailed depictions of particular eras and events. I take a middle path, drawing selectively from historical instantiations of human rights and humanitarianism with the aim of bringing conceptual clarity to some issues and positing what I hope are useful distinctions. Rather than start with a fixed definition of either human rights or

49

humanitarianism, I note my historical starting points. Scholars of humanitarianism sometimes distinguish the long history dating to the rise of
a humanitarian culture in eighteenth-century Western societies from
a shorter history dating to the latter half of the twentieth century.
Michael Barnett refers to the former as "The Humanitarian Big Bang"
and, of the latter, maintains that the 1968 response to the civil war and
famine in Biafra is "rightly credited with opening a new chapter in
humanitarian action."[2] A parallel distinction and fault line for debate
exists in the history of human rights, with some focusing on the eighteenth
century as the era in which human rights were "invented" while others
stress the 1970s as the "breakthrough" era.[3] I focus primarily on developments in the eighteenth century and the latter half of the twentieth
century not because that is all there is to the history of human rights or
humanitarianism, but because we continue to grapple with challenges
that are vividly manifest in those historical moments.

   In the section "Eighteenth-Century Encounters," I identify four paradigmatic ways in which a politics of suffering and a politics of equal status
intersected, or failed to, in the eighteenth century. In the sections "Rights
and Status" and "Stories of Suffering," I draw distinctions I take to be
crucial in thinking about status and suffering in relation to human rights
and humanitarianism. One aim here is to identify more and less ambitious
versions of the politics of status and the politics of suffering. Specifically,
the section "Rights and Status" distinguishes the way humanitarianism
has incorporated the idea of equal human value from the more radical
status-elevating function of human rights. The section "Stories of
Suffering" distinguishes the prevailing type of "humanitarian narrative"
from forms that have more powerful political potential. The politics of
suffering is particularly relevant to twentieth-century encounters between
human rights and humanitarianism as each took on novel forms – the
focus of the section "Twentieth-Century Iterations." An enduring challenge is whether the contemporary politics of human rights and humanitarianism can achieve the aims of more robust versions of either a politics
of status or a politics of suffering.

Eighteenth-Century Encounters

Two eighteenth-century developments that have indelibly shaped modern moral and political life in the West are the degree to which avoidable
(particularly physical) suffering increasingly came to be viewed as intol-
erable, and status hierarchies increasingly came to be viewed as
unjustifiable.[4] The first development is often identified as the very heart
of humanitarianism. Historian Norman Fiering is surely on to something

when he defines "modern humanitarianism" in just this way, as "the widespread inclination to protest against obvious and pointless physical suffering."[5] Something similar can be said about human rights in relation to status hierarchies: challenging them has been at the heart of what human rights are about.

These two developments are central elements of the modern "social imaginary," as the philosopher Charles Taylor uses the term to capture something "broader and deeper" than ideas or intellectual schemes. He uses the term to describe "the ways people imagine their social existence, how they fit together with others, how things go on between them and their fellows, the expectations that are normally met, and the deeper normative notions and images that underlie these expectations."[6] In this sense, various narrative forms, types of imagery, and repertoires for mobilizing collective action to alleviate suffering or to challenge status hierarchies can be viewed as key parts of the modern Western social imaginary.

Before considering the relations between the two developments, more substance must be given to each. Elements of the first included increasing philosophical attention to moral sentiments like compassion and sympathy, which was part of the spreading notion that human beings are naturally, perhaps irresistibly, moved to alleviate the suffering of others – a central character trait of the "man of feeling," who was such a prominent figure in eighteenth-century philosophy and literature.[7] There were also changing views of the individual body and its pains, and the rise of naturalistic as opposed to theistic accounts of suffering.[8] Beyond changing ideas, moral sentiment was mobilized in the form of "organized compassion," in social movements whose expressed aim was to reduce misery: from abolitionism to prison reform, to changing policies regarding poverty and mental illness, to campaigns against judicial torture.[9] The kind of sentimental narratives developed in the eighteenth century also made possible the powerful influence of Henry Dunant's passionate call to aid suffering soldiers in *A Memory of Solferino* (1862), the springboard for the founding of the Red Cross and the campaign to make war more humane. If there is a single thread running through these developments, it is how compassion has been socially mobilized in moving people to act, individually and in concert, to alleviate suffering. In this way, we can characterize a whole range of collective mobilizations under the heading of a "politics of suffering."

The best starting point for describing the second development is the status-leveling aims of the French Revolution. The philosopher Joel Feinberg describes precisely how "revolutionary the idea of equal human rights was" by contrasting it with European society prior to the

French Revolution, in which the "rights men had as a matter of status were theirs as royalty, nobility, clergy, serfs, and so on."[10] By contrast, "human rights, as a revolutionary idea, were associated with the idea of a single status society, where the powers of the high and mighty were limited everywhere by the rights of all persons derived from their 'status' as human beings."[11] In this sense, the French Revolution represents a sweeping break in its attempt to remake a modern social order without any status hierarchies. Other efforts have been less revolutionary, though typically quite radical. A "politics of status" is manifest whenever causes or campaigns reject inferior treatment, when the claims at stake are that the excluded be included, the oppressed liberated, or that those being ignored must count. If there is a single thread running through these developments, it is the way in which various social and political movements have mobilized the demand that no human being innately deserves a higher status than any other in the basic structures of a social or political order.

To capture the dynamism in these developments – that this is about ideals advanced by movements, not just intellectual debates about the nature of suffering or status – I refer to them as two forms of a "politics of humanity." A politics of suffering aims at alleviating human suffering, while a politics of equal status aims at elevating all human beings to the same status. But history is complicated; it is not always easy to place a single label on any particular movement. For example, some strands of anti-slavery activism sought to end abject misery while more radical strands aimed at abolishing status distinctions by making equal citizens out of former slaves. In fact, this difference is where I start in sketching four encounters, or in some cases missed encounters, between a politics of suffering and a politics of status.

Suffering without Status

The shared origins of humanitarianism and human rights, it is commonly said, can be grasped in eighteenth-century invocations of humanity. But starting there raises an immediate complication. While "humanity" could refer to a shared species category in that period, this was only one possible meaning. Another, dominant connotation was the humanity of the person who could feel for another, to humanity as a feeling of benevolence or sympathy for distress in some other being. This meant that appeals to humanity were often more about displaying and confirming one's *own* humanity than that of the other, and in a way that did not always challenge the belief that the creatures eliciting feelings of humanity were lesser beings.

In a brilliant essay, Lynn Festa analyzes how "most abolitionist writers" could slip almost indiscernibly between the two senses.[12] Not only were appeals to humanity ambiguous, but also the sentimental form they often took made such appeals doubly ambivalent. Although sentimental narratives could inspire readers to imagine new possibilities for alleviating the suffering of distant strangers, the structure of identification generated by sentimental sympathy often failed to support a stable definition of humanity. This weakness in the sentimental form of humanitarian sensibility – that it operates without a clear definition of humanity – was, as a practical matter, often a source of great strength. Being indiscriminate about content opened up the possibility for including all manner of populations – the impoverished, the disenfranchised, the enslaved – as worthy of sympathy, which could generate ameliorative action, without having to answer more difficult questions about moral status. The weakness in this mode of appeal is that without a categorical definition, specific individuals and groups can all too easily be "yo-yoed in and out of the human purview on a case-by-case basis."[13] In short, this way of deploying humanitarian sentiment provided a way of recognizing the needs of others while maintaining a hierarchy between a proximate community of affectively moved individuals and distant others who were often viewed more like sentimental objects. Sentimental appeals were not the only tool available to abolitionists. But Festa's work shows how powerful sentimental appeals were not always egalitarian, while more egalitarian status claims were often less influential. She rightly maintains that there is a "critical discontinuity between the sentimental basis of eighteenth-century humanitarian sensibility" and the more "categorical imperative of modern humanitarianism: its enjoinder to alleviate suffering based on" the equal value of all human beings.[14]

Imagining Equality

An altogether different tale about the power of sentimental stories is told by historian Lynn Hunt, who argues that mid-eighteenth-century sentimental literature is precisely what laid the groundwork for late eighteenth-century commitment to the Rights of Man. According to Hunt, a variety of cultural practices – in particular, reading immensely popular epistolary novels – led to new kinds of experience that ultimately led to radical social change. Such novels

made the point that all people are fundamentally similar because of their inner feelings, and many novels showcased in particular the desire for autonomy. In this way, reading novels created a sense of equality and empathy through passionate involvement in the narrative ... Epistolary novels taught their readers nothing less than a new psychology and in the process laid the foundations for a new social and political order.[15]

Hunt is rightly attentive to the degree to which the idea of equal rights "could only flourish when people learned to think of others as their equals, as like them in some fundamental fashion."[16] In effect, Hunt brings out the affective dimension of recognizing others as equals: "Equality was not just an abstract concept or a political slogan. It had to be internalized in some fashion."[17] She vividly captures the way in which various cultural practices transformed people's embodied and affective relations to one another through the experience of individual autonomy ("an increasing sense of the separation and sacredness of human bodies: your body is yours and my body is mine, and we should both respect the boundaries between each other's bodies") and empathy ("the recognition that others think and feel as we do, that our inner feelings are alike in some fundamental fashion").[18]

There is much worth exploring here in the idea that such cultural practices can enable people to imagine equality across various divides. But Hunt is on less stable ground in positing the historical link the way she does, between the rise of these practices and the later French Declaration of the Rights of Man (let alone the American Declaration of Independence) and subsequent struggles for equal rights. She concludes her book by provocatively maintaining that "the history of human rights shows that rights are best defended in the end by the feelings, convictions, and actions of multitudes of individuals, who demand responses that accord with their inner sense of outrage."[19] But the ways in which affective resources like outrage and indignation can be mobilized in struggles for rights is not a story Hunt's book actually tells. She leaves a gap between the practices she does analyze, which mobilize affect and rely on empathy in particular ways, and practices like social movements and struggles for rights, which may do similar things but in a way that the book fails to analyze.

Perhaps the most we can say is that Hunt uncovers a possible pathway from sentimental appeal to equal status. But Festa demonstrates just how unreliable such pathways can be. Indeed, even in the aftermath of the Declaration of the Rights of Man, as the next encounter shows, appeals to suffering could undermine the very equality that Hunt says they fostered.

The Politics of Pity

Hannah Arendt was the first critic to analyze the dangers posed to a politics of equal status by a politics of suffering – a kind of humanitarianization.

This critique, in *On Revolution*, is part of a larger worry about how public discourse on suffering in the eighteenth century undermined the political equality posited by the Rights of Man. Arendt was not just concerned about the pernicious aspects of a politics of suffering; she was deeply skeptical about the possibility of a genuine "politics" of suffering at all.[20] The argument depended on her distinction between compassion and pity, and on her understanding of the nature of democratic politics. Compassion, according to Arendt, is an affective response to particular individuals; it is "to be stricken with the suffering of someone else as though it were contagious."[21] Pity, on the other hand, is a more remote sentiment directed at an abstract suffering population – "it can reach out to the multitude."[22] Neither emotional response, Arendt argues, has a proper place within the politics of a democratic society of equal citizens.[23]

The philosopher Elizabeth Spelman aptly sums up Arendt's worry in terms of several related concerns: "One is that professions of compassion all too often are barely disguised forms of pity, that what is presented as an authentic and spontaneous concern for another human being is actually a selfish and cruel wallowing in the misfortune of others."[24] Second, while genuine compassion is both possible and superior to pity, compassion as defined by Arendt is apolitical. Its mode of directly sharing in the suffering of another is at odds with the kind of public debate and discussion she associates with shared political life. Finally, Arendt uses Robespierre's speaking and acting in the name of the suffering of *le peuple* to display the many dangers of public proclamations about others' suffering: it can be a way of declaring one's own virtue, it amplifies the distance between those who are not suffering and those who are, and it precludes the latter's participation in public discourse on their suffering by speaking in their name. The issue, Spelman rightly points out, is not whether Arendt's definitions of compassion, pity, or politics are decisive; rather, Arendt draws attention to perennial risks revolving around appeals to suffering and sentiment in politics.[25]

Arendt contrasts both compassion and pity with the kind of solidarity through which a group of individuals can potentially establish "a community of interest with the oppressed and exploited."[26] Rather than establish an inclusive community with the poor, the revolutionaries connected with them through pity. The political theorist Ayten Gündogdu maintains that "Arendt's critique suggests that the Jacobins took a profoundly anti-political approach to the Rights of Man ... Turning the poor into an undifferentiated mass of suffering victims, they undermined any possibility of organizing a politics centered on solidarity and equality."[27] If Festa's work shows how sentimental appeals to suffering can sustain hierarchy, Arendt raises the possibility that even the founding of a single-status society may not suffice in trying to avoid the pernicious effects of a politics of pity.[28] Nevertheless, a fourth case illuminates how new ways of mobilizing appeals to suffering can arise within such a single-status society.

The Politics of Dignity

The basic idea for this fourth encounter is that within the context of a social order in which the ideal of overcoming status hierarchies has taken root, certain forms of suffering that are integrally related to status take on a new salience – as experiences of "social suffering" that can be mobilized in struggles for equal status. The core of this dynamic is sketched by Jürgen Habermas in an essay exploring the connection between human dignity and human rights.[29] The rise in the eighteenth century of a modern single-status society, according to Habermas, gave rise to a transformation in the concept of dignity. While traditional forms of social dignity distinguish between higher and lower ranks, the new idea is that of human beings all having the same, very high rank.[30] This resulted from a fusion of three elements: the idea of dignity as a concrete social status was combined with a second, moral element – the moral idea of equal respect for all human beings – and a third, legal element – the idea of a legal person as a bearer of rights. The point is to see how equal dignity became a modern legal concept associated with the status citizens are accorded in a political order of subjects with equal rights.

Once this status is instantiated it can give rise, Habermas argues, to a dynamic social process in which experiences of violated dignity give rise to further claims of two basic types: claims for extending equal status to all and demands for expanding the content of the rights accorded to all. As T. H. Marshall put this in a classic essay, the "urge toward a fuller measure of equality" took the form of "an enrichment of the stuff of which the status is made and an increase in the number of those on whom the status is bestowed."[31] However fused these two moves may be in practice, for analytical purposes we can refer to struggles for equal status and struggles over what equal status entails. Habermas stresses that the specific meaning of human dignity, and so the need for particular basic rights, only becomes apparent through specific violations of dignity, as experienced by, for instance, marginalized social classes, disparaged minorities, undocumented immigrants and asylum seekers, and so forth. He refers to "historical experiences of humiliation and degradation" and how such "political outrage could find expression in the language of positive law."[32] The main point is that, in the context of an ostensibly single-status society, the appeal to social suffering can become a mobilizing force – by those suffering, and in generating solidarity from others – around equal status. Habermas merely provides an initial sketch. One way of filling it in would be to analyze various social movements against inferior treatment and forms of "social cruelty."[33]

To sum this up in relation to the other positive encounter between suffering and status: Hunt identifies a possible pathway from sentimental stories of suffering to imagining equality, while Habermas detects an ongoing role for appeals to social suffering in struggles to achieve equal status. The two critical takes, on the other hand, warn that the possible pathway is unreliable (Festa) and that the promise of equality can be undermined by a politics of pity (Arendt).

These four cases are not the only possible ways in which appeals to suffering and claims to status have intersected. But they are crucial cases for analyzing the relations between human rights and humanitarianism against the background of the relation between suffering and status, from the eighteenth century up to the present.

Rights and Status

The full story of how humanitarian discourse incorporated equal status – the shift from the sentimental to the categorical, as Festa puts it – remains to be told. This is one case in which asking whether the term "human rights" was literally invoked as part of an earlier discourse of "humanity" can distract from the equally important task of identifying precisely when, where, and to what ends the discourse of humanity has invoked conceptions of equal human status. The latter is evident, for example, in Dunant's aim of caring for injured soldiers on both sides of battle. It is surely evident in the early twentieth-century shift by aid organizations from focusing on "identity" (e.g., concern for co-religionists) to "need" in deciding who was worthy of their relief efforts.[34] Today, a "principle of humanity" is widely acknowledged to be a core tenet of humanitarian organizations, as evident in Jean Pictet's formulation of a central aim of the ICRC: "To prevent and alleviate human suffering wherever it may be found."[35] In this sense, the equal value of humanity is now widely considered a core norm of humanitarian practice.

Nonetheless, it is crucial to distinguish this important advance within the sphere of humanitarianism from the more radical version of status egalitarianism found in human rights practice. In a humanitarian context, the notion of equal status means that the only legitimate response to the question "Whose suffering matters?" is "Every human being's." As a principle of universal inclusion, it forbids discrimination when respond-ing to suffering. When it comes to human rights, however, the notion of equal status not only signals that everyone matters, but also brings with it a particularly robust way of saying how everyone counts – as a subject of rights – that has sweeping implications for how societies are organized. In short, when thinking about equal status it is important to keep in view the difference between saying *the suffering of all human beings matters* and saying *the equal status of all human beings as rights-bearers must be respected within every social and political order.* Here I want to focus on some of the implications of the latter claim.

There are different ways in which the equal status of rights-bearers gets instantiated. The primary site for the politics of equal dignity sketched above has been the politics of equal citizenship carried out over the last 200 years within the nation-state. But one way of thinking about developments in international human rights practice since the Universal Declaration of Human Rights (1948) is that the aim has been to secure this status for the individual both within each state and to some extent beyond states. Certainly nobody would claim that international human rights practice creates a single-status world society along the lines of a democratic nation-state. But there is a sense in which a clear aim (or effect, insofar as it is effective) of contemporary human rights practice is to elevate the status of certain types of claims to the international level and thereby elevate the status of each person. In his account of contemporary human rights practice, the political philosopher Charles Beitz maintains that "the doctrine of human rights is the articulation in the public morality of world politics of the idea that each person is a subject of global concern."[36] This global concern is expressed in practice by articulating a set of urgent individual interests that must be protected, and establishing a set of formal and infor-mal mechanisms for doing so at both domestic and international levels.

The philosopher Allen Buchanan argues that one of the most striking features of the international system of human rights is "the fact that, taken as a whole, this system of rights expresses a strong commitment to equal-ity of basic status for all people."[37] He calls this "status egalitarian func-tion" one of the primary functions of international legal human rights. The point of calling it "status" equality is to capture the idea of "equal standing" and distinguish it from distributive equality (regarding the distribution of resources, opportunities, or outcomes).[38] Buchanan cites five aspects of the international human rights system that are key to its performing the function of protecting equal status. These features display two aspects of the radical nature of the human rights system, and its commitment to the equal status of each person along with a long sub-stantive list of rights guaranteed to each person:

1. Inclusive (or universal) ascription of rights (international legal rights are ascribed not just to men, or whites, or so-called civilized peoples, but to all people).
2. Equality of rights for all (the *same* rights are ascribed to all in a very strong sense: they are understood to have (a) the same *content* (including the same correlative duties), (b) the same *weight*, and (c) the same conditions of abrogation, that is, the factors that allow abrogation do not discriminate among persons.
3. States are obligated to make *everyone's* rights effective, that is, they are not allowed to make any distinctions among persons that would disadvantage anyone with regard to the effectiveness of their rights.
4. Robust equality before the law (including an extensive set of *equal* due process rights and the requirement that governments are to ensure that domestic legal systems provide effective legal remedies for all when the rights are violated, with no allowance for discrimination among persons as to the legal remedies to be made available).
5. The inclusion of strong rights against discrimination on grounds of race or gender (where this includes both formal legal discrimination and informal practices of discrimination in the public and private sectors).[39]

It is certainly worth stressing the many ways in which that system still does not, as a matter of principle or practice, strive to overcome the material inequality that plagues the world today.[40] Nonetheless, in the context of comparing human rights and humanitarianism, we should not lose sight of how radical it is to posit that every human being must be respected as having equal standing to press their claims.

Even when humanitarian and human rights overlap in practice on some particularly important human interest or need, there is still a difference in the work each typically tries to do. Humanitarian action often provides what someone needs (and can use the language of rights in doing so), but human rights work, at its best, attempts to put one in a better position to stand up and effectively demand what one needs. In meeting needs, humanitarian actors typically try to carve out a "humanitarian space" from the surrounding context of social and political conflict – a kind of moral space, metaphorically and in reality, in which the humanitarian agent can come to the aid of the beneficiary.[41] Human rights work, on the other hand, tries to alter the social and political context itself, transforming it into one in which each individual can effectively make claims. This is the core of its status-elevating function.

Philosophers like Joel Feinberg have long stressed the kind of self-respect and respect for others that is constituted in this way among equal rights-bearers. "Having rights," he argues, "enables us to . . . look others in the eye, and to feel in some fundamental way the equal of anyone."[42] Of course, having equal rights is not the only way to constitute equality, but struggles to attain the status of rights-bearers are paradigmatic struggles for equality in modern societies.[43] When people struggle to become bearers of equal rights, they struggle to elevate their status. This practical political relation between human rights and status is evident in the work rights can do, or more precisely, what people do with them: they claim them. By positing that anyone anywhere can make such claims, the status-elevating features of the international human rights system can be empowering. As Beitz puts it:

> This empowerment is in part a result of the change in self-conception that the practice of human rights can induce among those who participate in it: they are encouraged to conceive of themselves, and to act, as "makers of claims." This is most obvious when legal enforcement is possible, but there is also a reflection of it in the political practice of human rights.[44]

Individuals who encounter human rights practice in this way "learn to act with the dignity of persons who can stand on their own feet."[45]

This is a refrain often heard in accounts of rights education and the role of rights consciousness. For example, in her ethnographic work on the "vernacularization" of human rights around the world, particularly in the area of combatting violence against women, the anthropologist Sally Engle Merry notes how, as local activists "promote the ideology of human rights, some women say they have learned to stand up for themselves."[46] It is important to distinguish this powerful status-elevating function of human rights, related to the activity of claiming them, from other, pernicious effects of human rights practice brought to the fore in recent ethnographic work on human rights. For instance, the anthropologist Lori Allen has developed a compelling critique of the role of the "human rights industry" in the rise of cynicism toward human rights in occupied Palestine. Nevertheless, she also carves out space for a positive conception of human rights as the basis for claiming and making demands: "Every protest against occupation, every objection to the indignities it inflicts, every effort to free political prisoners, and every vote cast is an assertion of dignity and, in some way, a demand for human rights."[47] This aspect of the political character of human rights tends to come out in approaches that contrast concrete political struggles for rights with bureaucratic or legalistic aspects of the global human rights system.[48]

Ethnographic work can bring out the emancipatory potential of human rights practice by showing how it poses a radical challenge to status hierarchies around the globe. A similar point can be made in relation to historical work. For this status-elevating function of human rights practice provides a salient point of continuity between post-1948 international human rights and the longer tradition of claiming rights within nation-states. For some purposes, such as trying to explain the sudden rise of human rights rhetoric in the 1970s, stressing discontinuities in the history of human rights is essential.[49] But there are also continuities, and they are not always found in the concept or content of human rights being used in a particular context, but in the common function of rights practices more generally. When a practice posits equal status for all as rights-bearers – as the French Declaration and the Universal Declaration of Human Rights did – it poses a direct challenge to status hierarchies, at least to the extent to which social movements or legal institutions put some force behind those claims. In this way, there are continuities in the status-elevating function of human rights practice from late eighteenth-century struggles for rights within nation-states up to contemporary human rights.[50] This radical promise of a politics of equal status animates human rights practice at its best, even if – as Arendt pointed out long ago, and contemporary critics continue to demonstrate – it can be undermined by a politics of pity.

Stories of Suffering

Just as it is important to distinguish equal value as instantiated in humanitarian practice from the more robust status-elevating function of human rights practice, it is important to distinguish different ways of telling tales about suffering. In short, the politics of suffering should not be reduced to a politics of pity. The standard view of humanitarian narratives is that they mobilize compassion in order to motivate action to alleviate the suffering of distant strangers. This picture needs to be expanded by noting two other kinds of story about suffering, both of which aim to move addressees beyond compassion: the first does so by drawing attention not only to distant suffering but also to distant perpetrators;[51] the second more radically challenges addressees by directly implicating them in the suffering. By not stopping at compassion, these types of narratives at least have the potential to move beyond a politics of pity.

Regarding the first alternative form, in his classic study on distant suffering, the sociologist Luc Boltanski traces eighteenth-century developments in various discourses about suffering – in pamphlets, political essays, and novels – that challenged spectators to take a committed stance on the spectacle of distant suffering. Boltanski pays particular attention to different ways in which emotional commitments are structured and organized in the face of distant suffering, distinguishing two directions moral sentiment can be channeled:

Tender-heartedness brings into the political world, that is to say into the world of considerations and actions at a distance, resources drawn from compassion, it extends over a range of *sentiments* and it points toward *beneficent* action. *Indignation* is supported by justice and, more precisely by political constructions which establish the possibility of a just world and, in a style which can be called *pamphleteering . . .* it points toward *denunciation* and *accusation.*[52]

The spectator may be drawn to one or another emotional response in part depending on the content of the image or "proposal" made by some form of media. Of course one can reject the proposal. But if the spectator accepts it, the content may move her in one of two directions. Drawing on two contemporary examples, Boltanski maintains one can "be indignant at the sight of children in tears being herded by armed soldiers" or "be moved by the effort of this nurse whose hands are held out to someone who is starving."[53] The key is that the initial moment of concern for the fate of a suffering stranger can go in different ways. It can remain within the register of compassion, with its pull toward beneficent action, or it can shift toward indignation at the sight of a perpetrator, pulling more toward denunciation and action oriented toward stopping the one causing the harm.

A second form of humanitarian narrative directly implicates addressees as part of the cause of suffering. Instead of simply saying "we must *help* them," it says "we must *stop causing them harm.*" Quaker abolitionist John Woolman was an early innovator here. A primary aim of his work, as historian Thomas Haskell illuminates in a classic essay, was to convince slaveholders of the distant consequences of their conduct by getting them to see that the "geographical remoteness of the scene of initial enslavement" could not provide a defense even for benevolent slaveholders.[54] As Woolman wrote in a 1746 essay: "To willingly join with unrighteousness to the injury of men who live some thousands of miles off is the same in substance as joining with it to the injury of our neighbours."[55] According to Haskell, Woolman and other early abolitionists were not necessarily more morally sensitive to others' suffering than earlier human beings had been. Rather, a shift in their cognitive ability to discern the kind of causal chains that had not been evident in the past enhanced their sense of moral responsibility for suffering at a distance. Haskell's explanatory story is that modern market relations brought about this transformation. Woolman, for instance, clearly saw how supply and demand worked: "The idea that by owning a slave (or even a product of slave labor)," as Haskell puts it, "one helped constitute the demand without which suppliers of slave labor could not stay in business gained plausibility in the decades ahead[.]"[56] Indeed, Adam Hochschild aptly captures this aspect of British abolitionism in saying that their "first job was to make Britons understand what lay behind the sugar they ate, the tobacco they smoked, the coffee they drank."[57] These humanitarian narratives do not simply draw on sentiment, but also point to causal connections that implicate addressees as sharing the responsibility for the suffering.

To take another example, consider the iconic image of the nameless starving child – rightly critiqued for attempting to elicit sympathy without providing any political or historical context. Even this imagery has, in classic cases, been combined with causal stories that make it function quite differently. For example, the founder of Save the Children, Eglantyne Jebb, no stranger to using images of starving children, was arrested in 1919 for distributing a pamphlet in Trafalgar Square entitled, "A Starving Baby and Our Blockade has Caused This."[58] This was around the time she formed the Famine Council, whose aim was to end the British blockade that was a contributing cause to postwar famine in Europe. In this case, it is the appeal to politics and collective action – the call to work together to stop this – that moves attention to suffering beyond just compassion for the suffering stranger.

These are just a few examples. More work needs to be done to excavate this theme in the history of humanitarianism. Bruce Robbins has recently proposed a "revisionist view" of the history of humanitarianism that would focus less on the "appeal to empathy" and more on "a somewhat more rarefied feeling: that your fate is *causally linked*, however obscurely, with the fates of distant and sometimes suffering others." Robbins maintains that "the idea that I am causally responsible for someone's suffering appeals to something in me that is stronger than fairness or empathy."[59] Even if it is stronger, it is arguably some combination of empathy and a causal link that does the work in these narratives. The causal story would only work if at one end of the causal chain there is someone suffering and at the other end there is someone sympathetic to the suffering.

It is often forgotten how the historian Thomas Laqueur, in his classic essay on humanitarian narratives, linked the two.[60] Laqueur was a forerunner in identifying core elements of eighteenth-century humanitarian narratives, and is often cited for stressing how they relied on details about suffering bodies to engender compassion. But he also explicitly builds on Haskell's classic study in analyzing how these stories display causal chains connecting readers to suffering bodies.[61] As Laqeuer put it:

most importantly for the actual politics of reform, humanitarian narrative exposes the lineaments of causality and of human agency: ameliorative action is represented as possible, effective, and therefore morally imperative. Someone or something did something that causes pain, suffering, or death and that could, under certain circumstances, have been avoided or mitigated.[62]

This narrative form was found in a range of genres including novels, autopsy reports and other clinical reports, all of which created "sympathetic passions" that "bridged the gulf between facts, compassion, and action."[63] What is less often stressed about Laqueur's account, perhaps because it is at odds with the dominant way of construing humanitarian narratives today, is that one of his primary examples was the new genre of "social inquiry" exemplified by parliamentary commissions and reports:

> Beginning in the early nineteenth century, variously constituted committees and commissions produced an extraordinary number of hitherto untold stories of human suffering ... Like novels and medical case histories, the parliamentary inquiry is characterized by rich layers of detail and by a more or less explicit commitment to expose the naturalistic origins of suffering.[64]

Laqueur focuses specifically on an 1835 parliamentary committee that began the process of turning mining deaths into a public issue and cause for reform. Prior to such inquiries, little was known about the dangers of mining. But as the genre developed, what had earlier been considered "God's work and outside the bounds of human agency" would later be attributed to human causes: "improper ventilation" and the "greed of mine owners."[65] The upshot is that these narratives "locate the lives and sufferings of others in a social context, making them intelligible to readers of other places and periods. [They] are the product, and in some measure the creator, of a mass public that feels implicated in the particular evils that befall others and able to control these evils by incorporating them into narrative and action."[66] In short, there is an entire genre of "social inquiry" – focused on tracing social causes of suffering and implicating a responsible public – that should not be ignored when we talk of "humanitarian narratives" and the politics of suffering.[67]

Such causal stories have the potential to challenge addressees and make it harder for them to wallow in pity. As Susan Sontag provocatively wrote, "so far as we feel sympathy, we feel we are not accomplices to what caused the suffering. Our sympathy proclaims our innocence as well as our impotence. To that extent, it can be (for all our good intentions) an impertinent – if not inappropriate – response."[68] She rightly indicates that our feelings of sympathy or compassion are criticizable in those cases in which they reveal a false judgment about either the social causes of suffering or one's blameless relation to those causes.[69] One can feel compassion for famine victims, but if one knows the truth – famines have political causes; there are always responsible parties – then indignation at an injustice is the proper response. To go one step further: denouncing distant perpetrators can be easy enough, but pity can find a home here too if one still sees oneself only in the superior position of potential helper. That position collapses, and with it pity as primary affect, when one is implicated not only in not helping, but also in contributing to a harm. In short, the toolbox for mobilizing concern for distant suffering has long included tools that go beyond mobilizing compassion, some of which have the potential to take a politics of suffering beyond a politics of pity.

Twentieth-Century Iterations

The radical potential of both a politics of equal status and a politics of suffering often goes unrealized. That this has turned out to be the case when the two have intersected within contemporary iterations of human rights and humanitarianism is no surprise. Diagnosing why, or how this potential might be actualized, are important, though far from simple, tasks. One obstacle has been that, until recently, academic study of humanitarianism and human rights largely proceeded on parallel tracks. Even prominent promoters of the view that a significant shift in the politics of Western societies occurred in the latter half of the twentieth century, a shift embodied in the rise of either the international human rights movement (Moyn) or a form of humanitarian government (Fassin), had little to say about the other phenomenon in their ground-breaking works.[70] This is now changing, and provides the impetus for the current volume.

In this concluding section, I sketch some aspects of the *shared* politics of suffering that animated the work of humanitarian and human rights organizations at a key turning point in the 1960s and 1970s. This politics of suffering embodied core features of what Laqueur identified as humanitarian narratives: attention to suffering bodies – in this case victims of famine and torture – and causal connections to suffering. To the extent that it is still a compelling force today, this politics of suffering leave us with considerable challenges: Can causal narratives effectively draw attention to the larger structures that cause suffering? Could a more robust global politics of equal status get a foothold without being undermined by attenuated forms of the politics of suffering?

Historians have begun exploring ways in which the human rights breakthrough of the 1970s drew heavily on a politics of suffering. As Daniel Sargent puts it:

while human rights are not commensurate with humanitarianism, their rise depended on engagement with suffering human beings, from Biafran infants to Soviet political prisoners. Seeking to redress distant misery in the name of natural rights, human rights advocates plumbed deep historical wells.[71]

This suggests that an upsurge in concern for distant suffering bodies laid the groundwork for the rise of the international human rights movement.[72] The explanatory move here is reminiscent of Hunt's thesis that an eighteenth-century humanitarian culture laid the ground for the rise of the Rights of Man. If Hunt is right about the eighteenth century, does the latter half of the twentieth century reveal a similar pattern? More critically, one could situate Hunt's project within the aftermath of the twentieth-century breakthrough of human rights itself.[73] Perhaps a politics of suffering, which saw a dramatic boost in the late 1960s, was indeed crucial to the breakthrough of human rights in the 1970s, and this in turn influenced Hunt's search for a similar catalyst for the Rights of Man.

I leave this question to historians of both periods. But it does not seem incidental that anti-torture politics played a key part in both Hunt's story about the Rights of Man and the rise of an international human rights movement in the 1970s. In fact, a key episode in the rise of the contemporary anti-torture movement can be traced to 1968. This was the same year that the response to the civil war and famine in Biafra initiated a turning point in the history of humanitarianism. Rather than positing a "humanitarian" catalyst for the rise of "human rights," however, it is more apt to note how fluid things were during that period. Various past campaigns, movements, and organizations that mobilized around responding to distant suffering had made certain kinds of narratives available, even as the new dispensations – what it would eventually mean to be a "humanitarian NGO" or part of "the human rights movement" – had not yet crystallized. Here I want to juxtapose two episodes – campaigns on behalf of torture victims in Greece and starving Biafrans – to illuminate the politics of suffering that they share, and then stress how Amnesty International and Médecins Sans Frontières (MSF) were hybrid organizations from the start.

The historian Barbara Keys sheds light on the early work of Amnesty, arguing that their anti-torture activism in the wake of the 1967 coup in Greece "helped lay the groundwork for the worldwide 'human rights boom' of the 1970s."[74] Amnesty was little known in the United States at the time. Its two reports on torture in Greece were the first of their kind and, coming out in January and April 1968, they could hardly compete for news coverage with the Vietnam War or student protests, let alone the avalanche of coverage soon to come out on Biafra. But Keys maintains that,

Greece generated enough attention in the United States to offer a testing ground for new strategies of political mobilization ... By the mid-1970s, condemnations of torture, tested in the context of opposition to the colonels' regime in Greece, had become a critical catalyst for surging interest in human rights. In the public mind, torture attained the status of the most recognized and most reviled of all human rights abuses.[75]

Holocaust consciousness provided a new urgency to the long-standing use of causal narratives to invoke a sense of responsibility: "A new sense of moral responsibility for crimes committed by U.S. allies coincided with rising public consciousness of the Holocaust, the central lesson of which equated silence with complicity."[76] The campaign challenged Americans to consider why their tax money should support governments that relied on torture. The solution: cut off US military aid to Greece, which the US House of Representatives would do in 1971.

Similarly, many British campaigners on behalf of Biafra, during a period in which starving "Biafra babies" plastered the covers of newspapers and magazines in the summer of 1968, were critical of the British government for providing support to the Nigerian federal government. The book *Biafra Story*, in which pro-Biafran journalist Frederick Forsyth likened British support of the Nigerians in their treatment of Biafra to the treatment of Jews in World War II, sold out in a matter of weeks in 1969.[77] Historian Lasse Heerten has argued that the language of genocide used to draw attention to Biafra – some worried about an "African Auschwitz" – helped constitute the meanings and public understandings of both events, in a way that summoned the imperative to act.

Indeed, a common theme in this period – from protesting US support of Greek torture or British support for Nigeria's alleged genocidal aims – was a worry about complicity with distant suffering.[78] This worry is central to the origin story of MSF, an organization as innovative for humanitarian practice as Amnesty International (AI) was for human rights advocacy. The now-familiar story is that some Red Cross doctors working in Biafra decided not to uphold the traditional International Committee of the Red Cross mandate of remaining neutral. Among those who decided to break with protocol and speak out was Bernard Kouchner who, upon returning to France, helped organize public events to raise awareness and founded a pro-Biafra committee. As Kouchner later wrote, "by keeping silent, we doctors were accomplices in the systematic massacre of a population."[79] He would ultimately go on to help found MSF in 1971. Even if there is some myth-making involved in the story, the salient point is that "witnessing" came to be an important part of MSF's modified version of humanitarian practice.[80] In taking up the latter as part of their mandate, MSF injected the kind of activism now viewed as central to human rights advocacy into a decidedly humanitarian context.

If MSF's innovation was to combine the politics of denunciation with the mandate of direct care for suffering individuals, Amnesty's innovation was to bring a kind of direct connection with suffering individuals into an organization whose mandate was advocacy. "What made Amnesty unique," Keys argues, "was that it focused on individual victims and involved its members directly in helping them."[81] This is evident in the letter-writing campaigns for prisoners of conscience that Amnesty International pioneered in the 1960s. Consider Stephen Hopgood's vivid reflections on their power:

One early Mexican evening in August 2003, walking up the stone steps into a large meeting hall, I along with the gathered leaders of Amnesty was confronted by an ex-brigadier-general, Jose Gallardo, and his family, surrounded by 35,000 letters. These were the messages he had received in prison from Amnesty members. They spilled out across the floor . . . Letter after letter expressed the same sentiment: you are not alone; don't give up hope. Here was an almost tangible kind of moral force. No wonder released prisoners talk with such wonder about receiving these letters.[82]

Here we see a form of solidarity with suffering that was forged by a direct connection to suffering individuals – a mode of humanitarian action at the heart of human rights activism. In short, stories connecting people with distant suffering and concerns about complicity with the causes of that suffering – central elements of at least some strands of eighteenth- and nineteenth-century "humanitarian narratives" – were crucial during this breakthrough period and inspired innovations in both humanitarian and human rights practice. Focusing on suffering individuals did not turn Amnesty into a "humanitarian organization," nor did the practice of witnessing transform MSF into a "human rights organization." Analyzing the shared politics of suffering animating their practice in that period may tell us more about them and that historical moment than if we insist on categorizing these organizations solely in terms of human rights or humanitarianism.

Turning from suffering to status, we can see the shared politics of status embodied in both the witnessing practiced by MSF and the aim of much human rights advocacy and activism – the demand that victims not be ignored. This as one of the core status-elevating elements of the politics of humanity today. Speaking out by, and on behalf of, the suffering and the oppressed can raise their status by making them into subjects of global concern. "We matter" or "These people matter" – that is the base level of public recognition of equal status called for in such campaigns. But how people come to matter also matters – an eighteenth-century lesson that is still relevant. A common critique of humanitarian discourse and practice today is that it can reduce those who are suffering into speechless objects – mere victims as opposed to subjects capable of speaking and acting.[83] Many critics draw on the philosopher Giorgio Agamben's notion of "bare life" to criticize a range of humanitarian practices that only sustain the barest form of survival rather than supporting the social and political lives of human beings. Contemporary humanitarian practice is infused with references to human dignity, but too often it merely preserves "existence while deferring the very dignity ... it seeks."[84] Equal status can lack a foothold in such contexts, in part because the aim of alleviating suffering always embodies some degree of hierarchy: someone is suffering and someone else is in a position to help. In practice the hierarchy is not always pernicious, and can be mitigated, but it is hard to eliminate it entirely.[85]

Human rights might be thought to be inherently immune to this danger, for the status-elevating features of human rights practice work against this asymmetry in self-other relations and pose a challenge to hierarchical relations. While humanitarian work always requires a needy beneficiary, human rights work can provide tools to those protesting their own treatment. Those whose status is at stake may become an object of concern for others, but they can also (ideally always) actively take part as subjects in struggles to enhance their own status. That is how human rights practice at its best should function. But reality often falls short. Echoing Arendt's worry that a narrow focus on suffering undermines the political force of the Rights of Man, critics today worry about the anti-political effect a humanitarian lens has on the contemporary politics of human rights.[86] The core worry can be described in terms of suffering and status. When the focus is on suffering, particularly suffering bodies, subjects of human rights violations tend to be viewed, and sometimes treated, merely as passive victims or objects rather than as active subjects of rights.[87]

Keeping such pathologies in view is essential. Equally important is that ideals not be reduced to practical pathologies.[88] Overcoming them in practice is no simple task, but there are ways forward. For instance, sympathetic critics of humanitarian practice like political theorist Jennifer Rubenstein have mapped out ways in which humanitarian international nongovernmental organizations (INGOs) can ensure that their commitments to saving lives and alleviating suffering do not undermine norms of justice and the equal dignity of beneficiaries.[89] Importantly, Rubenstein maintains that such INGOs must take greater responsibility for both the contributions they make to the global system of which they are a part and the influence they have on the public's understanding of the nature and causes of crises, poverty, and suffering more generally. The general lesson here is perhaps that the more robust causal stories – focusing on systems and structures – that have played a smaller part in the history of humanitarianism need a larger role in the politics of humanity today. As Sontag puts it, regarding ubiquitous images of suffering:

To set aside the sympathy we extend to others beset by war and murderous politics for a reflection on how our privileges are located on the same map as their suffering, and may – in ways we might prefer not to imagine – be linked to their suffering, as the wealth of some may imply the destitution of others, is a task for which the painful, stirring images supply only an initial spark.[90]

Such reflection is crucial, and is the kind that takes humanitarian and human rights practice beyond drawing attention to distant suffering, beyond inspiring compassion for victims or indignation at perpetrators, to implicate all of us in the larger structures for which we share responsibility – structures that cause suffering and oppression and from which many of us benefit.[91] Much of the unrealized radical potential of both a politics of equal status and a politics of suffering may lie here.

Of course much more needs to be said in telling the story of how human rights and humanitarianism relate. My aim has been to show how that story must include the rise of and relation between two explosive ideals that coalesced in eighteenth-century Western societies, have had a deep and lasting impact on modern life, and whose radical potential has yet to be realized. Whatever the future holds for human rights and humanitarianism, it is hard to imagine a world in which the desire to eliminate needless human suffering dies or struggles against status hierarchies disappear.

3 Humanitarianism and Human Rights in Morality and Practice*

Charles R. Beitz

My starting point is the conjunction of two observations. First, the portion of public international law that takes the individual human person as its subject conventionally divides into two branches: international humanitarian law (IHL) and international human rights law (IHRL), each with its own founding documents, scope of application, and institutional structure. Canonically the domain of IHL is the conduct of armed conflict whereas the domain of IHRL is (or, anyway, was initially imagined to be) governments' treatment of their people in peacetime. Second, within what we might call the world of transnational social action, we find what seems at least superficially to be the same distinction, between humanitarian action and action to protect human rights, each with its own organizational networks and culture. Humanitarian action tends to be regarded as a more-or-less immediate and politically neutral response to suffering whereas human rights action typically presents itself as a longer-term and inevitably political response to various kinds of harms brought about by the actions or omissions of governments and, occasionally, of other agents. The distinction has come under stress in both domains for some practical reasons we shall come to.

For the purposes of this chapter, I shall consider humanitarianism and human rights as the subjects of distinct normative practices expressed in both international law and transnational social action. My question is whether the distinction as we find it in practice can accurately be seen as grounded on a moral distinction – the familiar and deeply rooted one between beneficence and justice. The question arises because something like the latter distinction seems to be embedded in the norms of these practices and in much of the public discourse surrounding them. This should not be surprising. Beneficence and justice are the two principal other-regarding virtues, or classes of duty, found in the history of ethics in the West and in the moral senses of many people today. Some philosophers consider the distinction between them to run deep. It is natural – for a political theorist, at any rate – to wonder whether the mapping of these two practices onto two distinct social virtues might illuminate in some way the corresponding divisions in law and practice.

I begin, by way of introduction, by saying more about the idea of a practice in general and about the practices of humanitarianism and human rights as I understand them. In that context I say briefly why one might be tempted to interpret these practices as manifestations of the distinction between beneficence and justice, or doing good and doing right (or, more exactly, relieving harms and remedying injustices). As I then observe, there has been some blurring of the lines between these practices in the last few decades even though there has been a tendency within each practice to maintain its normative self-understanding. In the third section, I turn to the distinction between beneficence and justice considered as distinct moral virtues and try to describe briefly how philosophers who have thought the distinction basic to our moral sense have understood it. This is important because one line of philosophical thought about the distinction has penetrated deeply into what we might call common-sense morality. I also note some respects in which the philosophical distinction might seem to be problematic. With this as background we can ask how well the philosophical distinction fits the distinction as we observe it in law and practice. To anticipate, the answer is: not well. In the final section I ask what we might learn from this about the nature of the difference between humanitarianism and human rights, understood as social practices, and about the idea of social practice itself.

Two Sets of Norms, Two Social Practices

The aims and motivation of contemporary humanitarian practice are conventionally presented as deriving from the origins of IHL in the first Geneva Convention of 1864 and the founding of the International Committee of the Red Cross (ICRC). The conventional presentation is not wrong but it is incomplete. It neglects to take into account the growth of interest in ideas of sympathy, humanity, and beneficence in the philosophy and literature of the previous hundred years. It also fails to recognize various elements of what we might classify as humanitarian action in the earlier nineteenth century – for example, in the anti-slavery movement's objections to slavery as cruel and inhumane.[1] Nevertheless, the conventional story is correct that the circumstances of the origins of IHL were critical for the subsequent development of the culture and practice of humanitarianism. At the center of the story is the response to the terrible suffering of soldiers at the Battle of Solferino, famously described by Henry Dunant in *A Memory of Solferino*.[2] Dunant was instrumental in both the founding of the predecessor organization of the ICRC in 1863 and the movement for an international agreement relating to the relief of wounded soldiers that produced the first Geneva Convention.[3] At the outset IHL consisted of a set of rules for the protection of sick and wounded soldiers on the battlefield. It was revised and extended in the Geneva Conventions of 1906 and 1929 and comprehensively reframed in the Geneva Conventions of 1949 in light of the experience of World War II. Today IHL extends protection mainly to four categories of persons affected by armed conflict: sick and wounded soldiers in the field, wounded sailors at sea, prisoners of war, and noncombatants in war zones. The reformulation of these protections in the 1949 conventions shifts the characterization of the protections from duties of states to rights of individuals.[4]

Today, the idea of "humanitarianism" in international life has a broader range of reference than its embodiment in international law might suggest. It applies to at least two other realms of action in addition to IHL. One is the expanding sphere of international and transnational action in response to various kinds of emergencies, ranging from those brought about by armed conflict to those brought about by natural and human-induced disasters – "emergency humanitarianism," as Michael Barnett calls it.[5] The other is action in response to what are perceived as the causes of suffering and harm. Barnett calls this "alchemical" humanitarianism ("structural" might be more neutral). He gives development, peace building, and community empowerment as examples.[6] The distinction between these referents is blurred by several facts; for example, some of the agents involved in monitoring and responding to violations of international humanitarian law are also involved in peacetime humanitarian action (e.g., Red Cross/Red Crescent); some humanitarian emergencies (e.g., refugees and migrants) are caused by armed conflict even if some of their victims can only be considered "victims of armed conflict" by a stretch; the application of international humanitarian law to non-international armed conflict is unsettled; and emergency relief in some circumstances cannot be separated from structural assistance.

Notwithstanding the blurred lines, each of the three branches of humanitarian law and practice very clearly has distinct core concerns. This is especially pronounced for what I have labeled structural humanitarianism, which is not plausibly seen historically as an outgrowth of IHL or of the culture surrounding it. This diversity within humanitarian practice is something we shall return to. For the moment, the point I want to emphasize is that many people, including many practitioners, regard all three branches as expressions of a single, common normative posture, typically seen as a desire to reduce avoidable suffering to the human person and to remedy its effects.[7]

The history of human rights is more complicated.[8] Arguably something like human rights can be found in the history of international thought as early as Grotius, if not earlier. In more modern times the idea of international protection of human rights emerged in the negotiations for the Treaty of Versailles at the end of World War I. A human rights movement developed between the wars. Franklin Roosevelt included protection of "four freedoms" in his declaration of war aims early in World War II. All of this framed the effort to draft the 1948 Universal Declaration and the two international covenants – on Civil and Political Rights and on Economic, Social and Cultural Rights, finally completed in 1966 but begun in the late 1940s. Several human rights conventions came after – for example, against discrimination, on the human rights of women and of children, and others. For each treaty there is an international "treaty body" that monitors compliance. The human rights treaties specify a long list of protections of important individual interests ranging from core interests in life and bodily integrity to interests in civil rights and liberties, health and wellbeing, and much else.

For our purposes, three points should be underscored. First, international human rights law purports to establish in-principle enforceable standards suitable to serve as bases of claims by individuals against their governments (and, increasingly, other agents). Second, the protected interests are diverse and the protections, taken seriously, are quite demanding. Third, in its structure international human rights law anticipates that failures of commission or omission by a government will become matters of international concern, a fact reflected most clearly in the establishment of "treaty bodies" to monitor compliance.

At the beginning I characterized IHRL as the law of peacetime, but this of course is only partly accurate. The threats that human rights are supposed to protect against can also occur in both international and noninternational war. This fact raises the question of how the two bodies of law are related to each other in cases of armed conflict. The question is controversial for reasons that are tangential to our concerns here.[9] But the issue is worth noting because, as we shall see, it has been one source of a blurring of the distinction.

As in the case of humanitarianism, a social practice has developed from the central norms of IHRL extending into the realm of political and social action. Particularly since the Helsinki Accords (1975), we have seen the elaboration of a transnational politics of human rights in which a variety of agents (e.g., states, international organizations, nongovernmental organizations, business firms) play differing roles either directly or indirectly in bringing pressure on governments for remediation of human rights failures. The significance of the legal background varies among these efforts: in some cases, IHRL serves mainly as a kind of political-moral authority for essentially political claims, whereas in others, political action aims to bring legal pressure on governments to adhere to their treaty commitments. Moreover, the legal/political distinction is permeable; for example, NGOs regularly play a supporting role in the work of the treaty bodies.[10]

Both of these practices are normative: they consist of sets of public norms that apply to a class of agents, a more-or-less widespread belief that these norms ought to be complied with, and some formal and informal processes for their propagation and enforcement.[11] I do not have a well-worked-out theory of normative practices but it seems clear that the main idea is of a system of public norms that people accept, and know that others accept, as providing at least pro tanto reasons for action. It also seems clear that within public normative practices, agents tend to develop shared understandings of the purposes of the norms as well as beliefs about how these purposes are best accomplished, and these develop into distinctive cultures. In comprehending the practices of humanitarianism and human rights, we should aim not only for a grasp of their contents, considered as sets of norms, but also for an understanding of the beliefs about the basis and significance of these norms typically shared by their participants.

At this fairly abstract level, the main difference between the two practices' normative cultures may seem obvious from what I have said. Humanitarian action is self-consciously concerned with protecting against or relieving immediate suffering or responding to immediate need, whereas human rights practice aims to bring it about that states (and sometimes other agents) satisfy the standards that compose international human rights doctrine. Corresponding to this contrast, the discourse of humanitarianism is typically a discourse of beneficence, humanity, or charity. As Barnett puts it, humanitarianism is fundamentally an "international ethic of care" that expresses itself in an expansion of benevolence ("a readiness to come to the assistance of those in need") beyond borders: it might thus be said that "humanitarianism implies going beyond the call of duty." On the other hand, the requirements of human rights are not "beyond the call of duty"; they are more like duties. Barnett writes that in contrast to humanitarianism, human rights are not occasions for benevolence but rely instead "on a discourse of rights."[12] In philosophy we associate rights with justice, and it is not uncommon (although it might be an overstatement) to conceive of human rights as norms of global justice. One might almost say that the interpretive mapping of IHL and IHRL onto traditional ideas of beneficence and justice is baked into the social practices surrounding these bodies of law. I will not devote more time to documenting this claim, but let me mention one influential and familiar source. He is Jean Pictet, probably the most important contributor to the development of IHL in the postwar period and the most prominent theorist of the ICRC's mission. In a passage frequently quoted in the literature of humanitarianism, Pictet wrote that "modern humanitarianism" is a "form of charity and justice" but that in practice it is difficult to pursue both. "One cannot be at one and the same time the champion of justice and of charity. One must choose, and the ICRC has long since chosen to be a defender of charity."[13]

I have described the association of the distinction between humanitarianism and human rights with that between beneficence and justice as an "interpretive mapping." To say this is to suggest that the best or most fitting account of the moral basis of the protections contained in each normative practice, as understood within the practice, makes essential reference to the values of beneficence in the case of humanitarianism and justice in the case of human rights. Some practice theorists might regard such an account as part of the "meaning" of a practice.[14] The phrase "best or most fitting account" is obviously a gesture at a theory of interpretation of normative practices of the general kind advanced by Ronald Dworkin, though it need not be Dworkin's theory.[15] The role of such a theory would be to set out a method for understanding or making sense of a normative practice in terms of one or a few fundamental values or ideals that the practice seeks to respect or advance. A theoretical account of interpretation is well beyond my present scope so I simply assume that we have a pre-theoretical notion that normative practices can be understood as collective efforts to respect or advance certain values. When I refer to moral values as "underlying" a practice, I mean to say that they have this kind of an interpretive relation to it.

Changing Contexts of Law and Social Action

Developments of the last several decades have blurred the distinction between these practices. I anticipate these here in order to motivate what I shall say later, beginning with the realm of international law, where the blurring is more evident. Here there are two important developments: the changing nature of armed conflict, which clouds the distinction between war and peace presupposed by existing law; and the jurisprudence of the various courts and agencies charged with applying the law, which have increasingly drawn on both bodies of law to settle disputes.

First, the changing nature of war. The original distinction between IHL and IHRL supposes that we can distinguish between war and peace. The paradigm of war, as the main body of IHL understands it, is armed conflict between territorial states that have regular military forces under a command apparatus. The paradigm of peace is the absence of war in that understanding. This distinction may have been workable when the founding documents were written after World War II, but today it is clearly problematic. Most of the organized political violence in the last several decades falls outside the category of armed conflict between states.[16] Some of it consists of insurgencies and civil wars in which at least one party is a non-state actor and the contest is for control of part or all of a state's territory. This is what IHL refers to as "armed conflict not of an international character." Common Article 3 of the four Geneva Conventions, explicated by a 1977 additional protocol, applies to this category of war. Of course, although these standards are supposed to apply to all parties to a conflict, non-state actors have not subscribed to the conventions, so the legal basis of their obligation to comply is controversial.[17]

Some cases of armed conflict, however, are not obviously either international war or "conflict not of an international character." The following are some examples: civil war with foreign participation other than the sending of troops; terrorist violence where the issue is not control of territory at all; military occupation of a foreign territory for an indefinite period; or tactics like targeted killing by drones outside of areas where there are active hostilities on the ground.[18] We might add to these examples the use of violence by states in response to armed, transnational criminal activity like drug cartels. Since all of these cases fall outside the law's understanding of international war and conflicts "not of an international character," it is arguable whether IHL applies at all. This raises the possibility (exploited during the George W. Bush administration in the United States) that only a more permissive law of "self-defense" might govern some types of armed conflict.[19]

This is a problem within the law for the obvious reason that we cannot apply law without knowing which body of law is applicable. For our purposes, however, the more important point is that the kinds of violent conflict that fall outside the models of war between states and conflicts "not of an international character" represent different forms of interaction between different kinds of agents in different kinds of surroundings than conflicts within the models. These differences can be relevant to judgments about the moral status and rights of those affected by a conflict. For example, the moral status of bystanders in conflicts outside the two models might be different than that of noncombatants within the territory of a belligerent in conventional war. This is not an original point: it generalizes a problem that arises in connection with drones and targeted killing. This is the question whether to construe the typical circumstances of targeted killing according to a "paradigm of war" or a "paradigm of law enforcement."[20] The latter is, in effect, a paradigm of human rights. And, indeed, some commentators and practitioners believe that in cases like this the appropriate norms are those of IHRL instead of IHL. Since IHRL is generally understood to be more demanding, this matters.[21]

The second point concerns the jurisprudence of IHL and IHRL – that is, the "case law" of international and regional courts and tribunals, determinations of HR treaty bodies, declarations of UN agencies, and so on. On this point, only one brief comment. Courts and other authorities responsible for resolving legal claims about the use of force, presumably the domain of IHL, have increasingly been willing to import concepts from IHRL – a development that is incontestable.[22] The 1977 Additional Protocols to the Geneva Conventions acknowledge that legal protections of fundamental human rights apply in armed conflict (although the text is not as helpful as it might be about which rights apply in conflict situations, and how).[23] More recently both the Human Rights Commission and the International Court of Justice have accepted the point. The picture that emerges from ICJ jurisprudence is that IHRL is a body of fundamental norms that apply in both war and peace and IHL is an interpretation of these norms for (at least some) cases of armed conflict. This picture might be problematic for some doctrinal reasons but there is no question as a matter of fact that the distinction between these bodies of law is more eroded in legal practice than in black-letter treaty law. This makes my central question inevitable: if these two bodies of law are increasingly entangled in practice, at least partly because we face practical challenges that the basic architecture of the law of armed conflict did not anticipate very clearly, is there any underlying reason of moral and political theory for continuing to regard the distinction between them as having ethical significance?

A similar question arises in the realm of political and social action. Social action being what it is, a distinction between humanitarianism and human rights action could never have been drawn as crisply as in international law. Still, some markers of distinction are easily recognizable. Consider, for example, the contrasting cases of the postures of the ICRC and Amnesty International at least since the early 2000s with respect to political conflict.[24] The ICRC has historically maintained that humanitarian action should be politically neutral in order to minimize the extent to which governments might be tempted to deny humanitarian actors access to those in need of their services.[25] Amnesty, by contrast, has devoted considerable ingenuity to finding ways to hold governments accountable for failures to protect or respect various human rights.

Leebaw observes that Amnesty, like other human rights organizations, has sought to "transform the language of human rights into a set of impartial legal norms" yet, at the same time, has not hesitated to engage in public criticism of governments' internal conduct when it judges the norms to be violated.[26]

Notwithstanding the contrast at the level of what we might call procedural values, for various reasons it is difficult to maintain that these organizations stand for clearly distinct ethical-political postures. For one thing, in practice, each organization has borrowed strategic ideas from the other when necessary to attain political or social goals even while professing distinct identities. There is also a deeper point best illustrated by Amnesty. It was founded to draw attention to a particularly odious violation of human rights – the detention of persons on grounds of political belief and conscience. It has broadened its remit considerably since then but still identifies as a human rights organization. Yet from the outset volunteer participation in its activities relied for motivation on the idea of the suffering prisoner evoked by the image of a candle bound in barbed wire, a logo that has been maintained to the present.

The observation generalizes. Transitional justice institutions, for example, which aim, broadly speaking, to restore respect for human rights, occasionally turn to humanitarian tropes (e.g., relieving suffering) and procedural norms (neutrality) to win support for their missions.[27] Similarly, in the evolution of humanitarian action, in particular, there has been an increasing resort to ideas characteristic of the human rights movement to articulate the aims of humanitarianism and to shift emphasis away from the historical association of humanitarianism with sentiments of pity or sympathy (though it must be said that here, too, the range of human rights in question is narrow considered in relation to the normative breadth of human rights practice).[28] A striking illustration can be found in the "Humanitarian Charter" of the Sphere Project, which presents the "humanitarian imperative" to "prevent or alleviate human suffering" from disaster or conflict as based on the principle that "all human beings are born free and equal in dignity and rights."[29] As with the convergence of IHL and IHRL, what might appear to be a partial convergence in the normative discourses of humanitarian and human rights practices raises the question whether there is any stable moral basis for the distinction.

Justice and Beneficence

The received view maps the difference in law and practice onto the traditional philosophical distinction between the virtues, or duties, of beneficence or humanity and of justice or right. Is this mapping any help in understanding these practices?

Those who think so tend not to say very much about their understanding of the moral contents of these virtues or about the nature of the requirements they impose on action. So I would like to comment briefly about justice and beneficence in the history of moral philosophy and its meaning in common-sense morality today.

The distinction between justice and beneficence is fundamental in modern moral and political thought but it has ancient roots. Its best-known classical expression occurs in Cicero's *On Duties* (*De Officiis*), a work that exercised enormous influence on the thought of moral and political philosophers in the seventeenth and eighteenth centuries, including the early modern authors of classical international law – much greater influence than contemporary readers of those philosophers often realize. Early in *On Duties*, Cicero gives a catalog of four dimensions of honorable conduct. They track the four cardinal virtues of Greek moral thought, although Cicero does not name them as the Greeks did. The most straightforwardly social of these is the virtue by which "the common life [is] held together." He only once refers to this virtue as "justice," but it occupies the place in the catalog that is inhabited by justice among the cardinal virtues. Cicero goes on immediately to say that social virtue has two parts. The first is justice in a specific sense, whose content I shall come to shortly; the second is "the beneficence connected with it, which may be called either kindness or liberality."[30]

Cicero's distinction was the source of a distinction made by Grotius between "perfect" and "imperfect" right that was, in turn, restated by Pufendorf as a distinction between "perfect" and "imperfect" duties. Most of the main contributors to moral and political philosophy from Locke to Hume, Adam Smith and Kant read both writers and considered the distinction to be a basic feature of common-sense morality that needed to be explained.[31]

Here is a crude, broad-brush summary of the distinction, patching over disagreements in the tradition, and with apologies for rehearsing ideas that may be familiar.[32] A central part of common morality consists of norms defining what we owe to each other. Suppose we formulate what we owe to others as duties. (With some adjustments we might also speak of virtues, dispositions, or kinds of reasons for action.) The traditional view is that when we take inventory of our duties to others, we see that they fall into two categories. These are Cicero's duties (*officia*) of justice and of beneficence and Pufendorf's perfect and imperfect duties. Generally speaking, according to the Ciceronian view, duties of the first kind include not threatening bodily harm to others, respecting their property, keeping faith with promises and contracts, and, for some writers, defending others against violations of these duties by third parties. (This is conspicuously narrow, compared to some contemporary ideas of justice, a fact we shall return to.) Duties of the second kind include helping to satisfy the needs of people unable do so themselves, doing good for those close to us, reciprocating when others have helped us, and acting as we can to protect those who are vulnerable to various kinds of harm. Most writers have held that the strength of our duties of beneficence is related to the closeness of our relationships to potential beneficiaries. Most have also held that we have duties of beneficence to strangers (i.e., those with whom we have no preexisting relationship), but for the most part they did not believe these duties could impose significant costs on us, the duty-bearers. (Of course, not everybody agrees.[33]) The exception to this generalization is that, on some views, we have more demanding duties to help those in deep distress or urgent need; as Sidgwick says, they "have a claim on us for special kindness."[34] Although I will have to leave aside the interpretation of the distinction in Christian moral thought, what I have just said about beneficence in common-sense morality substantially applies also to the theological virtue of charity (*caritas*) as it was understood, for example, by Aquinas.[35]

These categories of duties appear to differ in characteristic ways. Some duties (say, the duty not to harm the innocent) seem to have a kind of precision that other duties lack (say, the duty to help those in need). My duty not to harm the innocent applies to every innocent person on every occasion when I am in a position to harm them[36] – it is "perfect" in the sense that I can know reasonably clearly what it requires of me and to whom it is owed. My duty to help those in need is not comparably precise because I have some discretion in deciding when and how to carry it out – it is "imperfect" in the sense that I am not obligated to help everyone who is in need on every occasion when I could do so. I have latitude to make choices about whom to help, when, and by how much. That discretion is contextual – there may be cases, like the philosopher's case of the child drowning in a pond, in which there is no question what beneficence requires of me – but on the whole duties of beneficence seem to be more open-textured than duties of justice.

The two kinds of duties also seem to operate differently in moral life. Duties of justice (or of "right") can be the basis of demands for performance by those to whom they are owed, whereas duties of beneficence generally cannot be (in most cases, because each of us gets to decide who should be the beneficiaries of our beneficence). This means that a certain kind of response to failures of duty is appropriate in the first case that is not appropriate in the second: I would be justified in resenting someone's treating me unjustly or violating my rights, whereas except in extraordinary circumstances I would not be if someone failed to help when I needed it. In that case disappointment (or, perhaps, hurt, if I have some relationship to the other) would be more appropriate. To put the general point another way, one has a status as the object of a duty of justice that one generally does not have as a potential object of someone else's beneficence. Joel Feinberg described this as having "the recognizable capacity to assert claims," that is, as being entitled to insist on a certain kind of treatment by others.[37] Being a potential object of beneficence confers a different status, roughly that of an agent whose needs, just because they are the needs of a human person, ought to be taken into account by others whose actions could possibly benefit that person. Some describe this as the status of a "patient," though it seems to me that the medical allusion risks being distorting. In any case, to have this status is not necessarily a bad thing: it is possible to be the object of someone else's beneficence without being either subordinated or shamed. But it is not the same as the status of an agent with "the recognizable capacity to assert claims."

In this section I have been trying to describe a common understanding of the ethical distinction. In calling this understanding "common," I do not mean to suggest that the distinction itself is either unproblematic or uncontroversial.[38] This is not the place for an extended critique, but it is worth noting two complications in the common view that will be pertinent below. First, as I observed earlier, the traditional idea of the scope of justice is narrow considered in comparison with conceptions of social justice that have developed since the end of the eighteenth century. This enlargement of scope puts pressure on the notion that all duties of justice are perfect.[39] Suppose, for example, that we believe that the reduction of inequalities of social status is a requirement of social justice and that we have (perhaps "natural") duties to act where possible to reduce injustices of this kind.[40] These duties appear more like imperfect than perfect duties because they afford some discretion in deciding how and when to act. So it may seem that not all duties of justice are perfect. What has happened in this case is that a historical change in the range of a moral concept has destabilized the traditional understanding of some of its attributes, yet that understanding has persisted, as it were, by a kind of inertia. But the problems in the common view are not limited to those arising from conceptual change. Consider, for example, the duties of parents to their children, which have tended to be classified as duties of beneficence. These duties have a peculiar, intermediate form: although in some circumstances parents have discretion about how to carry them out, there is no question to whom the duties are owed and in some circumstances no question what they require. Something similar might be said about duties of gratitude, also traditionally considered to be duties of beneficence. So duties of beneficence do not seem to be uniformly imperfect. As we shall see, parallels to these complications in the traditional distinction arise when we return to the mapping of the distinction onto that between humanitarian and human rights practices.

Humanitarianism/Beneficence, Human Rights/Justice?

We are working with a rough notion of a normative social practice as a system of public norms that people accept, and know that others accept, as providing pro tanto reasons for action. And we assume that within a public normative practice, agents tend to develop shared understandings of the purposes of the practice as well as beliefs about how these purposes are best accomplished, and that these develop into distinctive cultures. There are at least two normative questions that we might ask about such a practice: first, about whether and why the practice is a good thing to have – for short, about its value; second, about the kinds of reasons people might have to participate in the practice by filling the roles it defines and making themselves subject to its norms – for short, about the reasons that motivate participation. These are distinct questions even though it is possible, at least from some perspectives, that the answers will overlap.

The interpretive mapping of the distinction between the practices of humanitarianism and human rights onto the distinction between the virtues of beneficence and justice might suggest answers to both questions. Perhaps the value of humanitarian practice is that it serves the desirable social aim of reducing avoidable human suffering and relieving suffering that is not avoidable (or anyway was not avoided). The disposition to contribute to avoiding and relieving suffering is paradigmatic of beneficence as I have described it. At the limit, it is a disposition to respond to the needs of another agent that arises from recognizing that agent as relevantly similar to oneself – as we might say (though it is imprecise), from a recognition of common humanity. The exercise of this disposition might also explain how people can be motivated to participate in the practice. Similarly, we might think that the value of human rights practice is that it reduces the incidence of harms perpetrated by governments and other collective agents to the interests protected by human rights, both by bringing pressure on governments and by contributing to processes of institutional change. Resentment of injustices done, both to self and to others, might also be the most likely source of the motivation to participate in human rights practice. This is clearly painting with a broad brush, but something like it seems to me to be how the interpretive mapping I have described might seem to answer the questions of value and motivation. If accurate, this picture illustrates how the practices we observe in the social world might be connected to the distinct underlying virtues of beneficence and justice.

Is this picture accurate? Let me make three observations. The most general point is that when we look at the actual conduct of these practices (as opposed to the discourse of participants), the association of one with beneficence and of the other with justice is implausible on its face – not wrong, but at minimum excessively simple and in some respects a misrepresentation. It is true, as a historical matter, that IHL originated in something like beneficent or humanitarian concern about other people's suffering. That is what the response to Solferino was about and not a bad interpretation of the moral basis of the first Geneva Convention, which was concerned with treatment of vulnerable wounded and sick soldiers on the battlefield. However, as I noted earlier, IHL has changed significantly since the 1860s. It now covers several "protected classes." These include noncombatants. It also applies at least to some armed conflicts "not of an international character" in which it is plausible to think that many of those affected are entirely innocent of any involvement in the conflict. To the extent that IHL has legalized the traditional *jus in bello* principles of discrimination and proportionality, it is difficult to see it as devoted only to relieving or preventing suffering. The principle of discrimination, for example, says that it is not permissible to target non-combatants intentionally. In my view, the most natural interpretation of the moral basis of this principle is that the category of noncombatants includes large numbers of people who are innocent of contributing to the war effort and who have what, in human rights language, would be called a "right to life" – that is to say, a right not to be deliberately threatened with death without cause. According to the traditional view, this is a matter of justice, not beneficence.

Parenthetically, although we are not concerned here directly with the law of the UN Charter, it is worth observing that although the Charter prohibits intervention by states in the internal affairs of other states, many people believe that "humanitarian" intervention may be legitimate under some circumstances even if not strictly legal. In the aftermath of the Kosovo intervention (1999) this idea was formulated as the "responsibility to protect" ("RtoP").[41] A constrained form of the doctrine was adopted by the General Assembly in 2005 and some people now regard it as part of, or in process of becoming, customary international law. I do not wish to defend that position here, only to observe that its advocates (plausibly) defend it as a human rights norm. But this means that, strictly speaking, on this view it would be a misnomer to describe "humanitarian intervention" as humanitarian. It is intervention to protect human rights, and thus an effort to redress injustice.[42] (It is contested, however, whether intervention "to protect" is obligatory on every occasion on which it would be justified – that is, is a perfect duty. The majority view seems to be that it is not.)

If we turn to areas of humanitarian practice beyond IHL, we find a parallel incongruity. Certainly some elements of the practice can be seen as expressions of beneficence with respect to both their value and their motivations – relief of natural disaster, for example. However, as I observed earlier, humanitarian practice has grown increasingly diverse and today some elements are difficult to distinguish in their social and political goals (if not always in the motivations of practitioners) from action to protect human rights. This is most obviously true of what I called "structural" (and Barnett calls "alchemical") humanitarianism but the same might be said, for example, of action to provide health care in war zones. Of course, one might simply rule that in this respect the practice misunderstands itself, as perhaps it does. But we are interested here in the self-understandings of complicated social enterprises, so eliminating apparent incongruity by interpretive fiat would not be especially constructive.

A second point concerns human rights doctrine in its primary application to domestic-level societies at peace. The main function of international human rights practice is to make certain aspects of a government's treatment of persons under its jurisdiction matters of international concern. It represents an international and, increasingly, a transnational commitment to monitor, promote, and sometimes to enforce human rights standards within states. So one of the questions we must answer about human rights is why these rights ought to be treated as matters of international concern. I believe that how we answer this question depends on the nature of the right in question.[43] Some human rights – for example, the central "civil and political rights" like the right to life, right to due process, and rights to freedom of religion and association – fit naturally within a "justice" framework. They protect fundamental interests in what we might call the integrity of the person and the importance of that value across a wide range of lives helps to explain why the rights should qualify as matters of international concern. But what about social and economic rights – for example, the right to an "adequate standard of living," to health care, and to rest and leisure? Why should these be matters of international concern? As a matter of political theory, this is a complicated question. It can be argued that they are matters of social justice. But if we are to work with the traditional distinction, it seems to me more natural to regard them as high priority considerations of beneficence, addressed to improving wellbeing or meeting needs rather than protecting the integrity of the person.[44] This suggests that we need considerations related to both justice and beneficence to explain the moral importance of the wide range of protections that count as human rights within the practice, and thus the value of the practice taken as a whole.

Finally, a third observation. As I mentioned, traditionally justice and beneficence are associated respectively with perfect and imperfect duties. However, if we try to apply this distinction to human rights and humanitarianism, then for reasons we have already seen we quickly run into trouble. Beginning with human rights: as I have said, international human rights doctrine is normatively diverse. There are some rights about which it is plausible to think that the corresponding duties are perfect – for example, the right against torture. But there are many cases in which agents like governments, international organizations and non-state actors face choices bearing on human rights across large populations. Given the scarcity of resources, decisions must be made about who should act and for what ends. This is clearly the case for some economic and social rights, which may not be immediately satisfiable for everyone and may require long-term policy interventions. It would be hard to argue that there are perfect duties to satisfy these rights for each person today. The duties they imply look more imperfect than perfect; they are duties to adopt a certain end – namely, the good of others – rather than to perform a specific action. Although it is hardly unlimited, there is some latitude to decide the level of resources to devote to this end and how best to pursue it.

The reverse point applies to parts of IHL. For example, the duty not to deliberately target civilians is not "imperfect." It is clear from the Fourth Geneva Convention and its protocols that every protected civilian has a right not to be intentionally targeted. Conceivably that right might be overridden in some cases of military necessity, but it is still a right. Attackers do not have discretion about when to respect it and when not. So not only does this feature of what is called "humanitarian" law represent a concern for justice rather than beneficence, but it also expresses itself in a perfect rather than an imperfect duty. This is clearly at odds with the mapping of IHL onto the virtue of beneficence.

Where does this leave us? These points show that the distinctions between humanitarianism and human rights, on the one hand, and beneficence and justice, on the other, are orthogonal to each other. They are not parallel. To interpret the moral distinction as underlying the practical distinction invites misunderstanding the differences in practice. So, for example, members of protected classes under IHL have perfect rights and agents have perfect duties to respect them. Respecting these rights is not "beyond the call." Similarly, within some humanitarian aid operations, such as those occurring after armed conflict, it may be more accurate to regard the displaced as having claims in justice for relief than as suffering victims with claims to beneficence.

More generally, the evolving contents of each body of practice are not in any obvious way expressions of fundamentally distinct moral values and certainly not of an exclusive concern to relieve suffering on the one hand and to redress injustice or violations of basic rights on the other. Both practices aim to protect urgent individual human interests against predictable kinds of neglect or abuse. They differ in the contexts to which they centrally apply – their "target circumstances," as we might put it. In both cases these protections can take varying forms – sometimes as rights conceived as bases of claims, sometimes as rights conceived as priority goals of political action, sometimes as claims to help when resources and circumstances make it possible. Differences in the content and range of the protections must be explained by differences in the circumstances in which the urgent interests are subject to threat and in the forms of protection that are feasible. To look at the relationship of IHL and IHRL in this way is to think of them as continuous and sharing a common basis that takes predictable threats to urgent human interests as sources of reasons to act in ways that would protect against the threats. Similarly, to understand the humanitarian norm of political neutrality in this broader context is to see it as instrumentally necessary in circumstances of conflict for achieving ends that might also be formulated in terms of human rights.[45]

What I have just presented presupposes a view about the justification of human rights that I have defended elsewhere but do not have space to reiterate here.[46] So I will just suggest as a hypothesis that if we could begin to think this way, we might be able see our way past some of the dilemmas that the binary distinction of humanitarianism and human rights leads to. For example, we might be able to conceptualize norms for the conduct of armed conflict in contexts different from the target circumstances of IHL within the same paradigm of justification as IHRL. Earlier I noted the controversy about whether (or when) "targeted killing" should be judged as an act of war or of law enforcement. The present point suggests that we might instead conceptualize law (or rights) enforcement as the genus and international war as one species of it. This makes room for the thought that the circumstances of asymmetrical conflict might be another species.

I have been concerned in this chapter with what now appears to be a lack of fit between the way participants in (and some observers of) these practices often describe the moral ideals that motivate them and condition their understanding of the aims of the practices, and the way these ideals and aims have been understood in an influential part of the history of moral philosophy and in contemporary, common-sense morality in the West. So one might think that the interest, if any, in these remarks is primarily descriptive or sociological. But this might be myopic. The way we describe the moral requirements that apply to us as individuals and as participants in our shared practices can influence the way in which we understand the stringency of these requirements and the priorities we assign to them when they conflict with one another and with other claims on scarce resources. When our practices classify these requirements using categories that have independent significance in common-sense morality, descriptive distortions could warp practical judgments about how to act and how to allocate scarce resources when we cannot do all that we have reason to do. To put it more directly, inaccurate labels can encourage faulty choices.

Finally, a speculation perhaps worth considering elsewhere. I have maintained that humanitarianism and human rights are each the subjects of a normative social practice. There is no question that the "procedural norms" of these practices differ. As I have observed, for example, within the culture of humanitarianism, humanitarian action strives to be neutral between competing political forces whereas human rights culture tends to be explicitly partisan. This contrast is related to another. Humanitarian practice typically gives priority to the relief of urgent suffering and has less if any concern to bring about systematic change in the longer term. Human rights practice, on the other hand, takes a longer view and often aims explicitly at inducing legal and political change. These differences in "procedural norms" make sense in light of the practical differences in the "target circumstances" of the activities characteristic of each practice and may explain why participants in these practices are tempted to misconceive of the practices' underlying moral values. They call attention to a possibility that philosophers do not often recognize – that the functional needs of our social roles may encourage us to adopt beliefs about the values that we protect or advance in those roles that are unsound and might possibly distort our judgment as practitioners. I wonder (I have not said enough to do more) whether the cultures of humanitarianism and of human rights might be cases in point. If there is such a thing as a theory of normative practices, this is a possibility it should take on board.

4   For a Fleeting Moment
The Short, Happy Life of Modern Humanism

Stephen Hopgood

To say that there is a fundamental difference between human rights and humanitarianism, we need to be able to point to something that will allow us to say "that's human rights" and "that's humanitarianism." Some *core* to each that the other cannot replicate; some red line that signals an uncrossable boundary between the two. Even in the empirical case, where we simply describe the modern institutional manifestation of each, there is nothing, I argue, that meets these criteria. They are inextricably intertwined.[1] To take an obvious example: what humanitarians mean by "protection" is what human rights activists actually do on a daily basis. If we look at them conceptually, in their grounding principles, logics, and moral architecture, we find little to distinguish them. Indeed, they are social practices that might have developed in a variety of different ways such that we could call what each does as its signature form of action by the same name. Some already do. Hence, the forlorn nature of scholarly efforts to insist that X is properly "human rights" and Y is properly "humanitarianism" or "international humanitarian law."[2] Both human rights and humanitarianism are branches of the same broad humanist tree with its distinctive commitment to the life of the human person and her/his/their basic needs and desires. That is, a commitment in principle to the equal moral value of all individual human lives regardless of any aspect of identity or behavior. This is the cornerstone of liberalism.

After elaborating in part one of this chapter on the fruitlessness of a search for conceptual distinctiveness between the two major secular universal normative social practices of our time, the second part looks at their empirical similarities, going as far as to suggest that in our era of rapid transformation in global politics there is a case for strategic partnership, and perhaps even for merger between human rights and humanitarian organizations. That this would, in principle, be easy enough to effect at the level of ethos (less so organizational culture) tells us much. Médecins Sans Frontières (MSF) plus Amnesty working in prisons, Amnesty plus the International Committee of the Red Cross (ICRC) working on torture, Human Rights Watch and the International Rescue Committee working on refugees? No problem – indeed, they are all already working on these issues in broadly similar terms just not as parts of the same organization. What will make merger hard is not any core ethical incompatibility but cultural differences – human rights advocates tend to be less flexible (they are often lawyers) and more hubristic (or, more generously, optimistic) than humanitarians – and competing funding models, along with the more contested politics of human rights demands compared with those of humanitarians who can (and do) trade categorical principles for access.[3]

In part three, I will argue that for both humanitarians and human rights advocates the nature of the transformation of the international system we are witnessing condemns both to an uncertain and potentially less relevant future. Both can survive, as well-funded, highly esteemed symbolic institutions tend to do. But only through a kind of inertia. Whether or not they can do much good in the new world is less clear. Of the two, humanitarians have the better chance because in the end they can yield to the demands of even venal states in order to provide a very minimal form of aid to those who suffer terribly at the hands of their tormentors. Which will be, paradoxically, an argument against merger. This might give the impression that there *are* distinct differences between the two. More accurately, human rights are a form of overreach beyond their humanitarian origins. It is not clear that human rights bring any systemic benefit to states – being at best an occasional ally and at worst an impediment – whereas humanitarians help in situations of dire suffering to contain and stabilize the mess that states themselves have all too often caused. This is not evidence of any deep-seated empirical, ethical or conceptual distinction. It tells us one thing only – that a rhetorical commitment to the importance of all human life occasionally has functional value for states. The vast panoply of rights and mechanisms to promulgate and enforce them that human rights advocates have built is balanced on this one thin thread, the signature contribution of humanism to world affairs.

Humanist Origins

There are, broadly, two nonreligious origins – reason, and nature – given as transcendent sources for human rights and humanitarianism. These are groundings, anchors, beyond the caprice of human social invention and contingency. Here, it is the idea or concept, the intellectual and moral substructure, and its logical unfolding, that drives humans forward, not any choice we as a species or as individuals might somehow make about how we ought to act. We did not find our way to these universal moral prescriptions, they lay latent in our minds until we discovered them and put them into practice. There have always been a few far-sighted prophets who made universalist arguments of this sort, but it took until the Enlightenment for humanity as a species to begin to consider all human persons (only potentially, obviously, and dependent on who qualified as fully "human") as morally worthy and morally equal (for more on these and other cognate developments, see Flynn, this volume). A third option, God, has been a more popular answer to questions about what gives rights and organized compassion their ahistorical, transcendent moorings, but I take it as a given that under modernity such an answer is now too contested to command universal support even in theory (which God? which strain of which religion?).[4]

What *reason* tells us is that moral laws, like "thou shalt not kill," or "treat others as you would wish to be treated yourself" (the golden rule), are exactly the laws we would give ourselves if we only thought about it properly. The fact that the majority of human beings have not treated each other with such reciprocal respect is because we do not successfully listen to reason's voice. The *natural* origin claim, by contrast, sees us all having within us some shared moral sense, some capacity for empathy and compassion, which when effectively activated creates a more or less identical response to human suffering and urges us to help, to do something, to act ethically. Even if it took until the 1700s for this button to be pushed on a large scale, it was always there within us, waiting to be triggered. And so, the global ethical projects we call "human rights" and "humanitarianism" are simply the latest stage of our evolution toward being more civilized, moral, and thoughtful human beings.

If we accept either of these accounts, we can then ask what the core distinction is between "humanitarianism" and "human rights" in a different way. If each is somehow a "natural kind," then do they represent the unfolding of two different logics? Is one the "law" (human rights) and the other "love" (compassion for fellow humans in distress)? Perhaps these are Platonic categories that structure our world? But this does not get us very far. Identifying exactly what the natural kind is would be an exercise in anachronism unless we think that there are concepts, like "law," "love," "justice," and "freedom," that stand outside social time and are meaningfully definable in the abstract, even in some vague sense "pre-linguistically" (a deeply problematic notion), concepts that in some way were latent in the universe and existed before we did.

This requires us to hold that abstract conceptual parameters create limits to human social action. That what freedom is, or love, or justice, has limits that were set down for us, or in us, long before we roamed the earth and that no matter what we decide freedom to be, reason and/or nature has beaten us to it. The diversity of human social forms refutes this empirically. By what authority do any transcendent sources tell us that we are wrong, that we have made a mess of things? In whose voice could they speak if not in that of an embodied God? And even if this account is true, if it cannot be made to *seem true* to enough people to make it true, then we will always live in a world we define and make for ourselves, even if we have long since departed from the one true moral path.

Of what practical use is it to claim, therefore, that there is some kind of essence, "humanity," whether as a collective noun or an adjective, that persists beneath all and any of the various forms of human development? It helps bolster the courage of the faithful but does nothing to resolve the problem of counter-claims and heretical dissent, let alone the difficulty of defining concepts in terms of other concepts whose meaning can only be found in other concepts and so on. This is not to say that human rights advocates and humanitarians do not make origin claims. They use arguments for transcendent moral truth to bolster their here-and-now political claims. We should see this as socially constructed myth-making, necessary perhaps and even effective, but not "true" in any deep sense. This past has been constructed through a process of bricolage, fusing together ideas, events, texts, and stories from the distant human past, and by privileging one narrative, that of the inexorable process of moral improvement over another, the story of human killing, cruelty, and suffering. These pieces all came together on a *global* scale in the eighteenth century when for the first time there was a social phenomenon (European empire) that served as a vector to globalize what were otherwise culturally and geographically local social practices.

Accepting the social construction of human rights and humanitarianism means we will find it impossible to settle *with decisive authority* when a form of social action is, and is not, an example or contravention of one or the other. The Catholic Church dealt with issues on which it could not generate agreement by engineering consensus. When a collective understanding of what "the truth" was evolved (or, more likely, was manufactured), that "truth" was given the seal of approval by church authorities and became "true" allowing punishment to be meted out for denying it.

In his Apostolic Constitution, *Ineffabilis Deus* (*The Immaculate Conception*), issued in 1854, Pope Pius IX wrote:

We declare, pronounce, and define that the doctrine which holds that the most Blessed Virgin Mary, in the first instance of her conception, by a singular grace and privilege granted by Almighty God, in view of the merits of Jesus Christ, the Savior of the human race, was preserved free from all stain of original sin, is a doctrine revealed by God and therefore to be believed firmly and constantly by all the faithful.[5]

He added:

Hence, if anyone shall dare – which God forbid! – to think otherwise than as has been defined by us, let him know and understand that he is condemned by his own judgment; that he has suffered shipwreck in the faith; that he has separated from the unity of the Church; and that, furthermore, by his own action he incurs the penalties established by law if he should [d]are to express in words or writing or by any other outward means the errors he think in his heart.[6]

This approach (likely to be of limited efficacy for the modern Church) is far beyond anything that anyone promoting human rights or humanitarian ethics could hope for. Or, indeed, should aspire to? How do we want our believers? Behaviorally compliant out of habit, custom or instrumentality? Or self-policing and internally committed to the faith? Do we care why people comply, in other words? Either way, human rights and humanitarianism lack an equivalent authority that can wield the threats of excommunication and a fiery torment. They remain far more contested despite codes of conduct, credentialism and training courses, memoirs, peer pressure and socialization, heart-rending high-profile examples of suffering, publicity and promotional campaigns, laws and norms, court cases, and so on. In other words, even the UN, the ICRC, MSF, Amnesty, and many others have been unable to pronounce with finality that "X is not human rights" even when what is being proposed, like "the dignity of the human family" or "traditional rights," is something very different from what we would usually call rights. When discrimination is held up as example of "humanitarianism," who can say with authority it is not?

The obvious answer, perhaps the only answer, is: via agreement, especially one enshrined in the law. We can see this in the many conventions and covenants on human rights (not to mention the Universal Declaration of Human Rights (UDHR)) and in the Geneva and Hague Conventions. These are a more secular and discursive and (hopefully) democratic version of what the Catholic Church was attempting. We agree what we mean by "human rights" and by "humanitarianism" and try to make that a meaningful limit on social action. Like all international law these are an unusual form of law because in the main they lack enforcement capacity. The International Criminal Court (ICC) would, it was hoped, provide it for both human rights crimes (crimes against humanity and genocide) and international humanitarian law (crimes of aggression and war crimes).[7] In fact, the only major powers to join the ICC are in Europe, raising doubts about whether or not there is any consensus over the Rome Statute at all. Indeed, as Mark Goodale shows, in *Letters to the Contrary*, submissions to UNESCO on the topic of human rights in 1947 from luminaries of that age prove there was no consensus at all even at the start about rights as somehow agreed meta norms for the coming world order.[8]

Moreover, states, particularly in the West, talk about human rights while often rejecting them (US treatment of migrant children, Hungary's illiberal democracy, Poland's dismantling of its constitutional judiciary, the UK government's approach to the European Convention on Human Rights). That is before we look at the attitude to human rights and humanitarian action in China or Russia or Turkey or Brazil or Egypt. My suggestion is simple: what little consensus there was in the twentieth century has gone. There was just a preponderance of sympathetic power. We will no longer be able to turn to the law to settle the issue of what constitutes "human rights" on the one hand, and "humanitarianism" on the other.

One might argue: the law clearly defines what human rights and humanitarianism are, it is just that states ignore it. But if these same states refuse to recognize by consensus the substance and boundaries of the terms "human rights" and "humanitarianism" and if we can appeal to no other authority to tell us the answer, we are left with the reality that they float freely from transcendent origins and are not limited by explicit agreement.

An analogy is with Buddhism. What might we take as the fixed core of Buddhism, even beyond the absence of a real self and the disintegration of the ego, the need to avoid attachment and to embrace the void of emptiness, getting beyond the cycle of birth and death and achieving Nirvana? As the Dalai Lama puts it: be kind. The Nobel Eightfold Path, which even Theravada Buddhists of Sri Lanka and South East Asia are expected to follow, has moral virtues that include no killing or injuring and no self-enrichment in a material sense. Yet one goes to the Schwedagong Pagoda in Yangon with its roof of gold or reads of the blood-thirsty demands for violence against the Tamils or the Rohingya and asks: Are these really Buddhists? And of course, they are – they live the lives of Buddhists, occupy the temples, walk the path, have been anointed, dress, eat, pray, and act accordingly. By what authority do we say they are not? Yet they violate the peaceful and kind core of Buddhist practice and belief. Which suggests it has no such core. The *Bhagavad Gita*, the great Hindu epic from the Mahabharata where Krishna explains to Arjuna what selfless action and duty requires, was a favorite book of the Nazis, especially the SS.[9] By the same token, Jan Smuts, the highly educated South African leader and proponent of racial segregation, allegedly carried a copy of Kant around with him.[10]

With the necessary "lawfare," the concepts of "human" and "rights" can be so defined as to exclude members of certain ethnic, cultural, or religious groups (see Klose, this volume) without stepping beyond "humanity's conscience" (because in reality there is no "humanity" and thus no "conscience"). It is a short step from "humanitarian" to "humane" and thus to actions – for example, mercy killing – that might justify ending the lives of those whose quality of life we, not they, judge to be undesirable. There is, then, no way to draw a line around these practices and say what they are, what they are not, and what they should or should not be. We could even have lived in a world in which humanitarianism and human rights were not a thing at all. We can identify pivotal historical moments where things could have gone differently, and the subsequent development of our social lives would have been altered in unpredictable ways. Whether or not you are committed to the arbitrariness of human moral development can be answered by asking yourself: Do I think a world could have evolved in which treating people unequally was considered just? That used to be the world, and many if not most parts of the world still manifest many such beliefs. Why are we unable to imagine a future where this is explicit again?

In the end, therefore, even law is unable to hold against the tide and falls victim to a kind of *rebus sic stantibus* principle. Constitutional courts struggle with the politics of this constantly and that is *within* a system of relatively settled laws and precedents. How much harder is this codification in the world of human rights and humanitarianism where so much is vague and fundamentally contested. When words and concepts are seen as matters of conventional usage not prefigured meaning, then everything depends on what is taken to be authoritative resolution of differences of belief, fact, and opinion. Even the term "human" is now contested in terms of subjectivity, performativity, artificial intelligence, the posthuman, the xenofeminist.

Indeed, it suggests neither human rights nor humanitarianism is an ethical practice at all except to the extent that "we" say it is. And if that "we" fragments and is challenged by voices that have hitherto been silenced, voices that reassert Gods, alternative faiths and traditions, or biological essentialism, all things we might think have been relegated to the detritus of history, then we will be left with a vision that cannot be universalized any longer, even as an aspiration. How will a Hans Kelsen-style "grand norm," the unmoved mover, the point back beyond which we do not need to go, fare in such a world? The best we can hope for is an agreement – an "overlapping consensus" – about what we think are desirable social practices and try to commit to realize those ends with as much pressure and leverage as we can muster.[11] Without even the possibility of coercion, however distant and diffuse, to give weight to the charge that this is "*the* direction of travel" such claims will founder on the implacable resistance of many who stand to lose authority and power through yielding up their existing privilege.

Humanist Social Practices

We are left, then, with empirical realities, that is, distinct sets of practices. Human rights workers tend to advocate for law and justice, to seek prosecution and accountability, while humanitarians, in contrast, provide succor for the suffering, focus largely on medical and reparative (not retributive) intervention, meeting basic needs, before then moving on to social goods like public health and education. Charles Beitz (this volume) analyses this as a distinction between "beneficence" and "justice." When we focus on crises this division seems clearer. There seems less for human rights defenders to do when saving lives is the only priority. But things are not so simple.

What about institutions? We have our set of major humanitarian non-governmental organizations (NGOs), led by the ICRC, MSF, CARE, Oxfam, and Save the Children. And on the human rights side, we have Amnesty International and Human Rights Watch, along with FIDH, Human Rights First, and a whole series of other smaller organizations with global ambitions. The people who work in these organizations often have different formal qualifications, different sets of standard operating procedures, and different fundraising and marketing techniques. They compete with each other for money, publicity, and influence while all the time professing their strong affinities as parts of the humanist international. Within the major global institutional bodies, the UN, the EU, we have parts working on humanitarian issues and those working on human rights; for example, the United Nations High Commissioner for Refugees (UNHCR) and the Organization for the Coordination of Humanitarian Assistance (OCHA) vs. the Office of the High Commissioner for Human Rights (OHCHR); we have the European Civil Protection and Humanitarian Aid Operation (ECHO) and, in the Council of Europe, the European Court (and Convention) of Human Rights. We have two sets of laws – international humanitarian law and international human rights law. This should enable us to say, "I know you speak on behalf of human rights because you cite the UDHR and work for Amnesty." And yet, once we look more deeply, we discover an inextricable web of interconnections.

This was not always the case. When Western powers dominated the international system, especially after the 1970s, there was space for both.

Experts with formal credentials began to assert their own unique contribution to dealing with human suffering and depravity. At first sight, as noted, humanitarians seemed to act in crises without much explicit attention to law (excepting the ICRC), while human rights worked on the basis of finding out who was responsible for abuses and violations and prosecuting them. This meant that in natural disasters, barring claims for negligence, humanitarians had things to offer – concrete products like food, shelter, water, and medicine – that human rights defenders did not. It also explains why some of the very largest humanitarian organizations – World Vision, Catholic Relief Services – are both religious and engaged in compassionate social practices. They focused on needs alone and were not required to take a position on rights issues.

What brought the two together was the politics. First, the importance of conflict. I have argued elsewhere that the ICRC – in its attachment to the suffering human person – can be seen as the first human rights organization.[12] As conflict evolved and attempts to prevent it and ameliorate its worst effects became increasingly legalized, the ground that separated humanitarians and human rights workers narrowed. In the Rome Statute, as noted earlier, they closed. It is impossible to tell whether the International Criminal Court (ICC) is a humanitarian or a human rights court. In truth, where crimes against humanity are concerned, it is both. Killing is always an act against the human right to life even if some justifications might be thought to trump that right. Gustave Moynier, builder of the ICRC, proposed an ICC to try individuals rather than states as far back as 1872.[13] Second, it became clear from the 1970s on, especially as regards civil wars and non-state actors, that who was innocent (indeed, what innocence was) mattered hugely for both these forms of normative social action. In the case of civilians in urban and ethnic conflict, it could be hard to clearly identify combatants. Third, once they professionalized and bureaucratized in the 1980s, these NGOs started to fish the same waters for money, members, and supporters. There might be some distinctions here, prima facie. The lack of an explicitly religious account of rights might have made humanitarian NGOs more attractive than human rights for religious people. But the importance within Amnesty, for example, of its many religious members belies this fact.[14] Someone as high profile as Sergio Vieira de Mello could be UN undersecretary general for humanitarian affairs, and then UN high commissioner for human rights. Jan Egeland could hold the same humanitarian affairs brief then become deputy director of Human Rights Watch (having been chair of Amnesty International in Norway beforehand).

Even the crisis exemption – that this is where humanitarians are uniquely to the fore – does not hold up. The ICRC defines protection as "to ensure that authorities and other actors respect their obligations and the rights of individuals in order to preserve the safety, physical integrity and dignity of those affected by armed conflict and other situations of violence."[15] The seven fundamental principles of the International Red Cross and Red Crescent Movement – humanity, impartiality, neutrality, independence, voluntary service, unity, and universality – are very similar to those of Amnesty International's "core values": "Amnesty International forms a global community of human rights defenders based on the principles of international solidarity, effective action for the individual victim, global coverage, the universality and indivisibility of human rights, impartiality and independence, and democracy and mutual respect."[16] In its fundamental principle of "humanity," the Red Cross talks of "assistance without discrimination," and of its purpose as being "to protect life and health and to ensure respect for the human being."[17] Amnesty could make exactly this statement, minus the "health" element. But this is more a branding issue. In fact, Amnesty made a set of recommendations to the G20 in 2017 precisely about the right to health: "Amnesty International is providing a set of recommendations to G20 countries on the importance of universal health care for all persons without discrimination and the full realization of all aspects of the right to health, including through a human rights-based approach to healthcare services provision which, if implemented, would demonstrate their global leadership in this area."[18] The UN's OCHA – which sits atop the global humanitarian architecture – has five strategic objectives in its 2018–2021 plan of which number 4 is: "International acceptance of the centrality of international humanitarian and human rights law, access and protection that results in meaningful action for affected people, especially internally displaced people."[19]

Let us take a concrete case like Syria. Here, we find Human Rights Watch and MSF, to take two further examples, both with a great deal to say. Human Rights Watch points to the targeting of civilians, indiscriminate attacks, and the use of banned weapons, especially chemical and nerve agents. It also points to attacks on hospitals and unlawful restrictions on humanitarian aid.[20] MSF gives more empirical detail to these charges, as well as condemning the Assad government's crimes in a language that HRW could have used: "In reality, they amount to massive, indiscriminate and disproportionate civilian targeting in urban settings, and, in the worst cases, to acts of terror."[21]

What do these examples show us? That if we are looking for clear-cut distinctions between the social practices of human rights and humanitarianism, we will be hard pressed to find them. Crucially, the moral underpinning of each of these social practices is the same, the evolution of a specific view of the human person and the obligations s/he/they are owed. If there appears to be a difference between them, it is to be found in institutional culture. And most of all, in the fact that broadly speaking there are a lot more lawyers in the world of human rights and a lot more nonlawyers – doctors, religious people, and well-meaning generalists – in the world of professional humanitarianism. This seems to give human rights NGOs a particular idiom, or ethos, one about justice. But under the surface much is the same.

One objection might be that humanitarians deal with need, mainly but not exclusively in crisis, whereas human rights advocates are looking to remedy violations of the law that are not among our most fundamental needs. Even this is controversial, however: protection is as much a core need in the moments after catastrophe as anything else. Protection is that part of the UN cluster system that the UNHCR, the most operational of the UN's agencies, is directly responsible for, and it is clear that protection is intrinsically about human rights.[22] The ICRC also stresses protection in terms of the rights of individuals.[23] Meeting immediate need is not a foolproof test.

What about a more fine-grained operational analysis? Humanitarians provide medical treatment, food, shelter, and clean water, and human rights workers do not. Human rights groups would argue and advocate for a person's "right" to these basic requirements, but they do not have the expertise and resources to deliver them directly. They do not need to, of course, because others do. There is no problem working on the rights to these basic needs, in the same way that campaigning to stop the bombing of hospitals is an essential element of ensuring people's basic needs are met. We can make the same argument about more development-focused humanitarian NGOs – Oxfam, for example – and ESC rights, including the right to development, that many human rights groups work on. Here, much work is about the law, access to justice, government policy, aid, all core areas where human rights have as much a role to play as direct provision of services. MSF is working on conditions in refugee camps and in prisons, as is the ICRC, as is Amnesty. They could work together quite easily, each bringing different levels of expertise, donor and membership groups, contacts and networks, nuanced and slightly differentiated operational arguments, but all united on the same basic commitment to humane treatment and respect for all human individuals. Merger would be an operational, not an ethical challenge.

Humanist Futures

By focusing on the *differences* between human rights and humanitarianism there is a danger of missing the forest for the trees. That is, both rely heavily on the global liberal settlement for their efficacy and that settlement is coming apart. We are missing the big picture. Humanism itself, part of the core cultural fabric of Western-led global liberalism, in its imperial and post-imperial phases, is now under serious pressure. This period of 200–300 years is marked by vast hypocrisy, bad faith, atrocity, self-interest, and selective amnesia to name just a few of its ills. But, at the global level, we have rules, norms, and institutions that are broadly liberal in their intent.

By liberal, I mean, again with the caveats mentioned previously, nondiscriminatory *in principle*, universal *in principle*, and non-sectarian *in principle*. This in-principle commitment to the same opportunities and protections for all human persons regardless of identity is built into the majority of these global institutions. How could it be otherwise? In the last few decades a commitment to the idea of global space and global agreements has been intensified into something which has been present in the West since the beginning of modern empire – the urge to modernize other societies along lines considered appropriate first via Christianity and second via what it means to live a full, morally autonomous, fulfilled life where you get to decide how you yourself wish to live. This produces avid consumers, is heavily driven by the needs of modern capitalism, and your chances of realizing it are hugely dependent on your position in class and identity structures, but it has nonetheless embedded the idea that, to paraphrase Thomas Jefferson, "all human persons are born equal with certain inalienable rights" (again, however much that has been ignored in reality).

This version of liberalism is eroding. Identity was, in truth, never depoliticized for those who had that identity (think race in the United States and almost anywhere else, or gender, or sexuality). What has changed is the in-principle objection to rules and policies that discriminate. This is evident in the rejection of liberal rules and norms in many parts of the non-West (e.g., China, Russia, Turkey, Uganda, the Philippines, Cambodia) thereby fulfilling many Western fantasies about the advanced West and the backward South. But the assault on liberalism is now in full swing in the core of the West – Hungary, Poland, the United States, Austria, Italy, the Netherlands, and so on. Even Angela Merkel's progressive stance on migration in Germany has been tempered by political realities and the rise of right-wing parties.

In other words, two dynamics, inextricably linked, have come together. First the relative decline in the power of the West. At the core of this is the rise of China whose influence grows ever greater. Given China's at best problematic relationship to the whole discourse of human rights, it sees such demands as an infringement of its sovereignty but also as the kind of rank hypocrisy that Western nations have indulged in for centuries, a soft power form of coercion that belies the extent to which states like the United States ignore human rights when it seems expedient to do so. Second, the implosion of liberal ideals in a West under pressure economically and socially through competition, rapid technological change, refugees and migration, growing inequality, and environmental collapse.

In 2018, Freedom House recorded its twelfth consecutive year of declining freedom worldwide, with seventy-one countries registering a reduction in political rights and civil liberties.[24] Governments of rising powers, increasingly important in a world whose norms and rules they did not write, will be suspicious, rightly, that humanitarianism represents the soft power form of Western modernity, another vector for the transmission of liberal–capitalist values that threatens their hold on national power and resources. The degree to which humanitarians often attend crises that the major Western powers have been complicit in creating substantiates this concern (think Vietnam, Congo, Cambodia, Iraq, Syria, Libya). The implications of this are simple but profound: *Rules and norms that conflict in some way with the preferences of the rising powers, and especially the Chinese government, will no longer necessarily be enforceable at the global level.* We know what this looks like in the case of China because it is how the United States has behaved for much of the last 80–100 years. This is the prerogative of being a superpower. Now we have two superpowers again. As China's influence, its diplomacy, its money, its power filter into all areas of the international political system, so it will be harder and harder to persuade either indifferent or reluctant states that they have no choice in the longer run but to follow the West.

This means that there is a void, an interregnum, a vacuum, where no one really knows what the most important rules are and whether they will be enforced anymore (to the extent that they ever were really enforced) – think international humanitarian law, think torture, think freedom of speech. States at best have to hedge their bets (trying to retain the goodwill of both China and the United States) and at worst can simply flout those rules with impunity. The Philippines and Cambodia are the only Asian states that have signed the Rome Statute of the ICC, the humanist institution par excellence, to take just one obvious example. Who else will sign now the United States and China have made it clear they have no interest in the court? What does this mean for humanism? That the conditions conducive to the globalization of human rights and humanitarianism, which some have argued were rooted in the slow progressive teleology of a "widening circle of compassion" datable back to the European Enlightenment, are diminishing.[25] Whatever happens next in our global social and political life, there is plenty of reason to fear it will not be hospitable to the norms of human rights or humanitarianism, particularly their legal achievements. Has anything better exemplified the death (even if it is temporary) of the humanist ideal than the bombing of hospitals in Syria and Yemen by the governments of Russia, Syria, and Saudi Arabia? Or the use of torture by the US government? Was this not a norm "we" assumed would never openly be breached in the West?

These changes, including the possibility of a United States-China trade war and the United States's withdrawal from key Western-led transnational institutions (the Human Rights Council), as well as ambivalence about the North Atlantic Treaty Organization and the World Trade Organization, will take us back to a world of concrete solidarities where shared interests and identities (and threats) will bind people more tightly as a mobilizing principle than more abstract commitments to universal notions (like the moral equivalence of all persons) and the essential humanity that we all share. Which presents humanists with a fateful question: What responses are available when faced with rejection of the whole principle of equal moral worth? Humanitarian social practice encompasses a kind of silent witnessing, compassion for the suffering and the dying without words, without judgment. Its repertoire does not require public condemnation. Human rights advocacy is all about speaking out (making MSF of all humanist organizations perhaps the best hybrid example).[26] There can be humanitarianism in a nonliberal world, but little human rights (as a social practice; rights-like *ideas* will persist, of course). Liberalism is preferable for humanitarians, but they have things they can do without it. There remains a call for compassion in the death camp or in the hospital under fire. Whether or not such suffering is morally wrong, it is always pitiable and capable of inspiring empathy. No one would request help in such extreme situations on the basis that they had a right to it unless they were faced with someone refusing to assist them on principle (i.e., someone denying the *validity* of their request for help). The demand is: help me. And the expectation would naturally be that help would be given.

Consider three real MSF examples: should you provide medical assistance to a torture victim in prison when it means he will survive to be tortured again tomorrow; should you provide condoms to a child soldier so that when he rapes women in the villages he raids they will not get HIV; should you re-stitch an infibulated woman after childbirth rather than letting the local midwife do it with far inferior tools and in less hygienic conditions?[27] What is the human rights answer to any of these questions?

Do not torture, do not rape, do not practice female genital mutilation. Okay, now given that none of those morally desirable things will happen in these cases, what is the answer now? In the here and now, humanitarians have one, and must have one, whereas human rights advocates do not. In the cases above, is not the *right* thing to do: stay with the torture victim, hand over the condoms, and reconstruct the infibulation? This is a recognition of the moral importance of this specific human person, not of the abstract principle of "humanity." In each case you are complicit in an abuse. Humanitarians are used to these morally imperfect choices. The content of humanitarian books tends to be about crisis, failure, and defeat. Human rights advocates usually write about achievements, that is, their success in building a global human rights movement and establishing treaty and national human rights law.

Humanitarianism can survive in a million acts of compassion for those who suffer. It need not be justified, defended, explained, or articulated in any form. It can be just a moment of mercy, respite, of human kindness. We do not all have to manifest it, it does not need to be enshrined as a law or obligation. It might not even have to come from a place of love. It is an act of humanity outside the realm of conceptual justification. There will always be some, maybe only a few, people who help in this way under any regime of truth, regardless of the identity or moral character of those they are helping, and in this lies humanitarianism's inextinguishable mission.

Conclusion

All of this is an important indication of why the humanitarian "business model" is a more durable form of humanism in inhospitable conditions than its human rights variant. But humanitarianism has something else going for it also: it is difficult to see what value human rights have for states as a whole at the systemic level (beyond narrow areas of reciprocity like prisoner protection). They can be useful as a foreign policy tool to apply soft power pressure to other governments, but all states find them more or less irksome when they demand accountability or behavioral change. Human rights contribute little that is obvious to the functioning of the international system (assuming that they rarely deter atrocity and forced displacement, and indeed as this chapter suggests are increasingly less likely to do so). But humanitarianism *does* have system-wide functionality – it provides a mechanism to prevent the failures of the system as a whole (usually because of failures of state policy) that endanger the broad consensus necessary for the system to exist without the deployment of massive coercion and the overt suppression of dissent. Humanitarians mop up a little of the mess when state policies end in failure and collapse. They give states an alibi and a way out.

Take refugees for example. If humanitarians can keep refugees in their original country, they stop other states from facing the political costs of accepting, or refusing, refugee demands for asylum. Or disease. The frontline role of humanitarians in keeping Ebola "over there" – creating a quarantine zone that protected other states from danger – prevented a massive public health and political headache for other governments including those in the West. The UNHCR can be seen, in this way, not as the last hope for displaced and traumatized people but as complicit in a giant camp system designed to stop the negative side-effects of state actions from undermining the system of states en masse.

It is in this way that human rights, more strident, more principled, more monotheistic, will be the form of humanism that withers as the climate for global normative improvement deteriorates. The relationship between human rights and humanitarianism is a vertical one not a parallel one. The initial shoots from the core humanist principle of equal moral worth were simply about compassion, care, concern. From this grew attention not only to those who suffered but also why they suffered. The over-whelming influence of the West in the last two centuries, and especially in the twentieth century, the age of American power, meant that its attach-ment to ideas of law and justice, however partial and self-interested, could be globalized.

Nothing could better illustrate this than the victor's justice on display at the Tokyo war crimes tribunal after World War II (Japan having just been subject to the two greatest single examples of crimes against humanity in history). Human rights – in the guise of international justice – gave the United States a way out of the Balkan wars (by allowing something to appear to be done), it even – in the case of Rwanda – provided a mechanism for post-conflict reconstruction that facilitated the contin-ued functioning of the system as a whole (to give an example, contra my argument above, that human rights has no functionality). But these are all cases that depend on overweening power. Now that has gone, the "stretch goal" of human rights will need to be reduced to more feasible horizons. To provide a little solace for those who suffer and to look for those occasions on which the international system needs to deal, if only cosme-tically, with threats to its reliable functioning. It will fall to humanitarians, in other words, to keep the flame alive until the conditions arise once again within which it can grow into human rights. There is no reason, of course, apart from a belief in the ineluctability of liberal progress, to assume that that day will come any time soon.

Part II

Practices

5 Humanitarian Governance and the Circumvention of Revolutionary Human Rights in the British Empire

Alan Lester

Humanitarianism and human rights are often seen as having a shared late eighteenth-and early nineteenth-century provenance within the revolutionary fervor of the European Enlightenment, the anti-slavery campaign, and the rise of sympathy for distant strangers.[1] While Moyn points out that "humanitarianism and rights rarely crossed into (let alone defined) each other in the hierarchical global order and world visions of the nineteenth century," I want to push the distinction further.[2] I argue that these projects were not coeval in the sense that they sprang from a common orientation to the world. Their genesis was indeed related, but antagonistically rather than in alignment. Humanitarianism and human rights were oppositional assemblages. As Fabian Klose notes in this volume, "humanitarianism and human rights are presented in opposing terms, sometimes even as rival concepts by advocates on both sides," but often, I think, for the wrong reason. Often, humanitarianism is contrasted with human rights because of the former's reliance "upon a discourse of suffering and charity," and the latter's basis in "a discourse of justice and solidarity." Here, however, I argue that these discourses are opposed rather by their fundamental political orientation. Whereas the former had origins broadly in the amelioration of existing relations of power and privilege, the latter proposed revolutionary transformation. The former was forged directly to contend with the latter.

My focus will be on humanitarian *governance* specifically.[3] Humanitarianism has specific temporalities and geographies, but it is also manifest in specific registers. The combinations of words, text, and images that humanitarian agencies use to express and mobilize concern for vulnerable and distant others, so as to raise consciousness and funds, are different from those mobilized by political lobbies on behalf of state intervention, and these in turn are different from the various articulations by governmental figures of their own "humane" policies. Each humanitarian register corresponds to a particular project of humane intervention – a particular kind of change that the humanitarian is trying to effect in the world on behalf of vulnerable and precarious others. My understanding of governmentality is derived above all from Foucault, who sought to describe the practices of government of a population that emerged in Europe from the Renaissance. For Foucault, governmental rationalization within these societies "differs from the rationalisation peculiar to economic processes, or to production and communication techniques; it differs from that of scientific discourse." It "doesn't involve instrumental violence," but rather the inducement by various means to affect behavior, both of the individual and of the collective: "right from the start, the state is both individualising and totalitarian." The "aim of the modern art of government, or state rationality," for Foucault, is "to develop those elements constitutive of individuals' lives in such a way that their development also fosters that of the strength of the state."[4] Humanitarianism has been as much a part of this modern governmental project as any other.

Humanitarian "reason," as Fassin puts it, has always existed not solely in the extra-governmental realm of the nongovernmental organization or the political lobby. It has also "serve[d] both to define and to justify discourses and practices of the government of human beings."[5] Humanitarian governance allows for the functioning of the polity as a whole, by providing welfare to elements of the population in need.[6] As Reid-Henry puts it:

technologies of care were ... an unavoidable consideration both of and for the modern bureaucratic state ... if in his analysis of the emergence of the modern era of government [Foucault] was right to suggest that the new aim of punishing was not to punish less but to punish better, with more universality and to insert the power to punish more deeply into the social body, then the same is no less true of the desire to save.[7]

Humanitarian regulation as a function of government – a way of *being* governmental – was as intrinsic to the project of Britain's colonization of other lands as it was to the simultaneous emergence of a modern state system in Europe. As Fassin points out, humanitarianism is a "mode of government that concerns the victims of poverty, homelessness, unemployment, and exile, as well as of disasters, famines, epidemics, and wars – in short, every situation characterized by precariousness."[8] The acquisition of an expanded settler empire produced such precariousness in multiple, and previously relatively disconnected contexts, for all of which British governing men were now responsible. I contend here that humanitarianism arose, at least within the British Empire, in part as a counter-revolutionary practice of governance, precisely in order to defuse the radical potential of human rights to destabilize that empire.

Telling the story of two men who sought to govern the British Empire in different "humanitarian" registers helps us to delineate these tensions, and also to chart the longer history of dynamism within humanitarian governance. Both George Arthur and George Grey were proponents of humanitarian governance. The former developed what we might call a paternalistic register culminating in policies of Protection, and the latter an eliminationist one aimed at "amalgamation." Yet both were engaged in a project to fend off the radical transformation latent in the late eighteenth- and early nineteenth-century idea of human rights. This was a project that altered quite fundamentally during the course even of these two men's careers. George Arthur governed a diverse array of colonies between the 1810s and 1840s, while George Grey governed the settler colonies of South Australia, New Zealand, and the Cape Colony from the 1840s to the 1860s. Arthur was a pioneer of a form of humanitarian colonial governance rooted in the amelioration of slavery and translated into Protection for Indigenous peoples. Grey helped to reshape humanitarian governance as assimilation, or the eradication of difference, otherwise known to settler colonial historians as the attempted cultural genocide of Indigenous peoples. The two men elaborated quite different styles, or registers to use Fassin's term, of humanitarian governance, the former apparently premised upon a tolerance of difference and a desire to preserve community autonomy, the latter a form of social engineering designed to erase distinct communities and difference. Both were counter-revolutionary, and counter-human rights strategies, articulated by different individuals for different times and in different contexts.

George Arthur: From Amelioration to Protection

In 1837, Lt. Governor George Arthur, at the time governor of Upper Canada, wrote that the British government must raise in Canada

a race of Englishmen with the same Government, the same feelings, and the same love of freedom that fills our bosoms; and here we may by their assistance oppose the most effectual barrier to the demon of democracy, which is threatening all civilized Governments.[9]

For Arthur, freedom and democracy were antithetical concepts. Freedom consisted in being governed by those most qualified to exercise authority. Individuals were best protected from want, strife, and oppression by those most fitted to govern by education and upbringing. Democracy brings with it rule of the mob. It consists of individuals being trampled upon by political zealots. Within an increasingly global Anglosphere, the sincere pursuit of humanitarian objectives by imperial administrators such as Arthur was, in part, an attempt to head off the revolutionary potential of a human rights discourse that was seen to lay behind the American, French, and Haitian Revolutions and their dangerous notion of democratic governance. Humanitarian governance would help maintain an established regime centered on aristocracy, Church, and Crown.

By the time Arthur wrote of the contrast between British freedom and American democracy, he had fought in the French Revolutionary and Napoleonic Wars and been operating in colonial governance for some thirty years, in Jamaica, Honduras, and Van Diemen's Land. Recently posted to Upper Canada (Ontario), he had inherited a potentially revolutionary situation, with American Patriots or Hunters Lodges crossing into British Canada to stir up rebellion among disloyal colonists and spread revolt from Lower Canada (Quebec). It was in this context that Arthur made his most explicit delineation between freedom and democracy. Like so many other British imperial administrators, Arthur's formative years had been shaped by anti-revolutionary warfare. Along with most of his peers, he saw the amelioration of slavery as a prophylactic response to the revolutionary potential of the enslaved after the Haitian Revolution; the protection of Indigenous peoples as a strategy to counter anarchy in the settler colonies, and the genesis of human rights discourse in France and the United States as heralding revolutionary terror elsewhere.[10] Throughout Arthur's and other British colonial officials' careers, humanitarian "amelioration" of certain peoples' conditions of life was an antidote to the revolutionary potential of human rights. Humanitarian forms of governance were the way in which both enslaved peoples and settlers (equally liable to rebellion in Arthur's experience) would be incorporated as free and loyal colonial subjects.

Arthur's career in the military began at a critical time for the shaping of modern forms of governmentality in Europe and in colonial sites.[11] In the wake of the American Revolution, a modern British state was being created as a direct rival and conservative counterpart to first the French Revolutionary and then the Napoleonic state, through "fiscal-militarism," as a tax raising and spending civil bureaucracy was brought into alignment with military discipline and expansion.[12] Like so many of his generation of colonial officials Arthur first came to the attention of the British governing elite as a result of his distinguished conduct as a young soldier. He fought bravely in the skirmishes leading up to the Battle of Maida in southern Italy, the attempted occupation of Alexandria, and the disastrous Walcheren campaign.[13] Lieutenant-General Don, who assumed command of the survivors from Walcheren, offered Arthur a post as aide-de-camp in the military governance of Jersey in 1810 as a direct result of his distinguished service. Here, in close proximity to France itself, Arthur encountered the difficulties of governing in the face not only of invasion fears but also of radical critics within the civilian population. In 1779, popular agitation had forced the autocratic governor of the island to allow the election of magistrates on a broad franchise. Don complained about the "very great difficulty in carrying out the Executive business" in the face of "a growing spirit of insurbordination" from those magistrates who opposed him, and indeed resolutions opposing control of the island by the British parliament.[14] Arthur was struck, apparently for the first, but certainly not the last time, by the necessity for those who govern to be unimpeded by dangerous democratic notions.

Arthur's was a humanism founded on the rights of subjects, rather than of citizens, let alone those of "man" as a universal entity.[15] Arthur's understanding, developed through his relationship with Don, was that those who were best positioned to govern should be able to do so without interference from subjects who could not possibly comprehend the range of factors influencing any well-informed and reasoned decision. It was through his experience of military command that he came to straddle the transition from autocratic military governance to reforming, humanitarian-inclined intervention in colonial societies. Arthur's support for Don allowed him to take up a vacant majority in the 7th West India Regiment in 1812. This had been founded as a predominantly black corps in 1795 in response to the high mortality among British officers in the Antilles. By the time Arthur arrived in Jamaica the regiment had served with distinction against French units similarly recruited among enslaved populations in the Caribbean. During his eighteen months as assistant quartermaster-general and acting paymaster-general in Jamaica, Arthur expressed himself "a perfect Wilberforce as to slavery," and objected to planters' restrictions on preaching to slaves.[16] He also resented planters' attacks on his soldiers' freedom to operate outside the plantation economy. In Jamaica, Arthur became a more devout and convinced evangelical, "understanding," as he put it, "what Gospel really was in truth and power."[17] Rather than his evangelicalism predisposing him to oppose slavery, in Arthur's case it was the witnessing of slavery that made him more evangelical. It was also perfectly consistent for Arthur to become more autocratic at the same time. His exposure to planters made Arthur just as wary of "respectable" and powerful settlers who opposed humane interference in their affairs, as he was of radical agitators.[18]

The end of the Napoleonic War closed down opportunities for advancement in the army. Within a month of his wedding Arthur reluctantly accepted the less than glamorous vacant post of superintendent and commandant (as lieutenant colonel) at Belize, the capital town of a small

British commercial settlement on the Bay of Honduras. There, his evan-gelicalism took a more serious turn. Honduras was not, technically a British colony, but rather a settlement of some 150 British settlers, mostly mahogany cutters and merchants, 900 "free blacks" and 3,000 enslaved people tolerated on Spanish colonial territory. Until 1820 Arthur had believed settlers' representations concerning the relative "mildness" of slaves' conditions in the interior, beyond Belize. A slave revolt in that year, however, saw him travel inland encountering what he described as "very unnecessary harshness," for the first time.[19] Having previously reasoned that there was no need for them, Arthur now became determined to apply the ameliorative measures that Colonial Office policy demanded, as a result of the pressure of the anti-slavery lobby, in the rest of the Caribbean.[20]

Protectors of slaves were progressively appointed to all the Caribbean Crown colonies starting with the former Spanish Trinidad. Their appointments speeded up after the Haitian Revolution, to preempt the spread of revolt to British colonies. Their role was to enforce the new ameliorative codes limiting work hours and punishments, and to investi-gate enslaved people's complaints against masters who breached them. Significantly, the protectors were also intended to help prepare enslaved people for their freedom by encouraging their Christianization and "civilization."[21] This was a project which Arthur anticipated and pursued vigorously in Honduras. It represented the convergence of his evangelical awakening, his distrust of both privileged and radical settlers "who have ever been unceasingly troublesome and impatient of the most ordinary interference of the Crown," and his insistence on the primacy of church and state in the face of the French Revolutionary and Napoleonic threat.[22] The most concrete realization of this project included the appli-cation in Honduras of Jamaican law so that enslaved people had some protection from the arbitrary punishment of masters, and the freeing of descendants of Mosquito Coast "Indians" who had been enslaved illeg-ally by settler parties.[23]

Arthur's attempted prosecution of the British timber cutters and mer-chants responsible for keeping these "Indians" in captivity was evidence of his determination to enforce a discourse of humane governance. The fierce opposition that Arthur encountered when pursuing amelioration in Honduras affected his health, and he had to return to England on leave in 1822. While the settlers sent an agent to orchestrate legal proceedings against him in London and bar his return to the settlement, he had to defend his actions in a voluminous correspondence with the Colonial Office.[24] With the approval of the Colonial Office, Arthur had burnt his bridges with the settlers of Honduras and so he was offered the newly vacant post of lieutenant governor of Van Diemen's Land. There, he would be confronted by a new challenge for humanitarian governance: the resistance of a still independent, sovereign people to the colonization of their land, rather than the plight of an enslaved population.

Arthur began, nonetheless, by taking the notion of "amelioration," with its policies of individual and collective reformation of settler and slave subjectivities, with him to the penal settlement of Van Diemen's Land in 1824. There, at first, he attempted to apply the project again, to both convicts and Aboriginal people. He wrote to the leading anti-slavery campaigner in London, Thomas Fowell Buxton, that religious instruction would supply the convicts "with an inward regulator," which was "ten times more effectual in every case ... than all the fear and alarm that can be exerted from without," and produced two pamphlets for circulation in the colony and in Britain elaborating upon proper measures for the rehabilitation of transportees.[25] But while he admitted privately that he felt about a quarter of all transportees were "irreclaimable," he would not allow such of the Aboriginal inhabitants of the island.[26] Arthur's response to the Aboriginal resistance that he was about to encounter, "was more measured and gradual than his ruthless and decisive crushing of the bushranging gangs that roamed the colony."[27] One of Arthur's first acts in the colony to issue a proclamation affording Aborigines equal rights to settlers and promising "the same punishment as though committed on the person or property of any settlers" to those who harmed them.[28] Its effect was soon nullified by the imperative for colonial governance to facilitate British emigrant settlement.

The year before Arthur arrived, Samuel Guy noted that a new settler "will now have some difficulty in obtaining good land except he gets into the infrequent parts of the colony – among the wild natives."[29] Although only 132,500 acres had been awarded to emancipists (former convicts, now free to settle in the colony) and free settlers between 1804 and 1822, within seven years of Arthur's arrival, in accordance with instructions from the Colonial Office, he had overseen the allocation of a further 1,899,332 acres.[30] The central Aboriginal groups responded by initiating a guerilla war. Arthur continued to dispose of land to the Van Diemen's Land Company and settlers regardless of Aboriginal occupation and usage, but encouraged a small settlement of Aboriginal people on Bruny Island near Hobart as a humanitarian experiment to see if they could be redeemed and "reclaimed" for Christianity within a new, colonial environment. When Arthur advertised among the Hobart settlers for a superintendent of the Bruny Island settlement, the successful applicant was George Augustus Robinson, a former builder from the East End of London. Robinson wrote that he was "fully persuaded that the plan which your Excellency has devised is the only one whereby the aborigines of this territory can be *ameliorated.*"[31] Robinson's and Arthur's trajectories first became entwined as a result of this language of amelioration, of which Arthur had encountered relatively little since his arrival among the Van Diemen's Land settlers.

By the late 1820s settlers outnumbered Aborigines on the island by about twenty to one and significant numbers of them backed a campaign of Aboriginal "extermination" in the face of continued and well-organized resistance.[32] A settler newspaper presented Arthur with an ultimatum: if the Aborigines were not removed quickly, "they will be hunted down like wild beasts and destroyed" (*Colonial Times* 1826). Despite recurrent portrayals of him in much of the Australian historiography as a genocidally inclined imperial autocrat, Arthur was deeply affected, writing to the Colonial secretary that the violence "wholly engrosses and fills my mind with painful anxiety."[33] He declared martial law in 1828 in an attempt, as he portrayed it, to take the conflict out of the hands of settlers and into those of the state. But the move effectively licensed settlers to continue exterminatory raids on Aboriginal bands.[34] Arthur's attempt to use settler militias and the regular army to round up the remaining tribes of the central island so that they could be held in "benevolent captivity" on reserve land failed to bring the warfare to a conclusion. His naïve calls for settlers to treat Aboriginal resisters with humanity were denounced by the settler press as arising from "false notions of pity."[35]

Robinson, in the meantime, had been able to embark on an alternative plan that he called his conciliatory, or "friendly" mission. He would employ the Aboriginal people that he had first come to know on Bruny Island to travel with him on various expeditions across parts of Van Diemen's Land where independent tribes were holding out, and embark upon negotiations with them. These negotiations would result in their surrender and removal to a new settlement on Flinders Island.[36] Through Robinson, Arthur found a way to bridge the crucial differences between an established discourse of *amelioration,* based on the protection and reform of captive, enslaved people, and the conciliation and *protection* of a defiant Indigenous population. Even as all of the remaining Aboriginal people on the island were finally rounded up and exiled, the deterritorialization of amelioration in Van Diemen's Land and its reterritorialization as protection provided salvation for Arthur's reputation as a humanitarian governor. Arthur was sincere when he told the colonial secretary in London that

it cannot hereafter be said that [the Aboriginal people] were torn from their kindred and friends ... No! their removal has been for their benefit, and in almost every instance with their own free will and consent. They have been removed from danger, and placed in safety in a suitable asylum ... where they are brought under moral and religious inculcation.[37]

Robinson himself wrote, "I trust the time is not far distant when the same humane policy will be adopted towards the aboriginal inhabitants of every colony throughout the British empire."[38] Thus would Indigenous peoples become the nineteenth-century equivalent of refugee camp inhabitants within the settler colonies.[39] On Flinders Island itself, the 200 Aboriginal people who were the subjects of this "humane policy" resisted the program of schooling and agricultural training to which they were intermittently and inconsistently subjected. They continued to protest about their removal from customary resources and restricted mobility as malnourishment and susceptibility to disease diminished their numbers. In 1847, the remaining forty-seven were finally allowed to return to the Oyster Bay area of the Tasmanian mainland.[40]

Even while these "beneficiaries" of Robinson's plan ceased to exist as a viable community, Arthur himself was able to realize Robinson's vision for the wider adoption of his policy. He did so primarily through his connection with Thomas Fowell Buxton, whom the ailing William Wilberforce asked to take over the campaign to emancipate the enslaved in Britain's colonies. Arthur had met Buxton in London before sailing for Van Diemen's Land and maintained the connection through letters thereafter. As member of parliament for Weymouth, Buxton devoted much of his considerable energy to the pursuit of emancipation in the Caribbean. But he also maintained his own prior reformist interests. Giving a characteristic snapshot of the relationship between his domestic and overseas humanitarian concerns in 1823 he wrote:

How can I promote the welfare of others? In private, by ... sparing on my own pleasure and expending on God's service. In public, by attending to the Slave Trade, Slavery, Indian widows burning themselves, the completion of those objects which have made some advance, viz. Criminal Law, Prisons, and Police.[41]

By 1835, Buxton was planning for a House of Commons Select Committee to investigate the injustices that settler colonization was occasioning throughout the Empire. He argued that "Great Britain has, in former times, countenanced evils of great magnitude, – slavery and the Slave Trade; but for these she has made some atonement ... An evil remains very similar in character, and not altogether unfit to be compared with them in the amount of misery it produces. The oppression of the natives of barbarous countries is a practice which pleads no claim to indulgence."[42] Arthur returned to Plymouth in March 1837 and between then and December, when he received his next posting, he was able to talk directly with both Buxton and the Colonial Secretary Lord Glenelg about the measures needed to translate anti-slavery discourse into policies for the protection of Indigenous peoples.

Arthur's intimate reflections on British atrocities in Van Diemen's Land matched precisely the discourse of Buxton's committee. This too held that British colonization was just in principle but had been perverted in practice by particular British settlers.[43] That exteriorization and the projection of blame that it entailed necessitated a moral reformist commitment and it was this which led Arthur to urge for the establishment of Protectorates of Aborigines in other contemporary spaces of settler violence and dispossession. It was settlers, not the colonial government, who had created the destruction of Indigenous society, and it was government's task to protect Indigenous peoples from them throughout the process of colonization. Arthur insisted on the need for a new, humanitarian branch of colonial government. The idea of these Protectorates was written into the Aborigines Committee's recommendations and Glenelg was happy to hand over the process of determining principles and personnel for a New South Wales Protectorate to Arthur himself. By July 1837, he was proposing that Robinson be appointed chief protector, and by December he had chosen his four assistants.[44] I will return to the Port Phillip Protectorate later.

Arthur's next experience of governance was in North America, where we encountered him in 1837. It brought to prominence once more those antipathies to radicalism and democracy that Arthur had fashioned during his experiences of fighting the French. As soon as he arrived in Upper Canada, Arthur inherited the difficulty of deciding the fate of the convicted rebels from an abortive 1837 uprising that had been directed against the colony's ruling oligarchy and was loosely connected to the more serious resistance of French Canadians in neighboring Lower Canada.[45] The rebel leaders Samuel Lount and Peter Matthews had already received capital sentences and Arthur had to decide whether to proceed with their executions and what to do with the remaining captured rebels and American "patriots," who had engaged in cross-border raids in support of them. Whichever course he took would alienate one settler faction or another. Loyalist settlers, many of them having resettled from the United States after the revolution, demanded the severest possible penalties for all those who had engaged in acts of rebellion, while reformers, among them "respectable" recent British emigrants, called for clemency. Arthur compromised. He had the sentences on Lount and Matthews carried out, while "leniently" transporting the ringleaders among the other convicted rebels back the way he had come, as convicts to Van Diemen's Land. Arthur wanted more severe punishment of the cross-border raiders from the United States than his Legislative Council, writing "I have caused 17 of the Ruffians who invaded the province to be executed which has damped the courage of the Patriots ... They are the most Vain people in the world, and certainly believed that we did not dare to hang an American citizen."[46] Arthur's tenure in Upper Canada was short lived as the colony was soon confederated with Lower Canada under revised structures of government intended to prevent a recurrence of settler rebellion. In the meantime, Arthur's authoritarian conservatism, expectations of discipline, self-restraint and perseverance, and dedication to the relief of suffering were a paradoxical mix that characterized the particular kind of humanitarian governmental doctrine that Indigenous peoples in certain parts of the British Empire first encountered.

George Grey: From Protection to Amalgamation

While Arthur helped develop a discourse of Protection, entailing the safeguarding of Aboriginal people on reserves akin to the humanitarian camps of today, George Grey pioneered a quite different form of humanitarian governance – one that respected the cultural difference of its "beneficiaries" far less. Grey's governmental practices, and his representations of them, proceeded from the notion that Arthur's Protection had failed its intended beneficiaries. While it emphasized their ultimate "civilization" and integration with settler communities, Protection entailed preserving Indigenous communities' access to land and treating with them, to a certain extent as if they were still sovereign peoples within specific locales. Grey, however, established the terms upon which cultural genocide could be posited as the only humane alternative to racial extermination. Grey's promotion of "amalgamation" in place of an otherwise inevitable physical destruction went on to influence the highest levels of colonial administration. Amalgamation entailed both the elimination of Indigenous society and the transfer of its territory on the one hand, and the duty of care to Indigenous individuals newly assimilated into settler societies on the other hand. On behalf of the British Empire as a whole, Grey helped to reconcile "humanitarian" governance with settler colonialism.

Grey, who governed the colonies of South Australia, Aotearoa/New Zealand, the Cape Colony, and Aotearoa/New Zealand again between 1841 and 1868, remains one of the most enigmatic of British imperial figures. His biographer noted that "he has been denounced as an autocrat and a Conservative and hailed as a great Liberal and a radical reformer"; portrayed as "an ambitious self-seeker who humbugged the authorities by professions of philanthropy" and "a genuine humanitarian pursuing high ideals by dubious methods which exposed him to misinterpretation."[47] In 1830, commissioned as an ensign, Grey had been posted to Ireland, where he served for three or four years. In most biographical narratives, Grey's uncomfortable experiences there persuaded him of the necessity for a liberal, humane empire. Although instructed to counter an organized boycott of tithes, he could not help himself being inspired by Daniel O'Connell's nationalist oratory. Rather than being the cause of the conflict between his loyalty and his sympathy, however, the British Empire offered Grey a resolution to it. "Appalled by the poverty of the Irish people ... He reached the conclusion that emigration was the solution to Ireland's ills: new nations should be established, in lands of opportunity for the poor."[48] Although Grey left Ireland after three years to return to Sandhurst for further military training, he made it seem in later accounts, reproduced by subsequent biographers, as though the experience of service there had so radicalized him that he chose to leave the army and pursue a career as a colonial explorer, in order to help realize his vision of benevolent imperial expansion in new lands.[49] After exploring in Western Australia, Grey acted briefly as magistrate in Albany. He used his few months in office there to very good effect in the promotion of his career in Britain. Not only did he publish his exploratory journal and a vocabulary of Aboriginal languages, but also appended to his journal a pamphlet entitled "Report on the Best Means of Promoting the Civilization of the Aboriginal Inhabitants of Australia," which outlined a scheme for the humane governance of Aboriginal people undergoing settler colonization.[50]

Grey promoted his report assiduously, via James Stephen, permanent under-secretary at the Colonial Office in London, who enclosed it with the instructions sent to James Hobson for his first lieutenant governorship of New Zealand, as a potential model for humane governance of the Māori. It was published in Parliamentary Papers and republished in periodicals in Britain and the Australian colonies. As Damon Salesa notes, the report's "strength was that it tied together many diverse approaches to which the Colonial Office was already sympathetic, with a few detailed touches that were Grey's own." Nevertheless its effect was, in the words of Colonial Secretary Lord John Russell, to render Grey "a man destined to reclaim an aboriginal race and amalgamate them with civilization."[51] The contact that he had made with James Stephen enabled Grey to embark upon the governorship of South Australia, aged only 28, after his return to England, and it was there that he acquired particular favor with the Colonial Office for reversing the colony's slide into insolvency and complete dependence on the British exchequer.

Grey's subsequent influence within humanitarian governing circles was as much due to his reputation for ethnographic expertise acquired during his Western Australian exploratory adventure, as it was to his exercise of political economy as a governor. His direct experience of Aboriginal society and culture enabled him to join in debates about the likely future under Arthur's protectionist form of governance. And indeed it was the colony which Arthur had governed – Van Diemen's Land – which portended the fate that many believed lay in store not only for Australia's Aboriginal people, but for Indigenous peoples more generally. The almost complete elimination of the Tasmanian Aborigines – at least those of unmediated Aboriginal descent living on the main island – was reinforcing a new understanding in Europe that human extinction, like that of certain species of animals – could be a "natural," if unfortunate, process. Aboriginal "eradication" in Tasmania came to be understood as an inevitable consequence of the spread of a more advanced people and civilization – the first empirical example of a supposedly dying race.[52] It was this understanding which gave rise to the origins of ethnography as a project of salvage.[53] Before the British Association for the Advancement of Science (BAAS) in 1839, James Cowles Prichard outlined the tone for the new discipline:

Wherever Europeans have settled, their arrival has been the harbinger of extermination to the native tribes ... Now, as the progress of colonization is so much extended of late years, and the obstacle of distance and physical difficulties are so much overcome, it may be calculated that these calamities ... are to be accelerated in their progress; and it may happen that, in the course of another century, the aboriginal nations of most parts of the world will have ceased entirely to exist. In the meantime, if Christian nations think it not their duty to interpose and save the numerous tribes of their own species from utter extermination, it is of the greatest importance ... to obtain much more extensive information than we now possess of their physical and moral characters ... How can this be obtained when so many tribes shall have become extinct, and their thoughts shall have perished with them?[54]

If the Indigenous peoples of Britain's settler colonies (and of the United States' proliferating western territories) were dying out, then it was clear that the project of official Protection had failed. One of the key questions for colonial governors during the later 1840s and 1850s, then, was how to perpetuate the legacy of humanitarian colonial governance, inherited from the emancipationist, evangelical 1830s and early 1840s. George Grey provided perhaps the most persuasive and explicit rationalization of the dilemma and answer to this problem. The Colonial Office had Grey's report from Western Australia published and circulated the year before Prichard's explicit call for a salvage ethnography. Grey himself would soon become one of the most influential contributors to that project and at the same time, one of the most powerful figures in the governance of empire.

Grey began his report by noting that all previous attempts to civilize Aboriginal people in the Australian colonies had failed. This, he argued, was because colonial policies were founded on the protective principle that, until such time as Aboriginal people proved amenable to British laws, they should be allowed to exercise "their own customs upon themselves." While originating in the "Philanthropic motives" that were manifested in the Protectorates, such a position betrayed an ignorance of the real nature of these customs and of their effects upon the individuals subjected to them. Australia's Aboriginal people, as all good humanitarians knew, were "as apt and intelligent as any other race of men," but as long as their code of laws prevailed, it would be impossible for them ever to "emerge from a Savage state." Even a highly endowed, civilized race, Grey asserted, would quickly be reduced once more to savagery if such laws were ever to be imposed upon them.[55] The only solution was to insist, "from the moment the Aborigines of this Country are declared British subjects," that "they are taught that the British laws are to supersede their own." Far from being an aggressive assertion of sovereignty by right of conquest, this was "the course of true humanity." Individual Indigenous people persuaded of the benefits of British civilization might thus have an escape route from imprisoning and retarding customs. In order to exemplify, Grey invoked the kind of figure upon which anti-slavery and evangelical humanitarian narratives had centered in their attempts to garner compassion at a distance, writing of Aboriginal "girls who have been betrothed in their infancy, and who, on approaching years of puberty, have been compelled by their husbands to join them" in the bush. Such "barbarous laws" would "destroy and overturn" any strides made by Aboriginal individuals.[56]

Grey's ethnographic knowledge acquired a status among men and women of science because of his prolific correspondence with figures such as Thomas Hodgkin, Charles Darwin, and Florence Nightingale. Grey's early Aboriginal vocabularies were just the beginning of a prolific publishing career in and on Aboriginal Australians, Native Americans, and Māori.[57] As governor in the Cape Colony he was responsible for amassing the collection that became the South African Library in Cape Town, and for the appointment of the librarian Willhelm Bleek, who coined the term "Bantu" for southern Africa's pastoralist African peoples.[58] Stocking describes Grey as "one of the more perceptive ethnographers of his day and author of some of the most influential ethnographic work of the century."[59] By contributing to governmental and scientific assemblages from the late 1830s, Grey helped to establish that any policies which aimed to do more than just smooth the pillow of inevitably dying Indigenous races could be considered a worthy humanitarian intervention. As such he was a participant in humanitarian networks as much as he was in governmental and scientific ones. He persuaded a large trans-imperial constituency that amalgamation was not simply an expedient governmental exercise, but the only humane alternative to extermination, and thus the only means of exercising practical rather than merely sentimental humanitarianism. "As individuals and as a body, the [humanitarian Aborigines' Protection Society] ... eulogized Grey's benevolence and 'sound policy towards the natives'."[60] Throughout, Grey's ethnography, his humanitarianism and his governmentality were inseparable projects, empowered through his overlapping networks of correspondents.

In the Cape Colony, Grey's governorship coincided with (and helped to exacerbate) an existential crisis among those Xhosa polities bordering the colony. Following sequential losses of grazing land, successive attempts to regain it militarily (each of which had been punished with the confiscation of more land), and the spread of lung sickness further raising mortality among their cattle, from 1856 tens of thousands of Xhosa placed desperate faith in Nongqawuse, a 15-year-old girl's prophecies. She predicted that the sacrificial slaughter of remaining cattle would prompt the ancestors to arise and sweep the British away from the land once and for all. Grey capitalized on the ensuing catastrophe, known as the Great Xhosa Cattle Killing, in 1857, in which some 30,000 people starved the death. He reduced surviving Xhosa to a dependence on work for welfare programs, employing them in building roads which would enable more effective crushing of future resistance to colonial expansion.[61] Yet his humanitarianism remained unquestioned. In 1863 after his "successes" in the Cape, the famous missionary-explorer David Livingstone told him that "a word from you" on the need to act against the African slave trade, "is ever valuable and exhilarating."[62]

Among Grey's promoters was Herman Merivale, professor of political economy at Oxford from 1837 to 1842 and then, by virtue of his published "Lectures on Colonization and Colonies," assistant and then permanent under-secretary for the colonies at the Colonial Office. Merivale's lectures were cited by Marx in *Capital* as well as being a great influence on Trollope and, of course, in the exercise of imperial administration on a daily basis.[63] Merivale saw Grey as his informant on Indigenous peoples and the best ways of administering them within an empire which took pride in its anti-slavery tradition. For him, Grey was "an observer who has studied with no common diligence and success the characteristics of the natives."[64] In particular, it was Grey's posited alternative futures for

Indigenous peoples that Merivale helped to disseminate and implement. "What is the ultimate destiny of those races whose interests we are now discovering?" he asked. The answer was that "There are only three alternatives which imagination can itself suggest." The first was a process by now becoming widely accepted as probably inevitable: "The extermination of native races." The second was the outcome toward which existing policies of Protection, pioneered by George Arthur, were aimed: "Their civilization, complete or partial by retaining them, as insulated bodies of men, carefully removed, during the civilizing process, from the injury of European contact." The third was Grey's particular innovation: "Their amalgamation with the colonists." Merivale rationalized Grey's choice:

> Those who hold the opinion that the first is inevitable, are happily relieved from the trouble of all these considerations. Their only object must be to ensure that the inevitable end be not precipitated by cruelty or injustice. The second alternative I cannot but believe to be impossible . . . . Instruction in segregated communities is only to be carried on under the defence of laws hedging them in from all foreign intercourse with a strictness impracticable in the present state of the world . . . long before the seeds of civilization have made any effectual shoot, the little nursery is surrounded by the advance of the European population; the demand for the land of the natives become urgent and irresistible, and pupils and instructors are driven out into the wilderness to commence their work again. There remains only the third alternative; that of amalgamation. And this I am most anxious to impress upon your minds, because I firmly believe it to be the very keystone, the leading principle of all sound theory on the subject – that native races must in every instance either perish, or be amalgamated with the general [settler] population of their country.[65]

Merivale added a footnote: amalgamation had

> been carried out with more success in South Africa than in any other British possession . . . on the eastern frontier of the Cape Colony (especially since the strange collapse of the Caffre [Xhosa] power, under the influence of scarcity and superstition in 1857–1858), great numbers of natives appear to have taken voluntary service under the settlers, and to have performed it with reasonable steadiness . . . the experiment was superintended by one of those men who seem to possess the rare faculty of entering into the savage mind, and becoming themselves intelligible to it, the governor, Sir George Grey.[66]

Grey's own, and others' ethnography had, by the mid-nineteenth century, established a very low threshold for what qualified as humane governmental intervention in settler colonial societies: the maintenance of "bare life" at an atomized individual, rather than a social scale.[67] In offering a program for Indigenous peoples' future welfare as assimilated subjects, Grey seemed to offer more than this. He offered emigrant and metropolitan Britons a liberal empire founded on violent dispossession and cultural genocide without culpability for the physical eradication of races. The combination of Grey's geographical mobility and his expressive adroitness, facilitated by the enhanced communications and transport networks of a growing empire, enabled him especially to provide Britons with a narrative through which they could legitimate a "humanitarian" empire without biological determinism or the extremes of scientific racism, and certainly without the specter of revolutionary human rights for colonized subjects.[68]

Conclusion

The Career of Humanitarian Governance

Michael Barnett has written that "[t]he anti-slavery movement is the only major historical event of the nineteenth century that is claimed by both human rights and humanitarian scholars as one of their own. On what grounds? Is this where humanity coalesced? What does this tell us about human rights and humanitarianism?"[69] The anti-slavery movement is indeed often claimed as a point of origin both for modern humanitarianism and for a discourse of human rights. But in the light of an analysis of Arthur's and Grey's careers across a large expanse of the globe, we need to be more precise about the routines, techniques, and patterns that it did pioneer, and those for which it cannot possibly be held responsible. Evangelical anti-slavery activists in Britain and the United States, in combination with those who resisted slavery in the British Caribbean itself, can be said to have forged a certain kind of long-distance mobilization. In the context of the moral panic prompted by the loss of the thirteen colonies, the French and the Haitian Revolutions, they engendered transatlantic networks through which Britons "at home" could be made to feel responsible for the plight of distant, enslaved strangers with whom they would never have personal contact or familiarity. They pioneered the use of campaigning representations of passive, harmless recipients supplicating the help of more privileged Westerners. It was the period of amelioration (1806–1830s) in which something that we might recognize as humanitarian benevolence was inscribed into governmentality.[70] With no more slave "imports" after the 1807 abolition of the slave trade, Britain's slave-holding colonies were forced to govern their existing slaves in ways that complied with the expressions of concern that had resulted in abolition. Ameliorative codes, enacted by colonial governments along guidelines supplied by the Colonial Office in London, were the answer. But while amelioration brought what we might identify as humanitarian concern into the "art of government," this was still a project delimited by a primarily transatlantic spatial axis.

Between the early 1830s and the 1860s, what benevolent intent there was behind ameliorative legislation was translated into the colonization of new lands across a far more spatially extensive terrain. It was the new humanitarian governmental register of Protection which marked the first globalization of humanitarian governmentality. The transition from slavery to freedom in the Caribbean proceeded simultaneously with the mass emigration of British settlers to dispossess Indigenous peoples in North America, Australasia, and Southern Africa. The same individuals and families that had mobilized against slavery now turned their attention to the plight of Indigenous peoples facing invasion. Amelioration in the Caribbean was translated, not least through Arthur's capacity, into Protection, as Protectors of Aborigines were sent to certain colonies and officials elsewhere instructed to protect the lives, and preserve certain landholdings of, Indigenous peoples. On these landholdings they could maintain certain of their own customs and practices until such time as they were ready to be subjected to the same laws as the settlers around them.

Protection was the dominant register of imperial humanitarian governance for some thirty years, but by the mid-nineteenth century, the contradiction between colonization by hundreds of thousands of British emigrants and the protection of Indigenous difference and landholding was acute in all of the settler colonies. Grey utilized the expectation that Indigenous peoples were inexorably dying out when confronted by a superior civilization – an expectation engendered through the networks of both scientists and humanitarians – to bolster his own credentials as one of their most valuable ethnographic chroniclers. But his more striking innovation was to establish the supposition that any government which did more than simply making their extinction as painless as possible was perpetuating humanitarian governance beyond the initial, now failed, period of Protection. Grey's particular register of governmentality was founded not only upon the survival, but also upon the redemptive development of Indigenous individuals through their amalgamation with settlers. Thanks to his benign, assimilationist interventions, Grey and others could claim, individuals of Indigenous descent, released from the failed "nurseries" of their own land holdings, and thus from territory, would survive the death of the cultures that had circumscribed previous generations. As Merivale concluded, "amalgamation, by some means or other, is the only possible Euthanasia of savage communities."[71]

However, when we shift perspective and try to conceive of engagements with humanitarian governance from its intended beneficiaries' point of view, we see less an opportunity to change for the better, and more one to manipulate certain organs of the state so as at least to preserve a worldview intact, until such time as it can acquire its own material vitality and sovereignty once more. Here, perhaps, is where the revolutionary potential of human rights discourse stands most starkly at odds with humanitarian governmental practice. Neither Grey nor his contemporaries' articulation of humanitarianism ever included the word "rights." Indeed the word was anathema throughout this period, both to British imperial officials and to most humanitarian campaigners. It was associated with the American and French Revolutions which imperial officials, mainly drawn from the military, had fought directly against, and with the Haitian Revolution, which was itself blamed in part on rights fervor in France. When revolutionary sympathizers spoke of the "Rights of Man," British officials saw only the threats to individual liberty promised by the rule of the "mob." As Moyn points out, "In the recent search for a usable past ... the revolutionary origins of rights have been domesticated."[72] Moyn's argument is that the rights of the early nineteenth century have become narrowly focused on issues such as torture at the expense of material equalities and more structural injustices.[73] Taking the sting out of rights is not just a contemporary project though. It was why humanitarian governance was globalized, through different registers of protection and amalgamation, paternalism and elimination, by people like Arthur and Grey in the first place.

There is no linear path from an empire engaged in dispossession to the administrators of humanitarian camps for displaced people today. Nor is there any direct genealogy linking Indigenous peoples facing colonization in the nineteenth century to refugees dispossessed by a multitude of warring parties today. We should be wary of learning lessons from direct comparisons between discrete historical configurations, especially with no analysis of the intervening transitions. One such key transition was the dissolution of the imperial forms of governance within which men like Arthur and Grey pursued their careers. The post-imperial world, with new delineations of sovereignty and statehood saw the emergence of humanitarian intervention, which, as Fabian Klose argues in this volume, was premised to a great extent upon a convergence of both humanitarian and human rights ideas. It is tempting to ascribe some of the ambivalence of the doctrine and its implementation during the twentieth century to this very conflation of antithetical ameliorative and revolutionary political orientations. The humanitarian governmental registers that I have discussed here were peculiar to a globally extensive form of imperial governance, and the late eighteenth- and early nineteenth-century revolutionary human rights discourses that I have alluded to were very different from those which Moyn locates in the later twentieth century, geared as they were to the generation of an entirely new social order rather than remedying specific abuses of individuals.[74] There is nonetheless, I think, something profoundly unsettling in this work of historical recovery to any neat association between ameliorative forms of humanitarianism and the radical notion of human rights. Rather than rest content with their putatively common "genealogy of empathy," the realization of the historical antipathies between humanitarian governance and human rights, and their very different effects for the maintenance or undermining of an existing distribution of power and privilege, should force us at least to interrogate the different potentialities that they and their multiple registers offer to their intended beneficiaries.[75]

6 Humanitarian Intervention as an Entangled History of Humanitarianism and Human Rights

Fabian Klose

From the mid-1960s, especially in the wake of the Biafra conflict of 1967–1970, an intense debate on the concept of humanitarian intervention re-emerged among international legal scholars.[*] In his article "Intervention to Protect Human Rights" published in 1969, Richard B. Lillich, an important US scholar of international law and member of the influential International Law Association (ILA), vigorously pleaded for this concept and argued that the right to intervene should be implemented by the United Nations to defend universal human rights. Especially in regard to the human catastrophe in Biafra, he argued: "Finally, the situation in Biafra is one that would have been ideal for collective humanitarian intervention of the nineteenth century type."[1] From his perspective, the doctrine of humanitarian intervention seemed to be designed perfectly for the situation in the South Eastern part of Nigeria and accordingly should be implemented immediately. Thus, Lillich referred directly to a humanitarian practice, which emerged in the nineteenth century as a kind of model to protect human rights in the twentieth century.

The history of humanitarianism as well as of human rights has crystallized as two very prospering fields of research over the last decade. Both themes have been the subject of a lively debate among international historians, well documented by a vast amount of workshops, conferences, special issues of journals, edited volumes, pioneering books, and research projects.[2] Even though new intriguing research landscapes are opening before our eyes, the relationship between humanitarianism and human rights is still a "troubled rapport" as Michael Geyer trenchantly puts it.[3] The link between these two prospering fields remains often blurred and rather ambiguous. Frequently humanitarianism and human rights are presented in opposing terms, sometimes even as rival concepts by advocates on both sides.[4] According to them, humanitarianism rests upon a discourse of suffering and charity, while human rights are based on a discourse of justice and solidarity. Humanitarians focus on providing relief in emergency situations and are very cautious about speaking out against rights violations because of their fear of endangering access to people in need by politicizing their humanitarian action. By contrast, for human rights activists providing relief is secondary to their main goal of collecting evidence about atrocities and prosecuting perpetrators of human rights violations.[5]

Undeniably, humanitarianism and human rights indeed constitute two concepts with different approaches to achieve distinctive goals. However, instead of mainly elaborating on the opposing characteristics of both concepts, their obvious distinctions and even rivalries, from a historian's point of view it can be far more productive to focus on the relationship and entanglements of both fields – as Michael Barnett clearly indicates in the introduction of this volume. Humanitarianism and human rights are not the same, for sure, but they share some similar historical origins and developments. In theory as well as in practice there are manifold overlaps and links between the two fields. Both histories are often so closely entangled that it is difficult to analyze them completely isolated from each other. We can identify a fluidity between both concepts, which enables them to converge without becoming identical.[6]

The practice of enforcement is one of such issues, where this fluidity becomes obvious and where both fields are indeed very closely entangled.[7] Generally defined as military intervention across state borders into the domestic affairs of a sovereign state for the purpose of protecting humanitarian norms and universal human rights,[8] humanitarian intervention is intensively debated within both fields of research.[9] Accordingly, the question arises, in which field the history of humanitarian intervention should be located? Or is the concept an integral part of both historiographies? And if so, does it connect both areas in any way?

Investigating the historical emergence of the practice and legal doctrine of humanitarian intervention can serve as a significant lens through which entanglements of the history of humanitarianism and human rights can be identified, without mixing the two concepts randomly. In my eyes, one can identify a key transition at the beginning of the nineteenth century: the departure from the early modern concept of protection on the grounds of religious affinity to the practice of defending humanitarian norms for all individuals regardless of their religious affiliation and on the basis of an evolving notion of a common humanity. The concept of armed intervention to safeguard humanitarian norms thus arose during the course of the long nineteenth century in the context of the abolition of the slave trade; by the early twentieth century, it had become an established concept within international law.

However, the history of humanitarian intervention was not necessarily also a history of the advancement of human rights protection from the very start as recent studies propose.[10] The historical precedents of the nineteenth century contributed to the emergence of humanitarian norms within international law, but this was not synonymous with the emergence of the robust implementation of individual rights. Indeed, the protection of human rights became linked with policies of military intervention only in the course of the twentieth century. This happened first at the beginning of the twentieth century when prominent activists and scholars of international law, including figures such as Antoine Rougier, André Mandelstam, and Hersch Lauterpacht, linked humanitarian intervention directly to the emerging notion of universal human rights.

Thus, my main argument is that the theory and practice of humanitarian intervention emerged out of nineteenth-century humanitarianism. Various precedents of the nineteenth century then served as a crucial reference point and as a kind of model for legal scholars to transform this practice into an instrument to protect human rights in the twentieth century, thus connecting both fields in a significant way. This chapter consists of two parts: first, I will elaborate on how the concept of humanitarian intervention emerged in the course of the long nineteenth century and how it was directly connected to the evolving notion of not human rights but a common humanity; second, I will concentrate on the transitional period when humanitarian intervention became linked with the emerging vision of universal human right. Regarding the twentieth and twenty-first centuries, it is therefore more adequate to talk of the concept of human rights intervention instead of humanitarian intervention.

Enforcing Humanity in the Long Nineteenth Century

The notion of humanity is a malleable and dynamic concept, which exists in various languages and cultural contexts, having different meanings at different times.[11] It is evoked in a remarkable array of themes and it is the fundamental essence shared by humanitarianism as well as human rights. Despite the fact that in various languages the definition of the term varied over time and historical context, there are some core meanings, which are significantly and repeatedly associated with the word "humanity." In Samuel Johnson's *A Dictionary of the English Language*, published originally in 1755 and considered as one of the most influential dictionaries in the history of the English language, the word "humanity" (together with a direct reference to the French translation of *humanité* and the Latin translation of *humanitas*) was defined as the "nature of man" as well as "Human kind; the collective body of mankind."[12] Beyond this description as the natural characteristics of individual human beings as well as the collective noun for the body of the whole human species, the dictionary provided another significant definition, namely the practice of "Benevolence; tenderness." In order to explain this third definition more concretely to the reader, the dictionary explicitly referred to a quote of the English philosopher and influential Enlightenment thinker John Locke: "All men ought to maintain peace and the common offices of *humanity* and friendship in diversity of opinion."[13]

As the burgeoning body of historical research on the history of humanitarianism in the last few years has shown, we have to relate this emerging notion to a broader "humanitarian revolution"[14] taking place in the Enlightenment during the second half of the eighteenth century. People started to feel empathy for their fellow human beings, not only within their own country, but also across borders and even on distant continents. Individuals were mobilized by a sentimental and moral "humanitarian narrative" that motivated them to care for strangers.[15] Thus, humanity increasingly gained crucial ethical qualities and transformed evermore to a kind of "moral compass" for social behavior within human societies.[16]

In this context, British abolitionism is regarded as the driving force for the crystallization of humanitarian sentiments.[17] In an intensive campaign spanning several decades, abolitionists significantly mobilized public opinion and caused an outcry against the transatlantic slave trade. British Abolitionists started an unprecedented humanitarian campaign, lasting several decades.[18] However, it is of crucial importance to note that in their campaign the abolitionists articulated their political demands not in the language of rights but in terms of "humanity."[19] They could vigorously fight against the transatlantic slave trade and ask for state intervention, but at the same time endorse the paternalistic concept of a mission to civilize the Africans without granting them equal rights. For example, William Wilberforce, one of the leading voices of the abolitionist movement in parliament, was recorded as expressing this view in a debate on the abolition of the slave trade in the House of Commons in April 1791 with these words:

The Negroes ... were creatures like ourselves: they had the same feelings, and even stronger affections than our own; but their minds were uninformed, and their moral characters were altogether debased. Men, in this state, were almost incapacitated for the reception of civil rights. In order to become fit for the enjoyment of these, they must, in some measures, be restored to that level from which they had been so unjustly and cruelly degraded. To give them power of appealing to the laws, would be to awaken in them a sense of the dignity of their nature. The first return of life after a swoon, was commonly a convulsion, dangerous, at once, to the party himself, and to all around him. Such, in the case of the Slaves, Mr. Wilberforce feared, might be the consequence of a sudden communication of civil rights.[20]

Instead of rights it was the moral category of a common "humanity" that was crucial to the abolitionist argument and thus became the movement's undisputed leitmotif. Their primary goal was to raise awareness in public and parliamentary debates that African slaves were not ordinary commodities but human beings with feelings who formed an undeniable, integral part of humankind.[21] The abolitionist task was to revoke the process of dehumanization of the captives to mere goods in the Atlantic trade system by emphasizing their true human nature. The iconic image created by Josiah Wedgwood of the enslaved African kneeling with manacled hands outstretched, posing the rhetorical question "Am I not a man and a brother?," which swiftly became the official emblem of the movement, represented this notion most vividly.[22] The abolitionists tried to appeal to the humanitarian sensibility of their fellow citizens to evoke sympathy for the fate of African slaves and to demand action on behalf of suffering fellow human beings.

The abolitionist cause finally prevailed and gained official recognition in parliament. On March 25, 1807 the Act of the British Parliament for the Abolition of the Slave Trade was passed,[23] which stigmatized the slave trade as "contrary to humanity." The singular importance of this decision lay, above all, in the fact that the struggle against the transatlantic slave trade, which the abolitionists had up to that point conducted exclusively at the levels of civil society and politics, now became, by law, a matter of the United Kingdom. The British government had committed itself to deploy means of state against the traffic in human beings. Accordingly, the Act had practical implications, stipulating the seizure of slave ships.[24] In this way the Abolition Act laid the legal foundation for the military deployment of the Royal Navy off the coast of West Africa to enforce the ban on the transatlantic slave trade. From 1808 to the mid-1860s the United Kingdom continued to demonstrate its permanent military presence along the infamous Slave Coast, the first and longest humanitarian intervention in history.[25]

Thus, humanity and its violations became a guiding, legally recognized principle for the new paradigm of abolition, which eventually initiated and justified the new practice of humanitarian intervention. Beside the national level in the United Kingdom, this also came true on the international level. Following the international condemnation of the slave trade at the Congress of Vienna in February 1815,[26] which may be regarded as one of the first important documents in the history of international humanitarian law, the British government initiated diplomatic negotiations to install an international machinery of enforcement.[27] In the course of diplomatic negotiations lasting several decades, the United Kingdom successfully managed to establish a comprehensive international treaty network to enforce abolition. This included almost all states in Europe and the Americas as well as several African kingdoms.[28] Thus, by the mid-nineteenth century an international moral and legal consensus had emerged that human trafficking was indeed a gross violation of common humanity and international humanitarian norms, which justified the employment of violent means.

This significant consensus also found its way into such a fundamental text of international law as Henry Wheaton's *Elements of International Law*, first published in 1836. The renowned US legal scholar, explicitly stated in his study: "The African slave trade, once considered not only a lawful, but desirable branch of commerce, a participation in which was made the object of wars, negotiations, and treaties between different European states, is now denounced as an odious crime by the almost universal consent of nations."[29] By referring directly to the Vienna declaration and the related international treaty regime he clearly underlined this position. Moreover, in his later publications, he denounced the slave trade as a "crime against humanity,"[30] using a legal term long before it became a crucial element of international criminal law of the twentieth century.[31]

Some recent scholarship links this development and these historical precedents of humanitarian intervention directly to the rise of the modern human rights concept. For instance, legal scholar Jenny Martinez argues that international human rights law derives its origins from the fight against the slave trade and the related "Courts of Mixed Commission for the Abolition of the Slave Trade." In her opinion, this Mixed Commissions represent the first "international human rights courts" and were a significant forerunner of international criminal justice of the twentieth and twenty-first centuries.[32] Additionally, Brendan Simms and David Trim put forward the argument that due to the frequency of these early humanitarian interventions against the slave trade and for the protection of minorities, "'human rights' emerged as a term and legal concept in the mid-nineteenth century."[33]

However, this perspective provokes a clear objection, especially concerning the recent controversial debate about the origins of the human rights concept and its relation to humanitarianism. The historical precedents of humanitarian intervention indeed contributed significantly to the emergence of humanitarian norms in international law, but this was not tantamount to the rise of the human rights concept in a modern sense. Admittedly, prominent advocates of a legal doctrine of humanitarian intervention during the second half of the nineteenth century like the Swiss legal scholar Johann Caspar Bluntschli and his German colleague Aegidius Arntz referred in their works to the protection of "*Menschenrechte*"[34] and *"droits de l'humanité"*[35] as a justifiable reason to interfere. However, without defining the content and nature of these aforementioned rights, they left the term completely vague and did not codify these rights, as was later realized in the Universal Declaration of Human Rights in 1948. As already shown, abolitionists could passionately fight against the transatlantic slave trade and demand military intervention against this violation of common-sense humanity, but at the same time endorse the paternalistic concept of a mission to civilize the Africans without granting them equal rights. Even though the idea of protecting humanitarian norms by force was established in the long nineteenth century, this was not synonymous with the idea of protecting human rights according to the principles of equality and universality.[36]

Quite the contrary, the process of establishing humanity as an international norm and protecting it by violent means remained a rather arbitrary and ambiguous concept. Attacking the slave trade did not immediately and automatically lead to the end of the institution of colonial slavery itself and the final liberation of slaves by granting equal rights. The United Kingdom would passionately fight for its foreign policy paradigm of abolishing human trafficking, but at the same time leave colonial slavery untouched for nearly another two decades until the final Slavery Abolition Act of 1833. Other countries, also part of the international treaty regime, waited even longer to abolish human bondage eventually, such as the United States in 1865, Spain in Cuba in 1886, and Brazil in 1888.[37]

Moreover, there is a strong argument that the practice of intervening against the slave trade "in the cause of humanity" triggered a development in the exact opposite direction, thus revealing the ambivalence of humanity as a nineteenth-century norm. The concept could be successfully used to support abolition and even its military enforcement. However, at the same time abolishing the slave trade in the name of humanity could be an effective instrument for legitimizing colonial and imperial conquest in Africa as most infamously shown in the case of the Congo Free-State. Thus, the issue of intervening against the African slave trade in the name of a common humanity reveals most vividly the close entanglement of European humanitarianism with nineteenth-century colonialism and imperialism, but not with the history of universal human rights.[38]

Humanitarian Intervention as Human Rights History in the Twentieth Century

Over the course of the long nineteenth century, the concept and practice of humanitarian intervention had developed to the point that, by the start of the twentieth century, it had become an established doctrine of international law.[39] In July 1900 the historian William E. Lingelbach, professor of European history at the University of Pennsylvania, indicated that "intervention on humanitarian grounds" had peculiarly developed due to various historical precedents in the course of the nineteenth century.[40] Even though Lingelbach was fully aware of the importance of political and economic self-interests of the intervening states he argued that this practice was now recognized as a legal mean in international relations: "Intervention, therefore, instead of being outside the pale of the law of nations and antagonistic to it, is an integral and essential part of it; an act of police for enforcing recognized rights, and the only means, apart from war, for enforcing the rules of International Law."[41] During the nineteenth century, interventionist doctrine focused mainly on the abolition of the slave trade and the protection of minorities in the context of enforcing humanitarian norms. At the beginning of the twentieth century, it became increasingly associated with an international rights discourse and directly linked with the emerging language of universal human rights.

Antoine Rougier, a French law professor at the University of Caen, was one of the first to deal with this issue.[42] In 1910 he presented his "Théorie de l'intervention d'humanité," in which he also referred to the historical precedents of the nineteenth century and the first legal approaches by Bluntschli and Arntz.[43] In contrast to them, he not only described the violation of the rather abstract "lois de l'humanité" and "droits humains" as a legitimation for intervention, but also started to define concretely the content of these laws and rights of humanity. In this context, he identified three fundamental human rights, namely the "droit à la vie" (the right to life), the "droit à la liberté" (the right to liberty), and the "droit à la légalité" (the right to legality) as the only legitimate reason to intervene.[44] Thus, Rougier connected in his legal theory the concept of humanitarian intervention for the first time directly with the idea of the protection of defined fundamental human rights.

After the end of World War I, this development gained further momentum, especially in connection with the newly founded League of Nations.[45] Legal scholars such as Malbone W. Graham hoped that the Geneva-based international organization would become the central authority in charge of international security and provide an effective safeguard for the emerging concept of human rights. For Graham the creation of the League of Nations fundamentally altered the question of humanitarian intervention, because a legally recognized international organization could act on an objective basis as the enforcer of the law of nations.[46] Instead of a "subjective Law of Nature" and a "sentimental Law of Humanity" a new substantive law of nations was now clearly defining the right of humanitarian intervention.[47] Graham argued that interventions of a humanitarian character would occur henceforth "as the express result of the action of the League in selecting the appropriate country to act as its mandatory, its agent, in enforcing the terms of the mandate given for the purpose of removing unfortunate conditions violative of the most elementary human rights."[48]

Another strong advocate of the idea of collective mechanisms to safeguard human rights implemented under the aegis of the League of Nations was the Russian diplomat André N. Mandelstam. Being in exile in Paris after the Bolshevik revolution of 1917, Mandelstam became one of the central figures in the international struggle to establish human rights during the interwar years. He took part in various initiatives as a member of the renowned Institut de Droit International and played a leading role in securing the adoption of the "Déclaration des droits internationaux de l'Homme" adopted by the institute during its session in New York in October 1929.[49]

In one of his essays on the importance of the New York declaration, Mandelstam focused on the active international protection of human rights, making reference to the various European interventions in the Ottoman Empire during the nineteenth century.[50] However, the Russian exile rejected the idea that humanitarian interventions on behalf of international human rights could be grounded in the nineteenth-century division between "civilized" and "uncivilized" nations. In his perspective, the founding of the League of Nations and the associated move toward universality meant that all states were now obligated to protect these rights around the world without exception.[51] The "principle of universal protection of human rights," Mandelstam argued, should be enshrined in a "world contract."[52] He hoped that the New York statement by the Institut de Droit International would serve as the impetus for the adoption of such a world contract.

Thus, Graham and Mandelstam referred explicitly to the nineteenth-century model of humanitarian intervention, but now separated it from the "sentimental law of humanity" as well as the division of "uncivilized" and "civilized" nations. Instead, they linked the practice for the first time directly to an international organization such as the League of Nations and the emerging notion of universal human rights. However, neither Graham's nor Mandelstam's idealistic hopes that the League of Nations might serve as the new international authority for humanitarian intervention were fulfilled. The Geneva-based organization did not possess the kind of robust mechanisms needed to implement a "world contract" on human rights. Although a number of non-European states joined the League of Nations, including Abyssinia, Japan, and Siam, the League was strongly influenced by the old colonial hierarchies and the dominance

of the European member states.[53] During the interwar years, the imperial
nations that dominated the League – Britain and France – were both at
the height of their colonial power and had little interest in developing an
international system to carry out interventions on behalf of universal
human rights.

After World War II, the United Nations even incorporated a strict and
legally binding prohibition on the use of force and a clause on nonintervention in domestic affairs in its charter. Article 2, Paragraph 4 of the
Charter bans any threat or use of force in international relations apart
from the right to self-defense, while Article 2, Paragraph 7 forbids interference in the internal affairs of a sovereign state.[54] These two provisions
are fundamental norms in the UN Charter, which can only be limited
under exceptional circumstances such as a threat to peace or a breach of
peace. Despite this strict limitation placed on the concept of forcible
intervention, some experts on international law sought to establish
a direct link between the concept of humanitarian intervention, international human rights protection, and the newly developing system of the
United Nations.[55] One prominent proponent was no other than Hersch
Lauterpacht, who as a renowned professor of law at Cambridge
University, member of the UN Commission on Human Rights, and
judge at the International Court of Justice at The Hague, must be
regarded as one of the most influential legal scholars of the twentieth
century.

Lauterpacht, born to a Jewish family in Habsburg Galicia, was
a vociferous advocate of the incorporation of human rights in international law. His engagement was certainly also influenced by his own
personal history and the death of nearly his entire family in the
Holocaust.[56] In December 1942, during World War II, Lauterpacht
presented a paper before the British Grotius Society advocating the creation of an "international bill of rights" and demanding effective enforcement mechanisms.[57] The presentation also made explicit reference to the
theory and practice of humanitarian intervention in the nineteenth century as well as the international humanitarian treaty regime on slavery and
the protection of minorities.[58] Lauterpacht suggested, that these historical cases could serve as valuable inspiration for the development of an
effective mechanism to safeguard human rights.[59]

After World War II, he continuously argued in a large number of
publications, including his influential treatise "An International Bill of
the Rights of Man," that this protection could best be accomplished
within the framework of the United Nations.[60] As a supranational
authority, he believed, the United Nations would possess the means
to promote, monitor, and peacefully enforce international human

rights standards.[61] However, in the case that political means were exhausted, the United Nations must also be permitted to engage in more direct means:

in the last resort ... there must remain with the highest political authority of the Organization of States the legal power to give effect to the Bill of Rights by means of coercive action. Such action will be exceptional, but it is that ultimate power which will give to the Bill of Rights the impress of an organic part of the international legal order.[62]

In Lauterpacht's opinion, the enforcement of human rights by the United Nations – by coercive measures if necessary – was an important step in the development of an effective international human rights regime.[63]

However, during the postwar period Lauterpacht's hopes would remain unfulfilled. Instead, the violent conflicts that arose in the course of decolonization and the emerging East–West conflict hindered the development of a robust human rights regime.[64] Rather than implementing the enforcement mechanisms envisioned under the UN Charter, individual states instead retreated behind the charter's nonintervention clause and rejected humanitarian interventions in the cause of universal rights. It was not until the mid-1960s that the topic of humanitarian intervention gained fresh impetus when the issue became the subject of an intense debate among experts in international law. The passage of two UN human rights pacts in 1966 and the International Year of Human Rights in 1968, culminating in the first International Conference on Human Rights in Tehran, lent further momentum to the debate, which soon focused on fundamental questions regarding concrete and robust mechanisms to safeguard human rights. At its August 1966 meeting in Helsinki, the influential ILA passed a resolution announcing that it would henceforth shift its focus away from purely definitional debates in favor of discussions on the concrete implementation of human rights.[65]

One of the important contributions to this debate came from Richard B. Lillich, member of the ILA and director of the Procedural Aspects of International Law Institute in Washington, DC. In his already mentioned essay "Intervention to Protect Human Rights," Lillich defended the concept of humanitarian intervention, which he described as a form of state self-help, and argued that the right to intervene should only be implemented within the framework of the United Nations. As examples for his argument, Lillich cited several contemporary political hot spots, including the Congo crisis of 1964, the US intervention in the Dominican Republic in 1965, and the emerging humanitarian catastrophe in Biafra.[66]

Finally, it was the Biafra conflict of 1967–1970 that would lend even greater intensity to this emerging debate. As the humanitarian crisis threatening the Igbo people in the Nigerian secessionist region of Biafra continued to aggravate, Lillich's colleague Michael Reisman, an American professor of international law at Yale, submitted a petition to the UN in September 1968, demanding that the world organization should intervene immediately.[67] The petition concluded with a vigorous argument in favor of institutionalizing the concept of humanitarian intervention:

> Whether or not a U.N. humanitarian intervention in Nigeria will lay the groundwork for an institutionalized pattern of humanitarian intervention in the future, the United Nations must consider the creation of such an institution as soon as possible. . . . We have waited too long and have already lost our innocence; if we cannot perfect, as a minimum, a system of humanitarian intervention, we have lost our humanity. If we sit passively by while the Ibos [*sic*] suffer genocide, we have forfeited our right to regain it.[68]

After submitting his petition to the United Nations (which also explicitly mentioned the cases of the humanitarian interventions of the nineteenth century[69]), Reisman circulated the memorandum among international legal scholars both within and outside the United Nations in order to encourage further debate.

This discussion continued and the topic of humanitarian intervention thus did not recede from the international agenda. Indeed, since the mid-1960s, prominent scholars of international law have continued to address the central questions of whether forcible intervention in the domestic affairs of a sovereign state on behalf of the protection of universal human rights is permitted under international law, and whether such interventions may be carried out within the framework of the United Nations.[70] Thus, the concept and practice of humanitarian intervention was inextricably linked to the history and growing prominence of human rights in the twentieth and twenty-first centuries.[71] In this regard, in the twentieth and twenty-first centuries, it is probably more adequate to talk of the concept of human rights intervention instead of humanitarian intervention.[72]

Conclusion

The concept of armed intervention to safeguard humanitarian norms arose during the course of the long nineteenth century and it was directly connected to the evolving notion of not human rights but a common humanity. By the early twentieth century, it had become an established concept within international law. It was the first half of the twentieth century, especially the interwar period, when prominent scholars of international law, including Mandelstam and Lauterpacht, started to link the idea of humanitarian intervention with the emerging notion of universal human rights and international organizations. Even though the UN Charter of 1945 had anchored the principle of nonintervention within international law, scholars such as Lauterpacht continued to place great hopes in the emerging system of the United Nations, in which the ideas of humanitarian intervention were linked to notions of the international protection of human rights. By the mid-1960s, these discussions received fresh impetus as the concept of human rights increasingly began to move away from a purely definitional debate in favor of concrete measures to protect and implement universal rights, a development that was spurred by the passage of two UN human rights pacts in 1966 and the events and publicity surrounding the International Year of Human Rights of 1968. Legal scholars such as Richard B. Lillich and Michael Reisman assumed a leading role in these efforts. Over the course of the 1970s, the topic of human rights continued to gain prominence in international politics, which lent at the same time further weight to debates on humanitarian intervention to safeguard human rights.

Returning to the questions raised at the beginning, in my opinion the issue of humanitarian intervention is indeed an integral part of both historiographies – of humanitarianism as well as of human rights. As shown, I argue that this practice originated in nineteenth-century humanitarianism and then became more and more connected to twentieth-century human rights history. Thus, to fully understand the historical emergence of the concept and practice of humanitarian intervention it is inevitable to look at and to analyze both fields of research without mixing the two concepts. It is exactly these transition processes, which show the fluidity between both fields and enables them to converge from time to time. Again, to be clear, humanitarianism and human rights are not the same concepts, but they share some significant historical developments and practices. One of these is the history of humanitarian intervention and it is exactly this shared history, which makes it so interesting to look at both concurrently, not as completely separated, competing, and opposing concepts, but as related and complementary ones.

7 Mobilizing Emotions: Shame, Victimhood, and Agency

Bronwyn Leebaw

One way to think about the relationship between humanitarianism and human rights is to go back to the debate between Socrates and Thrasymachus at the outset of *The Republic*. Thrasymachus becomes angry with Socrates for talking about justice in a way that dances around what he takes to be most important about it – that justice is "the advantage of the stronger."[1] The powerful write laws that reflect their interests, he explains, they make other people obey them, and they call that "justice." Thrasymachus becomes increasingly frustrated and eventually walks away from the conversation. Their disagreement is not necessarily about the meaning of justice, as Hanna Pitkin observes, but centers on what kind of conversation people should be having about justice.[2] Socrates wants to discuss what the idea of justice might mean apart from the way it is conventionally understood, while Thrasymachus makes a sociological point about the conventional meaning of justice and how it is institutionalized in ways that legitimate domination and hierarchy. His departure seems like a victory for Socrates and for the reasoned pursuit of ideals over an emotional display of cynicism. However, his contribution also reminds readers that outrage, in response to hypocrisy and injustice, is an important starting point for those who invoke ideals to challenge established institutions. Thrasymachus would probably respond to contemporary debates on human rights and humanitarianism by raising concerns about how these ostensibly idealistic frameworks reflect and legitimate the interests of the strong. This chapter investigates differences in the way in which human rights and humanitarian frameworks are formulated with respect to their significance for this kind of concern. In evaluating what is at stake in these differences, the chapter suggests, it is useful to examine how humanitarian and human rights organizations have developed distinctive strategies for mobilizing emotions in order to hold powerful actors accountable for their responses to suffering and injustice.

Humanitarianism, whether conceptualized as beneficence, charity, or an effort to minimize "unnecessary suffering," is predicated on strategies for altering the way in which those in power define their own advantages. Humanitarianism has been associated with appeals for compassion and empathy aimed at soliciting support for life-saving assistance to those who are experiencing crisis.[3] In contrast, human rights have been conceptualized as a basis for empowering excluded and persecuted peoples to confront various forms of domination and hierarchy, as Jeffrey Flynn and Aisling Swaine stress in contributions to this volume. Professional human rights organizations have developed confrontational shaming strategies designed to exploit the hypocrisies of abusive authorities as weapons that can be turned against those who wield them.[4] Shame is "a felt ethic of obligation or regulation," writes Jill Locke, "that judges our thoughts and actions in terms of their relationship to norms and standards that one shares."[5] The feeling of shame is an important response to injustice, writes Chris Lebron, because in alerting people to their common failures, it also reminds them of their commitment to shared values.[6] Strategies for mobilizing shame are appealing as a basis for exerting pressure "from below" without conventional forms of material power, or "from above" without the conventional enforcement mechanisms associated with state power and military hierarchy.[7] Shaming strategies are also championed as a basis for establishing accountability through socialization aimed at cultivating the internalization of norms.[8]

Professional human rights advocates have positioned shaming as a kind of bridge between the diplomatic posture of humanitarianism and the broader, more transformative, aspirations elaborated in major human rights conventions. However, human rights shaming strategies are also associated with certain frictions and boundaries that set professional human rights advocacy apart from the kind of work that is associated with humanitarianism, as well as the kind of work that is associated with social justice. The effectiveness of shaming, as formulated by influential human rights organizations, depends on confrontational strategies that frequently clash with humanitarian commitments and a legalistic approach to justice centered on individual accountability for "physical integrity rights."[9] Although shaming strategies cultivated by prominent human rights advocates are at odds with familiar approaches to humanitarian diplomacy, then, they reinforce the minimalism associated with the "humanitarianization of human rights," as discussed by in chapters by Jeffrey Flynn and Samuel Moyn. Some see these limitations as necessary to the effectiveness of the human rights framework as a basis for holding powerful authorities accountable for their actions, while others contend that these shaming strategies place arbitrary limits on the transformative potential of the human rights framework. In evaluating these competing claims, however, most commentators share a tendency to focus on a very distinctive approach to confrontational shaming that is practiced by professional human rights organizations.

This chapter looks at how shame has been mobilized in other ways, by other actors, in relation to other emotions. It argues that prominent humanitarian organizations have also developed strategies for mobilizing shame, but in ways that are different from human rights strategies for mobilizing shame. Human rights organizations mobilize the power of shame in the form of threatened ostracism, by framing appeals that inspire outrage in audiences and encourage them to stigmatize abusers. Humanitarian appeals suggest that passive bystanders ought to feel personally ashamed if they do not respond with compassion and action to alleviate suffering. Shaming strategies are also routinely developed by authorities who seek to justify abuses by stigmatizing those who complain about them. Others have pursued accountability for human rights abuses by developing strategies for confronting shameful systems and institutions. In evaluating the relationship between human rights and humanitarianism, this chapter suggests it is important to consider how familiar "naming and shaming" strategies intersect with these other ways of mobilizing shame. To do so, the chapter builds on two general insights that have been widely recognized among scholars who have studied the politics of shame and shaming disciplinary perspectives. First, the order-reinforcing role of shame is thought to be especially powerful when it is most subtle, and operates by inhibiting people from challenging established institutions and authorities, by stigmatizing deviant behavior, by shaping daily habits, or by influencing the kinds of values that people take for granted in how they define themselves.[10] Second, although fear of stigmatization can be a powerful form of pressure, confrontational shaming tends to be double-edged and associated with fairly predictable forms of backlash, defensiveness, or emotional deadening.[11]

The first two sections of the chapter build on these insights to investigate how prominent humanitarians and human rights advocates have invoked shame in framing appeals for moral action and accountability in response to suffering and injustice. I suggest that these different strategies for mobilizing shame are associated with distinctive forms of backlash, but that both can backfire by intensifying the stigmatization of those who are singled out as uniquely deserving of protection. Prominent human rights advocates and humanitarians have responded to this problem in a similar manner, with appeals for action that frame accountability with reference to discrete choices made in response to the plight of uniquely helpless victims in need of urgent protection. This strategy positions human rights advocacy as a kind of humanitarian practice – one that centers on actions taken by privileged or powerful actors on behalf of those who are thought to be helpless. The problem with this is not that it limits scope of human rights advocacy per se. The problem is that when human rights are identified with advocacy on behalf of the helpless, this reinforces the stigmatization of those who pursue transformative responses to hierarchy and undermines efforts to mobilize human rights as a basis for political empowerment. The third section of the chapter locates an alternative approach to shaming in the writings of W. E. B. Du Bois and other thinkers who have conceptualized human rights as a response to institutionalized racism and structural injustices. In contrast with those who mobilize shame in response to helpless victims, Du Bois framed his human rights appeal as a call for political agency and solidarity needed to confront international norms implicated in colonial domination and white supremacy. In contrast with those who mobilize shame as a basis for individual accountability, such thinkers suggest that the role of human rights depends on strategies for exposing shameful systems, institutions, and hierarchies.

The Shame of Bystanders

"I was a mere tourist with no part in this great conflict," reports Henry Dunant in the opening pages of *Memory of Solferino*, "but it was my great privilege to witness the moving scenes that I have resolved to describe."[12] Dunant's account of the 1859 Battle of Solferino charts his own personal transformation and invites his readers to be transformed by sharing his experience. Having witnessed and admired the bravery of the soldiers as they prepared for battle, Dunant conveys his horror at the sight of the fallen, "faces black with flies," as they "gazed around themselves, wild-eyed and helpless." He recalls how he came to feel a sense of obligation to stay and tend the wounded soldiers despite the fact that he could do so little for them. The proximity to their suffering and to their pleas for help, Dunant discovered, inspired a "positive energy" and a desire to "relieve as many as one can."[13] The experience also led Dunant to become painfully aware that much of the suffering and death associated with war has little to do with military goals and might have been prevented if organized relief organizations had been in place. His account of Solferino features graphic details about the bodies of the wounded soldiers interspersed with reflections on his own instinctive impulse to assist them. "I moistened his dry lips and hardened tongue," writes Dunant, "took a handful of lint and dipped it in the bucket and squeezed water into the deformed opening that had been his mouth."[14] He was no longer a "mere tourist." Dunant suggests that those who read his account should not do so as vicarious tourists and that they should be moved by similar instincts and energies to lend support to his efforts. He proposed to channel the instinctive impulse to act in the presence of suffering into support for such relief efforts by facilitating cooperative agreements among powerful states that could be maintained in accordance with the principle of reciprocity. Such organizations could do a great deal to help, he suggested, if established in a manner that could be perceived as an advantage for powerful states and consistent with the way in which military leaders defined their own strategic interests.

Dunant's account exemplifies what Arendt refers to as the "politics of pity," characterized by appeals that draw power from their capacity to awaken sentimental responses to the spectacle of suffering.[15] Such appeals aim to inspire a commitment to general norms by awakening instinctive compassion in response to graphic particulars of suffering. Dunant was aware, however, that the sentiment of compassion would not be enough to sustain such commitments, and indicates that his sense of compassion was not the only thing that motivated him to remain with the wounded soldiers. He suggests that his instinct to act was not only a response to his experience as a *witness to* suffering, but also a response to his experience of being *witnessed by* the suffering. He recalls the outrage and sense of abandonment expressed by soldiers as they begged for help: "They desert us, leave us to die miserably, and yet we fought so hard!" In the presence of acute suffering, Dunant suggests, the moral obligation to assist becomes a uniquely powerful imperative – one that transcends borders and overrides hesitation.

Peter Singer's 1972 essay, "Famine, Affluence, and Morality," uses a kind of thought experiment to extend this logic to appeals for famine relief.[16] In the presence of a drowning child, Singer contends, inaction is obviously shameful and the obligation to assist is felt as an instinctive imperative. If a child is drowning in a pond and calling for help, it would be shameful to hesitate or to worry about one's expensive clothing, Singer argues. It is just as shameful, he proposes, when privileged people spend money on indulgences instead of sending support for famine relief. If we think about what we would feel obliged to do in the presence of those who are struggling to survive, Singer suggests, then life-saving assistance is better understood as a moral imperative, rather than a benevolent act. Like Dunant, Singer invokes an image of helpless suffering in order to compel privileged audiences to see themselves as bystanders confronted with a clear moment of decision that presents a choice between immediate assistance and shameful inaction. Both thinkers observe that in the presence of acute suffering, indifference and passivity feel shameful in very obvious ways. Both configure physical and emotional distance as unnecessary obstructions that stand in the way of efforts to develop the moral implications of this impulse and both assert that one should have to be physically present with those who suffer to feel a sense of obligation to assist them.

Jean Pictet invokes a similar logic in his commentary on the Fundamental Principles of the Red Cross. Humanitarian action is rooted in the instinct for pity, according to Pictet, and a duty to combat distress, "no matter how disproportionate to it are the means available."[17] Framed in this manner, humanitarian action is in tension with efforts to investigate and remedy injustices that cause suffering. However, Pictet suggests that this instinct to alleviate suffering can influence the elaboration of shared norms that might inform efforts to pursue justice. Because all humans are aware of our shared vulnerability to suffering, he contends, we also share a common intuition that it is wrong to abandon those who are struggling to survive. As a response to the sense of obligation felt in the presence of suffering, Pictet asserts, humanitarian action reflects and reinforces a distinctive approach to justice that aims at "correcting the inequalities of fate," as well as a Christian ethic of charity, extended "even to our enemies."[18]

The idea that it is shameful to abandon those who suffer puts humanitarians in a difficult position. The "forces of compassion" have an expansionary logic, Barnett suggests, propelled by greater awareness of suffering with the spread of ideas and technologies that dissolve boundaries.[19] There is always more that one could do to help, and "[o]nce a set of needs is attended to," observes Barnett, "then it becomes virtually impossible to refuse an adjacent set of needs."[20] This expansionary logic is intensified by the way in which humanitarian appeals shame the figure of the passive bystander, suggesting that it is inhumane or immoral to witness suffering without feeling compassion and an instinctive desire to help. The proximity to limitless suffering, whether physical or virtual, provides humanitarians with a constant reminder that there are limits to what they can feel and limits to what they can do to help those in crisis. This causes humanitarian shaming strategies to have an expansionary logic as well. "The feeling one has of one's own utter inadequacy," Dunant writes of such experiences, "is unspeakable."[21] This feeling of shame at the limits of what he could do made it difficult for Dunant to sustain his compassion for the soldiers, causing him to adopt a posture "akin to cold calculation" in order to avoid becoming overwhelmed with despair. "Your heart is suddenly breaking," he writes of such moments, "as if you were stricken all at once with a bitter and irresistible sadness."[22] Hugo Slim suggests that this complicated mix of emotions may be an enduring feature of humanitarian work.[23]

Scholarship on affect and shame would suggest that humanitarian appeals are likely to backfire in predictable ways that are consistent with Dunant's account of his own conflicting emotions. Appeals for compassion in response to helpless victims can backfire by causing privileged audiences to engage in emotional distancing, as Berlant observes.[24] Based on a study of responses to humanitarian appeals, Stanley Cohen suggests that this kind of distancing might have something to do with the way in which such images not only awaken feelings of compassion, but also cause people to feel a sense of helplessness, despair, or resentment in response to any overt suggestion that it would be shameful to look at such images without feeling compassion and taking immediate action.[25] Those who feel resentful in response to the inference that they are expected to feel ashamed may respond defensively by avoiding exposure to information about the suffering of others or by cultivating indifference. Humanitarians may try to mitigate this defensive response by appealing for beneficence from audiences with narrative strategies that dramatize the helplessness of victims. This underscores the message that even a small effort can help those who have very little. This strategy can also backfire, as a number of commentators have observed, when it turns graphic accounts of helpless suffering into a spectacle for privileged audiences. Citing the example of Bob Geldoff's "Save the Children" campaign, Jen Rubenstein notes that humanitarians are generally aware that images of helpless suffering reinforce distancing stereotypes and that their continued reliance on such images is an enduring ethical dilemma.[26] By portraying suffering as limitless, and by focusing attention on common experiences of extreme helplessness, humanitarian appeals depict victims as interchangeable, superfluous, and disposable, observes Christina Beltrán.[27] Such appeals can reinforce the stigmatization of those depicted as victims, as well as those who assert agency in ways that are at odds with representations that characterize deserving victims as helpless.[28] At the same time, however, such appeals release privileged audiences from any shame they might feel about their own insularity or apathy by suggesting that people will be grateful to them for doing something to help–even if it is something very small.

Humanitarian strategies for soliciting the beneficence from those positions of power and privilege can also backfire when they cause humanitarians to feel that they are becoming implicated in the legitimation of abusive authorities in ways that turn them into passive bystanders despite, or even as a result of, their own relentless efforts to help. Humanitarian norms have legitimated colonial conquest and dispossession, as well as mass killings characterized as "collateral damage" defined in relation to "military necessity."[29] In their efforts to save lives, Arendt suggests, humanitarians assumed a public posture of deference to the Nazi regime and played a role in normalizing the systemic logics of mass killing.[30] A similar set of concerns was raised in the 1990s, regarding the role of humanitarianism in relation to the Rwandan genocide and mass killings in Bosnia-Herzegovina. "I have to confess that what I feel most tonight is shame," stated Rony Brauman in 1993, regarding the humanitarian responses of the United Nations during this period.[31] As Médecins Sans Frontières's (MSF) general coordinator in Bosnia, Eric Stobbaerts agonized, in correspondence, over whether the emphasis on providing life-saving relief had put MSF in a position of legitimating abusive authorities. "Should MSF play the role of jailer/prison doctor in the service of . . . the parties in conflict?"[32] Stobbaerts asked, adding that the presence of MSF might have given the impression that everything was "going well."

In her influential 2001 article, "Bystanders to Genocide," Samantha Power proposed that powerful liberal states should be shamed as bystanders if they fail to pursue timely military intervention to stop genocide.[33] In Power's formulation, the shameful bystander is one that hesitates to use the force required to stop mass killings in order to rescue people threatened with genocide. Power called for an approach to humanitarianism that would set aside the principles of impartiality and neutrality, which had been crucial to Pictet, yet framed her case for humanitarian intervention as the logical evolution of the humanitarian idea that it is shameful to be a passive bystander. She compared the role played by the Clinton Administration in response to the Rwandan genocide with the role played by Canadian General Romeo Dallaire, who served as head of the UN Peacekeeping Mission. It was Dallaire who stayed behind and, with only a few hundred remaining peacekeepers, resolved to remain present and to save as many as he could. "He feels that the eyes of those killed are constantly watching him," writes Power, after detailing Dallaire's inability to move on after the genocide with business as usual. Power's account invokes Dallaire's personal experience of bystander shame in order to invite readers to imagine that their own responses to suffering are also being witnessed by those who beg for assistance in moments of acute crisis.

Power's case for humanitarian intervention exemplifies the double-edged power associated of humanitarian shaming strategies. It identifies moral action as an urgent imperative to alleviate the suffering of helpless victims – one that depends on choices made by powerful actors in discrete moments of decision, without regard to the implications of history or long-term calculations. As outlined in "Responsibility to Protect Doctrine," such interventions are to be regulated in accordance with political and legal accountability mechanisms. Power's formulation of humanitarian intervention, suggests that these accountability mechanisms are to blame for shameful inaction and urges powerful leaders to cast them aside.[34] By condemning United States leaders as shameful bystanders to genocide, Power's formulation displaces concerns regarding the state's role in sponsoring perpetrators of war crimes. US leaders are too inhibited, she suggests, by diplomatic strategies and by their concern for the unintended consequences of interventions.[35] This denigration of diplomacy is consistent with the kind of thinking that reportedly contributed to the breakdown of diplomatic initiatives in response to violence and abuses in Syria, suggests Asli Bâli, who notes that Kofi Annan resigned from his role in such initiatives in 2012, followed by Lakhdar Brahimi in 2014 – both citing US preconditions that had rendered diplomacy untenable.[36] The disregard for the unintended consequences of humanitarian intervention is consistent with a general indifference or denial of responsibility, in political debates within the United States, for the violent aftermath of the US intervention in Libya.

For Arendt, the humanitarian "politics of pity" is also double-edged in the sense that it can undermine efforts to cultivate solidarity and political responsibility in response to those in need of assistance, as Flynn observes in his chapter for this volume. In "We Refugees," Arendt suggests that when persecuted populations feel compelled to suppress their identities and voices to appear as deserving recipients of aid, this can lead to a destructive form of self-abnegation, causing people to internalize their own stigmatization and to carry shame quietly as a private burden instead of working together to contest oppressive logics.[37] To some extent, Pictet shared such concerns regarding this "dark side of charity," as he put it, observing that recipients of aid feel obliged to cultivate a posture of deference and unending gratitude for a debt that can never be repaid. This problem could be mitigated, he suggests, through efforts to institutionalize the provision of aid in ways that would enable it to be claimed as an entitlement and received "as a right."[38] Many thinkers have proposed that the limits of humanitarianism, as predicated on appeals for beneficence, could be addressed through efforts to mobilize human rights in ways that would empower people to assert agency to confront abusive authorities and institutionalized forms of injustice. Like humanitarians, however, human rights advocates have pursued shaming strategies that are double-edged as responses to systemic forms of abuse, and at odds with efforts to confront structural injustice.

Naming and Shaming

"The newspaper reader feels a sickening sense of impotence," wrote Peter Benenson, in "The Forgotten Prisoner," the 1961 op-ed that is credited with launching Amnesty International. "Yet if feelings of disgust all over the world could be united into common action, something effective could be done," he argued in his appeal for a collective response to the unjust imprisonment of "prisoners of conscience."[39] The goal of Amnesty International, as outlined by Benenson, would be to mobilize global support for the rights outlined in Articles 18 and 19 of the UDHR, which call upon all states to protect freedom of thought, religion, expression, and opinion, as well as the right to import information through the media, "regardless of frontiers." Whereas Dunant told audiences that they should be outraged by the indignities suffered by brave young soldiers, Benenson rallied his readers to outrage at the plight of the "nonconformist," imprisoned without due process for opinions deemed threatening to the state. Benenson's appeal did not incorporate graphic accounts of physical suffering endured by political prisoners, but emphasized the pain of being silenced and forgotten. He appealed to readers for support by introducing specific "prisoners of conscience," sharing their names and providing a brief overview of their stories. Benenson's call for action centered on a case for mobilizing "the force of public opinion." The force of opinion could be uniquely powerful, he suggested, when people with very different views and opposing political identities come together in a manner that is "broadly based, international, non-sectarian, and all party." Benenson hoped to cultivate a sense of community for idealists that had become disillusioned with leftist politics, according to Hopgood.[40]

The trial of Adolf Eichmann also took place in 1961. As prosecutor in the Eichmann Trial, which was held in Jerusalem, Gideon Hausner invited survivors to share extensive testimonies regarding their experiences of abuse, loss, daily life, and resistance in a range of forms.[41] His decision to air lengthy victim testimonies would have a major influence on global perceptions of genocide and victimhood.[42] In the decade prior to the trial, the divisive "Kastner Affair" had centered public attention and shame on the actions of Jewish leaders, such as Rudolph Kastner, accused of bargaining with the Nazis to save select friends.[43] More generally, Holocaust survivors had encountered pervasive forms of shaming and silencing in portrayals that stressed their passivity or expressed skepticism regarding what they might have done to survive.[44] Hausner was explicit in framing his decision to invite survivors to share lengthy testimonies as a strategy for countering this stigmatization. Despite their very different political agendas, Hausner and Benenson shared a common concern with the way in which victim-shaming is bound up in claims about resistance. Those identified as victims are either stigmatized for their failure to resist or for having resisted in shameful or treasonous ways – as "terrorists" or as "subversives" that threaten the integrity of established order. Both Hausner and Benenson proposed to confront victim-shaming by mobilizing public outrage in response to the guilt of perpetrators. Stigmatizing perpetrators can be a way to destigmatize the persecuted, both suggest, and cultivating empathy for victims is a way to galvanize support for the institutional order that empowers advocacy on their behalf.

As Amnesty International and other organizations expanded the scope of human rights activism, they pursued strategies for strengthening the force of stigmatizing shame. In theory, such efforts would complement humanitarian relief work by addressing what Pictet referred to as the "dark side of charity." Human rights shaming strategies would expose powerful authorities to public criticism, which could enable human rights organizations to address the limitations of humanitarianism as a challenge to the advantage of the strong. Human rights shaming strategies differ from those developed by prominent humanitarians and aim to mobilize different emotions. Instead of mobilizing bystander shame, human rights appeals aim to awaken outrage by stigmatizing specific abusive authorities. Like humanitarians, however, human rights advocates direct their appeals to privileged audiences and aim to galvanize support by cultivating empathy in response to accounts of victimhood. To be effective, Keck and Sikkink observe, efforts to mobilize stigmatizing shame must be framed in ways that resonate with values that are already deeply held and widely shared. And they are unlikely to work on those who commit abuses openly and shamelessly.[45]

Human rights shaming strategies are associated with different, and more public, forms of backlash than the shaming strategies cultivated by humanitarian organizations, yet share a common reliance on accounts of helpless victimhood that are framed to solicit empathy. Mobilizing around the binary of criminal guilt and innocence has been a prominent strategy for defending the integrity of victims against such attacks, as Ticktin observes in her chapter for this volume, yet this strategy can backfire when the binary is flipped by those who wish to legitimate exclusion by stigmatizing the persecuted.[46] When presumptive innocence is established with reference to indicators of helplessness, this can reinforce the logic by which political exclusion is justified or rationalized through the stigmatization of those who assert agency to challenge abusive authorities and institutions.[47]

In the 1970s, the Madres de la Plaza Mayo began to make weekly processions to demand information regarding children "disappeared" by the military dictatorship in Argentina, incorporating imagery that identified motherhood with innocence. The military dictatorship was shaming women for their political engagement and that of their children, writes Diana Taylor. The Madres worked to counter this stigmatization and to establish their own moral authority by incorporating symbolism identified with maternal self sacrifice and the Virgin Mary.[48] However, this did not prevent them from being shamed for the way they challenged authority, observes Taylor. "I can't imagine the Virgin Mary yelling, protesting, and planting seeds of hate," one commentator asserted, "when our Lord, was taken from her hands."[49] The concerns of the Madres were taken more seriously by representatives from Amnesty International, members of the Carter Administration, and the Inter-American Human Rights Committee, who visited Argentina in the late 1970s. However, the human rights strategy of cultivating empathy by stigmatizing perpetrators is associated with predictable forms of backlash. When appeals for empathy make people feel judged or shamed, it is common for them to react defensively by cultivating indifference, rather than compassion. This strategy is likely to reinforce the kind of failures of empathy that Feldman identifies in response to Palestinian suffering, in her chapter for this volume.

Political backlash raises the stakes for human rights organizations that are invested in mobilizing stigmatizing shame. Stigmatizing shame functions as a public accusation, and the accused are likely to respond with counter shaming strategies, aimed at discrediting or intimidating their accusers. Backlash can embarrass human rights advocates when abusive authorities respond to stigmatization with public displays of shamelessness. This kind of backlash exposes the limitations of confrontational shaming strategies and weakens the subtle force of shame as a basis for cultivating the internalization of international norms by exposing their politically contested character. In order to mitigate such challenges, human rights organizations have borrowed shaming strategies associated with humanitarianism, which appeal for beneficence from privileged and powerful actors in response to acute bodily suffering. They have focused on stigmatizing those who violate human rights that are also prohibited in international humanitarian law, and worked to develop enforcement mechanisms that criminalize violations of the laws of war. These efforts have altered international humanitarian law and led to the incorporation of human rights principles into the laws of war.[50] However, they are in tension with the aspiration to mobilize the human rights framework as a basis for empowering political agency in response to unjust hierarchy and systemic forms of abuse.

In an essay written as executive director of Human Rights Watch, Kenneth Roth argued that in order to mobilize shame effectively, human rights organizations must be in a position to establish the identity of a "violator," the identities of "the violated," and an effective remedy for the violation. If any one of these three elements is missing or ambiguous, he added, "the capacity for shame is greatly diminished."[51] Roth outlined this analysis of human rights methodology as part of a larger discussion of its limitations as a basis for pursuing economic, social, and cultural rights. It makes sense for human rights organizations to focus primarily on abuses of "physical integrity rights" that are associated with specific abusers and legal remedies, Roth argued – not because they are more important than economic, social, and cultural rights, but because those who commit such abuses can be effectively shamed. Shame cannot be effectively mobilized in response to structural injustices, Roth contends, because stigmatization loses its power when people cannot perceive clear lines of accountability.

Roth does not explain why those committed to confronting human rights abuses would want to bind themselves to such a limited strategy. He implies that the answer to this question is somewhat obvious, and that human rights organizations and institutions depend on such strategies if they are to be effective in challenging powerful authorities. These comments exemplify some of the striking internal contradictions associated with prominent human rights strategies for mobilizing shame. Although human rights are championed as a basis for confronting systemic, institutionalized, and legalized forms of abuse, Roth and other influential advocates suggest that human rights advocacy should be limited to discrete violations abuses of established law. Although human rights are championed as a basis for empowering people to assert agency in response to hierarchy and domination, human rights shaming strategies are only effective as a basis for aiding those who are helpless and thought to be incapable of acting on their own behalf. In his response to concerns about this minimalist approach to advocacy, Roth insists that the power of shame can be mobilized in ways that are inherently benign, as a basis for strengthening legal norms that does not displace or undermine efforts to address structural injustices. However, such shaming strategies are double-edged, as many critics have observed. By identifying some forms of abuse as uniquely shameful and outrageous, human rights organizations suggest that other forms of abuse are not as shameful or worthy of concern and that those who experience such abuses may be less deserving of empathy.

Human rights organizations have championed international criminal justice institutions, such as war crimes prosecutions and truth commissions, as a basis for accountability for crimes against humanity and other systematic forms of abuse. As discussed by Ilana Feldman, the influence of such institutions is associated with the way in which they intervene in the politics of memory. Such institutions have been championed for their pedagogical role in confronting systemic, institutionalized, and legalized forms of abuse. This basic aspiration is reflected in the way in which South Africa's influential Truth and Reconciliation Commission (TRC) introduces the findings presented in its final report by observing that legalization of apartheid-era abuses had been a powerful strategy for legitimating the apartheid state – a strategy that influenced global public opinion for many years by shielding the state from concerns regarding the institutionalized brutalities of the apartheid state: "Laws tore millions of workers from their families ... Laws forced people to work for grossly insufficient remuneration ... Laws forced people from their homes and communities."[52]

In order to effectively stigmatize individual perpetrators, and cultivate empathy for victims, the TRC adopted a narrow interpretation of its legal mandate to investigate "gross-violations of human rights," by focusing on *jus in bello* violations of international humanitarian law. This meant that the TRC would not investigate the denial of voting rights, dispossession, forced labor, forced removals, and other institutionalized forms of abuse. South Africa's TRC also urged victims to let go of anger and embrace forgiveness. As a number of commentators observed, this would discourage participation from those who wanted to express anger, discuss grievances beyond the scope of the mandate, and share accounts centered on experiences of agency and resistance.[53] In theory, human rights advocacy addresses the limits of humanitarianism by mobilizing shame to confront abusive authorities. In practice, human rights shaming strategies obfuscate the systemic logics of abuse and reinforce various forms of stigmatization that maintain such logics.

Shameful Lands and Systems

> We sing: This country of ours, despite all its better souls have done and dreamed, is as yet a shameful land.
>
> W.E.B. Du Bois, "Returning Soldiers"[54]

In his 1919 essay, "Returning Solders," Du Bois invokes the collective voice of black soldiers to lament the hypocritical idealism of wartime rhetoric meant to justify their sacrifices and the reality that they had been forced to fight for an America "that gloats in lynching, disenfranchisement, caste, brutality, and devilish insult." Written in the first person plural, "Returning Soldiers" catalogues a list of institutionalized injustices and appeals for action. This appeal is not directed at America, which Du Bois refers to as "It," but imagined as a song that is sung about America by the soldiers to themselves: "It keeps us consistently and universally poor ... then feeds us on charity and derides our poverty," they sing. "It insults us" through a "world-wide propaganda of racism" and "it looks upon any attempt to question or even discuss this as arrogance, unwarranted assumption and treason." American shameless- ness has been institutionalized, Du Bois suggests, to such an extent that "It" cannot hear the voices that of those that would expose its worst hypocrisies. The song they sing is imagined as a fight song, meant to fortify those heading from one battle into another: "We return from fighting / We return fighting ... Make way for Democracy!"

A system cannot be made to feel ashamed. It is difficult for people to perceive the systemic logics of abuse, as Du Bois observes, because those same logics generally function to normalize and rationalize abuse. The work of challenging social and political hierarchies requires "unashamed citizens," writes Jill Locke, including those who may or may not have formal citizenship, to "interrogate and denaturalize the terms of shame and shaming ... and fight for a reconstituted social order."[55] It is difficult for privileged audiences to hear narratives that challenge established institutions and the systemic logics that have come to define what they take to be natural or normal. When people are asked to reflect on their responsibilities as beneficiaries of a shameful system, it is common for them to respond in a defensive manner. For people who are accustomed to appeals for beneficence, such challenges may appear to be misguided and destructive. For people who identify accountability with social ostra- cism, the prospect of being implicated in systemic forms of abuse may feel deeply threatening. When people are accustomed to feeling empathy in response to helpless victims, they may be less inclined to respond with empathy to those who attempt to engage them as political agents or those who ask them to consider their responsibilities as beneficiaries of, and participants in, institutionalized forms of abuse.

People who mobilize human rights to challenge structural and systemic logics of injustice confront a problem: they will find it difficult to be heard by those who wield power within those institutional settings. They can frame narratives that appeal to the beneficence of privileged audiences, yet it is difficult to do so without participating in the silencing or erasure of their own most pressing concerns. Ida B. Wells addressed this dilemma in a 1900 speech entitled, "Lynch Law in America," with journalistic stra- tegies aimed at exposing the shame of courts that accepted the "unwritten law" that African Americans would not receive a trial for allegations made by others, and could not go to the courts to seek justice for wrongs committed against them. She worked to expose the normalization of white supremacist violence with accounts that would document the role of lynching as a systematic pattern of abuse. Her accounts draw attention to details aimed at exposing the role of bystanders, including "leading citizens," who may not have carried out such acts themselves, but continuously condoned them with their presence.[56] Wells drew attention to the shamelessness of American bystanders to lynching in order to expose it as an institutionalized atrocity, rather than an aberration, while observing that in the eyes of the world, America was a shameful country. "No American travels abroad without blushing with shame for his country on the subject," wrote Wells.[57]

If the influence of shame is bound up in its subtle order-reinforcing role, then it might seem sensible to set aside concern with shame and shaming. However, the order-reinforcing role of shame can cause stigmatized populations to internalize the burden of shame in ways that complicate efforts to organize as "unashamed citizens." Du Bois characterized "double consciousness" as a "peculiar sense of always looking at the world through the eyes of others, of measuring one's soul by the tape of ... contempt and pity."[58] "Learning to see and hear only what the priests and brothers wanted you to see and hear," recalls George Manuel of his experiences with the Indian Residential School System in Canada, "even the people we loved came to look ugly ... can there be a more elegant violence than this?"[59] Internalized shame can be profoundly destructive and violent, yet facilitate the appearance of consent in ways that make it especially difficult to contest institutionalized injustices. In "Returning Soldiers," Du Bois imagines a way of working with the power of shame that would respond to this problem. The soldiers announce their refusal to continue tolerating the normalization and silencing that perpetuate structural injustices. They do not frame their appeal as an effort to compel those in positions of power to feel outrage or compassion on their behalf. Instead, they issue a call to those who share the similar burdens to shed the internalized shame associated with such stigmatization through the collective work of exposing what is shameful in established systems and institutions.

In 1947, Du Bois addressed those involved in drafting the Universal Declaration of Human Rights with "An Appeal to the World: A Statement on the Denial of Human Rights to Minorities in the Case of Citizens of Negro Descent."[60] Du Bois invokes human rights principles to frame racial injustice in the United States as an international problem. The United States was lending support to white supremacist regimes, Du Bois observed, and participants traveling to meetings of the United States would be highly vulnerable to American racism. "Peoples of the world, we American Negroes appeal to you," wrote Du Bois, "our treatment in America is not merely an internal question of the United States. It is a basic problem of humanity ... and as such it demands your attention and action." Only through pressure from "peoples of the world," Du Bois, suggested, would it be possible for the United States to begin to confront profound injustices embedded within its very justice system – legalized and normalized to the extent that white Americans could not even seem to see their own abuses well enough to grasp the nature of the appeal.

The appeal was not taken seriously by those who institutionalized human rights. This is not because Du Bois failed to grasp the power of shame, but because he pursued an approach to working with that power that stands in stark contrast with the "naming and shaming" practices of prominent human rights organizations. The appeal that Du Bois submitted to Eleanor Roosevelt was not framed in a manner that was designed to appeal to the sensibilities of privileged audiences. He did not articulate a plea for empathy and outrage aimed at stigmatizing individuals for uniquely egregious and deliberate cruelty. His appeal was meant to embarrass American elites and unsettle their assumptions about victimhood, guilt, and rights. Like "naming and shaming" however, the strategies favored by Du Bois were confrontational and inspired backlash. Backlash can be useful to those who aspire to expose and weaken the order-reinforcing role of shame, yet it is also costly and dangerous, and it can provoke repressive violence that makes it difficult to continue the work of challenging established norms.

Human rights organizations and institutions can play an important role in supporting efforts to expose shameful systems, then, when they provide strong collective support, as well as support for the civil and political rights claims of those engaged in asserting political agency. The assassinations of high-profile environmental justice activists, such as Tomás García and Berta Cáceres, leaders of the Civic Council of Popular and Indigenous Organizations of Honduras (COPINH) underscores the salience of their appeals for civil and political rights protections as an integral dimension of their efforts to challenge economic exploitation, dispossession, racial injustices, and corruption.[61] Following García's assassination in 2013, Cáceres was routinely threatened for her leadership in COPINH's efforts to stop logging projects and secure communal land titles for Indigenous communities in Honduras. COPINH responded by demanding that the Inter-American Court of Human Rights investigate the 2016 assassination of Berta Cáceres, and that the banks invested in extractive projects and dams in the region investigate Indigenous rights violations associated with such projects. They also called for congressional representatives in the United States to support the Human Rights in Honduras Act.[62]

Mily Treviño-Saucedo also cultivated strategies for empowering agency by responding to stigmatization when she began organizing Lideres Campesinas in response to the abuse and sexual harassment of undocumented migrant workers in California's Coachella Valley. Treviño-Saucedo found that the men did not want to discuss it and that the women had been intimidated by a culture of blaming and stigmatizing women who spoke out. As part of a master's thesis project at Cal State San Bernardino, Treviño-Saucedo surveyed women working in the fields to document the scale of the problem and to solicit their ideas about how to address it. Lideres Campesinas builds on insights from this work by providing a network of support for women that aims to "strengthen leadership of farmworker women and girls so that they can be agents of economic, social, and political change and ensure their human rights."[63] The organization now has chapters throughout the state of California and works to educate farmworkers and their families regarding rights issues associated with pesticide poisoning, wage theft, asylum, and workplace safety, in addition to sexual violence. As Ramona Felix puts it, "[W]hen we realize that there are many who feel like this, we unite in order to stand up for human rights."[64] Human Rights Watch and other rights groups provide support for legal strategies associated with the work done by organizations such as Lideres Campesinas and COPINH. However, these organizations do not identify justice with law enforcement and they do not position themselves as helpless victims in order to appeal for empathy and outrage among privileged advocates. Rather, they work to empower agency by countering internalized shame and stigmatization, and they offset risks associated with the inevitable threat of violent back-lash by providing networks that can offer legal expertise, as well as collective political support.

Conclusion

In his chapter for this volume, Stephen Hopgood contends that human rights will likely decline in significance because there is little consensus on what is essential about them and they are an annoyance for powerful states that underwrite international laws and institutions. As this becomes increasingly clear, he adds, it will also become clear that human rights advocates can no longer rely on the legal frameworks and institutions they have established. Thrasymachus might respond approvingly, while not-ing that if human rights laws and institutions are generally framed in ways that advantage the strong, then their unreliability is not really a new development. Socrates night observe that there is little consensus regard-ing what is essential to justice more generally, but many people think it is still an important point to debate and to pursue. Ideals are generally institutionalized in ways that benefit those in power, but it is difficult for people to critically evaluate such institutions and to assess the logics of legitimation when they get in the habit of conflating the meaning of concepts and ideals with their institutional expression in a given order. Attention to the order-reinforcing role of shaming strategies is useful in pursuing Thrasymachus's concern with unmasking the logic by which ideals are invoked to legitimate the interests of the powerful, as well as Socrates's concern with the process by which people critically evaluate institutions by debating the meaning of their ideals.

Prominent shaming strategies enable privileged audiences to remain shameless in denying responsibility for their role in policies and strategies that perpetuate systemic forms of abuse. To the extent that they inhibit political agency and obfuscate systemic logics, these strategies can reinforce resignation, even as they demand moral action. By defining moral action in relation to stark binaries, shaming strategies are associated with predictable logics of backlash and defensive maneuvering in response to grievances and critiques that expose the limits of established institutions. These dynamics can reinforce the silencing and stigmatization of those who pursue the kinds of political engagements that are needed to transform systemic and structural logics of abuse. Such strategies establish subtle, yet powerful incentives for those who seek support to share stories that are likely to appeal to the sensibilities of those in positions of power and privilege. They can also discourage those who might wish to share stories that privileged audiences might find unsettling or off-putting. This makes it difficult for humanitarians and human rights advocates to hear the voices of those best positioned to explain what kind of assistance they need, and the voices of those who might explain how the appearance of peace can be maintained by the normalization of violence. Such strategies can make it difficult for those most affected by persecution, exploitation, and abuse to share stories that might convey full weight of the invisible burdens they bear and what it would really mean to take responsibility for addressing them.

A well-known Aesop's fable "The Dog and the Shadow" tells the story of a dog crossing a river with a bone in its mouth when it looks down and sees another dog with a bigger bone sitting in the water. Eager to acquire a better meal, the dog opens its mouth to reach for it. This causes the original bone to fall into the water, revealing that the desired bone was nothing but a shadow of the one the dog already had and has now lost.[65] The fable teaches a lesson about the importance of valuing modest, yet life-saving, achievements. It invites audiences to reflect on whether their impulse to ask for more might be driven by foolish illusions and imagined visions of what could be. Humanitarian organizations convey a similar message when they mobilize shame in ways that position deserving recipients of aid as helpless victims, grateful for assistance no matter how limited or inadvertently destructive it may be. Human rights shaming strategies reinforce this message to the extent that they cultivate habitual obedience in response to conventional norms and institutionalized authority. These strategies also inhibit and stigmatize those who assert agency to call for more expansive approaches to justice, implying that they, like Aesop's foolish dog, risk losing what they have been given if they open their mouths to chase shadowy illusions. We could question the logic of the fable by imagining a different and more just kind of order that would grant the dog access to a supply of bones. To pursue such goals would also require different approaches to formulating moral action and just order – approaches that are not designed for audiences that are expected to behave like foolish dogs, but for those that are expected to participate in the process of elaborating, maintaining, and revising legal orders through the continuous exercise of critical judgment and political agency.

Efforts to confront suffering and injustice will be limited, Arendt suggests, without support for those who assert agency to confront institutionalized forms of abuse. In her view, this would also require new ways of thinking about authority that do not identify the achievement of just order with evidence of success in enforcement and compliance, and do not limit the scope of moral action and accountability to intentional choices made in discrete moments of decision. Wells, Du Bois, and Treviño-Sauceda may be viewed as exemplars of an approach to working with the power of shame that advances such goals, and one that is not uncommon among those who mobilize the human rights to confront structural and systemic forms of abuse. The significance of such strategies cannot be evaluated with reference to their success in gaining support from powerful actors because this is not their primary goal. Such strategies are premised on a common assumption that those who confront systemic forms of abuse must work to expose, unsettle, and transform the kinds of subtle order-reinforcing logics that preclude meaningful access to institutional remedies for abuse and injustice. It is an approach that challenges silencing and political exclusion by repudiating internalized shame and by exposing what is shameful in established institutions and familiar conventions.

8   At Odds?

Human Rights and Humanitarian Approaches to Violence Against Women During Conflict

Aisling Swaine

In 1999, working with an international aid agency on the Albanian border with Kosovo during the NATO bombing of that territory, I encountered an issue that was to become central to the ways in which international human rights and humanitarian organizations would establish their approach to women's experiences of conflict. As thousands of Kosovars streamed over the border to the growing camps and services on the other side, the stories of atrocity by the Milošević regime on those people were pouring out too. My work, and research that I was conducting, led me to speak with adolescent girls. Through conversations with them, I learned that almost every one I spoke with had experienced some form of sexual assault and/or rape; that this violence was part of the range of threats that their families were fleeing from; and for some girls, their families had spontaneously married them to men from their communities during flight as a form of protection from rape that was targeted at "virgin" Kosovar girls.[1] When I raised this issue with the humanitarian agency that I was working with, and with others on the ground, and explained that almost every girl I met with was describing sexual violence as part of their experience of the conflict and refuge from it, I received consistent responses: "We don't do that," "It's too sensitive," "That's not within our remit, we deliver aid."

Fast forward to 2018: since the turn of the century, the foremost multilateral system that oversees response to the impacts of armed conflict on affected populations, the United Nations and its entities and partners, have dramatically changed their tune. In the human rights arena, human rights monitors on the ground, working with entities such as the Office of the High Commission for Human Rights (OHCHR) and UN political and peacekeeping missions, specifically document conflict-related sexual violence (CRSV[2]);[3] the UN Human Rights Council's Commissions of Inquiry now include sexual violence within their mandates and experts on sexual violence in their teams conducting investigations in conflict-affected settings globally,[4] with a roster of people with these specific investigatory skills established for deployment;[5] the UN Human Rights Council has adopted several resolutions on this issue;[6] the Committee of the Convention on the Elimination of All Forms of Discrimination Against Women (CEDAW) has adopted a specific General Recommendation advising states parties of their obligations to address women's rights in conflict, including sexual violence;[7] while in 2015, the UN General Assembly adopted a resolution nominating June 19 as international day against CRSV.[8] In the humanitarian arena, prevention and response to CRSV as part of humanitarian relief emerged through the UN Security Council's specific resolutions condemning the use of sexual violence in war;[9] in 2005 (and updated in 2015) the UN Inter-Agency Standing Committee on Humanitarian Action (IASC) first published its specific guidelines for the sector on addressing what they term "gender-based violence" (GBV) through humanitarian response;[10] a specific sub-cluster on GBV was established under the process of reform of the global humanitarian response architecture in that same era;[11] a state-led high-level global conference on the prevention and response to CRSV was held in 2014;[12] the G8 issued a declaration condemning the issue;[13] international aid agencies are now measured on their level of response to GBV programming;[14] while international donor governments are now assessed and critiqued for their levels of funding to policy and programming addressing this issue.[15]

Attitudes and approaches to conflict-related violence against women (CRVAW[16]), and particularly CRSV, have clearly changed dramatically since 1999. Normative and operational changes toward these issues are conspicuous in the rapidity at which they have developed and the degree to which the UN system and its associated entities have embraced CRVAW as relevant to their remit. Also conspicuous is that these developments traverse both the human rights and the humanitarian fields of global policy and practice in response to conflict-affected settings. As evidenced here, issues of women's rights, particularly CRSV, have become very much entwined in the global policy systems of human rights and humanitarianism. In fact, comparative to my experience in humanitarian operations in 1999, the neglect of CRSV in a complex humanitarian setting on the part of either human rights or humanitarian organizations on the ground is now unthinkable and would be subject to serious critique, and identified as a failing.

What do these developments represent? Are they simply evidence of a growing cognizance of women's experiences of conflict and their relevance to the mandates of the human rights and humanitarian actors? Or more than that? Do they represent evidence of fragmentation within the UN system in terms of its structural and normative approach to issues that are common to, but are evidently developing separately within, its differentiated human rights and humanitarian regimes?[17] Or of the merging of these regimes and norms within practice, a complementarity galvanized around a singular issue, where human rights workers document violations, including sexual violence, that have led to the displacement of people across conflict settings, while humanitarians get nearer to those frontlines, witness those violations, and make addressing them part of their operations? Critical questions arise in respect to what has motivated these developments and what they say about each sectors' approach to the impacts of conflict on affected populations. Of most interest to this volume is a consideration of what they say about the relationship between and areas of intersection across the fields of human rights and humanitarianism when it comes to the issue of CRVAW.

This chapter examines the relationship between the human rights and the humanitarian fields through the lens of their normative and related practice response to the issue of CRVAW. In its exploration of these issues, the chapter focuses on the approaches to practice that have come to characterize the human rights and humanitarian fields. By this, I mean, the body of normative laws, policy, and operational approaches that have emerged through the United Nations system and associated actors. For the purposes of this chapter, each field of practice is understood in respect of its evolution within the international system of governance, representing "regimes" within the UN system. The human rights regime is understood as the genealogy of the post-World War II international legal system which established an "adjudicatory model" with the "ultimate normative power" to make human rights "protectable."[18] The adoption of the UN charter, the Universal Declaration of Human Rights, and the evolving body of international human rights treaty law that followed espoused a new mode of legal accountability for human rights ideals.[19] The concept of human rights thus became "premised on the idea that outsiders must judge the way in which states treat their own citizens."[20] Accordingly, the UN human rights regime as it is referred to, is made up of a body of human rights conventions, with an associated architecture designed to oversee monitoring of their implementation by states, with the aim of accountability for transgressions of legal obligations. This practice field is made up of, among many actors, the UN Human Rights Council, the treaty bodies that are attached to international human rights conventions, and operational agencies such as the OHCHR which establishes many "missions" around the world to monitor implementation of human rights law.[21]

The humanitarian field of practice, on the other hand, is understood to be founded in international humanitarian law which "does not set out to end war or eradicate civilian casualties but rather to tame war by minimizing death and suffering."[22] Traced back to Henry Dunant's creation of the International Committee of the Red Cross, the humanitarian practice field has evolved to become "the impartial, neutral, and independent provision of relief to victims of conflict and natural disasters," with its own architecture, or governance system.[23] The humanitarian "regime" within the UN (very loosely conceived) would broadly include the UN Inter-Agency Standing Committee on Humanitarian Action which draws together many of the more prominent UN and other international actors in the field such as the Red Cross movement, to establish and oversee UN-led normative rules and policies for the operation of humanitarian assistance,[24] and UN Secretariat entities such as the Organization for the Coordination of Humanitarian Affairs (UNOCHA), which coordinates the activities of UN and other actors in sites of operation. Associated actors in the humanitarian space are departments on humanitarian action within governmental donor agencies, nongovernmental and UN agencies with specific mandates to operate humanitarian relief. The practice of this field involves provision of basic services, water, food, shelter, as part of the relief response to those displaced and otherwise impacted by humanitarian crises, and is "undertaken in the name of compassion, care, and responsibility."[25] The field of humanitarian practice is largely preoccupied with addressing the consequences of a crisis, rather than its causes per much of the human rights regime, even though this is changing for many actors.[26] It is important to note that what is referred to here largely represents what has emerged as a "formal or institutional humanitarian system … mostly Western actors whose raison d'être is humanitarian and who are linked together by established codes, shared principles and jargon … [which] has become increasingly institutionalized and centralized under UN leadership for the sake of improved coherence and coordination."[27]

Through examining the issue of CRVAW within and across each of these sets of regimes and associated practices, this chapter considers whether there are commonalities and/or distinctions in the ways in which each deals with the impacts of conflict on women's and girls' lives, and specifically, their experiences of conflict-related violence. The chapter explores the perceived boundaries in terms of the foundational basis of both fields, identifying that they are not so clear cut when examined in respect of specific thematic areas of human rights and humanitarian operations; namely, in the case of CRVAW. It is, however, in the *strategies* that both sets of actors use to fulfill these conceptual aims that divergence emerges, as well as opportunities for synergies. The chapter first sets out an overview of the development of approaches to CRVAW within the field of human rights and then humanitarianism. It then identifies areas of divergence between the fields in respect of conceptual and practical approaches to CRVAW. On the basis of these key areas of tension, the chapter then uses a gender interests framework to explore the potential for future complementarity across the fields for the fulfillment of women's rights within and across each field of practice.

Human Rights, Humanitarianism and Conflict-Related Violence against Women: Developments in Each Field

The fields of human rights and humanitarianism have offered much to the formal and substantive advancement of women's rights. Historic and informal civil society activism on women's liberation and rights, which largely took place outside of governance structures, gained a foothold in the evolving and increasingly formalized and rule-based paradigm offered through the emerging multilateral systems of the United Nations. Initially an imperative for women's rights activists that post-World War II multilateralism was informed by and engaged with women's equality, it is now the case that critical issues that arise for women, such as specific forms of crime, violation, and inequalities, are normatively shaped and molded by this very system.

The "global governance" role that spheres of human rights and of humanitarianism have come to occupy have been documented by scholars of both fields.[28] It is perhaps the issue of CRVAW that has most predominated, gained traction and is the most commonly addressed women's rights issue across both of these fields in recent times. Curiously, it is an issue that is quite tangible in respect to rights and delivery of services and around which, not without controversy, states have galvanized.[29] This is most evident in respect to sexual violence by conflict actors, where both human rights and humanitarian organizations have increasingly carved out a specific role for themselves in respect of their mandates and modes of working. In a short time-span, primarily from the late 1990s to the current time, the issue of CRVAW, and particularly specific forms of CRSV, namely rape, has become quite central to whether and how each field engages with women's equality. There appears to be critical synergies between what becomes normative through public international law (e.g., forms of CRVAW as human rights violations), and what then also becomes normative to and a legitimate concern for the field of humanitarian response (programmatic responses to CRVAW). To explore these synergies further, I first map out the genealogy and key characteristics of the approach taken to CRVAW by the human rights system, and then by the humanitarian system.

Human Rights and Violence Against Women

The human rights field is the earliest site of feminist engagement with international law, with women's rights becoming quite central to that body of law relatively quickly.[30] The need to overcome the gendered bias in the founding human rights instruments[31] and to promote the inclusion of specific rights pertaining to discrimination impacting women was a primary site of initial "liberal inclusion" and "structural bias" scholarship of the 1980s and early 1990s.[32] The rights entitlements formally articulated under early human rights frameworks, such as the UN Convention on Civil and Political Rights (1969) and Economic and Social Rights (1969), although in theory available to "all," were found to have "blind spots" with respect to women's rights.[33]

The introduction of the idea of a "bill of rights" for women at the time of the proliferation of human rights treaties in the 1960s resulted in a "declaration on the elimination of discrimination against women," eventually culminating in the adoption of a specific treaty on this same topic.[34] The Convention on the Elimination of Discrimination Against Women (CEDAW) was adopted in 1979.[35] It advanced the overall human rights doctrine in general terms, formally articulating a legal definition of discrimination for the first time, while firmly situating specific areas of discrimination relating to women's lives as central to the evolving human rights field: the family, reproduction, employment and legal identity, among others.

The human rights field thus offers a very specific frame through which the lives of women are articulated: discrimination, which derives from and causes inequality, and which is tackled in terms of a legal definition and means. This differs quite significantly from the humanitarian sphere, which as will be discussed later, is very much about operational programming and still questions, on the part of some operational actors, whether or not longer-term gender *equality* issues are even relevant. The lens of discrimination implies that there is an explicit bias to be tackled, and its human rights and legalized framing means that the direction of accountability and redress is the state.

It was not until the 1990s, with the wave of human rights attention following the end of the Cold War, that the issue of violence against women (VAW) came formally under the frame of human rights. The proximity of the Yugoslav wars and the reports of sexual violence emerging from the region to the 1993 Vienna Conference on Human Rights inevitably held significant influence on the resulting attention to VAW. On the heels of CEDAW's General Recommendations 12 (1989) and 19 (1992)[36] which articulated the applicability of the Convention to VAW,

166   *Aisling Swaine*

the Declaration on the Elimination of Violence Against Women (DEVAW) was adopted.[37] These developments in the human rights field did a number of things for the issue of VAW. First, VAW was above all defined as a violation of human rights, which was an important development in respect of gaining the political and legal legitimacy and symbolic currency needed to be addressed within the vertical regime of accountability under the UN's state-based system of human rights.[38] Second, the instruments denoted VAW as a "gender-based violence," framing it in respect to the social construction of harm in a gendered social world, and relating it directly to gender inequalities experienced by women. Third, it framed VAW within the founding basis of formal legalistic ideas of women's rights, namely under CEDAW's articulation of "gender-based violence [as] a form of discrimination that seriously inhibits women's ability to enjoy rights and freedoms on a basis of equality with men."[39] The violence in women's lives thereby became framed as a form of discrimination requiring legal redress for violating women's human rights and potential in respect of equality.

Humanitarianism and Violence Against Women

The development of approaches to VAW within the humanitarian sphere has not been quite so formalized. A distinctive body of multilateral state-driven consensus-based frameworks on VAW specifically for and within humanitarian governance has not evolved over time. Rather, engagement with CRVAW by humanitarian actors is arguably grounded in the UN's existing legal and normative frameworks outlined before and developed elsewhere i.e. in the human rights and development regimes of the UN. There has however been the adoption of ad hoc and derivative policy statements under the IASC that have progressively come to shape a distinctive humanitarian body of policy approaches to such issues. The first related major policy development in the humanitarian "regime" of the UN system came in 1999, with the adoption of a "Policy Statement for the Integration of a Gender Perspective in Humanitarian Assistance" by the IASC, which oversees articulation of standards and norms for humanitarian policy and programming.[40] Following the adoption of "gender mainstreaming" as a UN system-wide strategy for the advancement of gender equality by the UN's Economic and Social Commission in 1997,[41] the IASC, recognized that in complex emergencies "the human rights of women and children are often directly threatened, i.e. the right to physical integrity and to lead a life free of violence, and women become more exposed to violence, especially sexual violence."[42] The policy is underpinned by principles of "gender equality and the equal protection of human rights of women and men."[43] A later 2008 policy aims to ensure that "gender equality is addressed adequately in all aspects of the IASC's work."[44] These policy developments were followed by the aforementioned IASC policy guidelines on GBV and on gender mainstreaming in humanitarian action.[45]

Humanitarian agencies have been slowly developing programming responses to VAW in humanitarian operations since the 1990s. The UNHCR was the first agency to develop a specific policy and set of guidance on addressing "sexual violence against refugees" in 1995 (alongside the events in the former Yugoslavia), and a later edition in 2003.[46] Numerous aid agencies followed suit and have focused on the broader frame of GBV, which is understood as "an umbrella term for any harmful act that is perpetrated against a person's will and that is based on socially ascribed (i.e. gender) differences between males and females. It includes acts that inflict physical, sexual or mental harm or suffering, threats of such acts, coercion, and other deprivations of liberty. These acts can occur in public or in private."[47] The United Nations Population Fund (UNFPA) has led this field with a focus on GBV within and outside of humanitarian settings, while NGOs such as the International Rescue Committee became the first of the international aid organizations to establish a specific institutional unit and expertise on responding to GBV. The Sphere Minimum Standards, evolving in the late 1990s, failed to adequately address gender or GBV issues, but later updated in its handbook of 2011 and 2018, setting out critical standards for attention to gender and GBV within humanitarian operations.[48]

It was not until the UN Security Council adopted its women, peace, and security (WPS) agenda that specific links between humanitarian action and response to CRVAW, and particularly CRSV, were formally adopted by decision-making political organs of the UN system. Its resolutions articulate the need to "ensure the protection of all civilians inhabiting such camps, in particular women and girls, from all forms of violence, including rape and other sexual violence, and to ensure full, unimpeded and secure humanitarian access to them"[49] and "urges United Nations entities and donors to provide non-discriminatory and comprehensive health services, including sexual and reproductive health, psychosocial, legal, and livelihood support and other multi-sectoral services for survivors of sexual violence."[50]

The outline given here has offered some clues as to the areas of convergence and divergence between the fields of human rights and humanitarianism with regards to normative responses to CRVAW. I use this as a basis for next exploring the critical issues that arise in terms of their interrelationship and interconnections in how they approach these issues.

Divergence and Symbiosis in Approaches to CRVAW in Human Rights and Humanitarian Fields

The purpose of this volume is to explore the interrelationship between the fields of human rights and humanitarianism, their symmetries, as well as the boundaries and distinctions that may set them apart. Considering the relationship between human rights and humanitarianism in respect to the issue of CRVAW is far from a simplistic or straightforward exercise however. Whether the human rights field's approach to CRVAW is similar to or distinctive from that taken in the humanitarian field, and whether distinctive boundaries exist, and how they relate, might be somewhat more difficult to discern than other debates and themes set out in this volume. Arguably, preventing and responding to violence against women, whether through the legal redress process (human rights) or provision of medical care following an assault (humanitarian response), are endeavors aimed at fulfilling women's rights. Parsing out one from the other as distinctive is not only tricky, but also negates the framing through which multiple women's movements globally have brought visibility to and attempted to tackle violence against women – to fulfill women's rights and achieve gender equality. It is the very fact of boundaries such as those discussed through this volume that feminist scholars and women's rights activists have for decades decried as being the central problem to the ways in which the international governance system, and particularly international law as the basis for its actions, has responded to women's lives.[51] As I discuss some of the divergences between both fields in respect to CRVAW, I do so solely on the basis of distinctions in normative and programming approaches, and in places point back to the synergies between both fields as it is critical that their shared approach to CRVAW because it is a violation of women's rights is recognized as inherent to my argument and to the work of both fields. In discussing the divergences, I do so on the understanding that human rights actors are those in conflict settings wishing to document and seek legal redress for violations of international law by parties to a conflict, while humanitarian actors are those providing a range of services which are otherwise absent in a conflict crisis setting. I attempt here to set out three observations on the ways in which the human rights and humanitarian fields, and their differentiated histories and substantive approaches, first demonstrate divergence, and then commonality, in how they address CRVAW. In so doing I also underline the problems that boundaries present in compartmentalizing women's needs and rights in complex humanitarian settings.

First, divergence between human rights and humanitarianism primarily emerges through the ways in which the mandates of each field are interpreted and implemented in operations and programming. The human rights field and its approach to CRVAW has evolved on the basis of its founding in legal and judicial approaches to human rights violations, while the humanitarian field has been led and is characterized by its response to life-saving and addressing the bodily needs of people, which has prompted a medicalized and health-centric approach. These are divergences that characterize each field's understanding of the issue and have implications for how it is substantively addressed. These differences have critical implications for the fulfillment of women's rights and needs in conflict settings, and adherence to mandate-specific formulas thereby have implications for women's lives. This is particularly the case where human rights violations are understood by human rights actors as state-centric phenomenon. The solution thereby rests with tackling state responsibility in respect to omissions or the commission of violations. Humanitarian actors focus on the needs of the population that is suffering as a result of an event outside of their control, likely resulting from state lack of/actions.

In global policy, and increasingly in humanitarian programming, there has been a significant and substantial turn to legal redress as the solution to the "problem" of CRVAW, and particularly of CRSV. Evident is an increasing securitization and legalization of CRSV normatively.[52] As feminist activists have turned to global governance institutions to respond to the prevalence of CRVAW, there has been a growing "carceral feminism" that has espoused a response grounded in legal redress and punitive criminal responses.[53] The solution to both prevention and deterrence of CRVAW and responding to its occurrence is increasingly a legal punitive criminal redress issue. This is evident through a number of normative means: the framing within the UN Security Council resolutions on WPS, the only multilateral normative frameworks setting out the UN systems' approach to this issue, as a focus solely on CRSV and specifically "tactical" and "systematic" rape by parties to conflict, with a primary focus on legal redress by the system;[54] and the focus on "tackling impunity" for CRSV as the primary solution driven by global state-driven responses (including, for example, the UK's Preventing Sexual Violence Initiative (PSVI)).[55]

In practical terms, within humanitarian settings, this has meant that there has been a growth in the number of human rights and "rule of law"-focused organizations operating legal programs providing support for victims/survivors to secure legal accountability for sexual harms that are attributable to the state.[56] The inclusion of "Women Protection Advisers" in UN peacekeeping operations[57] to collect data on forms of CRSV that come under the UN Security Council's WPS agenda are also a new development in the UN-mission response to the issue,[58] as is the reporting and "naming and shaming" of those state and non-state actors known to enact sexualized violence.[59] The framing of the WPS agenda on sexual violence is, however, a very narrow and reductive focus on "sexual violence when used as a tactic" in conflict, that is, a very specific and political form of violence that is attributed to armed actors for the purposes of their political aims. This has advanced a degree of divergence within the field of humanitarianism itself, where the peace and security realm intersect with that of the humanitarian. Some cleavages are evidently emerging between the legal, peacekeeping and security-focused actors that will focus on a specific form of CRSV under a "peace and security" umbrella, while humanitarian actors take an approach based on the wider "GBV" frame and its capture of wide-ranging forms of harms impacting women in humanitarian settings such as intimate partner violence (even though for many agencies, funding and resourcing a program may depend on framing it as a response to the same narrow forms of sexual violence specific to the conflict).

For humanitarian agencies, the original development of on-the-ground programming responses to GBV evolved as a public health response. This mirrors the initial engagement on VAW in national jurisdictions in the global north outside of conflict, where state and non-state policy responses have primarily developed as a public health response. The medicalization of GBV in humanitarian action was initially sustained by international humanitarian organizations, led by NGOs mirroring and establishing what they saw as the most pressing concern with respect to this issue – providing a practical response to the physical life-threatening injuries and sexual health issues that VAW results in for women and girls. This has been and remains the primary focus of humanitarian agencies. It fulfills the life-saving imperative of humanitarian agencies and means that they can provide life-saving services, even if and where the harms they are responding to are highly politicized as being part of conflict tactics. In the case of humanitarian action, the service response is inclusive of broad-ranging forms of GBV as a response to urgent need. This service is provided to victims/survivors of GBV regardless of who enacted the violence (combatant/civilian), where it took place (the home/battlefield), and its outcome (injury, political gain, sexual opportunism). Humanitarianism, in its mission to serve all on the basis of impartiality, provides services regardless of distinctions in what is occurring, while human rights law and its practice, as evidenced, tends to reinforce them.

There are implications to these divergent approaches that I set out here as being characteristic of the boundaries that exist in practice for both fields. First, there is little cohesion between these actors on an overall

agreed and consistent approach to CRVAW within a humanitarian setting, with divergent approaches even among and across UN entities. In
a humanitarian setting there will be a range of organizations that may
determine their mandate as human rights focused or humanitarian
focused, or both. All of that work, human rights and humanitarian in
focus, is about fulfilling an individual's right to life, livelihood, and
services and is a thread that runs through the work of both sets of actors.
Nonetheless, on the one hand, in any one setting there are a range of
human rights organizations that promote a legal response, encouraging
victims/survivors to "report" their rape and seek legal redress, primarily of
violations by state and non-state armed actors. Advocates for justice and
redress argue that without accountability, the potential for legal deterrence is lost and the roots of the problem will never be addressed,
particularly where prosecution is understood as a deterrence to violations
of human rights and humanitarian legal norms in political violence. On
the other hand, there are a range of humanitarian organizations that
provide humanitarian services for CRVAW in the form primarily of
a health and personal-safety response. While they may also provide programming, information or referral to legal and justice services, the organizations that predominate the responses to GBV, primarily encourage
victims/survivors to seek, in the very least, a medical response to the
physical and psychological harms they have endured to receive basic
treatment. Many advocates argue that the most urgent need is
a medical response to the very real physical, emotional and psychological
injuries that are experienced as a result of violence. While for the human
rights organizations the process of seeking legal redress for violations by
culpable actors is of primary concern, for the humanitarian organizations
it is not only secondary, but also may in fact counter their means of
providing confidential and safe services, which is central to their service
provision. Each set of actors claims to "know what's best" in the interests
of those affected. The focus in human rights on "the state over civil
society, and of civil and political rights over economic and
social rights"[60] is seen by many as an obstruction to what humanitarianism terms "women-focused" or "survivor-focused" approaches to GBV.
These approaches increasingly come into tension with one another, particularly in complex political humanitarian emergencies where legal
accountability is paramount for actors who require reporting and data
to achieve legal redress, and for health service providers, maintaining
confidentiality rather than reporting is paramount to ensure the safety
of women who do come forward.

For both, in an increasingly donor and funding-led environment, the
need for reporting of how many victims/survivors accessed their medical

or legal support services is very real. In fact, as I have witnessed myself in humanitarian programming, there is a guarded protectionism over clients. While confidentiality and the security of the woman herself is paramount and central to much of the good practice that is happening, there is also a protectionism whereby some service providers may act as gatekeepers for those who report, unless and until that woman expressly requests access to legal services. On the other hand, such protectionism may be necessary in an environment where UN agencies and NGOs are under pressure to be seen to be acting or to "deliver" on justice in their programming, and are breaching much needed confidentiality principles that are necessary for the safety and security of women who report in highly politicized contexts.[61] There is a competitiveness emerging. As has been noted in the DRC, where CRSV has received hyper-visibility and politicization, and where multiple international organizations are wanting to be seen to respond and are motivated to do so on the basis of the broad availability of funding, this has resulted in the "creation of a 'market' for services for prevention and protection."[62] There results significant divergence over policy terminology (legal human rights vs. health-focused language), or agreement on the causes (political neglect or deliberate political intent vs. gender and a gender-based harm resulting from inequalities) and solutions to the problem of violence in women's lives (legal vs. health). The divergent language also determines how the issue becomes represented to those that human rights and humanitarian actors are trying to influence, that is, the UN system, donors and funders, and influencers.[63]

Second, the two fields have offered distinctive responses in respect of the feminist endeavor to address violence in women's lives. Feminist engagement with human rights and other bodies of international law has been a political project, politicizing the interests and concerns in women's lives. From the outset of engagement, feminists identified the boundaries that international law establishes with respect to women's lives.[64] The dichotomy between the public and the private sphere, where women and the issues impacting them were relegated to the private sphere and noninterference by the state and its regulatory apparatus (except in regards to reproduction), is the most fundamental boundary that feminists identified.[65] A reconceptualization of human rights law was envisaged by activists to reform and overcome this distinction, a move largely taken forward in the 1990s and through the developments in law that were earlier outlined. The ultimate achievement was the re-framing of VAW from being a private concern, to a human rights and thereby state-based and political concern, making the issue a concern of the public and political sphere.[66] While there has been much critique of the "depoliticization" of women's rights that occurs within global policy spheres, securing a framing of this issue as a concern of rights, equality, and discrimination has been a wholly political endeavor and a necessity to make it an issue of high politics.

In contrast, the approach in the humanitarian field is estimated to have had the opposite effect. The centrality of medical practical responses to CRVAW has a reductive effect in delineating forms of violence as an "apolitical 'injury', a 'harm done',"[67] rather than a violation or form of discrimination as is framed by the human rights field. "Medicalisation has had the strange effect of erasing gender – that is, the power relations that produce and inform gender – leaving in its place suffering bodies, without perpetrators or causes, each of which can be treated by the universal 'humanitarian kit.'"[68] While the "gender-based" framing of VAW is essential to humanitarian engagement with CRVAW, that is, addressing GBV because it is a violation aimed at women because they are women, arguments abound that tackling the underlying inequalities, gendered and political in respect of conflict-driven violence, is not an imperative for humanitarian settings. While GBV advocates will argue that GBV programming is about advancing gender equality, evident is a distinctive suspicion and skepticism among wider humanitarian actors as to the relevance of social change issues like inequalities to the humanitarian field. Gender may, on the one hand, be essential to understanding the basis for why women experience violence, but on the other, addressing inequalities are not essential to delivery of services and is thereby questioned by some (even though the very recent securing of inclusion of GBV response in humanitarian "packages" has arguably been a progression toward achieving equality for women in humanitarian response in itself). Further, the focus on a medical response has been noted to address the outcomes or impacts of the violence, rather than the gendered and structural causes, a dynamic that is again the focus of the human rights field.[69] "Medicalisation directs attention away from the structural inequalities that are so intimately linked to this human rights violation, for both western women and women from the global south."[70] This approach "depoliticizes the (female) victim/survivor of sexual violence in order to render her, as a recipient of international aid, 'palatable, legitimate, even sympathetic.'"[71] That status of "social suffering" rendered to the conflict-affected female population[72] and the foregoing process of attributing legal status to the issue of VAW within the human rights field has arguably been integral to ensuring that responses to CRVAW are among the panoply of concerns, namely human rights concerns, that humanitarian organizations consider as within their remit.

These developments within the humanitarian sphere are clearly framed around the imperative of humanitarian action in response to a humanitarian need. In the articulation of this imperative comes the concept of need and with it the concept of vulnerability and victimhood. The "refugee" or "displaced" or "conflict-impacted individual" is at the center of its approaches. It is about "addressing need," the basics of survival, and also of protection. The very recent UN system and humanitarian institutional engagement with CRVAW signals another way to understand and to approach it – the events of a conflict and of a humanitarian crisis causes something that is done to an individual that requires response, differing from the human rights regimes' positioning of the issue as an outcome of structural discrimination. Humanitarian action starts from this frame – that vulnerability and dependency arise in acute ways in humanitarian contexts, where "victims" are blameless and warrant immediate support, which now includes women who have experienced GBV. Human rights arguments, and particularly those from women's rights constituencies, affirm and re-affirm that addressing GBV requires addressing structural inequalities that impact women and girls. The politicization of the issue through human rights stymies the ability to deliver services, while the depoliticization of the issue through humanitarianism misses addressing its structural causes.

Third, international legal frames conversely establish boundaries between forms and locales of violence. The human rights, and later criminal law developments on CRVAW in the 1990s, brought a necessary gaze to and regulation of the conflict-time violence of armed combatants targeting women. This has, however, resulted in a dichotomized stance in relation to that violence – the violence of warfare now receives inordinate attention under international law, while the "private" violence outside of conflict, and that continues during conflict, does not get captured, nor achieve redress under these legal regimes.[73] Human rights, derived from its basis in public international law, sets out clear parameters for what it considers state-based violations to be and its role in respect to state accountability for the same, including for CRVAW. This is a specific approach derived from the tenets of international law. While the inclusion of VAW within human rights regimes represents a gain for many rights activists, it is critiqued for the boundaries it sustains in respect to public/private distinctions in the legal, social, and political constructions of difference in that violence.[74]

It is at this point of legal construct that perhaps humanitarians and human rights operators most clearly part ways. Conceptually and theoretically, feminist scholars have pointed to the continuums in the violence that appear in women's lives across time and space. They have argued that there are connections in forms of violence across women's lives, underpinned by the social, cultural, and gendered norms that inform this violence.[75] Thereby there is need to theoretically understand that, regardless of its location or form, VAW appears because of its basis in and continued presence of gender inequalities across time and space. Empirically, some violence is experienced or understood as distinctive relative to the normative levels of violence in women's lives, such as mass or tactical rape occurring during warfare.[76] However, this violence may also be understood as still connected to their normative basis outside of conflict, their appearance in conflict deriving meaning and function due to their connectedness back to pre-conflict gendered norms.[77]

The human rights project is generally surmised as an endeavor to bring a singular focus toward individual rights violations and is characterized by a "One victim = One violation = One perpetrator" paradigm.[78] Arguably a reductive approach, this not only singles out specific violations for attention, but can also inculcate hierarchies in harms, which are an anathema to the humanitarian actors (in my personal experience). This fundamental basis to the human rights field is what creates a boundary with the humanitarian field. In an example I have recounted elsewhere,[79] on the ground practice may also reinforce these legal distinctions. When working in Darfur, Sudan, I was working with an international agency providing first-response and clinical services to women and girls who were experiencing GBV. Through our services we regularly provided support to women and girls who had experienced rape by armed parties to the conflict. The majority of reported violence we saw through our services were, however, violence occurring within the camps – by family and community members, ranging from physical and sexual domestic violence, to sexual assaults within the community. One extremely challenging case was a teenage girl who had been raped by someone within her community and discovering that she was pregnant, her family had tied her up and were attempting to kill her for the sake of hiding and preserving the family's "honor." In seeking assistance from the UN human rights office serving the camp community in dealing with this, I was informed by the human rights officer that this was not technically a human rights violation, at least not in respect to their mandate in that location, that is, to monitor and report on the violations perpetrated by the state and parties to the conflict. This violence fell into the "private" category. It was thereby something that as a humanitarian organization we were compelled to deal with, but the human rights officers did not find relevant to their mandate, modus operandi, and legal basis of their work in that specific context. This kind of distinctive approach is emerging more commonly within humanitarian settings, where international organizations focus on the violence of armed actors for the purposes of political and legal accountability, to the neglect of the broader harms that women may be experiencing. For example, in Northern Uganda, a study found that services were distinctly directed at those who had experienced sexual violence by armed combatants, even though broader forms of harm were more prevalent among the population.[80] Dichotomies in the forms of VAW that in reality map across women's lives, from intimate familial spheres, to public and political spaces, and from non-conflict to conflict spheres, have been established and reinforced by the boundaries that have characterized the legal and policy framing of that violence available through the UN human rights system.

A fourth observation identifies a synergy between both fields that derives from how each conceptualizes and engages with the issue of CRVAW. A point I made earlier must be reiterated to underscore the complexity, and to some degree the futility of arguments that point to any hard and exclusive boundaries between human rights and humanitarianism. Both fields essentially engage with CRVAW because it is a violation of women's human rights. Approaches to "GBV" that have evolved within humanitarianism have done so on the basis of broader human rights principles. In the primary policy guidance document for addressing GBV in humanitarian action, the IASC is clear that GBV is both a public health and a *human rights issue*.[81] Humanitarian agencies address GBV because it is a violation of women's rights. The nature of the impact of that violation on women, bodily, materially, practically, and socially, requires a practical and programmatic response, primarily understood as medical. It is only, however, because of the progress made on framing VAW as a human rights issue that feminist activists within the humanitarian field have had the normative basis from which to advocate for and secure a distinctive response to it, so that addressing GBV has become a standard part of the humanitarian aid package. Further, as noted earlier, addressing the harm done by GBV through a health response is nonetheless fulfilling women's right to health care in the event of a violation, demonstrating the complexity of attempting to parse out the difference between human rights vs. humanitarian response when it comes to addressing GBV. However, in respect to my overall argument, there is a difference in focus of each set of actors in conflict settings, where human rights actors are understood to be solely focusing on securing vertical accountability for violations by parties to a conflict. Ultimately, humanitarian response is focused on repairing the harm done, rather than seeking that same legal rights accountability and redress as per human rights actors (even though humanitarian actors will facilitate access to legal services as part of GBV responses). That is the difference between the modus operandi of human rights vs. humanitarian agencies. As discussed by Jeffrey Flynn in this volume, "[h]umanitarian action often provides what someone needs (and can use the language of rights in doing so), but human rights work, at its best, attempts to put one in a better position to stand up and effectively demand what one needs."[82] That essentially sums up the complementarity between the two fields when it comes to addressing women's rights concerns and certainly CRVAW. How that complementarity could be further advanced to the advantage of both the institutions and women in those settings is discussed next.

Turning Tensions into Opportunity: Exploiting the Gender Equality Imperative across Human Rights and Humanitarian Mandates

As noted before, a simplistic assessment of the boundaries between these two fields is naïve. The complexities of the issue of CRVAW and the evolving nature of both fields reveals intricacies in both relations and boundaries between the fields beyond a clear dichotomous assessment. As discussed, feminist scholars have critiqued the dichotomies that have been established through international frameworks in respect to women's lives. The divergence outlined in the previous section reflects not just this conceptual and normative divergence between the fields of human rights and humanitarianism, but also those within the practice of humanitarianism and human rights in response to conflict settings.

As humanitarian interventions in armed conflicts become increasingly complex, protracted, and embroiled in the political contestations that cause them, the work of humanitarian agencies takes them to the frontlines of witnessing and responding to human rights violations as they occur. The question arises as to whether it is enough anymore for humanitarian action to deliver just basic services. This question also appears to be bothering the actors in the architecture of global humanitarian response: evident is a bending and re-shaping of its role in recent times in response to the complex emergencies that it is now involved in. Humanitarian response has come to include "protection" as a central concern. The establishment of the IASC's "protection cluster" in the humanitarian reform process in 2005 is indicative of this. The protection cluster's articulation of its mandate states that: "Human rights protection is at the core of humanitarian action."[83] It is thereby the case that if the protection cluster goals are to be achieved, and ostensibly the goals of the entire humanitarian operation, then humanitarian workers must understand their role as contributing to the protection of human rights. It is not just that rights-based approaches to programming are espoused, but also that human rights are increasingly seen as part of what humanitarianism is about. Humanitarians may, by virtue of being present and delivering services, also see their work thereby as delivering on human rights, albeit, as noted before, in a service-oriented manner. Evident in the articulation of approaches above is a founding origin in the idea and field of human rights – humanitarian needs and the humanitarian imperative to address these needs and the protection of those in need is founded in the normative frames of human rights offered by the UN system.

What doing protection or "doing human rights" means for one sector appears to be very different to what it means for another however. Engaging in protection, placing human rights, and even women's rights, as central to what you do, may differ for different actors and thereby create some areas of distinction. For example, many humanitarian agencies in complex emergencies, such as Médecins Sans Frontières, draw clear lines between what they do, that is, humanitarian response and delivering services to affected populations[84] vs. what "human rights work" is, that is, dealing with the rights violations that are occurring and addressing the big "P" politics of seeking state-level accountability for those violations. As is argued by Charles Beitz elsewhere in this volume, it may be that the two are intricately tied conceptually, however, it is in practice that their approaches diverge. As he notes, humanitarianism is more of a short-term focus, with little concern to "systematic change in the longer term," while human rights "often aims explicitly at inducing legal and political change."[85] Even where normatively they may in principle and practice converge, the "procedural norms" may differ.[86]

Feminist scholars have advanced conceptual and practical ideas for "how" issues of women's equality may be advanced in practice. I draw from one of those frameworks here to try to identify how some of the tensions between the two fields identified in this chapter may be understood a little differently. In doing so, I see this as an endeavor to put forward a way to imagine the possibility that the overlapping synergies and divergences between the fields of human rights and humanitarianism could be seen as complementary rather than in tension with each other, in both concept and practice. The idea that VAW is "gender-based" was coined to signify the relevance of inequalities between men and women as significant in the manifestation of the violence in women's lives, promoting an understanding that this is ultimately violence as a result of the context of prevailing patriarchies. The argument goes that there is a difference between pointing to gender in respect to the demographics of a population and to the inequalities of structural oppressions that exist between men and women.[87] It is through the latter understanding of "gender" that the similarities and distinctions between these fields might be made visible and more fully exploited. When issues such as VAW become institutionalized, through human rights, humanitarian, or international development frames (where much of this early thinking derives), feminists have espoused that attention to both the gendered practical and the strategic aspects of women's rights require attention.[88] In advancing women's gendered interests in context (either through human rights or humanitarianism), the complexity of women's social positioning requires attention, that is, attention to their systemic gendered positioning within a given social context. The oppressions that lead to the inequalities and discrimination that are understood to underpin VAW must be understood as "multicausal in origin and mediated through a variety of different structures, mechanisms and levels which may vary considerably across space and time."[89] The best or most appropriate approaches to addressing VAW in practice are thereby divergent and debated, varying between engaging with men as the problem, with social power relations or with institutions, or with all of these.[90] This debate and divergence of approach is evident in the previous account of the differentiated operational approaches taken by human rights and humanitarian actors.

The proposal made here is to address the issue of CRVAW relative to how it arises within a given social context, that is, outside of constructed ideas of "women" and "violence" to an understanding of the gendered social context in which it occurs, and how that influences the construct and meaning of that harm for women in that specific context. Maxine Molyneux has proposed that this requires a multilevel response that simultaneously engages with the structural, institutional factors as well as with the basic everyday interactions and issues that give rise to gender inequalities. These are framed as, first, "strategic gender interests" found at the level of the structural and which "are derived in the first instance deductively, that is, from the analysis of women's subordination and from the formulation of an alternative, more satisfactory set of arrangements to those which exist."[91] Second, these are formulated at a "practical gender interests" level, which

are given inductively and arise from the concrete conditions of women's positioning within the gender division of labour. In contrast to strategic gender interests, these are formulated by the women who are themselves within these positions rather than through external interventions. Practical interests are usually a response to an immediate perceived need, and they do not generally entail a strategic goal such as women's emancipation or gender equality.[92]

The differences are evident. Strategic gender interests are those that relate to the macro structural and legal level frames that relate to the concerns of the human rights field, where the strategy taken to address CRVAW is very much about addressing discriminations and inequalities and state accountability at formal structural levels. The field of human rights is largely about responding (in this case) to the human rights violations that increasingly characterize armed conflicts and fuel complex humanitarian crises globally, that is, CRVAW. The human rights system, its constituent components, and its actors are focused on the macro and strategic level where accountability for entitlements to rights can be secured through the fulfillment of the duties of states. The motivation on the part of human rights workers is to advance the strategic interests of women in respect of gender inequalities and discriminations that cause the harms incurred and ensure states fulfill related responsibilities.

On the other hand, humanitarian response has largely evolved to ensure the provision of a "salve" to the affected populations, ensuring access to what are perceived to be essential life-saving services, such as shelter, water and sanitation, food, and in the case of CRVAW, health care and safe spaces. The humanitarian operation exists and accomplishes aid provision at a very practical and micro-individual level, and increasingly, ensuring that any gender disparities in access to those service are tackled as part of humanitarian operations.[93] The practical gender interests level characterizes those taken by the humanitarians, providing practical life-saving needs provision to the harm that has occurred. They allow women to decide for themselves what they need – a health response to injury or a decision to seek legal redress through relevant actors. The motivation here is in providing a practical solution to the practical experience of the harm and resulting need. There is acknowledgment that "these practical interests do not in themselves challenge the prevailing forms of gender subordination, even though they arise directly out of them."[94] That, in some way, fits with the perception within humanitarianism that provision of services is apolitical and impartial and is a short-term, immediate fix rather than a longer-term, strategic-level intervention aimed at structural change.

There is a further level of complexity to be acknowledged than this straightforward division of strategy between the fields, and this is where some of the synergies between the fields might be identified. As noted, humanitarian programming in response to CRVAW has evolved in a way that has centered around provision of life-saving services, in this case service delivery to victims/survivors of GBV. The specific mandates of humanitarian organizations delivering those services are framed around this idea. However, and this is where the boundaries blur, it must be acknowledged that the very tenets that underpin the delivery of those services to those impacted by violations derive from and are considered as essential to the fulfillment of basic human rights: the right to health care in response to rape; the right to bodily integrity and protection from violation; the right to safety and security and freedom from violence. These are all related to acts of harm that the state may be responsible for, whether through commission or omission. As argued throughout this chapter and is evident here, there is some degree of cross-over between these fields when it comes to the perceived centrality of human rights to their work. There is overlap in respect of the fulfillment of practical gender interests (services) with strategic gender interests (the right to access and decision-making over services), and both of these as an entry point for fulfilling broader strategic-level-related legal rights. Is this a place where the blurring of boundaries between these fields could in practice be exploited so that the operational approaches of each set of actors are maximized not just in reducing tensions between them, but also in enhancing potential for the fulfillment of women's gendered interests and rights in a given context?

Problematic with the strategic end of this approach is that "[h]uman rights positions itself as a neutral field of equality for all. Such a claim of neutrality, however, denies the myriad ways in which ideas about what it means to be a woman, about the proper relations between men and women, about the existence of a private and a public sphere, for example, structure the demands and expectations of rights."[95] What that means in respect to my argument here is that, whereas human rights aim solely for the strategic interests of women, it ignores that fact that women's ability to even seek the strategic, for example justice and fulfillment of those rights, is in itself disabled by the very context in which women must seek those rights, that is, a starting point of inequality and discrimination. The context to rights-seeking for women in an unequal playing field in which practical concerns, such as ability to secure basic needs, or in the case of VAW, to practically deal with a serious physical injury as a result of rape, an unwanted pregnancy, or being ostracized from home and family as a result of stigma, all determine whether the strategic end of their interests could ever be attained. Human rights implies that all are equal before the law, occluding how unequal gender power relations determine whether access to those rights and the enjoyment of them ever occurs. Humanitarians practically try to overcome inequality of access to fulfillment of practical interests, on the one hand negating attention to the strategic, while on the other, importantly, enabling access to the strategic at some point should women so choose – by the very virtue that their practical interests are fulfilled.

It is thereby the case that the practical interests fulfillment is very much required, or an entry point at least, to advancing the strategic rights of women at macro structural and "justice" and remedial levels. It is perhaps in this critical overlap between these two, in the strategic and practical strategies that are espoused by human rights and humanitarian fields, that there is significant overlap, interconnection, and potential for synergy and complementarity. It is in a co-dependence of the relationship between the practical and the strategic that we can understand the potential to move beyond the boundaries imposed by the normative and operational frames of human rights and humanitarianism toward a complementarity, as well as an ability of the humanitarian field to advance its claim to sustain a co-existing interest in both a practical response and a strategic and human rights focus to its work.

For actors in the fields of human rights and humanitarian practices, and in response to an issue such as CRVAW, there exists a range of potential actions. A critical question is what do you choose to do when, and why? Many scholars have argued the need for context-specific approaches to addressing VAW, that is, while this issue is universal, it manifests in different ways in different contexts, and the response should be tailored to different realities.[96] While many international organizations follow this kind of approach, the increasing institutionalization of issues such as CRVAW and their subjection to the framing offered by international legal norms also means that agencies with specific mandates often work back to those mandates more readily than they do to the context in which they find themselves and in which violations arise. This is perhaps the greatest challenge in respect to whether and how each of these fields might work in more congruent or complementary ways. Where the human rights field offers means and methods for advancing strategic gendered rights and interests and the humanitarian field addresses the practical gendered interests that must be met for longer-term rights fulfillment, a critical step is the need for each set of actors to respond to specific settings and the reality of those harms in context for women. This means working with and across different organizations, and while they will need to work to respective mandates, that should be done in ways that enable complementarity rather than competition, and overall enable women to make their own choices in context. This might require each of the fields reneging some control, ownership, or traction in respect of their stake in the very attractive issue of "GBV." This is a risk, after all, it is only recently that GBV "became the poster child for humanitarian aid"[97] and actors with a stake in the game will not easily let go of the credibility it might offer to be seen to act on this issue. This is particularly true in the increasingly data- and measurement-led aid industry, where donors will want to know how many victims/survivors have received legal aid, even where it may actually be precarious for any woman to seek legal redress in a context where rape has become highly politicized. While the human rights field requires the idea of the benevolent state as the central actor in human rights violations, and the humanitarian field requires the innocent and blameless victims[98] who require their stewardship through the experience of violence they have just undergone, women are the ideal subject. Addressing the practical and strategic gender interests of women relative to a given context in complementary ways would mean that the micro- and macro-level concerns of human rights and humanitarian actors are advanced, but in ways not restrictive to mandates, but complementary to them. The challenge is that boundaries between the fields are at times stark, however it is in the areas where they are more fluid that opportunity arises. The multisectoral model of response to CRVAW now established in humanitarian settings[99] allows complementarity to occur, that is, true ease for a victim/survivor of GBV to navigate the health and justice models if they so wish and in ways that are safe and led by that woman. The potential for more complementarity is perhaps in responding to the context of women's rights and interests over and above but in line with complementary in fulfilling institutional mandates.

Conclusion

In summarizing the complexity of the relationship between the practice of human rights and humanitarian organizations, the following should be borne in mind: "existing inequalities certainly are not natural. Inequalities are produced and reproduced by society and its institutions. Because neither inequalities nor the systems that produce them are inevitable, they can also be objects of reform."[100] Not only are the inequalities and violences that women experience in conflict settings thereby critical subject matter of human rights and humanitarian operations, but also the potential for those organizations to reproduce and generate further inequalities through their institutional ways of working make reform on the basis of complementarity an imperative. The case study that begun this chapter, where addressing CRVAW in the conflict setting of Kosovo was seen as entirely outside the remit of international organizations, has changed utterly. It is now essential that these organizations address CRVAW as part of a comprehensive response to women's rights and interests in any conflict setting. However, the wrangling about mandates, the need to respond to institutional requirements and reporting to donors, has largely meant that the tensions between those organizations have been to the detriment of the efficacy of their work and of women subject to that violence. If the change in understanding and perception of both the issue of CRVAW and of its relevance to the remit of international responses to humanitarian crises can occur so rapidly, then a change in attitude toward the tensions between these sets of actors in any one setting may also be possible. Further, there can also be changes in the perception that gender equality is not relevant to the work done in a humanitarian crises and that change can be furthered by an approach of complementarity through work practices. In the practices of each field lies the potential to congruently promote transformational change in the lives of women and girls, that is, by ensuring that their practical gender interests are adequately fulfilled in the event of an experience of harm, while at the same time ensuring that macro-level reforms and strategies are in place to deter, prevent and prohibit such harms from occurring in the first place, and of course, providing redress where it does. Both fields have a contribution to make in this regard. There is need for a more conscious willingness to work in complementary ways, or to let go of strict adherence to mandates or reporting requirements where necessary. Otherwise, they become part of the problem, sustaining and contributing to inequalities, reinforcing ideas of women's victimhood, potentially furthering more harm and ultimately placing their own fields' imperatives before those of women themselves.

9 Innocence
Shaping the Concept and Practice of Humanity

Miriam Ticktin

The ethical category of innocence is central to modern secular notions of humanity; indeed, humanity, in its purest form, is imagined as innocent, fresh, and full of potential. We need only think of the images associated with organizations that protect humanity: innocence is figured centrally on webpages and in publicity materials, particularly in the form of the child. As former director of Médecins Sans Frontières (MSF) USA Nicolas de Torenté writes, "deeply rooted images put a premium on the innocence of victims, making children, who are by definition blameless, the ideal recipients of care."[1]

The connection between humanity and innocence is not new, of course; we can trace it back to early theological interpretations. These locate innocence in the story of Adam and Eve, wherein innocence means not knowing the difference between good and evil; it means lacking worldly knowledge. Innocence is represented as a state of calm and repose, particularly in the Garden of Eden, before the fall of humanity, when Eve eats from the tree of knowledge. According to theological interpretations, the Fall helps to define humanity afterward; the loss of innocence is *how* we become human. But this changes with Enlightenment thinkers such as Jean-Jacques Rousseau and John Locke, who overturned the Judeo-Christian notion of humanity as soiled by original sin. Recalling the Garden of Eden, they saw humanity at its truest in the state of nature, as unsullied simplicity – as life that preceded the social contract and the political life of citizens. But they saw this purity as the essence of humanity, rather than its precursor – as the uncorrupt base from which all potential to act in the world arises. Innocence – as blank slate – is what enables us to imagine we can be the authors of our own future.

While the relationship between innocence and humanity is inherently unstable in that innocence derives from a mythical or imaginary past, and is thus always shifting, innocence nevertheless plays a central role in modern, secular discourses and practices of humanity. Where humanity is grounded on the principles of equality and dignity, innocence helps

185

define these principles, sometimes as their constituent outside, sometimes as their precursor, and often as their hope for the future. To be sure, innocence itself never embodies equality or dignity – it simply marks their limits. While I will be discussing the world of humanitarianism and human rights – a largely secular, liberal world, concerned with individual autonomy, freedom, justice, and rationality – innocence has persisting Judeo-Christian contours that give it power in these secular worlds, and even in the worlds that may border on illiberal or authoritarian. For instance, as with the Garden of Eden, our departure from the innocence of the "state of nature" (according to philosophers like Rousseau) is the beginning of our social existence, our state as political animals – this is the beginning of humanity as both a religious and a secular category. Perhaps unsurprisingly, then, those associated with innocence tend to be at humanity's edges; they mark its border, in the sense that they are not corrupt (as is a normative humanity), yet nor are they fully human in the Enlightenment sense of having reason, will, or autonomy – they are not fully socialized creatures, and often get figured as incapable of being thinking, active, or informed subjects. As such, innocence acts as the boundary for liberal ideas of personhood, where this constituent outside is simultaneously idealized and denigrated. In this sense, playing with the borders of innocence also means playing with the borders of humanity: this is its power, and its danger.

In this chapter, I trace the way innocence and humanity come together in contemporary practices of human rights and humanitarianism. What does innocence show us about the ways humanity is practiced, and indeed, how it is practiced differently by these movements? Humanity is often understood as an equalizing principle; for instance, we say that all human lives have equal value and dignity, and all human beings have equal rights. Yet innocence plays a complicated role here; even as it promises to further such notions of equality by way of giving everyone the benefit of the doubt (in secular thought, innocence is the grounding of our potential as human beings) in practice, it inexorably constitutes hierarchies, distinguishing between deserving and undeserving. That is, while both human rights and humanitarian movements rely on and deploy the concept of innocence in their work, I am interested in exploring how far innocence goes to further the recognition of universality (whether as shared suffering, or as rights), and when it works instead to institute moral hierarchies. Sometimes, this depends on whether innocence functions as a noun rather than an adjective (i.e., an innocent action); that is, whether innocence is seen as an essential identity characteristic, or whether it simply concerns an act. I will argue that humanitarianism and human rights both work to buffer the tendency to use innocence to create moral distinctions, albeit differently so, one through the concept of life, the other through the practice of law; despite this, I suggest that innocence primarily works to divide humanity, rather than to unify it as an affective, ethical, or political collectivity. Ultimately, innocence cannot escape its conceptual history as the limit of humanity; as we will see, in practice, this plays out by way of the unending redefinition of that limit, through moral distinction. For instance, innocence often works by protecting the rights of the exceptional, with a promise that this will eventually lead to rights for all – but this is an ever-elusive goal. In this sense, how might we begin to imagine humanity without innocence – can we decouple these concepts?

Innocence in Theory and in Practice

According to the *Oxford English Dictionary*, *innocence* means "freedom from sin, guilt or moral wrong in general," "freedom from specific guilt," "freedom from cunning or artifice."[2] This space of "freedom *from*" – this negative freedom – is so free indeed that it is seemingly free of content; it purports to be a state of *moral and epistemic purity*. Innocence is defined as a state of guilelessness, artlessness, want of knowledge or sense – in the terms of the *OED*, it is a state of ignorance, even a state of "silliness." But innocence is a concept that – either because of or despite its very emptiness – has been deployed politically in more or less vigorous ways over time; and indeed, it is critical in the work of both human rights and humanitarian organizations. Insofar as these movements are instrumental today in shaping our political grammars, it behooves us to take innocence seriously.

Innocence promises a space of experiential or epistemic purity. Of course, innocence has many meanings: it comes into being in relation to various binary others, such as guilt, knowledge, and sexuality. While the concept does different work in relation to these binaries, in each case innocence works to regulate a space of purity: sometimes this means to be without knowledge, sometimes to be without intention, sometimes to be free from desire, and sometimes free from guilt. It works as a boundary concept, and in the process it helps produce and regulate human kinds and their constituent outsides – it helps to imagine "humanity." It becomes relevant to human rights and humanitarian organizations insofar as it helps to define the contours of the secular humanity that grounds these organizations; but insofar as purity structures moral categories, it also fills out binary notions of deserving and undeserving, the innocent and the guilty. How does this tension play out in practice? Under what circumstances does innocence work to construct moral distinctions, and when does it enable a belief in and practice of universal equality? I ask this in the interest of fostering a politics of equality.

To further understand, let us begin with the archetypal figure of innocence: the child. Capturing innocence in the figure of the child reflects this search for purity in the secular world, this deep yearning for a time before corruption, a space beyond social norms. The child represents a mode of experience that is protected, controlled – it performs the part of tabula rasa, and as such it offers proof that as humans we can be anything, that we are not condemned by our sinful past. Of course, childhood was not always considered the epitome of innocence; this is a modern invention, dating to the eighteen century.[3] Following theories of original sin, which held that all humans carry the guilt of Adam's disobedience, children were understood as inherently sinful; they were small, faulty adults in need of discipline, correction, or worse, since they had no idea how to control their various impulses.[4] Notions of childhood as soiled by original sin shifted to the now more well-known ideas of romantic childhood, thanks in part to John Locke, who situated the child as simply a subject without experience and memory.[5] For Locke, the child was an instance of natural humanity, revealing humanity's *capacity* for knowledge and reason, without being tainted by the prejudices of actual knowledge in society. The child was pure and uncorrupt potential.

That said, locating innocence in the figure of the child leaves little space for actual childhood experiences. What happens when these experiences do not fit the parameters of innocence? Innocence carves out a conceptual space and time of unsullied hope, one that is linked to a freedom from knowledge. Yet the borders of this space are profoundly contested; rather than a given, this space is a political battleground. Understanding the work of innocence in relation to humanity requires tracing which types of knowledge are named or counted as pure (which experiences slip into a space of epistemic purity, unnoticed) and, by contrast, which ones somehow tip the balance and result in an expulsion from innocence.

Child soldiers, for instance, trouble the image of the child as innocent. And as Liisa Malkki has argued, child soldiers are seen as an abomination, a category mistake that leads to their being labeled "youth" or "teens" as opposed to "children" whenever possible, to set aside and protect a time of innocence, when they are still unworldly and untainted.[6] Similarly, the undocumented minors crossing into the United States from Central America in great numbers in the summer of 2014 were not categorized or treated as children; they were called "minors," no matter their age, and imprisoned in detention centers. While child soldiers are sullied by their involvement in war, the undocumented children were tainted by their association with gangs, drugs, and violence; they were rendered complicit in these crimes by virtue of coming from the same place – racially, geographically, and socioeconomically.

As these examples demonstrate, the concept of innocence does not describe a clear-cut state of epistemic or other purity. Rather, it helps distinguish morally acceptable forms of knowledge, action, and experience, and these are inevitably tied to one's being in the world. That is, innocence is defined not simply by a period of life called "childhood" or by outside standards such as age but by, as we just saw, class, gender, and racial background, among other positionalities, histories, and experiences. Certain conditions enable the space for an unsullied childhood; clearly class formation is important here, in configuring a space and time understood as pure, as empty or free of knowledge. But so is race: as feminist theorist bell hooks has noted, black children in the United States, particularly black boys, are never allowed to be children.[7] This is also true for black girls, who, starting as early as five years old, are treated as more adult than their white counterparts, with presumed knowledge of topics like sex.[8] Racial regimes mean that they are never allowed this period of untroubled and ignorant life; they are immediately interpellated into the structures and hierarchies of society, which render their knowledge suspect. Historian Robin Bernstein argues, in fact, that childhood innocence was from the very beginning racialized as *white* in the United States; it came into being in the second half of the nineteenth century in relation to its Other, the black child, who was constructed as a nonfeeling, noninnocent, juvenile *worker*.[9] In this sense, childhood was forged in the context of capitalism and slave labor – and innocence worked to mark the boundary of allowable, exploitative, racialized labor. Innocence thus not only evokes moral distinctions, but also produces and regulates ontologies of human kinds. When one is a noninnocent child, one is no longer a child – one is simply expelled from the category.

Nearly every humanitarian and human rights website figures children prominently. This is perhaps not surprising; the most iconic images of suffering figure innocent children, from Kevin Carter's 1993 photograph of a starving Sudanese child, crouched on the ground while being preyed upon by a vulture, to the 2015 photograph of Alan Kurdi, the three-year-old Syrian refugee whose body washed up on a Turkish beach in 2015. In the summer of 2018, figures of the migrant children separated from their parents by Trump's draconian detention policies were featured all over the news, successfully pressuring the government to change their policy; unfortunately, the new proposed regulation does keep children with their families, but in a challenge to what is known as the "Flores settlement," this would allow all of them to be kept for indeterminate periods in detention centers. It is images of suffering, solitary children that most galvanize public response. The ideal victim – the innocent – is appealing, particularly for fundraising efforts. And yet, having just seen that innocence not only draws attention to children, but also works to determine who counts as a child, and therefore, who gets recognition, attention, rights or aid, we must ask: How do the organizations manage innocence's tendency to categorize and qualify some as more deserving than others? In the name of humanity, how do they work to draw attention to those who are not deemed innocent – how do they protect these others?

One more aspect of innocence is worth noting here. Innocence helps to create a pure space for humanity, and both human rights and humanitarian regimes regularly draw on the concept to both ground and enact their missions. Yet both end up producing and enacting what Didier Fassin has termed "hierarchies of humanity."[10] Not only do they produce hierarchies among the people they seek to help or defend, but innocence also enables a distinction between those who help – human rights and humanitarian workers – and those whom they help. That is, while the concept of innocence shifts according to the constellation of experiences and histories in which it is located, it nevertheless always carries with it the desire to protect and the impetus to take responsibility for those whom – in their want of knowledge – cannot take care of themselves. Guilelessness evokes the need for care; innocents cannot take responsibility for themselves. But this means that it props up a feeling of control in those who care for the innocent; it assures them not only of their power but also of their knowledge, insofar as the innocent person is oblivious. It creates a class of saviors. As a space of purity, innocence itself appears outside history, and as such, it allows those who work as saviors to ignore the political and historical circumstances that created these victims.

This not only allows saviors to feel powerful or knowledgeable but also enables them to simultaneously capture innocence – to purify or absolve themselves. In other words, innocence also creates a savior class or subject, and they too make claims to innocence. If the people one is saving are understood as innocent, outside time and place, and one is intervening only to stop the suffering, how can this not be considered innocent too? For instance, while those inspired by humanitarian sentiments may try to bypass politics, claiming to act only as witnesses to injustice or in response to the immediacy of suffering, the political innocence they proclaim often ignores the privilege that allows them to act – it can masquerade as a refusal to acknowledge the structural inequalities that allow them to *be* humanitarians, witnesses, or saviors. And with human rights, innocence manifests in a belief that human rights are timeless, and that by protecting them, we protect a universal humanity; this ignores the historical and political contexts that produced the idea of human rights, and that enshrine certain political ideals while precluding others. Is there a way to act in the name of humanity, without capturing or claiming innocence in the process – without using it to reify differences in power?

Scales of Innocence in Humanitarian Action

I move now to think about the place of innocence in human rights and humanitarianism, to see how innocence figures both theoretically and practically, and where moral distinctions come to play. While I focus primarily on the Euro-American context, I trace what I see as a transnational deployment of innocence; that is, I suggest that political and affective dimensions of innocence travel across borders and work to shape transnational spaces – we cannot keep these spaces or politics distinct as domestic or international. Even something like the Innocence Project – which I will discuss in the last section – has chapters in various countries now, shaped by similar affective and legal goals.

Contemporary humanitarianism is largely understood to address humanity as a collection of suffering victims. Innocence is only relevant insofar as it is understood to be the condition of all of humanity in the face of suffering: no one deserves to suffer. MSF's four key principles clearly lay out the absence of moral or political distinction in their version of humanitarian action. According to de Torrenté, these include humanity (all people have equal dignity by virtue of their membership in humanity), neutrality (organizations must refrain from taking part in hostilities or conflicts that advantage one side over another), independence (humanitarian action only serves the interests of war victims, and not political, religious, or other agendas), and impartiality (assistance is provided based solely on need, without discrimination among recipients).[11] Of these four, the last – impartiality – is the most relevant here. The innocence or guilt of those who suffer is irrelevant; suffering is not ascribed to moral failure.

Humanitarians work hard to stick to their principle of impartiality, and to avoid moral distinctions about who deserves aid, and one way they accomplish this is by a focus on the sacredness of life. That is, rather than a virtuous, dignified, or deserving life, the ultimate moral value in humanitarian action is human life itself – it is the survival of each individual. As Redfield states in his insightful ethnography of MSF, "they [MSF] assume that the lives of people around the world are precious and something to be saved through human intervention."[12] Human suffering in whatever form requires a response: all human life is worth saving.

An overriding ethical focus on life – any life, all lives – means that humanitarians agree to treat anyone who needs urgent medical attention, whether victim or perpetrator. They do not make distinctions. In this sense, they recognize what Erica Bouris has called the "complex political victim," and the way in which victimhood is never pure or simple.[13] Indeed, they work very pragmatically, making compromises and interacting with whomever they need to get access to conflict zones – this includes armed militias. For instance, MSF's Marc le Pape relates that in Caritas's work in Congo Brazzaville in the late 1990s they decided to accept military escorts on aid convoys in order to avoid being attacked, which was still common at that time, when groups of armed men would set up roadblocks to commit rape and other forms of abuse.[14] Yet this occasionally involved taking on military escorts who carried the spoils of their plunder, which could provoke other groups, and threaten understandings of neutrality. He tells this story to say that humanitarians are constantly making decisions about which compromises to make: the point is that life itself is what drives their mission, not the moral status of those with whom they interact or treat.

A brief history of MSF reveals how life – particularly life in crisis – came to be held as the highest moral value; and yet this history demonstrates how innocence nevertheless still plays a role in defining what counts as "life." The founders of MSF – doctors and journalists, largely Marxist and Maoist inspired – were initially guided by the belief in a universal humanity grounded in equality and solidarity. But after the failure of 1968 to transform the social and political order and after the disappointment of anti-colonial revolutionary Marxist movements, Bernard Kouchner – one of MSF's founders – and many of his comrades from 1968 radically changed their views. They turned away from engagement with what they thought of as politics – engaging with power relations in the struggle for a collective future – and instead embraced the belief that one can ultimately address only individual suffering; in this sense, they attended to what they conceived of as a universal humanity composed of suffering victims.[15] Kouchner and MSF brought a form of action that appealed in its purported ability to *avoid* Machiavellian politics.[16] It was an ideology grounded in individualism, one that no longer allowed for the possibility of larger political change.[17]

This "new humanitarianism" was shaped by a frustration with and refusal of politics; consequently, it was driven by the search for an uncorrupted space of action. Innocence offers such a space of imagination, even as it calls forth and protects different versions of epistemic and moral purity. In this sense, the suffering victim driving humanitarian action quickly inhabited the conceptual space opened by the notion of innocence, even if it was not always identical to it – of course, humanitarianism is not *simply* a politics of innocence, and innocence clearly travels beyond its humanitarian deployments. While MSF maintains impartiality as a key principle, meaning that it offers assistance to people irrespective of their race, gender, religion, or political affiliation, in many humanitarian contexts – on the ground – innocence becomes the necessary accompaniment to suffering, required to designate the sufferer as worthy. That is, the suffering victim is best and most easily recognized by humanitarians when considered innocent – pure, outside politics, outside history, indeed, outside time and place altogether.[18]

So while humanitarians are guided by the principle of impartiality, in practice, finite resources limit their action.[19] The goal is to treat everyone equally, adjudicating based on need whether or not they are perpetrators or victims, but they themselves admit that they must triage, prioritizing those considered in the most serious and immediate danger. The concept of innocence helps in this process, as a way to grasp and measure vulnerability. Indeed, former MSF president Rony Brauman has criticized how moralist positions have marked humanitarianism, noting that the symbolic status of victim can in effect "only be granted in cases of unjustified or innocent suffering . . . . The point is that he [sic] must be 100% victim, a non-participant."[20]

This process of triage is evident in the case of sexual violence. Before the early 2000s, survivors of sexual violence were not included in standard models of humanitarian aid delivery (see Swaine this volume). In the collection of essays by MSF about humanitarian practices in the Congo Republic in the late 1990s, *Civilians under Fire*,[21] former MSF-USA executive director Nicolas de Torrenté and former MSF president Jean-Hervé Bradol admit that this is because relief organizations search for the "ideal victims." On the one hand, they acknowledge that this is strategic, insofar as it is a way to get donors interested. On the other hand, they suggest that this focus, instrumental or not, pushes other categories of victims into the background. Survivors of sexual violence were not seen as innocent – as Bradol writes, "The raped woman rarely represents the ideal victim."[22] This is because such survivors raised a number of unsettling issues for practitioners around violence and gender roles, which they felt were too political to engage. As a result, de Torrenté states that MSF reproduced forms of prejudice against women in general and survivors of sexual violence in particular. These discussions are haunted by the histories and treatment of women victims of rape, who were (and still are) seen as responsible for and consenting to their own rapes because of how they dressed or behaved, or where they had chosen to be. They are seen as too knowing and too agentive to be innocent.

In many ways, MSF's collection of essays marks the shift in the humanitarian mandate; sexual violence now merits an immediate response from aid workers. This was not because humanitarianism stopped looking for innocent subjects; rather, there was a shift to seeing these women as innocent enough to be compelling humanitarian subjects. This happened, in large part, through the medicalization of gender-based violence, which is a longer story related to its changing treatment by regimes of human rights and global health.[23] Attention was transferred to health consequences such as infection with HIV, physical injury and trauma, unwanted pregnancies, reproductive health, and STDs. This medicalization of rape and sexual violence ended up shifting the blame and rendering the victims innocent of the harm they endured. More specifically, a focus on the vulnerable body in biomedical terms brackets off social and political identities and realities. The medicalization was helpful insofar as it allowed women to be abstracted from their political contexts, rendered blameless, and treated; it has been less helpful, however, insofar as it has worked to depoliticize the larger gendered inequalities that lead to such harm. Even if humanitarian aid now seems to be more inclusive, it risks perpetuating inequality by writing out politics, and the causes of such inequalities. This further enables the capture of innocence by those who provide aid; they frame their work as addressing the pure horror of gender violence. Yet, as Lila Abu-Lughod and Leti Volpp have argued, this yearning for innocence in certain feminists whose politics are grounded in the desire to save others, such as Muslim women, is based on their will to not know about their complicities in the disenfranchisement of those they are saving.[24]

As Fassin notes in his book on humanitarian reason, humanitarian government tends to set up a "scale of innocence and vulnerability" that works to privilege some, like HIV-positive children who are the ultimate innocents, but in the process, it also works to penalize others, like their mothers.[25] While humanitarianism purports to serve and protect a universal suffering humanity, with the conceptual help of innocence, it nevertheless enacts hierarchies on the ground.

Human Rights: Just for Innocents?

If in humanitarianism, humanity is understood primarily by way of life in crisis, for human rights movements, humanity is about protecting the basic rights of individuals, joining humanity less with a biological or medicalized conception of life than with a philosophically and legally defined one, whether real or ideal. All human beings, so the familiar phrase goes, are bearers of rights by virtue of their humanity (of course, who protects those rights is another matter). And if, in humanitarianism, innocence's tendency to create moral distinctions and hierarchies is mediated by a focus on life itself, in human rights practices, the focus on the law attempts to serve as safeguard.

Human rights are for everyone, not just for the innocent. Human rights organizations claim to protect every person whose basic rights are being violated, including, for instance, those on death row, whose right to life is being threatened. That is, in theory, one can be both a perpetrator and a victim of human rights violations, as the idea of "complex political victim" suggests. As with humanitarianism, if one's rights are being violated, innocence should not matter – it should not depend on who one is, or one's past history.

But, as with humanitarianism, innocence nevertheless comes to play in human rights claims and responses. I will discuss two different ways that innocence is written into human rights struggles and protections, despite the affordances offered by the law to protect against moralisms. The first involves women's rights; and the second pertains to the death penalty.

Women's Rights

Women's rights bring the question of innocence to the fore in a way like almost no other group. While women have been figured as innocent, particularly in the form of mother and child, for women by themselves, chastity or sexual integrity has historically been the most important thing about them, and in this sense, innocence is still inextricably tied to sexual innocence.[26] As we know, sex is a particularly dense site of struggle between knowledge and ignorance; the term *carnal knowledge* illustrates the battle over how to categorize different forms of action and experience.[27] Kincaid describes innocence as simply "virginity coupled with ignorance."[28] For women, then, sex is considered the primary corrupting form of knowledge. To be innocent is to be chaste.

Sexual innocence comes to play in various ways in struggles for women's rights. The most written about, perhaps, is the case of trafficking. While current anti-trafficking laws are concerned with trafficking for forced labor as well as for forced sex, trafficking for the purposes of sex still receives the most publicity and emphasis transnationally, and one reason for this is the focus on and appeal of innocence. As anthropologist Carole Vance has long argued, the central characters in stories of sex trafficking are teenage girls and young women, putatively devoid of sexuality or knowledge, and sold into brothels.[29] This requires a focus on the blameless – not on the sexually active young women. Here, victims lack not only (sexual) knowledge but also intention.

These accounts successfully frame sex trafficking as a human rights issue, and yet there are limits to who can benefit from these rights; Vance states, "sexuality is made a special case in which only those who are sexually inexperienced, or those who frame their stories that way, are recognized as victims of human rights abuses."[30] More specifically, only those who are considered sexually innocent are given protection; they have to present very particular, scripted stories about how they were smuggled over borders or kidnapped into prostitution or modern slavery. Indeed, Vance continues, "nowhere in human rights doctrine and activism are protections and remedies reserved only for the innocent."[31] The necessity to perform innocence was true in my own research, in France, when I worked with undocumented immigrants;[32] nearly all the undocumented immigrants who were categorized as "modern slaves" and who were therefore granted documents and rights were young girls who had supposedly come to France naively, sexually innocent, and often without a choice. There was no room for their complicity in wanting a better life or to provide for their kin. The girls were described as vulnerable, defenseless, lost, and excluded. They were portrayed as unable to comprehend their situations. Those with sexual knowledge or experience, who chose sex work as part of a better life, or took opportunities to leave their homes, often with the help of their families, did not qualify for these human rights protections. In the process, sex work as work was either rendered invisible, or criminalized.

We see similar kinds of questions about sexual innocence coming to play in claims to reproductive rights. Advocacy groups argue that women's right to comprehensive reproductive health services, including abortion, is rooted in international human rights standards guaranteeing the rights to life, health, privacy, and nondiscrimination. Many of the international human rights bodies protect reproductive rights as part of already existing human rights obligations. The Committee on the Elimination of Discrimination against Women (CEDAW Committee) and the Committee on the Rights of the Child are two of the UN bodies that have worked to protect these rights, but cases have also been heard in the Inter-American human rights system, and the European human rights system, which have recognized state obstructions of lawful abortions as rights violations. In jurisdictions that generally prohibit abortion, claims aim to ensure access in exceptional cases such as to preserve the life of a woman or where pregnancy results from rape.

In an essay about abortion rights litigation in Latin America, Lisa M. Kelly makes a compelling argument about the centrality of narratives of innocence, and how these immediately circumscribe who gets rights.[33] This is relevant in that these have become landmark cases in international human rights law, and the strategies and tropes of course circulate, just as do the laws and the activists. Starting from the 1990s, she covers five successful claims in the Inter-American Human Rights system, each of which involved denial of a lawful abortion at a public hospital. Interestingly, these all involved young girls, who were raped or sexually abused, and became pregnant as a result. Of course, the lawyers chose cases that they felt would be high-profile internationally and could win both at law and in the court of public opinion. As we know, naming and shaming is one of human rights organizations' tried and true strategies, and for this, engaging with public opinion is critical (see Leebaw this volume). As Kenneth Roth, executive director of Human Rights Watch (also involved in advocating for abortion rights in Latin America), stated, "We are at our most effective when we can hold governmental (in some cases nongovernmental) conduct up to a disapproving public."[34] With this in mind, the lawyers chose those who could best foreground the exceptional elements of cruelty and inhumanity in current abortion laws, creating the possibility for shaming: innocent sufferers.

Anti-abortion advocates and similarly inclined civil society groups are active in these Latin American countries. And in fact, anti-abortionists frame their struggle in terms of innocence: they pit a universal *fetal* innocence against the guilt or lack of moral fiber of the person requesting an abortion. In the Latin American cases, the lawyers arguing for abortion rights did not challenge this frame. Instead, they chose to take on the cases of those whom they could also configure as innocent, and who could therefore compete with the status of the fetus: they chose the figure of the child-like rape victim to personify innocence. In this sense, they limited their cases to girls, with no sexual experience, and who did not consent to sex. For instance, there was the case of Paulina de Carmen Ramírez Jacinto vs. Mexico. Paulina was a thirteen year old who became pregnant as a result of rape, and was unable to get an abortion because medical staff dissuaded her mother, citing the dangers of abortion. In the Inter-American Commission, Paulina's team argued for compensation, and that by failing to provide adequate procedures through which she could access lawful abortion, the Mexican state had violated its obligations under human rights treaties and declarations.[35]

Kelly demonstrates how the language of childishness ("la niña") is used in each of these cases, to distinguish girls from teenagers, who are more likely to be seen as sexually active. Once again, we see innocence being used to draw the line between human kinds: girls deserve abortions, teenagers do not. Their arguments for abortion rights involved demonstrating the mental and physical health consequences of having their girlhood innocence violated – their grievous suffering – and as girls, their particular vulnerability.

Insofar as human rights movements agitate for political change, one can say all these cases were successful. However, they all draw on rape exceptions, which only provide safe access to abortion for a very few. They rely on women's nonconsent to sex – their sexual innocence; this means that women who do consent to – or desire – nonprocreative sex do not have reproductive rights, and must resort to informal means of termination or take on unwanted pregnancies. It also disqualifies women who are economically vulnerable and financially unable to raise a child. In general, arguments based on innocence cast the majority of those who want abortions outside the realm of rights, framing only the exceptional as deserving. As with the case of trafficking, innocence in the form of *sexual* innocence steals into these struggles, making moral distinctions about who deserves certain kinds of rights.

The lawyers and human rights activists argue that they use these exceptional cases for incremental change, that is, they hope that these cases will clear the way for further exceptions and for the eventual liberalization of abortion law and access. But can these exceptional conditions translate into more generalized arguments for universal rights? Or do such limitations fundamentally alter who we consider worthy of rights – do they work to sediment hierarchies of humanity? So far, looking at abortion debates in Latin America and in places like the United States and parts of Europe, such moves have simply narrowed the space of struggle, writing out others not only as different in age or experience, but as different in kind.

The Innocence Project

I turn now to another project that makes the case that protecting the rights of the exceptional will eventually lead to rights for all: the Innocence Project. Of course, this movement, unlike the others we have discussed, explicitly takes on innocence – but of a different kind. It refers to the presumption of innocence, or the idea that everyone should be considered innocent until proven guilty. This principle is enshrined in Article 11 of the UN Declaration of Human Rights – it is an understanding of innocence as universal, as something everyone should be granted if accused. Under the presumption of innocence, the legal burden of proof is thus on the prosecution, which must collect and present compelling evidence to the trier of fact. According to the deputy executive director of the Innocence Project, Meryl Schwartz, the Project was put into place to counter what they understood to be a creeping reversal of this presumption of innocence – it was to counter a turn to the racialized presumption that certain people are a priori guilty. They wanted to show that innocence still matters.[36]

Before I say more, I want to clarify the difference in the meanings of innocence here. If I have so far foregrounded the ethico-moral concept of innocence – as experiential or epistemic purity – and largely approached it in the secular, liberal context, the concept of innocence at play in the Innocence Project is based on its juridical version, to be free from specific wrong or guilt.[37] In contemporary legal terms, innocence is about acquittal – a decision to acquit means that the judge or jury had a reasonable doubt as to the defendant's guilt. It may be based on exculpatory evidence or a lack of evidence to prove guilt. It does not mean that there is absolute certainty, only reasonable doubt. To find someone innocent is not necessarily to make a judgment on who they are but on whether they committed a particular act. There is a distinction between innocent or guilty actions, and innocence as a kind or category of person. In other words, the legal concept has developed to judge acts, not identities (although, as Janet Halley has demonstrated, acts and identities may not be as easily distinguished as we might think).[38] The legal concept leaves room for uncertainty; it does not presume absolute truth. This is not the case of innocence as an ethico-moral concept, which is much less flexible, much less compromising, and which helps to constitute identities or kinds in relation to purity.

With the Innocence Project, there are several versions of innocence at play. These include actual or factual innocence, and legal innocence. Actual or factual innocence means that the defendant did not commit the crime they are accused of, even if found guilty at trial – one might say that they are "truly" innocent. Legal innocence, again, is where one starts: with the presumption of innocence. For legal innocence, as stated above, one only needs to be acquitted based on reasonable doubt. The goal is not to prove that they did not commit the crime.

While the Innocence Project started with the goal of preserving and defending legal innocence in the United States, where the number of people incarcerated is extraordinary, they have expanded their network to other common law countries like Canada, the UK, and Australia; but in the United States, they now work only with actual innocence, to show that innocent people do get wrongly accused. They do this by way of DNA evidence, to exonerate those wrongly accused. They started in the early 1990s with the advent of DNA technology, which offered them a tool with which to push back against racist analyses; they saw forensic evidence as a way to make a case more "objective." The Innocence Project's legal team makes a point of staying up to date on the latest scientific technologies, holding firmly to these as the way to "truth." For instance, as they recount in their materials, they helped to exonerate Steven Mark Chaney, who was convicted in Texas for a grisly double murder on the basis of bite marks on the victim's body. Drawing on forensic analysis, they challenged this evidence, and demonstrated his innocence. This resulted in a moratorium on the use of bite mark evidence in future criminal prosecutions in Texas, since it is a technique that cannot be scientifically validated.

In this sense, they do work to produce system reform by fighting for more sound procedures for everyone, from access to DNA testing, to police procedure reform in relation to eyewitness testimony; and they have also pushed mandatory video-recording of interrogations. But despite this, a desire for moral purity compels their work. DNA evidence is only available for a tiny fraction of cases, so right away, the cases they take on are exceptional. In looking for actual innocence, there is a claim to purity – to *real* innocence – that is grounded not just on legal, but moral distinctions. In an article "In Praise of the Guilty Project" – critiquing "innocentrism" – Abbe Smith writes about a flyer put up by one of the chapters of the Innocence Project, seeking clients, but stating in big font, "We do not help guilty inmates lessen their sentences or get off on technicalities." This language purports to distinguish the deserving from the undeserving, the real from the malingerers or the fraudulent; and such moral distinctions get repeated in remarks like that of one of the founders, Barry Scheck, who stated that "he had not represented a guilty person in twenty years."[39] The Innocence Project comes armed, as Smith states, "with both justice and certainty, a lethal combination."[40] Here, we see moral distinctions not only between the innocent and the guilty, but also between the lawyers who claim their own version of innocence by way of helping only those they deem factually innocent.

There is no room for political complexity in those they defend; no place for the not-quite-innocent, who, with the presumption of innocence, still deserve to be fairly treated. They focus on people who are untainted, and separate them out from the rest – those who have not committed the crime, full stop – not those who might have been unfairly sentenced, or sentenced for something different from what they did, or who have extenuating circumstances that might explain why they committed a crime. It does not focus on local-level crimes, and those held for violating parole or minor drug crimes, which bloats the prison population. This emphasis on the pure reinforces the idea of good and bad criminals, and like the distinctions made between good and bad immigrants when innocence is used to give papers to some and deport the rest, this allows for the further mistreatment of those designated bad. In looking for truth, rather than proof, this type of innocence slips from legal to ethico-moral, and once again, moves to create distinctions between people rather than protecting rights for all.

While the work of the Innocence Project is undoubtedly pathbreaking and important – some have called it a "new civil rights movement" – it nevertheless seems to cast doubt on the ability of the language of innocence to be flexible enough or to stretch enough to be able to address the injustice of those sentenced to life in prison for the most minor of crimes, such as stealing $50, as was the case with Alabama resident Alvin Kennard – or more broadly, for the injustices of the ever-expanding carceral system. So, we might ask, does the slippage in the concept of innocence (from legal to moral) preclude struggles for a different kind of justice? For more systemic equality?

A Humanity without Innocence?

Human rights and humanitarianism both depend on the concept of innocence to enact their work, and in so doing, both create distinctions and hierarchies in their practice of humanity. However, they have slightly different consequences. Humanitarians draw on the concept of innocence to determine who is most in need – tying need to vulnerability, which in turn is measured by way of innocence. But this is a practice of triage that could, presumably, have different measures. That is, precisely because of its minimalism – which is grounded in saving life itself, unqualified life – humanitarianism does not generally work to distinguish between human kinds; it makes distinctions based on the urgency of need. While this can and does result in the privileging of some over others, such distinctions are less about who one is or what one has done than how vulnerable one *appears* at a particular moment. In other words, the framing of need is flexible, and changes over time and context.

With human rights practices, however, it seems that innocence may (inadvertently) work to construct distinctions in human kinds; perhaps counter-intuitively, it is the identities that come to matter most, not the acts. I see this as related to the maximalism that is often a part of human rights practices, which, unlike humanitarianism, includes installing and protecting fuller versions of what it means to be human (i.e., dignity). As Michael Barnett describes in the introduction to this volume, this is linked to the progress narrative built into human rights projects. The goal of human rights discourses and practices is to create the conditions in which individuals can better flourish; as such, they try to support and amplify different qualities in the humanity they protect. Insofar as innocence is evoked as a special quality to be protected, betterment for a few is accompanied by the exclusion of many. That is, innocence works to value some forms of life at the expense of others. People may fight for the rights of innocent young girls who have been raped – and in this sense, a different, better world is imagined, one that does not countenance these forms of gender-based violence. And yet, when the language of innocence is used to further these girls' rights, their innocence necessarily produces the guilt of others (in this case, all women, or anyone with sexual experience). Innocence is a boundary concept, always working to create a space of epistemic or experiential purity, but in the process, it produces a constituent outside for the impure, contaminated or guilty. All those in this outside space are cast as unworthy or undeserving of rights or protections.

As such, when innocence comes into play in both humanitarianism and human rights work, it actually functions to further inequality: in the case of humanitarianism, while it may not be producing different and unequal human kinds, the use of innocence nevertheless can produce inequality in terms of life chances. In the case of human rights, it turns out, only some people deserve rights. We saw this in the case of anti-trafficking discourses; these not only exclude – but actually further penalize – those who cannot show they entered into sex work unknowingly and unwillingly. In the case of the Innocence Project, those who are not actually or factually innocent are similarly criminalized and condemned in a stronger sense, and deemed deserving of whatever sentences they may receive.

Innocence slips between its meaning as a lack of agency (helplessness, vulnerability, defenselessness), a lack of knowledge (naiveté), a lack of desire, and a lack of responsibility (blamelessness). It is a flexible concept that intimately shapes why and how we should care, for whom we should care, and whose lives matter: it constantly engages with the category of humanity, but it does so by defining distinctions in the category, and by circumscribing its limits. It seems unlikely, then, that humanity and innocence will be disentangled anytime soon. Even if humanity is differently practiced and understood by humanitarianism and human rights, with humanitarianism at least less dependent conceptually on the innocence of those it saves or helps, nevertheless, humanity is almost impossible to think without innocence; and insofar as innocence furthers distinctions rather than equality or inclusiveness, we must accept that humanity as a concept provides an inadequate basis for struggles for political equality.

10 Reckoning with Time
Vexed Temporalities in Human Rights and Humanitarianism

Ilana Feldman

In 1981 a mukhtar (village leader) in the Balata refugee camp near Nablus in the West Bank sent a petition to the high commissioner of the United Nations Relief and Works Agency for Palestine Refugees (UNRWA) complaining about a significant curtailment in UN rations provided to Palestinian refugees. The demand for rations restoration was explicitly couched in the language of rights: "The Palestinian refugees, who are suffering under occupation, appeal to you to extend to them immediate assistance, as an act to safeguard their rights and their dignity which is diminishing day by day and one month after one month."[1] And the petition also marshaled the specific language of human rights: "Where is humanity and what they call Human Rights? The rights that were granted to them by the United Nations in-lieu-of their usurped lands? Where is justice? Where is democracy? Where is the Human Rights that protect all the refugees ... women, children, and widows who are left without rations and on the verge of extinction." Even as he asked for rations, the mukhtar distinguished his request from charity: "we are not seeking charity or almsgiving. We are after our many usurped rights – the rights which were recognized unanimously by the United Nations."

The petition mobilized the language of human rights in pressing a self-defined humanitarian organization for a widely recognized humanitarian good. It demanded action in the present to both redress a past wrong and secure future rights. This sort of multiplicity is common in Palestinian discourse. In the seventy years since the displacement and dispossession of the majority of the Palestinian population, they have made rights claims of at least three sorts: humanitarian rights, human rights, and national rights. They have made these kinds of demands in multiple fora and to many parties. And they have generally presented them as, at most, different registers of a single rights universe. The concept of humanitarian rights, especially, showcases the porousness of the boundaries between human rights and humanitarianism. The way these rights are pressed for by Palestinians highlights the multiple parties involved in constituting these fields.

Some of the addressees of Palestinian claims, at least some of the time, view the conjoining of human rights and humanitarianism, and related demands for action across multiple temporalities, as a form of category confusion. Humanitarian organizations often view their jurisdiction as the provision of care, rather than the protection of rights. And human rights efforts are often more targeted at violations of individual rights than the national rights that Palestinians insist upon. Humanitarian activity is most comfortably situated in the present – providing aid to people in need now. Human rights, in partial contrast, takes up reckoning with the past and working for a different future as fundamental tasks. But even as many humanitarian and human rights organizations see boundary maintenance as fundamental to their ability to do some good in the world – the argument being that it is better to do a few things well than to do many things badly – the circumstances these organizations confront render such distinctions tenuous at best. And the demands of recipient communities are only one aspect of these circumstances.

The aim of this chapter is not to render a judgment about whether these distinctions are right or real, but to explore the terms in which they are both articulated and muddied. It is organized in three sections, each focused on a particular temporal dimension. The first part of each section considers how past, present, or future have been taken up in human rights and humanitarian communities, both scholarly and practitioner. The second part turns to the Palestinian instance to see how people on the receiving end of these interventions not only engage these terms, but also participate in their making and remaking.

The content, limits, and viability of human rights and national rights are all contested. But their existence is widely acknowledged. Humanitarian rights, on the other hand, seem to many to be an oxymoron. For some critics the problem with humanitarianism is precisely that it relies on compassion, rather than the more stable ground of rights.[2] The language of rights is not, though, alien to humanitarianism. Nor is it new. Bruno Cabanes traces the emergence of the concept of humanitarian rights to the aftermath of World War I, as part of the European turn away from war.[3] Both the international obligation to respond to circumstances of suffering and the expectation on the part of victims that such a response should be forthcoming were part of this conceptual framework. Cabanes describes the humanitarian rights of the 1920s as a transitional concept on the path toward the articulation of human rights. But humanitarian rights have persisted into the post-World War II human rights era even as they remain, as in the 1920s, "far from self-evident."[4]

The Office of United Nations High Commissioner for Refugees notes that the cornerstone document for refugee protection, the 1951 Refugee Convention, is "both a status and rights-based instrument."[5] The principle of nonrefoulement, the right not to be returned to danger, is at the heart of the refugee protection regime. The convention also specifies other rights, including nondiscrimination, access to courts, and that "the unity of the family ... is an essential right of the refugee."[6] The protection of civilians in armed conflict is a matter of concern for both international humanitarian law (IHL) and international human rights law (IHRL). The legal scholar Dan Kuwali has argued that the notion of humanitarian rights – articulated at the intersection of IHL and IHRL – is necessary to maximize these protections: "humanitarian rights can be the symbiotic concept regarding the protection of fundamental human rights and humanitarian norms in order to enhance the protection of civilians."[7]

If human rights are "not enough," as Samuel Moyn puts it, humanitarian rights are arguably even less adequate.[8] I would not go as far as Jacques Rancière, who describes humanitarian rights as "the rights of those who cannot enact them, the victims of the absolute denial of right." He views these rights as charity, "sent abroad, along with medicine and clothes, to people deprived of medicine, clothes, and rights."[9] But in addition to their articulation in legal domains, protection regimes, and discourses of distant concern, humanitarian rights are also claimed by people such as Palestinians, who insist both that humanitarianism is a right and that humanitarianism entails specific obligations. Their demands may not have the force of law, but, at least sometimes, they have been effective in changing practice.

Human Rights and Memory

The challenge of confronting the past has been one of the central questions in human rights practice. Bringing perpetrators to justice for crimes they have committed is one of the clearest ways that human rights advocates can take concrete action in support of their principles. The international tribunals that have been established to deal with particular atrocities – such as the International Criminal Tribunal for the Former Yugoslovia (ICTY) and the International Criminal Tribunal for Rwanda (ICTR) – and the broader International Criminal Court (ICC) are key means for a global reckoning with the past. And societies that have directly experienced these crimes have sometimes pursued local forms of human rights justice, such as the gacaca courts in Rwanda. Whether international or local, memory plays an important role in retributive justice, as people serve as witnesses in the trials.

Retributive justice is not the only human rights idiom for reckoning with the past. Generally considered as part of transitional justice practice, the truth and reconciliation model takes the past as its terrain and memory as a key means of acquiring the data for its accounting.

Truth and Reconciliation Commissions in South Africa, Canada, and Peru, for example, sought to deal with the violations of, respectively, apartheid, Indian Residential Schools, and insurgency and counterinsurgency, by providing thorough and unsparing accounts of these crimes. Lea David notes the growth since the 1980s (Argentina's truth commission was established in 1983) of "the human rights vision of memorialization as a process of remembering the wrongs of the past and honoring the victims."[10] Kimberly Rae Lanegran identifies a number of challenges in the T&R approach: "By demanding to know 'the truth' about past atrocities, do societies risk oversimplifying their pasts? Should remembering the past always be privileged over forgetting? To what degree does collective memory of atrocities contribute to society's healing? To what degree does it maintain wounds?"[11] Her conclusion is that such commissions are often "fundamentally limited and indeed flawed because those efforts are products of political processes."[12] In other words, perhaps too much memory and not enough justice.

Still, as important as it is to human rights practice, memory does not always sit easily in that frame. Andreas Huyssen laments this distance and asks: "Where would today's international human rights movement be without memory of the killing fields of the twentieth century? The dignity of the victims, their struggles, and their fate must be preserved in memory, all the more so since it was the express aim of the masters of genocide to obliterate all memory of their victims."[13] Why might memory pose a challenge for human rights? It may lay, in part, in the multiplicity of tenses in which human rights needs to operate. Huyssen argues that too often the past has been neglected for the sake of the future, indicating that "the human rights movement, however, remains firmly oriented to the future goal of establishing an international, perhaps even global, rights regime."[14] But Lea David suggests that human rights memorialization can engage multiple temporalities.[15] She quotes a UN report that describes such memorialization as not only past-oriented, but also oriented "equally to the present (healing processes and rebuilding of trust between communities) and the future (preventing further violence through education and awareness-raising)."[16]

In tribunals and truth commissions, memory is a mechanism for human rights redress. In other contexts – one can think of the demonstrations of the Madres de la Plaza de Mayo in Argentina[17] or pilgrimage marches to former prisons in Morocco[18] – memory makes a claim for the necessity of human rights action. Memoralizations that are intended to honor victims of past atrocities are presented as a form of action themselves; these other performances of memory use remembrance as a lever to push for other kinds of action. Participants in groups such as the Mothers of the Plaza place themselves in public space in order to make embodied memory (and grief and anger) a potent force. The tension that Susan Slyomovics notes between the "muffled, secretive nature of prison and disappearance" and the "qualities that make for verbal performance in the public domain" can make this embodied appearance difficult.[19] And yet people do it. Past and present blend together here as these performers insist that memory is neither private nor closed: memory is offered up as a force that makes a demand on the present.

Palestinian Memory

Palestinian memory has often been denied a place in the global world of human rights memory, though Palestinians are pushing back on that exclusion. Memory has certainly been central to Palestinian political practice and life experience, and to local human rights discourse. The central focus of this memory practice has been the *nakba* (catastrophe): the displacement and dispossession of the majority of the Palestinian population in 1948. Rosemary Sayigh and Nadera Shalhoub-Kevorkian have tracked the glaring absence of the Palestinian nakba from the "trauma genre."[20] The collection and circulation of trauma memory (the Holocaust is the paradigmatic case for the genre, but it has expanded considerably) is a key way in which memories of suffering are given a place on the global stage and rendered part of the universal field of human rights.[21] Nakba memory has been excludable, Sayigh argues, because of a broad politics that makes Palestinian lives less "grievable"[22] and because "in many Western academic circles today, anti-Palestinianism is a permissible form of racism."[23] The Palestinian circulation of nakba memories has been important for both the continuity of their community and the global recognition of their experiences and claims.

Nakba memory is also not about a single displacement event. Much of this memory is about life "before their diaspora."[24] It includes the circulation of stories of *ayyam al-balad* (village days) and the printing of "village books" describing these lost spaces.[25] It entails materialized memorialization in the regular naming of Palestinian institutions after lost Palestinian places (such as the Haifa hospital in the Burj al Barajneh refugee camp). It involves social expressions of such memory in marriage patterns that long retained preference for unions among descendants of the same village. Nakba memory is also about life in the aftermath of dispossession. Stories about the early years in refugee camps, about aid distribution, and ongoing precarity are all part of this landscape. For many years the dominant international (and Israeli) approach to Palestinian memory has been that such recollection is an impediment to "peace." The Palestinian (and some dissident Israeli) response is that it is the refusal to confront the past that is the real impediment.[26]

Palestinians have never considered the nakba a bounded event, and in recent years the idea of the "ongoing nakba" (al-nakba al-mustamirrah) has become an increasingly central lens for framing their continued experience of colonization, dispossession, and occupation. The term itself has been around for a number of years. At the 2001 Durban conference on racism, Hanan Ashrawi spoke of "a nation in captivity held hostage to an ongoing Nakba [catastrophe], as the most intricate and pervasive expression of persistent colonialism, apartheid, racism, and victimization."[27] Its prevalence has increased significantly over the past decade. Not only does it underscore the relationship between current conditions and past events, but it also highlights the shared experiences of a dispersed population.

In 2009, Badil (a Palestinian research center in Bethlehem focused on "Palestinian residency and refugee rights") published a special issue of its journal with the title: Palestine's Ongoing Nakba.[28] Published right after a punishing Israeli assault on Gaza, the editorial described that attack as "the latest chapter in a sixty-year nakba."[29] The articles in this issue described "ongoing forced displacement" in Jaffa, Jerusalem, the Negev, and the West Bank (among other places). Palestinian citizens of Israel protesting the Lyd municipality's demolition of their homes included the term "ongoing nakba" on their signs.[30] Even Mahmoud Abbas, president of the Palestinian Authority and no cutting-edge political thinker, used the term in advocating for Palestinian statehood at the UN.[31] If memory becomes "human rights memory" when it both stakes out a universal relevance and makes a claim for redress, restitution, or another form of justice in the present, the language of the ongoing nakba must be understood as part of the work of giving Palestinian memory a place in this field. And it has certainly been important in Palestinian demands for humanitarian rights.

Humanitarianism and the Challenge of the Durable Present

Human rights work is often slow and exacting, involving the careful accumulation of evidence of past violations that can be prosecuted for future deterrence. Humanitarian work, on the other hand, is meant to be quick and nimble, able to move speedily to respond to a crisis and ready to move on to the next disaster as the situation improves.[32] The idea of crisis response is at the heart of the humanitarian imaginary. The goal is to save lives and move on.[33] A consequence of this orientation is that the present is humanitarianism's "natural" time.[34] Humanitarian practice is often focused on addressing needs that are both urgent now and can be addressed now, rather than on planning for change. And humanitarian interventions frequently have short mandates and funding streams, limiting their planning horizon. The present crisis, though, often extends into uncertain futures. The UNHCR, for instance, estimates that two-thirds of the global refugee population experience protracted displacement.[35] The humanitarian sector is also often in conversation with fields such as development that are explicitly future-oriented. The humanitarian take-up of concepts such as "resilience," which addresses a society's ability to withstand and manage a future shock, is a product of such engagement. So even as present-focused, crisis intervention has seemed to be the heart of the humanitarian field, this natural time is not humanitarianism's only temporality.

The future is part of humanitarianism's existential challenge.[36] A significant portion of humanitarian work is long term, extending across the lives (and lifecycles) of individuals and communities, even as that future is not highly conceptualized.[37] The longevity of humanitarian operations in many cases calls the "temporariness" that is central to its self-definition into question. In these circumstances temporariness is not replaced by permanence, but rather by an uncertain in between. Not only is it difficult for humanitarian practice to actively engage with change over time, but also the very fact of a humanitarian future is evidence of (humanitarian) failure. The parenthetical marks indicate that the failure is perhaps more properly assigned to the political actors who have primary responsibility for producing and resolving conditions of humanitarian need, and humanitarian actors would certainly so wish to assign it. One of the ongoing debates in the field is about the extent to which humanitarian presence can abet a lack of resolution. Regardless of responsibility, the continuation into the future of humanitarian work feels like a failure and certainly presents a problem.

Even though situations of long-term displacement are common, they strain the limits of the humanitarian imaginary, and also of humanitarian resources. Long-term humanitarian work poses both operational and existential difficulties for what Peter Redfield terms its "minimalist biopolitics," the use of biopolitical techniques in an effort primarily to keep people alive rather than to help them thrive.[38] These conditions require organizations that are oriented toward emergency to respond to circumstances that are "protracted." Common in the dynamics of long-term humanitarianism is movement between the "humanitarian situation" – the emergency that presents itself as an urgent need and which mobilizes a humanitarian machinery – and the "humanitarian condition" – the less acute, but no less fundamental experience of living and working in circumstances of long-term displacement and need. One of the challenges that humanitarian actors face is being buffeted between the catastrophic and the cruddy and trying to respond alternatively to both situations.

If the future lurks as a definitional challenge, the past is sometimes absent from humanitarian consideration. For humanitarianism *how* people came to be in need in less important than the fact that they *are* in need. But again, since humanitarianism is in fact often a long-term proposition, there are humanitarian pasts as much as humanitarian futures. These pasts form part of the lexicon through which recipients, and practitioners, understand their current condition. The past becomes a ground for judging the present: that aid *used to* be better is an oft-heard complaint by recipients.[39] That "best practices" have evolved and improved is a belief shared by many practitioners. The past helped define the relationships that structure the present.

The humanitarian experience, furthermore, often involves living with time out of joint, and experiencing multiple temporalities at once.[40] Certainly circumstances of displacement – whether products of war or natural disaster – often upend people's sense of where they are in time. Not only does it take time to come to understand what has happened – that home is gone, that communities are sundered – but also the daily rhythms of humanitarian assistance are so dramatically different from those of what had been ordinary life that it can be extremely difficult for people to temporally orient themselves.[41] Waiting in line for rations as opposed to getting ingredients from one's own supplies (whether from a household garden or purchased as a store) indicates a different source of sustenance, and also takes a different kind of time in one's day.[42] So too does baking bread over a fire outside a tent instead of in a village or backyard oven. The rending of daily time that accompanies displacement makes temporality unstable. Even as the first crisis passes, temporal confusion can continue. Does the experience of a day (or days) define the present for the displaced? Or does the present still abide in their former experiences? Can a refugee's future have any continuity with the past or will it only be rupture? These questions are both existential and political. And they persist.

Humanitarian Rights and the Palestinian Present

Not only have Palestinians claimed multiple sorts of rights – humanitarian, human, and national – they have made these claims around multiple temporalities. The insistence that nakba memory be recognized as part of the landscape of human rights memory is a claim to acknowledgment of past wrongs. The language of the ongoing nakba is a reminder that these wrongs are not only in the past. Humanitarian rights demands have been another venue for making claims on the present – for insisting on international engagement in halting these ongoing wrongs. Refugee responses to Israeli occupation policy in the Gaza Strip offer a case in point. The occupation of Gaza was met, from the outset, with resistance. Organized armed struggle peaked in the years between 1969 and 1971, and then it was largely crushed by the Israeli military under the command of Ariel Sharon.[43] As part of its security measures, and its territorial expansionist policy, Israel both encouraged emigration from the strip and forcibly moved refugees out of camps.

In 1971, usually in the name of fighting terrorism, the Israeli military began demolishing shelters in Jabalia, Shati, Rafah, and Deir al Belah camps. Some demolition was done to widen roads in the camps, in order to enable easier patrolling. A 1972 demolition project in the Rafah camp was described as a matter of town planning, rather than security. UNRWA vociferously objected to the forced movement of refugees and repeatedly sought Israeli agreement to provide adequate alternative housing for refugees who were evicted. Many refugees, and Israel itself, reported that the only alternative housing that was made available was either in El Arish in the Sinai or in the West Bank. That is, the project of "thinning out" the refugee camps was also a project of depopulating Gaza. Even when people could not be moved from the strip, Israel sought to move them out of camps, claiming to transform them, as an editorial in the *Jerusalem Post* put it, from "refugees into people."[44] Commenting on this editorial, an UNRWA official dismissed it as "strictly propaganda."[45]

As refugees protested against forced removals, they used the language of humanitarian rights to press their claims. Demonstrations targeted UNRWA in an effort to enlist the agency's help. On July 24, 1971, a group of demonstrators, mainly women and children, gathered at the gates of the UNRWA headquarters early in the morning. According to a report by the responsible official on site, they came "from the direction of Jabalia camp, crying, shouting, and demonstrating."[46] The gendered character of this protest was surely not accidental. In part, it may have reflected a division of political labor, with men more likely to be engaged in militant action. In part, it also reflected different vulnerabilities in public assembly. Women and children are not wholly insulated from the threat of violent response, but they are slightly more sheltered from it.

The protesters pushed their way into the compound and could not be persuaded to quiet down. A small group of protesters was brought in to meet with the director and, in the meantime, those outside obstructed staff members from entering their offices. When the meeting concluded, the representatives told the rest of the protesters that "they were sure and confident that the director of UNRWA operations, Gaza is taking the matter seriously and he has promised to make all his efforts to help them." At this point the demonstrators agreed to return to the camp.

Other petitions accompanied this assembly in defense of the right not to be further displaced. The president of the UNRWA staff association wrote to the commissioner-general in the latter's "capacity as the representative of the Secretary General and the United Nations, the guardian of human rights, to put an end to their pains and suffering."[47] He cited legal and political bases for the objection to the Israeli demolition plan: "Compulsory movement individually and collectively of the inhabitants of the occupied territories is prohibited in accordance with Article 49 of the Geneva Convention IV . . . . It is prohibited for the occupying State to destroy movable or immovable belongings of individuals or groups of persons as stated in Article 53 of the above mentioned convention."[48] The letter also argued that these compulsory movements were political in nature, and that the UNRWA should work to stop them so that it "will not be involved in these political currents which are in conflict with its humanitarian mission." The language of humanitarian rights was paired with the presence of Palestinian bodies as an assertion of their demand to stay in place.

As demolitions and evictions continued, the UNRWA registered its dissent, but largely in vain: "The Agency requests an assurance that the Israeli authorities will proceed urgently with the provision of housing within the Gaza Strip for the refugees moved to El Arish and that they will be free to return to the Strip as soon as the accommodation is ready."[49] The agency viewed the entire operation as a violation of both the Geneva Conventions and General Assembly resolutions. And it expressed concern about its employees. A special report to the General Assembly in September 1971 noted that "despite assurances given by the Israeli military authorities . . . about 70 Agency staff members had had their shelters demolished."[50] Challenging an Israeli claim that refugees moved to El Arish "of their own free will," the commissioner-general wrote to Israeli General Shlomo Gazit that it seemed "inconceivable" that UNRWA employees would willing move so far from their place of employment "and if UNRWA employees were treated in this way, there must be considerable doubt about the consent of many others to their movement to El Arish."[51]

UNRWA files include numerous letters from local UNRWA employees describing the process by which they were forcibly removed, often to

El Arish. One teacher described how soldiers took all of his family's identification cards and told him that they were being moved: "I then addressed the following question to them: Where to will we be emigrated? They said: 'We do not know.' I then said to them: 'I work with UNRWA as a teacher.' They said: 'You will find schools there in which you will work.'"[52] Other employees reported similar treatment. Israeli officials continued to insist that the home demolitions were necessary for security, that it sought to "avoid undue hardship," and that no one was sent to the West Bank or El Arish "against his will."[53] And UNRWA and refugees continued to protest, to little effect.[54] This failure is a reminder of the limit of politics in the humanitarian space, a limit that is not simply attributable to the relative weakness of refugees. Rights to humanitarianism and humanitarian rights came together in UNRWA's later acknowledgment of its obligation to provide shelter assistance for persons whose homes were destroyed, making "no distinction between destruction by military action, by punitive demolition and for such reasons as the security 'road widening' operation in the Gaza Strip in 1971."[55]

Just as Arendt noted that the "right to have rights" is more fundamental than any of the specific rights of citizens, so, too, do Palestinians claim a general right to humanitarian rights that underlies any of the specific rights they demand as refugees. This right to humanitarian rights entails recognition, however limited, of Palestinian inclusion in an international community. To have humanitarian rights does not mean that Palestinians are not refugees; it does not entail a change in status in that sense. But the claim to these rights does constitute an argument that as refugees they should not live in the condition of arbitrariness that Arendt views as the lot of the stateless.[56] "What they do, did, or may do" should matter, Palestinians argue. And in so claiming they try to redefine the condition of being a refugee.

Can Human Rights Govern the Future?

If human rights engagement with the past is often about adjudication, human rights take up of the future is frequently about deterrence. One of the key purposes of human rights activity – including criminal prosecution of past wrongs – is to set precedents for the limits of acceptable behavior and to constrain future state action. Human rights practitioners also often view themselves as responding to an obligation to future generations to help make a better world. The memory work described earlier plays a central role in these future concerns as well. As Elizabeth Jelin argues for the Argentine case, the human rights response to the political violence of dictatorship moved through several phases, from an urgency around discovery and publicity, to "the vindication of the historical and collective memory struggling against oblivion," and then to demands for punishment and "the future projection of human rights in education and in new legal provisions."[57] She further indicates about the operations of memory in this instance: "The moving idea is that only through remembering can avoidance of such violations be ensured – as if 'never again' could only be guaranteed by the constant remembrance of the terror experienced during the dictatorship. Is memory the key to deterrence?"[58]

To the extent that human rights seeks to govern the future, it does so in several ways – through the social and political transformation of possibility and through specific legal mechanisms of deterrence.[59] Considering the US government's use of torture in the "War on Terror," Francesca Laguardia contends that there is significant evidence to suggest that state actors have been deterred by the prosecution of human rights violations. She further suggests that these efforts are part of a broad strategy of future-oriented human rights practice which recognizes that "rather than interrupting or punishing abuse, it would be far preferable to prevent its occurrence entirely. Perhaps surprisingly, criminal sanctions offer great promise in this regard."[60] Not only might prosecution deter human rights violation, Laguardia indicates that "deterrence theory also suggests failure to prosecute is likely to breed more lawless behavior if it is allowed to stand."[61] According to this argument, failure to act has its own future effect: the production of more human rights violations.

Prosecution is a key venue for human rights' future work. Education is another. Elif Babul has explored the importance of human rights training for Turkish government officials to the process of accession to the European Union. This process has several (future-oriented) aims. It seeks to transform the character of Turkey and Turkish governance to make it suitable for a place in Europe. In so doing it works to reconfigure the relationship between Turkish bureaucrats and the Turkish population. And it also tries to reorient human rights violations themselves from "manifestations of state violence" to "symptoms of deficiency in governmental capacity and expertise."[62] The training process has a present effect on the participants – shifting their understandings of their own positions, but this present effect is embedded within a future-oriented project. Like prosecutions, these trainings are intended to have a deterrence effect – in this instance as much through changing subject positionings as through shifting their calculations about the possible outcomes of their actions. Whether sanctions or human rights education can actually shape the future as proposed is an open question. So too is whether the international human rights regime has a future at all.[63]

Deterrence does not, though, exhaust the landscape of future-thinking around human rights. There is also a great deal of human rights talk that centers around the obligations that the present has to the future: "What kind of world will we leave our children?" It makes sense that the language of intergenerational obligation looms large in arguments about the environment and in efforts to stake a place for environmental activism in the human rights arena. Edith Weiss argues that "intergenerational equity finds deep roots in international law" and that environmental protection – specifically preservation of resources, planet quality, and access – is a central part of fulfilling this obligation.[64] Richard Hiskes acknowledges the difficulty, for a range of philosophical reasons, in sustaining an argument about intergenerational justice and avers that "emergent environmental rights supply a strong argument for justice across generations, because environmental rights logically presume concern for the future."[65]

When a group of young Americans (ranging in age from 9 to 20) sued the federal government to demand greater action on climate change, they explicitly used the language of obligation to the future in claiming that inaction was a threat to their "fundamental constitutional right to life and liberty."[66] When the court granted them a right to a trial on the matter, it acknowledged that there was merit to the claim. As the presiding judge wrote: "I have no doubt that the right to a climate system capable of sustaining human life is fundamental to a free and ordered society."[67] Whether environmental justice will be recognized as a fundamental human rights remains an unsettled question – though as the effects of climate change increase it will only become more pressing – but it seems clear that if it is so recognized, it will be in significant part through efforts to make claims for and on behalf of the future.

Palestinian Futures through Human Rights

From the condition of the present, the Palestinian future looks bleak. There have been many moments of hope and possibility along the trajectory of Palestinian suffering: the years of the "revolution" (*thawra*) in Lebanon (1969–1982) when the Palestine Liberation Organization (PLO) not only promised to fight for Palestine, but also offered protection and opportunity to refugees in Lebanon; the time of the first intifada (uprising) (1987–1993) when grassroots resistance to the Israeli occupation of the West Bank and Gaza Strip not only mobilized Palestinians in the territories, but also energized the community in exile; even the early period after the Oslo Accords, the 1993 agreements that created the Palestinian Authority (PA) in the territories and which many hoped would lead to an independent Palestinian state. But each of these moments has ended in defeat, leading many people to feel that there is little hope for the future.

As bleak as things seem for Palestinians today, today is not all there is. Looking at the Palestinian experience over time makes the recurring movement between possibility and impossibility evident. And there is no reason to think that the present constitutes the end of (Palestinian) history. It is true that certain futures are irretrievably foreclosed in the passage of time. As we have passed the seventieth anniversary of the nakba, the passing of the Palestine generation without return or resolution appears inevitable. The deepening infrastructure of occupation and settlement in the West Bank makes some political outcomes (namely a two-state solution) increasingly difficult, many argue impossible. But even as Palestinian political organizing and leadership is at a low ebb, and therefore ill-equipped to resist these conditions, the fact of continued Palestinian existence – perhaps the signal Palestinian political achievement over these decades – means that other possibilities can still emerge.

Human rights has had a vexed place in the landscape of future feeling among Palestinians. In her study of the world of human rights work in Palestine, Lori Allen describes the tension between faith in a better future and cynicism about achieving it through the system of NGO operations. She notes that Al-Haq, the oldest and most venerable Palestinian human rights organization, was explicitly founded with the aim of laying the groundwork for the future in that it "endeavored to prepare the population's collective consciousness for its future task of organizing Palestinian society in a just and equitable manner."[68] Indeed, in a context of occupation and the absence of national sovereignty, rule of law work such as human rights can only be future-oriented. For many in the field the work "gives a sense of doing something, even if results come only in the future."[69] And as the founder of Birzeit University's human rights program told Allen, "the flocking of students to a program in democracy and human rights is itself an indicator that even the pessimists, in their hearts, are persuaded of a promising future."[70] It may equally be that they are persuaded of the utility of the degree in an employment market that is NGO-heavy and RFP (request for proposals)-driven.

The international aid world shapes Palestinian engagements with human rights in other ways as well. Things like human rights education are increasingly built into donor demands. Promoting respect for human rights among Palestinians was a key impetus behind the development of a human rights curriculum for UNRWA schools. After beginning with a pilot program in Gaza in 1999, and then extending to other fields, in 2012 UNRWA formally adopted a policy for incorporating human rights education into its curricula in all five fields where it operates. The policy asserts that as a subsidiary organ of the United Nations UNRWA has a responsibility to uphold and promote the human rights instruments adopted by the General Assembly. And human rights education is described as part of the Agency's overall requirement to achieve "alignment with the international human rights system."[71] It calls its program "education for human rights, conflict resolution, and tolerance [HRCRT]."

UNRWA's advancement of this curriculum is part of a broader landscape in which human rights education (HRE) is developing as a field (and as an industry).[72] And the lessons and principles that UNRWA suggests to its teachers are well aligned with this broader field. It is more usual, however, for HRE to be pursued by self-defined human rights organizations, rather than a humanitarian organization like UNRWA. But UNRWA is an unusual humanitarian organization in having such a sustained responsibility for the education of so many children.[73] UNRWA schools follow the host-country curriculum in each of its area of operations. Incorporating human rights into this curriculum requires developing specific educational materials that can either be folded into other lessons or deployed as a stand-alone module (as was done in Gaza). The human rights curriculum is meant both to introduce students to the international human rights system and its instruments (UDHR, the convention on the rights of the child, etc.) and to bring a human rights approach into the life of schools – teaching children tolerance of difference, promoting educational inclusion, and developing techniques for nonviolent conflict resolution. And the goal is to have these lessons extend far beyond the classroom. As a toolkit developed for educators describes, a key aim of this education is to promote the spread of a "culture of human rights"[74] throughout the community.[75]

What does this culture consist of? As outlined in the materials: "A culture of human rights is one in which the full potential of Palestine refugee students is realised. It is a culture where the students develop attitudes and behaviours that are respectful of human rights." The goal is to "promote lifelong respect for human rights and tolerance as they mature and become active citizens in their communities."[76] Human rights are described as resting on five basic principles: human dignity, universality, equality and nondiscrimination, participation and inclusion, and tolerance.[77] There have been objections to aspects of the curriculum. Some see the focus on conflict resolution and tolerance as an attack on what they view as legitimate resistance to Israeli occupation.[78] Others have argued that the rights emphasized are too generic (such as the right to play) without giving sufficient attention to the precise ways in which the

Israeli occupation persistently violates Palestinian rights.[79] Certainly human rights education has emerged from donor interest and UN requirements rather than community demands. To this extent the future that is envisioned and enacted through human rights work is only partially a Palestinian future.

Impossible Distinctions

What do these different engagements and temporalities tell us about questions of boundary maintenance and encroachment in human rights and humanitarianism? They offer some indications about why boundary maintenance might be viewed as important by actors in the field. And they also highlight some of the reasons why such separation might also be viewed as undesirable and even impossible. Actors in both fields of humanitarianism and human rights, along with the communities where they intervene, regularly confront the limits of their capacities to have the effect they hope to in the world. Insisting upon a clearly defined task and jurisdiction is one response to these limits. But even as some actors claim the ground of distinction as a means of improving their chances of doing good, others argue that expanding activities and forming alliances with closely related actors is a better way of unsettling limits of possibility.

As scholars and practitioners debate boundaries and intersections, politics is a central concern. Some people worry that human rights will lose its capacity to deliver justice by blending too much with humanitarian compassion. Others fear that humanitarian access will be imperiled by an entanglement with political claims and fault-finding. The temporal distinctions in these modes of engagement with human vulnerability and suffering are part of this terrain. In the face of the human rights demand for redress of past injustice and a claim to offer future deterrence, the needs of the present can seem "tradeable." From a humanitarian perspective, inadequate attention to the urgent needs of now is an ethical failing of the highest order. And the reverse is true as well. Human rights actors (and others) argue that meeting the needs of the people in front of you – the doctor's oath and the humanitarian imperative – cannot be considered an unmitigated good if the past that brought people to that need and the future that is likely to extend it are not made a matter of concern. Whatever ground people try to stake, in human rights and humanitarian work temporalities get muddied, interventions overlap, and recipients work across all these lines of distinction to try to achieve better outcomes for themselves.

11 Between the Border and a Hard Place
Negotiating Protection and Humanitarian Aid after the Genocide in Cambodia, 1979–1999

Bertrand Taithe[*]

In 2017, a veteran of border refugee camps and medical development work in Cambodia mused on his professional journey and on the evolution of humanitarian work in the country. In a short anecdote he recalled how, when Ta Mok, "the Butcher," was still in hiding, optimistic humanitarians had convened for their human right workshop in his house, deep in Khmer Rouge territory.[1] This short story embodied many of the paradoxes of Cambodia in the 1990s but also illustrated how human rights issues had become salient among the many needs of a country being rebuilt with humanitarian assistance. Like my informant, many humanitarians of the 1990s had first experienced Cambodian politics from the margins of the border camps which represented one of the largest "emergency" relief operations between 1979 and 1992. With many others, he had joined in Cambodia a range of other humanitarian workers whose organizations had chosen to act within Vietnamese-controlled Cambodia during the same period.

Over nearly a generation, humanitarians engaged with the consequences of the Cambodian genocide, responded to the many demands of large refugee populations, and after 1990, to local and international expectations of state building. Humanitarians thus worked for over two decades with or alongside the perpetrators of genocide even as they engaged with human rights practices. In 1979, many humanitarians perceived the immediate response to emergencies to be the provision of basic protection and services. They reinterpreted these services as the guaranteeing of the rights of the refugees – sometimes in paternalistic terms.[2] This period was a very significant episode in the development of protection practices and in their assimilation to a rights-based approach to humanitarian relief. In the later phase, by the mid-1980s, this chapter argues, some imagined their role at the Thai border to be that of witnesses and promoters of human rights beyond refugee rights.

In significant contrast, development international nongovernmental organizations (INGOs) operating in Vietnamese-occupied Cambodia campaigned against the relief work at the border, arguing that it was a form of support for Khmer Rouge war-mongering. Throughout their work they favored more holistic programs of social and political renewal. In the debates around the future of Cambodia after the genocide, those working in Cambodia began to dream of a postwar order based on the rule of law and the promotion of human rights. In 1991, two understandings of humanitarian and human rights practices thus merged when the repatriation of border refugees entailed the mass arrival of emergency INGOs in Cambodia and the proliferation of small organizations within the country.

Following this merger, coalitions of INGOs sought to establish a rights-based polity. In what they convinced themselves was *their* project, international humanitarian organizations sought holistic and rights-based solutions. By the early 1990s, the UN-sanctioned peace agreement had brought into an unstable alliance the enemies of yesteryear. The ghost of the genocide hung over this new Cambodia and continues to inspire political debate.[3] Facing the full consequences of mass genocide for the first time since World War II, humanitarians attempted to establish their legitimacy and practices by using the terms of human rights discourses. For the purpose of exploring the complex relationship between human rights and humanitarian practices there are few case studies as relevant as that of the twin humanitarian interventions which took place in the border camps and inside Kampuchea/Cambodia[4] between 1979 and the era of liberal peace building.[5] Few sites have proven as complex and enduring as Cambodia since. There are a few other examples of continued presence and political activism by INGOs (excepted perhaps Sudan, Ethiopia, and Afghanistan) that shaped so significantly both humanitarians and their "beneficiaries." Cambodia became a *locus classicus* of the transformation of humanitarian protection practices into so-called rights-based humanitarian ones.

This chapter explores the context of this development of humanitarian work, the concepts of protection and rights it gave rise to, how humanitarians sought to bear witness of human rights violations and of the impending threat of a return of the Khmer rouge and how they took sides, in order to promote human rights as they saw them, in the reconstruction of Cambodia. This complex story of a humanitarian landscape responding to and being reshaped by the specificity of Cambodian politics may be coming to an end as the political usefulness of INGO works recedes in a developing economy under autocratic rule.

Context

The Cambodian humanitarian project was complex and multisited. It began in earnest in 1979 though there were some precursor interventions as early as 1975 on the border between Thailand and Khmer Rouge-controlled Kampuchea. From 1975 until the forced repatriation of most Cambodians in 1992–1993,[6] seventy-two temporary camps were established.[7] The United Nation's Children's Fund (UNICEF) and the International Committee of the Red Cross (ICRC) managed most border camps until the UN enabled the creation of a specific organization, the United Nations Border Relief Operation (UNBRO), which oversaw responsibility in 1982 of all camps with the exception of the resettlement camp of Khao I Dang, managed by the United Nations High Commissioner for Refugees (UNHCR).[8]

Originally a part of the World Food Programme and under the authority of the special representative of the secretary general for humanitarian assistance to the Kampuchean people, UNBRO managed relief work for the dozens of displaced persons and refugee camps set up in the no-man's-land between Cambodia and Thailand. These camps contained the flow of refuge-seeking Cambodians and kept their population in situ. Meanwhile the UNHCR managed the emblematic Khao I Dang camp. Unlike other camps, Khao I Dang was a site of transit. Though mostly built of mud, straw, and bamboo to satisfy the Royal Thai Government's (RTG) demands that nothing permanent might be established, the camps formed large urban centers. The largest housed up to 180,000 people in one composite urban complex in Site 2. Site 2 was really a conglomerate of camps sitting at the border of Thailand and vulnerable to occasional Vietnamese assaults; Khao I Dang was by far the most visited and public camp within the Thai territory. It became the subject of constant studies, visits, and academic engagement. In contrast, other camps remained under the control of political factions and for some, such as the Khmer Rouge camps, almost entirely outside any kind of humanitarian oversight.

Humanitarians working at the border soon discovered the complexity of late Cold War politics in the Indochinese peninsula. Far from being a simple "hot spot" between East and West, the Cambodian situation combined regional rivalries, Sino-Russian competition, postcolonial influence, and the fallout from the Indochinese wars since the 1940s. The Thai military had overall control of all refugee camps, but they surrendered management to competing Cambodian armed factions opposed to the Vietnamese. The Royalist FUNCINPEC party, the Khmer People's National Liberation Front, and the Khmer Rouge ruled parts or entire various camps (site B, Site 2, Site 8 respectively), while the Thai Task Force 80 governed access to these sites.[9] The Cambodian parties present at the border eventually formed the Coalition Government of Democratic Kampuchea in 1982 under the leadership of Prince Norodom Sihanouk. The Khmer Rouge under

Khieu Samphan, the foreign secretary of the coalition, remained in control of the UN representation for Kampuchea and led militarily in the anti-Vietnamese guerrilla resistance. For their American, Chinese, and Thai backers, these camps created leverage against the Soviet-backed Vietnamese. A covert war ensued throughout the 1980s during which the Vietnamese controlled the ground over the dry season while their foes were most active in the rainy season. Following the Vietnamese offensive of 1984, most of the camps were regrouped on the edge of the border zone of Thailand. The end of the Cold War removed some of the international actors but did not end the ideological divides within Cambodia or the regional tensions around it.

After many false starts, the international political process ending war in Cambodia was formally agreed in Paris on October 23, 1991. It ended both a civil war of twenty years and a thirteen-years-long war with Vietnam. Deliberately ambiguous, the peace process gave precedence to national reconstruction over the resolution of all conflicts or retribution for the unspeakable crimes of the 1970s.[10] In practice, this "peace" remained fragile until the Khmer Rouge weakened. On losing Chinese support in 1992, the Khmer Rouge retired to their forest hideouts once again and withdrew from formal politics to resume guerrilla warfare. Claiming to be a government in waiting in 1994, the Khmer Rouge were by then harassed by governmental forces and proved unable to resume full-scale warfare. In 1996 the so-called "win–win" offer from Prime Minister Hun Sen led to the defection of most of the remaining combatants, the split of the movement, the death of Pol Pot, the surrender of Khieu Samphan in 1998, and the arrest of Ta Mok in 1999.[11]

The 1991 accord also formally ended all humanitarian work at the border of Thailand. Relief INGOs that had grown dramatically over the period, for instance, Médecins Sans Frontières (MSF),[12] relocated to mainland Cambodia. This shift profited NGOs focusing on wider development issues rather than emergency relief work. UNBRO folded gradually into the UN-controlled authority. Sergio Vieira de Mello masterminded its final mission and transformed its mandate in March 1992.[13]

Accessing Human Rights: The Politics of Protection

Over the border camps period, from 1979 until 1991, humanitarians working with displaced people and refugees reframed their practice in relation to protection needs and human rights issues. Humanitarians on the border were addressing the needs of people at a juncture when most world refugees were fleeing communist oppression. Human rights issues were clearly underpinning the political understanding of this oppression. The concern with the delivery of practical relief and the need to offer protection to displaced people and refugees merged with a general sense that these guaranteed also the protection of human rights.[14] In practice humanitarians were increasingly managing a growing range of needs. Binding both ideology and practice, humanitarian protection became an overarching concept. The concept of protection in humanitarian aid had evolved dramatically since its first uses. Originally it denoted access to the bare wherewithal of survival – what Agamben calls bare life.[15] Manuals on protection from the 1940s referred to the basic human needs of water, food, and shelter.[16] At the Cambodian border the concept of protection remained in the first instance attached to providing very basic needs.

For humanitarians the notion of protection then developed empirically in relation to two specific aspects of the border: physical protection from structural camp violence inflicted by Khmer and Thai armed groups and protection from brutal "refoulement" or undesired repatriation.[17] All three dimensions of protection responded to abuses of "basic human rights" which humanitarians observed and reported on from 1975 onwards.

The arrival of refugees from 1975 onwards was limited to a handful of usually educated individuals who could communicate with the media some of the atrocities ongoing in Kampuchea.[18] Despite their repeated testimonials, European and American media kept on asking what had been going on in Cambodia since the evacuation of Phnom Penh by the Khmer Rouge. Until 1977 much debates between the left and right rested on the validity of refugees' testimonials.[19] The debate ended with the sudden collapse of Khmer Rouge control and the advance of Vietnamese forces when new arrivals in 1979 bore witness to extraordinary sufferings.

In 1979 the bulk of the refugees were fleeing the invasion and war rather than the Khmer Rouge dictatorship. The catastrophic situation at the border was thus not a direct result of genocide but the product of a different type of "red" terror. Throughout the 1980s the flow of refugees fleeing the Vietnamese occupation never ceased. This perspective from Thailand was strongly framed by anti-communist rhetoric. Yet some of the earliest Cambodian refugees, mostly ethnic Chinese, were encamped in communist Vietnam or Laos and awaited there for their visas for resettlement to the United States or France for much of the 1980s.

Throughout the 1980s the Royal Thai Government reluctantly tolerated such a large a potentially hostile crowd on its land – itself largely populated with ethnic Khmers. In the early days, it occasionally attempted to push them back whence they came. Humanitarians were thus weary of the host and their understanding of protection as against brutal repatriation was grounded in facts.[20] The most significant act of brutality on the part of the RTG in June 1979 was the forced repatriation of freshly arrived Khmers originally hosted in the Nong Chan camp. The Thai authorities pushed back through the Dangrek Mountain some forty-five thousand refugees. The crowds were sent straight in the direction of minefields surrounding the passage of Preah Vihear. Much like during the Khmer Rouge genocide itself, Cham and ethnic Chinese were apparently singled out, pushed first, and left to die when they detonated anti-personnel mines.[21] The events were reported by UNHCR and known at the border but remained largely silenced in the press. Only since 2010 has the Cambodian diaspora started commemorating the events and attempting a class action against Thailand at the International Criminal Court.[22]

Beyond the permanent risk that Thai authorities might change their attitude toward Cambodians, humanitarian workers in camps were also cognizant of the violence that armed bands, the notoriously brutal Task Force 80 and Cambodian political groups, inflicted on civilians in the camps. Though humanitarians had to leave at 4 pm for curfew, they heard on the grapevine tales of night-time terror. Despite these known and suspected atrocities, the official line was one of collaboration and cooperation with the Thai armed forces and the Cambodian authorities in exile.

Within this uneasy setting, UNBRO and the UN defined the purpose and meaning of humanitarian action. They structured humanitarian work by coordinating their INGO partners according to their core mission. At the border, the most active partners were the American Refugee Committee, the Christian and Missionary Alliance church (CAMA), the Catholic Relief Services (CRS), the Japan International Volunteer Centre (JVC), Operation Handicap International (later Handicap International, HI), Concern, Youth With a Mission (YWAM), IRC, Japan Sotoshu Relief Committee (JSRC), and ZOA refugee care from the Netherlands. MSF grew from being a partner in medical provisions to dominating the medical landscape and being in charge of referent hospital provisions. A number of other providers including the order of Malta resumed their traditional role in looking after lepers and, occasionally, lunatic asylums.[23]

Beyond "bare life" necessities, humanitarians sought to develop their roles and expand their protection in order to meet human rights needs. In particular, humanitarians developed educational provisions which met the rights of children that were themselves being refined in the 1980s. From the early 1980s, they developed educational premises suitable for a largely illiterate population. UNBRO's mandate was officially extended in 1984 to encompass new definitions of protection that took into account these needs (resolution 34/22).[24] By 1988, UNBRO delivered primary education for 61,748 primary school children.[25] Primary education was defined as a human right since 1959[26] but the 1980s were a key period in the development of the legal status of children, embodied in the 1989 UN declaration. As the border camps had a very high birth rate, many refugees in camps were born refugees. To address their needs, many NGOs volunteered their services such as Écoles sans Frontières. Yet in this crucial role UNBRO decided to manage alone. UNBRO devised a new Western style curriculum inspired by the French colonial precedent (though UNBRO replaced French with English as the main foreign language of instruction). Despite these efforts, the provisions of education in the camps failed to match those of the Vietnamese PRK regime according to UNICEF's own assessment. By 1987, the UN thus indirectly admitted its inability to meet the basic rights of children.

To its critiques, humanitarian protection and its provision of basic services to refugees failed to meet a more emancipatory understanding of human rights. In educational terms many commentators criticized UNBRO for its heavy-handed neocolonial attitudes to Cambodian culture:

With an appropriate Khmer-oriented educational vision, some of these western methods may help foster community and other indigenous, self-help forms of empowerment, but they also run the risk of promoting western patterns of behaviour (individualism, mindless consumerism, secularism, materialism) that would again act as solvents on Khmer culture and society.[27]

Critics of the modernizing agenda of INGOs in camps highlighted the significance of the arts for not only the survival of Khmer culture in the new diasporic communities but also for the survival of a sense of self: "He emphasized the importance of Khmer children learning artistic skills (creative writing, drawing, singing, dancing, acting) through which they can express, and thereby cathartically release, their inner, and cultural struggle to regain identity or, as he put it, 'to know themselves'."[28]

Expanding the remit of humanitarian aid to fulfill rights, restore cultural identity, and fulfill entitlements demanded the endless broadening of focus and an increasingly vast project going well beyond the provision of basic refugee rights. JSRC, ZOA, and IRC under UNBRO developed protection in the general direction of social care issues. During the 1980s, Japanese and EEC funding increasingly went to projects intending to relieve more than the physical needs of the refugees. Humanitarians were defining a rights-based response which transcended the emergency relief work they had originally been contracted for. They promoted notably higher-level education responses in an effort to make camps and their population self-reliant. This went beyond the established rights of refugees but was line with the wider remit if the 1980s definitions of children's rights. Ironically, as the protagonists of one of Rithy Panh's documentary "The Tan family" complained, they neglected agricultural training so necessary after repatriation: "I am a child of the camps. I have never done this [agricultural work] and I am afraid ... I do not have a job, I have only ever studied medicine."[29] Humanitarian protection addressing the needs of the soul, mind, and body found its justification in terms of health benefits. But the evidence provided from the camps soon framed a much more disturbing discourse on the sociocultural needs and required correctives to the malfunction of a traumatized and post-totalitarian society.

Cambodians were presented as broken and post-traumatized. Following the genocide of 1975–1979, Cambodians were often compared with the victims of concentration camps of the Nazi period. Much science developed to address the needs of Holocaust survivors was deployed in relation to Cambodians.[30] Ironically of course, most, if not all, refugees had fled not the killing fields of the 1970s but the food shortages and political violence of the Vietnamese occupation. Unable to distinguish between different causalities, much of this science addressed thus not the trauma of genocide but the ensuing trauma of humanitarian relief camps. Some of the science that humanitarians enabled, sometimes very reluctantly, sat on the boundaries between exploitation and problem solving.[31] A key focus was on the development of children, many of whom were born in a prison-like environment.[32] Site 2 and Khao I Dang enabled longitudinal studies of group psychology and the study of adolescent responses to stress.[33] American specialists such as Richard Mollica were at the forefront of this experimental engagement with refugees in camps. On the one hand, Richard Retchman and Didier Fassin argued,[34] this episode was part of a wider shift in the development of victim-based approaches to trauma and the rise of post-traumatic stress disorder (PTSD) as an umbrella term.[35] Retchman, himself one of the main critics of PTSD in France, worked clinically with Cambodian refugees resettled in France.[36] This emphasis on PTSD later impacted on the proceedings of the justice process devised to "heal" the genocide. As the anthropologist Anne Yvonne Guillou puts it:

many narratives of the Tribunal have focused on the "healing" of the victims as its most important role, as if post-genocide justice were foremost a matter of health. By doing so, the accounts given in many areas of the Tribunal have tended to impose an overall pattern of what social suffering should be and how it should be expressed and relieved, by using the idioms of "trauma" and "post-traumatic stress disorder" as their only models.[37]

The paradox of all these well-intentioned studies remains the lack of agency of the refugees themselves or the definition of their rights in a very abstract manner. The "humanitarian research" agendas were designed to address wider socioeconomic questions and sought to address actual needs and rights of refugees in camps or following repatriation, but they often seemed to have been an imposition on camp dwellers. Nevertheless, through this research, humanitarians maintained the needs of refugees in focus at a time when UNBRO and humanitarians needed the oxygen of publicity. By the late 1980s, private funding had gradually dried out precisely as humanitarian work had become more complex.

Witnessing Human Rights in and out of Cambodia

Humanitarian access was always conditional on either the specifics of the border refugee regimes or the close control of the Vietnamese regime and this conditional access framed how "political" or vocal humanitarian organizations could be. On the rumor of famines which alone might have explained the constant flow of refugees from Cambodia, French humanitarians mobilized in 1979 to denounce a new genocide separate from the Khmer Rouge genocide. In a momentous public debate on French national television, the missionary priest François Ponchaud denounced a new "subtle" genocide while MSF president Dr. Claude Malhuret described the continuation of the genocide by other means.[38] Despite the flow of migrants, the fear of a major famine in Cambodia proved unfounded.[39] In a publicity stunt and in the hope of gaining access to mainland Cambodia, humanitarians at the border gathered in a symbolic march for Cambodia. As Eleanor Davey has shown, the "march for Cambodia" in 1980, which featured Joan Baez and French anti-communist *nouveaux philosophes*, represented a watershed in the shift toward hard anti-communist humanitarianism.[40] What the marchers demanded – and did not obtain – was the opening of the border to their relief convoy and the right to intervene in occupied Cambodia.

If those at the border claimed their political integrity against Soviet oppression, they opposed those who had made the choice of collaborating with the occupiers of Cambodia. In the French humanitarian context, this split had brought medical practitioners who were closer to the French communists, the *comité français d'aide médicale et sanitaire à la population Cambodgienne* led by Dr. Jean-Yves Follézou[41] to join forces with Soviet,

Polish, and East German humanitarian aid. This socialist humanitarian effort had begun to arrive immediately after the Vietnamese invasion.[42] The French communists claimed the backing of Secours Catholique as well as the communist French NGO Secours Populaire Français.[43] Socialist humanitarians, including Warsaw pact state-sponsored efforts, unlike their conservative opponents were landing medical supplies directly in Phnom Penh in the name of solidarity. Among the British NGOs, Oxfam also took the view that to stand with the regime of Heng Samrin (led from 1985 by Hun Sen) was to stand with the real opponents to the genocide and was thus grounded in rights-based politics. This stance became the moral justification of the regime and of its identity. This of course brushes aside the fact that the entire pro-Vietnamese leadership originated from a split within the Khmer Rouge and that its leaders had only defected when the regime had launched major purges.

While the main events of the refugee crisis were the years 1979–1983, the actual end of the camps became a debated issue from 1989. With the fall of the Berlin wall and the end of military support from the Soviet Union, the Vietnamese army withdrew from Cambodia leaving Hun Sen to manage his own affairs. By that stage Hun Sen had self-educated in international relations largely through his frequent encounters with UN and NGO deputations.[44] The camps themselves remained an object of contention until the final Paris agreement and mass repatriation in 1992.[45] Ironically, the peace talk years were also the period during which competing Cambodian political groups remilitarized in order to guarantee their presence in "democratic" Cambodia. As the end of the border camps became more likely, humanitarians begun to express more vocally their repulsion at being manipulated.[46] Since 1982, UNBRO relied on the financial expediency of Cold War great games as well as on the continued support of the United States, Japan, France, and Thailand. The end of the Cold War freed critiques of international humanitarian work within and on the border of Cambodia.

In 1989, the thirteen INGOs operating in Site 2 denounced American-backed military rearmament of Sihanouk's nationalists partisans.[47] Paradoxically, the Vietnamese withdrawal and the prospect of peace also reopened the prospect of the Khmer Rouge's return and the possibility of a new genocide.[48] As Hun Sen's army ceded territory to the west of the country, the Khmer Rouge regained military control over many mountainous areas – including much of the border zone. In effect, the Paris Accord signified the return of the Khmer Rouge in Phnom Penh through a broad coalition of all political forces.[49] To mitigate this risk, the UN set up a transitional authority in 1992, led by the Japanese Yasushi Akashi, and staffed its largest military and policing deployment to date with a peacekeeping force of some 18,000 under Australian command.[50] Nevertheless NGO workers and international observers vociferously denounced the risk taken by allowing the unrepentant Khmer Rouge back.[51]

By 1993, Cambodia's recent history had been entirely rewritten in the light of the genocide and through a historical comparison with the Holocaust/Shoah. From the writings of François Ponchaud[52] to the march for Cambodia, the concept of genocide and systematic abuse of human rights had been applied to both the Khmer Rouge and their opponents. The initial shock of the revelation of the Khmer Rouge atrocities was constantly reinvented through documentaries and cinema – most significant in the 1980s was the 1984 film *The Killing Fields* and its main character, the photojournalist Dith Pran, himself a genocide survivor.[53] Even naïve humanitarians working at the border could not ignore the serpent in their nest. By August 1990 more than 120 humanitarian workers from the border camps signed a petition against any peace treaty with the Khmer Rouge.[54] Even as their role was about to end, humanitarians at the border used their cultural capital as witnesses to lobby on the nature and outcome of the Cambodian peace process. Major actors in the international response such as ICRC and UNHCR were unwilling to deal with the Khmer Rouge but remained silent.[55] Others, such as MSF denounced the political situation they were part of while they also denounced the Vietnamese puppet state which refugees continued to flee throughout the 1980s.

But the INGO which had most explicitly taken a side was Oxfam. Since 1979 Oxfam had chosen to engage with the food-based protection of Cambodians under Vietnamese control, distributing, despite some considerable political and logistical difficulties, food, bright fabrics which could challenge the ubiquitous black pajamas of the Khmer Rouge and nets which might restore the Khmer fishing industry.[56] In many ways true to their development ideals, Oxfam, which had raised much of its funding on the ultimately inaccurate portrayal of a famine in Cambodia in 1979–1980, sought to provide the essential means of reconstructing Cambodian society.[57]

This insider position entailed a systematic rejection of humanitarian protection through camps. Tony Jackson, who acted as an "independent member" of a World Food Programme evaluation mission in 1987, did not mince his words in his report, "Just Waiting to Die?":

It should be emphasized that the very efficient delivery by UNBRO of relief items, and the good technical work by the NGOs is not in question. Rather the overall result of the effort, particularly the support it gives to a resistance movement dominated by the Khmer Rouge and the hopeless future it creates for the people in the camps are the major concern in this report.[58]

Jackson went on to describe the absence of rights and protection affecting even the largest UNBRO camps[59] pointing out that the Thai authorities having not signed the international treaties on refugees made no difference between immigrants, migrants, aliens, and refugees. If their rights were unclear, their entitlement was much more clearly defined and, by the time Jackson visited in 1986, the quality of food supply and even health provisions at the border exceeded that in Cambodia itself – with the border camps being the best resourced refugee settlements in the world at that time:

where the voluntary agencies have fallen down is not on the technical side of their work, but on another aspect where we pride ourselves of being strong – in serving as a voice for the people for whom we are working. If ever a group needed a voice, someone to speak up for them, it is the Khmers in the border camps. However the agencies have been effectively muzzled by their close association with UNBRO.[60]

Oxfam policy leaders concluded that the rights of Cambodians could not be served by the political recognition of the coalition government. From 1979 it convened a Consortium for Cambodia which included thirty-three NGOs working within the country including Oxfam, Catholic Relief Services, and the Lutheran World Federation, which also represented the World Council of Churches.[61]

From 1988 it set out to broaden this group into an international forum which met in Brussels and London and which purposed to gather all NGOs working in the camps and Cambodia. Though it never quite managed this feat, it nevertheless represented sixty-seven international NGOs in 1990 and eighty-seven by 1991, when it became more formalized. Its range extended from Socialist Solidarity to Caritas, Christian Aid, Lutheran World Service, and a range of faith-based organizations across Asia, Europe, and North America. Oxfam Belgium and United Kingdom convened in the late 1980s and were joined by Christian Aid in 1991.[62] MSF was part of the forum but also conducted other human rights initiatives through its anti-communist offshoot Liberté sans Frontières.[63]

By the late 1980s, humanitarians on both sides of the border joined forces to claim for themselves the legitimacy of human rights guardians. In 1989, MSF and Médecins du Monde issued a joint call which stressed the importance of their volunteers as "our teams are on the ground. They have the support of public opinion and international organizations, our volunteers will act as the sentinels of human rights."[64]

Rebuilding Cambodia on Human Rights

This focus on human rights led to stark political choices. The NGO sector as a whole chose to align itself with one faction of the Paris negotiations. The forum and its members thus ended up backing unequivocally the Hun Sen government in Phnom Penh which many of them had denounced a decade earlier as genocidal in its own right. Party to the politics of the peace process, the NGO forum sought legal advice on its potential role in the peace negotiation and decided, on the advice of Tony Jackson of Oxfam, to focus its activities on the Khmer Rouge presence as seat holders at the United Nations and to ask specifically for the "non-involvement of the Khmer Rouge at the UN."[65] On November 6, 1989 Oxfam and the International Council of Voluntary agencies, who represented eighty-five NGOs, called for the Khmer Rouge to desist from the United Nations. Meanwhile, in 1989, the forum hired the British diplomat John Pedler as its diplomatic advisor, later replaced by the Belgian consultant Raoul Jennar in 1990.[66] Jennar's brief was to lobby on human rights ground all twelve states of the European Economic Community (EEC) and the Scandinavian states to convince them to withdraw support from the Sihanouk coalition and to divert their funding toward the reconstruction of Cambodia.[67] Jennar served as an expert witness on Cambodia to parliaments in Europe and to the US Senate on the Khmer Rouge threat.[68] Area studies academics added their own spin on the "new Khmer Rouge" threat.[69] INGOs which had grown dramatically in setting up national branches used their franchises to lobby locally. The Quaker United Nations Office lobbied for the forum at the UN.[70]

On the face of it, INGOs failed to win the initial battle. The Khmer Rouge remained part of the Accords and were only sidelined later by the combined efforts of Sihanouk and Hun Sen. Though briefly part of the transitional Conseil National Suprême, they were now without further political use for their allies. Consequently, the genocidal political party was targeted by sanctions through Resolution 792 in the United Nations on November 30, 1992. On April 13, 1993, the Khmer Rouge fled to Phnom Malai, to resume life in the bush regrouping around their military headquarters of 1985.

If the human rights diplomatic lobbying had failed to win outright, it nevertheless set INGOs in what they thought was their natural position: as the rebuilders of Cambodia and guardians of human rights. The NGO forum set itself out as a partner and match to UN presence in Cambodia and sought to coordinate and shape humanitarian provisions in the new Cambodia.[71] In February 1993, the INGOs issued a common declaration calling for sustained UN effort and for the exclusion of all active Khmer

Rouges (but not repentant Khmer Rouges).[72] A rush to rebuild, reshape, mend, and heal flooded Cambodia with NGOs. A whole district of Phnom Penh became known as "NGOland." This unprecedented rush brought together the NGOs of the border and the ones who had long collaborated with the Hun Sen administration.[73] On the one hand, the forum set up in Cambodia represented the coming of age of a humanitarian system, while on the other it made unsustainable claims for humanitarians to contribute to development while guaranteeing the most extensive understanding of protection and the guarantee of formal human rights for the "voiceless people" of Cambodia. Courted by the Hun Sen government, NGOs became associates in a "democratic project" arising from an uneasy compromise and much silence on genocide.[74]

Between 1992 and 2015, NGOs developed and invested every aspect of Cambodian life and developed in Cambodia new rights-based approaches to their practice which referred explicitly to the need to expand local understandings of human rights. Oxfam thus trialed gender mainstreaming in Cambodia in the 1990s. MSF, MdM, and other medical NGOs developed programs which sometimes combined high-level training and basic primary health care. Primary health care provisions were, in the spirit of the Alma Ata declaration, fulfilling a fundamental human right.[75] Yet even as INGOs experimented new fields of intervention or as new NGOs were set up by backpackers to address specific inequalities or human rights issues, the political narratives of Cambodia had become more focused on sovereignty issues.

Ever since 1992, the internal politics of Cambodia have been characterized by their constant return to the events of the late 1970s. Throughout that era Hun Sen, the champion of the leading NGOs, outmaneuvered all his political opponents and, arguably, his international supporters too. Hun Sen had to demonstrate, over and over, his independence from foreign interventions. Arrived as the man of the Vietnamese, he had to strike a diffident position toward meddling foreigners. Calling for US reparations for the secret war of the 1970s, chastising unprofessional volunteering organizations or anyone paying too much notice of land grabs or corruption, Hun Sen proved to be a difficult partner for his advocates of yesteryear, particularly if they claimed to defend human rights.[76]

On July 13, 2015, Hun Sen's government passed a new law on associations and NGOs[77] which effectively ended thirty years of free for all interventionism. The law "had a severe chilling effect on Cambodian civil society," according to Chak Sopheap of the Cambodian Centre for human rights cited by the *Cambodia Daily Newspaper*, shut down since by the government in September 2017.[78] The result has been that humanitarians have returned to the grind of their immediate objectives, favoring protection duties over more abstract needs and leaving human rights activists vulnerable to the increasingly illiberal policies of a regime backed by Chinese investments. A fine example of this can be found in 2009 when Hun Sen's regime reflected on its own priorities in relation to human rights and thus decided to forcibly repatriate Uighur refugees to China.[79] There was no Year 0 for a humanitarian and human rights Cambodia. Cambodian politicians had other priorities.

Conclusion

The boundaries between short-term immediacy around needs-based protection, and long-term principles of human rights were constantly blurred.[80] The shift that humanitarians embraced logically was to set themselves as the protectors of the rights of camp refugees, uphold their human rights, and campaign for a new Cambodia free of the Khmer Rouge. Since the latter were holding the UN seat and formed the main plank of the anti-Vietnamese coalition funded by China, the United States and its allies, this emphasis on human rights led key humanitarian organizations to take sides in internal Cambodian politics and support the Hun Sen government in the Paris Accords and political settlement of the early 1990s. From humanitarian practices – often at the bedside and through complex cultural encounters – a situation of permanent emergency had allowed the maturing of humanitarian concerns into broader and longer-term objectives. The humanitarians of the emergency days of 1979 could develop their goals toward developmentalist objectives first under the guise of humanitarian protection and later as rights-based practice. In mobilizing they reached new degrees of political militancy and arguably enlisted themselves in political projects over which they had little control.[81]

Arguably, this also corresponds to a period of profound hubris for humanitarian organizations, which were courted by a cunning political regime to provide them with legitimacy, expertise, and resources.[82] The human right agenda underpinned the humanitarian agenda for Cambodia while encouraging NGOs to claim Cambodia as *their* model project for post-genocide and post-trauma reconstruction. Cambodians themselves had different notions of what a world put right might entail – it included the past, ghosts, and spirits whose deranging presence haunts the landscape. As the psychoanalyst Rechtman points out, the rights of the survivors of genocide were not fulfilled by the granting of formal human rights – they had to include the dead for whom no healing process based on rights could exist.[83] The genocide was not so easily corrected[84] and in the granting of humanitarian relief, UN warranted security might not bring real peace.[85]

The absence of boundaries between human rights political campaigning and humanitarian practices appear with hindsight a strategic mistake. One could argue that the Hun Sen regime managed very well its relationship with the NGO sector by playing up the risk presented by the Khmer Rouge while allowing delivery NGOs to become guarantors of its human right legitimacy. Ironically, as Caroline Hughes argues, the formalistic demands of human rights NGOs may have stunted the growth of "civil society" in favor of an increasingly autocratic regime better equipped to meet the KPI of international norms.[86]

Twenty years hence, the Cambodian government (once considered a developmental model for the World Bank) is repressing and containing the activities of NGOs, even the least politically motivated. Hun Sen's regime seems indifferent to being regularly accused of violating human rights.[87] The coalition between politicians and international NGOs has outlived its initial political usefulness. Cambodia has embraced economic reforms which set it on a course for Chinese-funded economic development. This is a model of development in which neither humanitarian nor human right agendas feature highly. In July 2018, Hun Sen could thus declare without any sense of irony his belief in democracy and human rights as his party won every seat available in parliament: "People showed great will in exercising their rights to vote for any political party they liked freely without pressure or coercion."[88]

Conclusion
Practices of Humanity

Michael N. Barnett

How to distinguish human rights from humanitarianism? The standard method is to consult an authoritative source, such as a dictionary, high-profile rights and relief agencies, and classic texts in the field, and inventory the differences. For instance, the *Oxford English Dictionary* defines human rights as "rights possessed by humans; spec. the set of entitlements held to belong to every person as a condition of being human; (in sing.) an entitlement of this kind."[1] In contrast, humanitarianism is defined as "concern for human welfare as a primary or preeminent moral good; action, or the disposition to act, on the basis of this concern rather than for pragmatic or strategic reasons".[2] Amnesty International defines human rights as basic rights and freedoms that all people are entitled to regardless of nationality, sex, national or ethnic origin, race, religion, language, or other status. The ICRC and other medical aid organizations often refer to humanitarianism as the independent, neutral, and impartial provision of relief to victims of humanly made and natural disasters. According to one classic text on human rights, rights are entitlements that are natural (every human has them), equal (all humans have the same rights), and universal (applicable anywhere and everywhere).[3] Various articles and book on humanitarianism refer to the attempt to save lives of distant strangers that are *in extremis*.[4]

Yet dictionary entries, mission statements, and scholastic nominalism are acts of stipulation – human rights and humanitarianism are what we say they are – and fail in two important ways, as evidenced by the contributions to this volume. First, they border if not cross over the line into essentialism. Essentialism "consists in the identification of kinds by singling out some relevant property (or set of properties) that are possessed by all and only those [units] that belong to that kind."[5] For instance: humanitarianism is about saving lives, and human rights flourishing lives; humanitarianism is about charity, and human rights justice; humanitarianism is about addressing harms, and human rights reducing status inequalities. Such discussions often include a consideration of the characteristics the kind *cannot* possess. Many in the human rights community will challenge the credentials of those human rights organizations that favor group over individual rights. Samuel Moyn discusses the humanitarianization of human rights, questioning whether it is hollowing out human rights. Many in the humanitarian community insist that to be a humanitarian requires having the right motives – it is not enough to save lives, it also requires selflessness.

A second problem is that human rights and humanitarianism, like all social kinds, are not homogenous but rather heterogenous. A cursory reading of the writings on humanitarianism and human rights immediately reveals considerable variation in each community, which accounts for the contestation of the characteristics and boundaries of the field. Moreover, what is being contested can itself change historically; core debates over the constitution of human rights and humanitarianism have altered over the decades. This ongoing, evolving contestation reinforces the claim that both human rights and humanitarianism can have different and disputed meanings. The human rights and the humanitarianism of today look quite different from their predecessors of the previous century.

The tendency toward essentialism and failure to recognize diversity and contestation within each kind underscores the necessity of treating human rights and humanitarianism as the social constructions that they are. Social construction is a thicket of a process – produced by structure and agency, interests and ethics, practices, power and principle, history, and contingency and experimentation. Socially construction means denaturalizing something that appears quite natural, recognizing that things exist not because of genetics but rather because of human agreement. The agreement might be so powerful that it becomes taken-for-granted, at which point it becomes a social fact. But there is a difference between essential and enduring characteristics. To claim something is essential to a kind is to insist that the kind will cease to be a kind if it no longer has that characteristic. In doing so, it tends to treat a social kind as if it is a natural kind. But to claim that something is enduring to a kind is to recognize that what groups might believe is core can, in fact, change historically. For instance, elsewhere I have argued that some of the core members of the humanitarian community, including the ICRC, get their history wrong: they have insisted that humanitarianism has always been the impartial, independent, and neutral provision of life-saving relief to distant strangers, when, in fact, this is a bit of myth-making as it overlooks a near century of humanitarianism, defined quite differently by the participants and that existed prior to the establishment of the ICRC.[6] Enduring suggests a resilience because it fended off alternative views, interpretations, and meanings. But such endurance should not obscure a history of contestation. Even during periods in which meanings appear to be settled there are nonconformists. And then there are periods that are considerably unsettled, such as the current one.

What follows is not a search for their core and contrasting differences or an inventory of the forces that have shaped human rights, humanitarianism, and their relationship. Instead, it uses a practice perspective to consider the critical points of contrast between the two since the 1990s when scholars and practitioners began exploring their relationship.[7] Human rights and humanitarianism are practical activities. They are intended to achieve concrete results that improve the lives of vulnerable populations. It is not only practitioners that use the language of practices, but also scholars. There is an expansive literature on the concept of practices, it is well represented in the literature of human rights and humanitarianism, with important contributions from several of those in this volume.[8] Not surprisingly, there is neither a common definition nor agreement on the conceptual elements of practice or how human rights and humanitarian practices relate. My effort to do so consists of decomposing practices into four elements: the problem to be solved; the material and mental technologies that are viewed as most appropriate to address the problem; the background knowledge that subtly guides action and forecloses options; and meanings. These elements provide critical points of comparison for scholars and practitioners between human rights and humanitarianism. And to the extent that practitioners believed such differences must be maintained, they become posts for creating a border between the two.

Before launching into how a practice perspective can capture differences and distinctions between the two, I want to qualify my remarks in several ways.[9] First, I offer stylized comparisons of human rights and humanitarianism along these four dimensions, and in doing so potentially reify the very elements that are contested and in flux. Second, although I treat these four elements as analytically distinct, the chapters underscore their connections and co-constitution. For instance, Swaine and Taithe argue that the kind of suffering to be addressed can shape what counts as competent technologies and background knowledge; and the technologies and background knowledge can affect the definition of the problem to be solved and what kinds of suffering gets attention. Third, the chapters suggest how human rights and humanitarianism affected each other, including how each adopted characteristics of the other. Fourth, while human rights and humanitarianism are increasingly connected, my observation is humanitarianism was more vulnerable to human rights than the reverse, for reasons I suggested in the Introduction. The simplest piece of evidence of this unequal vulnerability is that the humanitarian field appeared to be much more concerned than the human rights field with drawing boundaries between the two.

Fifth, while the chapters examine differences, comparisons, and boundaries at the macro, meso, and micro levels, the following discussion focuses on the former two. The macro level concerns the conceptual underpinnings, principles, and broad self-understandings that define the community. Many of the chapters operate at this level, both histori-cally and philosophically. The meso level regards the formal and informal institutions that are places where discussions about the field occur; rules are created, diffused, and enforced; and boundaries are created between one field and another. Within each field many of these institutions are intersecting and overlapping, and thus are both creatures and effects of networks. The practice literature tends to operate with the concept of community of practice to capture this institutional dimension.[10] The micro level concerns local, historically situated, and culturally embedded actors who understand the boundaries between the two. As Feldman's chapter demonstrates, working at the micro level can help recover how these meanings and practices associated with each category can interpel-late and produce categories such as "humanitarian rights."

Feldman's chapter also does something that is critical but largely neglected in most volumes (including this one) on human rights and humanitarianism – the view from recipients. Including their views is important for reasons of politics and theory. Human rights and humani-tarian scholarship can silence and exclude those who are supposed to benefit from these interventions. In doing so, it turns the suffering objects of concern into passive actors that are denied agency, or at least makes invisible their agency. They can do nothing more than suffer in silence (and if they choose to make noise, then possibly become unworthy of compassion). Ignoring the recipients also means failing to include how they also imagine the relationship between humanitarianism and human rights, their vernacularization, whether they view them as differences without a distinction, and how they can strategically choose which dis-course makes most sense to them.[11]

The Problem of Suffering

When does suffering become a problem? Sometimes it doesn't. In fact, a reasonable observation is that most of the people most of the time do not register the suffering of others. Martha Nussbaum cites three, almost necessary, conditions that are required to spur action: the suffering is serious and not trivial, the person did not deserve to suffer, and there exists an emotional identification between the observer and the sufferer.[12]

But which suffering? Humanitarianism and human rights are offering alternative claims regarding what kind of suffering is a "problem": the former is organized around the needs that threaten physical survival, and the latter around the violation of rights that affect individual wellbeing, autonomy, and the ability and capabilities to choose how to live a full and flourishing life.[13]

"Needs" refers not to anything and everything individuals claim to require, but rather, inputs that are deemed (objectively) essential to the propagation of life itself.[14] Food, shelter, clothing, medicine, clean water, and sanitation are essential for "bare life" and are fundamental for a "regime of life."[15] Yet not all unfulfilled needs fall into the box of humanitarianism. Instead, humanitarianism focuses on "emergencies" that threaten mass suffering and death.[16] Emergencies can be caused by either natural or humanly made forces (even though there is widespread recognition that there are humanly made reasons for why some populations are more vulnerable than others to natural causes). "Natural" disasters are often likened to "acts of God." Violence and conflict are the most common cause of humanly made disasters. In either case, though, these are emergencies because time lost means lives lost.

Rights, on the other hand, refer to the entitlements that individuals purportedly possess that foster their freedom and flourishing.[17] In contrast to the handful of needs identified by humanitarianism, discussions of rights and entitlements can be wide-ranging.[18] There are rights that derive from natural and positive law. There are negative and positive rights. Some rights are seen as "basic" because, without them, other rights cannot exist. The Universal Declaration of Human Rights includes dozens of rights, and the subsequent decades have added new generations of rights that often become attached to specific populations. There are political, civil, cultural, religious, economic, and social rights that can be claimed by minorities, refugees, women, children, prisoners disabled, aged, and other categories of people. This rich tapestry of rights, though, serves a basic function: to help individuals preserve their freedom and protect them from tyranny, oppression, and unwanted interference; to allow them to express their opinions, beliefs, and views without fear; and to create the space to allow them to live their lives as they see fit and to pursue their flourishing as they define it.

Suffering is not objectively "out there" but rather must incite, be recognizable, and be meaningful. The concept of framing is often invoked at such moments to capture the social organization of reality. Frames "are specific metaphors, symbolic representations, and cognitive cues used to render or cast behavior and events in an evaluative mode and to suggest alternative modes of action."[19] Frames shape how actors situate and fix meaning to events, understand that there is a problem and how that problem connects to shared interests and identities; fashion a shared understanding of the world; galvanize sentiments as a way to mobilize and guide social action; and suggest possible and appropriate resolutions to current plights. Different frames, therefore, will have different kinds of effects.

The chapters suggest how humanitarianism and human rights have alternative frames of suffering.[20] These frames share the goal of mobilizing action and often implicitly suggest that a little compassion can be the difference between life and death. But they nevertheless rest on different evaluative, prescriptive, and normative foundations. The frame of humanitarianism casts the suffering as part of an emergency that demands immediate action; tends to mobilize action on the basis of sentiments and pity; demands that action be defined by principles of neutrality, impartiality, and independence; and limits action to the immediate symptoms of suffering.[21] In contrast, human rights frames elevate the obligations of the state to protect and respect basic rights; advance principles of nondiscrimination justified on the basis of universalism; demand that the state and other political authorities be accountable to victims; look to law to define rights and determine whether rights have been violated; attach suffering to the categories of victims and perpetrators; demand punishment of perpetrators; and seek justice.[22]

Discussions of frames and their potential impact often stress their cultural proximity to existing ways of understanding a problem, but the most effective frames rely not on reason but rather on emotion.[23] We are not expected to think about suffering but instead to feel it. Images of injured, sick, and dead children are expected to be a gut punch and rip out our hearts. Images of prisoners in stress positions and in long-term solitary confinement are intended to trigger outrage, anger, and call for justice. These victims might not be "innocent," but they nevertheless deserve decent treatment. Leebaw discusses the importance of different kinds of shame for understanding why and how individuals are prepared to contribute to human rights and humanitarian action. The West's occasional outpouring of assistance to victims of famine are intended not only to help them but also to make it feel good about itself.[24] Indeed, the desire to care about distant strangers might be driven not by any change in their circumstances but rather because of their need to recover a sense of moral goodness after national shame or disenchantment, as Brown observes in his study of British abolitionism and Keys in her account of the rise of human rights in the United States in the 1970s.[25]

Visual images can be critical to framing processes and framing processes are important to the potential impact of visual images.[26] Mark
Twain gave credit to the "incorruptible" Kodak camera for the international campaign to end the horrors in King Leopold's Congo.[27]
Disinterested and indifferent bystanders can be shaken by the image
of the body of a little boy washed up on a beach or a vulture lingering in
the background as a malnourished girl has collapsed as prey in the
foreground. But whether such images resonant emotionally depends
in part on how they are framed. As Ticktin observes in her chapter,
pictures of suffering people might not produce an emotional reaction
unless they are defined as innocent and undeserving of their fate.[28]
Humanitarian and human rights agencies have learned that such images
can be quite effective, but also costly. Some might be excited or even
aroused by them.[29] Agencies also have become increasingly uncomfortable with commodifying, exploiting, and using images of people's
suffering. At their worst, these images are tantamount to "humanitarian
porn" and snuff films. In response, human rights and humanitarian
agencies have developed norms regarding what kind of images can be
used, how, and when.[30]

Aware of the power of frames, humanitarian and human rights agencies
will compete to frame events so that they mobilize action in their desired
directions. When Doctors without Borders declared soon after the Asian
Tsunami of 2005 that it no longer needed funds because there no longer
was an "emergency" because those who had died were dead and the living
were in little danger of joining them. This message directly undermined
other aid agencies' siren for urgent action, and they countermessaged that
MSF's position was irresponsible and harmful to the survivors. This
competition can represent a sincere difference of opinion or be strategic.
Lester's contribution highlights how the British imperial state self-
consciously adopted the language of humanitarianism – and not human
rights – because it was more consistent with civilizing discourses and
imperial interests. If the suffering of aboriginal populations is
a humanitarian issue, then the solution is to protect them from settlers.
If the suffering, on the other hand, is a matter of human rights, then the
solution is to confer rights, including self-determination. For empires that
aim to maintain their rule, humanitarianism has its obvious advantages.[31]
States also have learned that framing their actions as humanitarian has the
advantage of suggesting that they care while avoiding the necessary political action that might be necessary to end the roots of the conflict that is
causing mass suffering. Humanitarianism serves as a "fig leaf" and real
solutions require switching away from the humanitarian frame to another
that is more political.[32]

How to Solve Suffering: Material and Mental Technologies

The chapters in this volume suggest that human rights and humanitarianism have developed distinct technologies that are related to their goals. Technologies are means to ends. But technologies are not just born from function. They also are deeply sociological. They are produced by a community, and the community will often advance technologies based not only on evidence of effectiveness but also on beliefs about appropriateness. The community also will determine the standards used to determine not only what counts as competent action but also who is competent, which increasingly depends on proper training, accreditation, education, and knowledge. Competent action is more than garden-variety pragmatism – it also requires the proper mindset, attitude, and cultural understanding, combining the cognitive, physical, normative, and even a "state of mind."[33]

The chapters suggest that the human rights community of practice is deeply imprinted by law and the humanitarian community of practice by the medical profession and public health. Law has come to dominate the human rights field.[34] A fair bit of human rights is nonlegal because it concerns outreach and teaching individuals what are their rights. In this activist role, human rights lawyering resembles social justice action and investigative journalism.[35] But law increasingly defines what counts as a human right, what is a human right violation, what evidence is needed to demonstrate the violations of human rights, and how human rights violators should be sanctioned. Law also imprints human rights as it shapes what are the competent methods, skills, and tactics.[36] Human rights activists try to pass and revise laws, litigate, provide legal counseling, and use law to change behavior. Human rights work also "has developed a very specific practice that deploys investigation, exposure, and confrontation to identify and rectify violations of people's human rights. This is the practice of the courtroom taken directly to the war zone."[37] There has developed a field of forensic human rights that combines medical, archeological, and detective skills to recover and exhume bodies, identify victims, and collect evidence to build cases against suspected criminals.[38]

The humanitarian field is shaped by those skills and professions that are best suited to the goal of saving lives, which has meant primarily medicine and public health and secondarily sanitation, water engineering, logistics, and other highly technical fields. Humanitarian medicine has made tremendous strides in treating malnutrition and managing cholera through the invention of new technologies and strategies of intervention.[39] There are more manuals that create minimum standards of care and provide guidance for how to respond to and work in an emergency. The 2016

World Humanitarian Summit showcased technological advances, such as drones and 3D technology, to improve the ability to locate, protect, and assist populations in need.

The different goals of human rights and humanitarianism can lead to different kinds of strategies, tactics, and best practices. Human rights is well known for the tactic of naming and shaming. As Leebaw discusses in her chapter, the hope is that publicizing those who have violated basic rights will cause them a high degree of shame. Central to this tactic, consequently, is making noise.[40] In contrast, the humanitarian community emphasizes "humanitarian diplomacy." Aid actors want immediate access to populations at risk; to that end they must negotiate, including with those who are responsible for the harms being committed against the victims. They must practice quiet diplomacy and adopt a "much less adversarial focus on assessment, appeal, and negotiation."[41]

Mental technologies also include reasoning. There are many kinds of reasoning, though students of international practice have elevated four to understand human rights and humanitarianism. Practical reasoning: getting things done and accomplishing some goal. Technical reasoning: the development of specialized methods for restricted domains of problems. Moral reasoning: doing the right things for the right reasons, frequently with reference to a broader ethical codes that determine right from wrong or the broader values of the community, public, or humanity.[42] And, legal reasoning: uses law and legal norms, including the centrality of precedent, rules for handing evidence, and the guidelines for which arguments are admissible and available, to justify decisions and guide action.[43] These forms of reasoning are not mutually exclusive, and often they are combined in processes of analysis and argumentation. In any event, different reasoning processes help constitute the competent.

Human rights draws heavily from legal reasoning.[44] There are certainly strong elements of moral reasoning: all humans are born with inalienable rights because of their humanity, and when those rights are violated, they must be defended.[45] Human rights law refers to "the system of law that establishes fundamental individual and group rights, and the obligations of states relative to those rights."[46] Importantly, human rights and law, according to many observers, have been mutually reinforcing, to the point that it is nearly impossible to think of human rights in terms other than law. Precisely why and how law became nearly constitutive of human rights is a matter of debate, but it has undeniably undergone a process of legalism.[47] The concept of legalism, as introduced by Judith Shklar, highlights how law shapes what counts as a right and whether a right has been violated, and what kinds of harms are a matter of political and moral concern.[48]

Humanitarianism is constituted by moral, technical, and legal reasoning, arguably in that order of salience. The very idea of humanitarianism is driven by a powerful emotional and moral reasoning that directs "our attention to the suffering of others and make us want to remedy them."[49] This "humanitarian imperative" – that "action should be taken to prevent or alleviate human suffering arising out of disaster or conflict, and that nothing should override this principle" – suggests acting first and asking questions later.[50] There also is technical reasoning. A central technology is triage. The presumption is that there is a diagnostic assessment that can be used to determine the order of treatment and how to allocate scarce resources. Legal reasoning, especially when compared to human rights, is relatively modest and limited to international humanitarian law.[51] When Doctors without Borders justifies its interventions in faraway places, it typically points not to legal justifications (the right to be present according to this or that law) but rather to the moral claim that all humans deserve medical attention. When aid organizations began incorporating the language of human rights, it was softened, became "rights-based," used strategically and rhetorically, and rarely referred to human rights law.[52] And when aid organizations do adopt the discourse of law, they mainly do so to emphasize that individuals have certain rights in areas of armed conflict, but humanitarians prefer the nonlegal language of protection and security. Indeed, much of human rights law presumes that individuals can make claims on others who have duties, but humanitarians refuse to accept that they are dutybearers; at most they are second best actors and the first best is the state.[53]

There is mounting evidence that the growing technical nature of human rights and humanitarianism is shifting their forms of reasoning. One study of human rights suggested that the increasing reliance on technology might be changing the nature of decision-making from moral and legal to more technocratic and managerial.[54] There has been a perceptible rise in technical reasoning in the humanitarian sector over the last several decades, owing in part to professionalization.[55] Although humanitarianism lists volunteerism as an important principle, volunteerism does not mean amateurism. Instead, it now means those who work in the sector without ulterior motives such as profit. Aid workers should be professionals and experts, with training and skills that allow them to provide effective and efficient life-saving interventions. Relief agencies must move tons of aid over long distances in short order, which places a premium on logisticians and those who expertly coordinate many moving parts. Because aid workers operate in increasingly dangerous environments, there is a growing demand for security experts, often recruited from the private sector, and with law enforcement and military experience. Inside and outside aid agencies there is greater pressure to provide evidence of results and efficiency, leading to a heightened presence of those trained in epidemiology, cost-benefit analysis, and evaluation methods. A consequence of this rationalization and emphasis on results and efficiency is an expansion of opportunities for private and for-profit firms. After all, who knows more about moving mountains in a cost-effective way than Walmart or Federal Express?[56]

The material and mental technologies of human rights and humanitarianism are developed, taught, learned, and revised in different places. Increasingly, to gain knowledge and become an expert in human rights requires being trained in law, which, in turn, elevates the importance of law schools and clinics, and law-shaped human rights centers. Although those who want specialized knowledge in international humanitarian and refugee law might also head to law-related institutions, most seeking a career in the field go to medicine, public health, and other areas that are central to human survival and health, such as sanitation. Not only do those who want to be credentialed in human rights and humanitarianism head in different directions, but the creation of these institutions of training and accreditation help to maintain the boundaries between the two.

Background Knowledge

Background knowledge exists in the shadows, is implicit rather than explicit, is on the tip of the tongue and often built into muscle memory, and is "just understood." It serves several functions that pertain to getting things done, including helping actors make sense of the meaning of events and developments, guiding their response, coordinating with others, and working toward collective action.[57] In this way, background knowledge is situated between mental and material technologies and meanings. The volume and other writings suggest that humanitarianism and human rights operate with different background knowledge, including the following.

First are principles that help organize action. Many discussions of humanitarianism's principles begin with the famous desiderata by the International Committee of the Red Cross's Jean Pictet.[58] He identified seven core principles: humanity, impartiality, neutrality, independence, voluntary service, unity, and universality. The first four principles, though, arguably constitute the core. Humanity commands attention to all people. Impartiality requires that assistance be based on need and not discriminate on the basis of nationality, race, religion, gender, or political opinion. Neutrality demands refraining from taking part in hostilities or from any action that either benefits or disadvantages the parties to the conflict. Independence requires that assistance should not be connected to any of the parties directly involved in armed conflicts or who have a stake in the outcome; accordingly, there is a general rule that agencies should either refuse or limit their reliance on government funding, and especially those that are involved in the conflict. Also, aid agencies are constantly fiddling with the principles in the everyday, on the ground practices of relief.[59]

The human rights community also refers to the principles of impartiality, neutrality, and independence, though with different interpretations.[60] In human rights, impartiality is determined in relationship to human rights principles and documents that are treated as having a universal status.[61] Amnesty International's claim to impartiality, for instance, "reflects the premise that the expansion of international human rights law is transforming human rights norms from a set of political aspirations into a body of impartial legal norms."[62] Like humanitarianism, human rights also treats impartiality as part of instrumental reasoning: it can be a strategy to portray a stance of "distance or disinterest needed to discriminate between victims and perpetrator."[63] In the world of human rights, neutrality, at least as understood by humanitarianism, makes little sense. The point of human rights is to pick sides and to promote social change. Independence can be a hinder to getting things done. Human rights advocacy is precisely designed to appeal to states and other constituents, which often requires making strong alliances.

The divergent interpretations of these principles also are bound up with alternative stances toward politics. As discussed in the Introduction, human rights unapologetically engages in politics while humanitarianism presents politics as a moral pollutant.[64] In brief, humanitarianism wants to save lives in immediate risk and worries that if it engages in politics it will potentially jeopardize its access to those in need, while human rights must engage politics if it is to punish perpetrators, challenge human rights violations, and create a more just society. These differing objectives are most keenly observed on the question of assigning responsibility for harms. Humanitarians are reluctant to assign blame, at least publicly. In natural disasters, or acts of God, no one is to blame. And while it is possible to blame God, and question why God would permit such suffering, the important point is that individuals are not held directly responsible.[65] Although in humanly made emergencies it is quite possible to identify the perpetrators, humanitarian agencies avoid assigning blame because the moment they do they potentially jeopardize their access. Rights approaches almost always see a human hand behind suffering

and deprivation. This conclusion is practically baked into the very discourse of human rights – victims are those who have had their rights
violated, and human rights violations cannot exist without a violator.

The Meaning Behind the Act

Meaning is central to the concept of practices.[66] Action absent meaning is
mere behavior. Meaning has an instrumental and existential dimension.[67]
Instrumental or functional definitions of meaning tend to focus on specific short-term tasks. The meaning of humanitarianism is to save lives
and human rights to stop oppression. In this way, meanings reinforce the
problems to be solved and practical action. Meaning also can have a much
more encompassing dimension, including the transcendent that necessi-
tates a consideration of the whole of reality and "something beyond or
transcendent to their lives." Action can be part of a "search for meaning":
the attempt to position oneself in relationship to others and the cosmos;
the need to fend off questions of emptiness and alienation that might
otherwise intrude on our sense of self; and the almost existential need to
make sense of suffering.

Humanity can help provide answers to these questions and address
these demands. It can be part of the sacred that binds the members of the
community and points them toward something that is "larger than themselves." Although such beliefs used to be primarily associated with a deity,
since the nineteenth century secularization processes contributed to the
sacralization of the human, resulting in humanity becoming "the object of
a sort of religion . . . a common faith."[68] This intertwining of the theological and secular recalls John Dewey's approving reference to William
James's understanding of religious experience (as distinct from religion),
in which the "self is always directed toward something beyond itself and
so its own unification depends upon the idea of shifting scenes of the
world into that imaginative totality we call the Universe."[69] The capacity
of individuals to link their everyday actions to the transcendental, to find
meaning and enchantment in practical and worldly activities, is reminiscent of the distinction between the immanent and the transcendental.[70]

Human rights and humanitarianism are part of the transcendent as they
connect to humanity and a world that is bigger than us.[71] But do they have
the same meaning? The chapters and other studies of these fields provide
strong hints that they offer contrasting meanings that are potentially
based less on metaphysics and more on practice. One influential version
of the practice perspective argues that the act precedes the meaning. If so,
the different actions associated with human rights and humanitarianism
will produce different meanings of humanity. A humanitarianism that

focus on needs and keeping people alive will tend toward a humanity defined by bare life. In contrast, a human rights that aspires to produce a full and flourishing life might be more likely to operate with a fuller idea of humanity. Not only might they operate with different meanings of humanity, but also their limited versus expansive actions and meanings of humanity might be more or less likely to create space for alternative views of humanity. Humanitarianism minimalism possibly provides greater possibilities than does a human rights maximalism that is constituted by Western culture.

The meaning of humanitarianism and human rights might also function to help us make sense of the world. Humans search not only for material advancement and security but also meaning. The search for meaning is likely to be most intensively felt during moments of chaos, despair, and bouts of inhumanity.[72] Different communities will have different ways of making sense of disorder, which invariably draw on the cultural material that binds the members. The post-Enlightenment West leans heavily on the idea of the sacredness of the human and the idea of progress. As discussed in the Introduction, progress has material and moral dimensions, but it is the fragmentation of the moral that is most likely to trigger the search for meaning. When do those in the post-Enlightenment West tend to engage in an urgent search for meaning? When war and other apoplectic-like events challenge the belief in rationality, learning, and the march of progress. Where does the West turn at such moments of loss, despair, and senseless suffering? The religion of humanity and its progeny of human rights and humanitarianism. There are many ways to explain why the West and the international community have institutionalized human rights and humanitarianism after great cataclysms, and one possibility is the spiritual need to restore the belief in humanity. The turn to humanity, human rights, and humanitarianism as a response to inhumanity can be understood as a form of coping and theodicy.[73] But only time will tell if the international community continues to find solace and hope in them.

THE WORLD AHEAD

It is indisputable that the modern world order has made a greater space for human rights and humanitarianism over the last century. There have been setbacks, plenty of them, but the record suggests an overall march forward. Yet contemporary discussions of the future of humanitarianism and human rights suggest they must prepare not for the occasional potshot but rather a pummeling. The current fear is that the long durée in which the milder forms of cosmopolitanism enjoyed considerable popularity is yielding to populism, narrow-minded nationalism, chauvinism, and xenophobia. Why this is happening is split between various hypotheses, including shifting geopolitics from the West to the East, widening domestic and global economic inequality, migration flows, and the rumored decline of the West and liberalism.

Another, somewhat ironic or perhaps tragic, factor might be the very discourse of humanity.[74] What sort of humanity has been constructed? Humanity demands the recognition of the humanity of all others, but we tend to offer such recognition only when they are in pain, when their rights are violated, or when they are on the verge of death. Those who are in positions to give often do so because of pity and know little about these people that are reduced to stick figures and their suffering. Is this cosmopolitanism of suffering up to the challenge of producing a meaningful community. As Hannah Arendt observed, "The world finds nothing sacred in the abstract nakedness of being human."[75] And those who rely on such a humanity to create connections are selling themselves short – or stunting their emotional life.[76] In the spirit of Orwell's infamous eulogy of Gandhi, the person who loves humanity perhaps is not capable of love, because love depends on knowing the person.[77] The connections associated with humanity are abstract and bloodless, especially when contrasted with a local that provides intimacy, chromatic emotion, and genuine we-feeling.

If humanity becomes questioned or recedes, then what happens to a human rights and a humanitarianism that are constituted by it? In closing I want to suggest that their fates are dependent on how they have practiced humanity and how closely associated they are to the West and liberalism. Those looking ahead seem to identity three possible paths. There is the occasional statement that human rights and humanitarianism will do just fine, or even that one or the other provides hope for the future. For instance, Kathryn Sikkink concludes that growing "wealth disparities, intolerance, and regressive nationalism signals a difficult struggle ahead to create a just and sustainable planet. The universal, supranational, emancipatory, and expansive character of human rights is poised to serve as a connective tissue binding disparate movements and awakening a global citizenry in a supra-movement capable of accelerating a Great Transition."[78] I cannot find a comparable statement in discussions of the future of humanitarianism; I suspect that this is partly because humanitarianism has never fully embraced the idea of progress or the possibility that humanitarianism might serve this end. In any event, the idea that human rights or humanitarianism might provide the light in these dark times could be based on a careful reading of history or theodicy and other coping mechanisms.

Another possibility is that both will suffer, and not only because these are less compassionate times but also because of their association with liberalism and the West. Even those in the human rights community who see the possibility of hope nevertheless acknowledge that the combination of long-term trends and missteps by human rights movements have contributed to these troubled times.[79] Human rights, rightly or wrongly, is associated with the West and liberalism. A prevailing view is that international human rights rose on the shoulders of Western states that wanted to create a world in their image for reasons of vanity, wealth, and security. And the version of rights that became hegemonic – political and civil, not economic and cultural – were closely associated with the version preferred by Western states and human rights organizations. Human rights also engaged in politics, proudly spoke truth to power, which made powerful enemies. In the past human rights organizations could look to Western governments for support, but they are increasingly absent as they are developing their own strands of illiberalism, becoming much less inclined to defend human rights abroad and friendlier with serial violators of human rights. These are dark days for human rights.

Many of the same factors that sponsored the rise of human rights also propelled humanitarianism, but arguably humanitarianism was never as reliant on discourses associated with liberalism as it proclaimed that saving lives has no ideology.[80] It insisted on working outside of politics. Most were heavily reliant on Western states for their funding, but that did not stop them from trying to project the appearance of independence. The supposed universalism of humanitarianism never experienced the barrage of critique that human rights did. But humanitarianism confronts considerable difficulties. It is constantly instrumentalized by states and others who found it useful, and there is now a growing fear that that this instrumentalization will become even more intense and force aid agencies to choose between compromise and complicity.[81] Also, while humanitarianism might not be as susceptible to cultural fragmentation as human rights, there are a growing number of non-Western attempts to construct locally generated forms of humanitarianism that might or might not include principles of neutrality, independence, and impartiality.

The third possibility is that human rights and humanitarianism will continue to exist, but not as we know it and without the same meaning. Humanitarianism and human rights, as we know them today, are products of age and their interactions with each other. But, if these currently unsettled times are but a passage toward a different world order, then the likelihood is that there will be a change in the kind of suffering matters, whose suffering matters, what counts as unnecessary suffering, and what are the acceptable remedies to suffering. Will humanitarianism and human rights extend their concern to the suffering of different kinds, such as animals and even androids? As the effects of climate change become more keenly felt, what will be come of the meaning and practices of human rights and humanitarianism? Will the Earth have rights? Will humanitarianism shift toward the prevention of the climate change, as is happening at the ICRC?[82] Or will climate change cause a shrinking of humanity and the international community as people retreat to their territories and look to defend the homeland?[83] Will the desire to prevent suffering lead humanitarianism to associate with modern eugenics?[84] Will human flourishing become tied to genetic engineering? COVID-19 makes a compelling case for the need for more humanitarianism, not less, but the evidence so far suggests that states are focused on their own. And in the name of public health, the state is introducing new surveillance techniques that all governments seeking power find to their advantage. But the hopeful premise of many of these questions is that individuals will continue to embrace a concept of humanity that includes the desire to prevent and relieve the unnecessary strangers. But, as in centuries past, will suffering strangers become pitiable but not grievable? For quite some time, human rights and humanitarianism have been expressions and guardians of global ethics, representing a world that many hope to exist and a set of principles to guide them there. What lies ahead?

Notes

Introduction: Worlds of Difference

1. Gordon 2007.
2. Teitel 2011. Also see Fortin 2012; Meron 2000; Droege 2007 and 2008; Hampson 2008; Lubell 2005; Leebaw 2007 and 2017; Reidy 1998; Heintze 2004; Crowe 2014; ICRC 2010; and Benison 1999.
3. We Robotics 2018; Emery 2016; Tapak 2019.
4. Nascimento 2004; Dutton 2001; Fox 2002.
5. Cuttitta 2018; Sciubra and Furri 2018; Perkowski 2016.
6. Feldman 2009; Ticktin 2016.
7. Slim 2001; Chandler 2001; Leebaw 2017; Dixon 2019.
8. Pflanz 2009. Also see Beison 1999; Kendall 2015 and 2018.
9. Geneva Macrolas. COVID-19: Privacy Versus Health. April 29, 2000. http://er bguth.ch/COVID-19_tracing_privacy.mp4; Mark Latonero, "Stop Surveillance Humanitarianism," *New York Times*, July 11, 2019; www.nytimes.com/2019/07/11/opinion/data-humanitarian-aid.html; Petra Moinar, COVID-19: Can Technology Become a Tool of Oppression and Surveillance?" *OpenDemocracy*, May 1, 2020, www.opendemocracy.net/en/pandemic-bor der/covid-19-can-technology-become-tool-oppression-and-surveillance/; Amnesty International, "COVID-19, Surveillance, and the Threat to Your Rights," April 3, 2020, www.amnesty.org/en/latest/news/2020/04/covid-19-surveillance-threat-to-your-rights/
10. Slim 2004; Viero de Mello 2004; Ogata 1997.
11. Stevens 2016; Dubois 2009.
12. Liu and Salignon 2003; Ticktin 2011; Kelsall and Stepakoff 2007; Schopper 2014, 593; and Kendall and Nouwen 2018, 7.
13. Hilhorst and Jansen 2012; Hilhorst and Jansen 2010, 1135–1136; Feldman 2007.
14. Dubois 2009.
15. Lubell, 2005, 738. Also see Gillard 2005.
16. Slim 2015, 16.
17. See note 2.
18. Sikkink 2011 and 2018; Simmons and Strezhnev 2017.
19. Moyn 2012; Keys 2014; and Iriye, Goedde, and Hitchcock 2012; Jensen 2016.
20. Goodale and Merry 2007.

21. Nash 2015.
22. Moyn 2017; Rutazibwa 2019.
23. Laqua 2014; Hilton et al. 2018.
24. Cooley and Ron 2002; Weiss 2013.
25. Ticktin 2014; Fassin 2011.
26. Agier 2011; Duffield 2019; Clark 2016; Weitzman 2012.
27. Festa 2010; Spelman 2001.
28. Kinsella 2011.
29. Manfredi 2013, 15–19; Geyer 2016.
30. Also see Slim 2015, 47.
31. Barnett 2011.
32. Wichmann 2019.
33. Foucault 1994, 708. Cited from Finkielkraut 2001, 88.
34. Shapcott 2010, 3–4.
35. Habermas 2010; Flynn 2003; Rorty 1999; Joas 2013; Bayefsky 2013.
36. Singer 2010.
37. Brudholm and Lang 2018; Burke 2017.
38. Faulkner 2014.
39. Arendt 1963; Boltanski 1999; Chouliaraki 2010; Wilkinson 2014.
40. Fiering 1976; Haskell 1985.
41. Fassin 2007, 15.
42. Arendt 1963, 79–80.
43. Weinert 2015.
44. Wilson and Brown 2009, 43.
45. Wilkinson and Kleinman 2016.
46. For a discussion, see Barnett 2011. Also see Oxfam 2019; Nelson and Dorsey 2018.
47. Zaman et al. 2018; Hunt et al. 2018.
48. Dunant 1862.
49. For a different understanding of the politics of life, see Fassin 2007.
50. And, as the old joke goes, the fish is then sold to the ex-pat development worker. For other jokes based on this saying, see www.iluenglish.com/give-a-man-a-fish-funny-adaptations-of-the-proverb/.
51. Brown 2004.
52. Moon 2016.
53. Brysk 2013.
54. Festa 2010, 8.
55. However, for discussions on the relationship between needs and justice, see Barry 1982; Buchanan 1987; Valenti 2015.
56. Cited in Leebaw 2007, 261.
57. Cited in Rubenstein 2015, 207. Also see Redfield 2013, 229–244; Leebaw 2017.
58. Cited in Leebaw 2007.
59. Valenti 2015, 736; Spivak 2004, 523–524; Festa 2010, 16; Kurasawa 2007, 204.
60. O'Flaherty and Ulrich 2010, 8.
61. Barnett 2016.

62. Appiah 2010; Hollinger 1985; Shapcott 2008.
63. Hollinger 1985, 59.
64. Festa 2010, 6, 7. Also see McManus 2017 and Nguyen 2010.
65. Branch 2011, 8.
66. Hutchison 2014; Balaji 2011.
67. Sluga 2013.
68. Keohane 1982; Alexander 1990.
69. Sikkink 2017 and 2018. Also see Teitel 1997; Moyn 2012; Hopgood 2013; Cmeil 2004; Dawes, Gupta, and Jayasinghe 2014; Slaughter 2014.
70. This progressive spirit in human rights is also sustained by similar sentiments in international law, which connect progress, humanity, and universalism. Altwicker and Diggelmann 2014.
71. Sikkink 2011.
72. For counternarratives, see Lacroix and Prachére 2018; Moyn 2012; Hopgood 2015; Afshari 2007; Dawes, Gupta, and Jayasinghe 2014; Slaughter 2018.
73. Fortrun 2012, 447.
74. Lacquer 2009; Rorty 1993; Linklater 2007.
75. Terry 2002.
76. Bradol 2004.
77. Redfield 2013, 229–244.
78. Dawes 2007, 18–19. Also see Bradol 2004.
79. Dawes 2007, 5.
80. De Waal 2010, S131.
81. Marx and Engels 1848, Ch. 3.
82. Donini 2010.
83. Swamy 2017.
84. Whyte 2019.
85. Also see Perugini and Gordon 2015.
86. Robbins 2017, 19; Giridharadas 2018.
87. Young 2006.
88. Donini 2012.

1   Human Rights and Humanitarianization

1. For the distinction, see Jeffrey Flynn's Chapter 2 in this volume.
2. Robbins 2017.
3. Moyn 2006 and 2017.
4. Davis 1966, 523–556.
5. Fulton 2002.
6. See Crane 1934, and the successor literature by Geoffroy Atkinson, G. J. Barker-Benfield, Michael Bell, Markman Ellis, Peter Uwe Hohendahl, David Marshall, John Mullan, Janet Todd, Ann Jessie van Sant, Anne Vincent-Buffault, and a host of others.
7. Laqueur 1989.
8. Arendt 1965, 65.

9. Pinker 2011, 129.
10. The first diagnosed "sadist" in world history was the man who got off on Harriet Beecher Stowe's graphic humanitarian imaginings of whipped slave bodies. See Halttunen 1995, 303–334.
11. See Davis 1975 and Bender 1992.
12. Brown 1999; Festa 2006; Barnett 2011; Benton 2011; Lester and Dussart 2014; Benton and Ford 2018. For popular studies of humanitarianism that acknowledge then run away from the connections, see Hochschild 2006. For a very different account, see Moniz 2016.
13. See, most revealingly, Lauren 1998, 37–70, which dealt with humanitarianism not as an old or new generalized phenomenon in the modern age but mainly when it came to "protecting the wounded" in the codified law of war in the nineteenth century. With the 1990s canonization of the Universal Declaration, much attention to the 1940s followed, perhaps most famously in Glendon 2002. For more details, see Moyn 2012, 123–140.
14. Hunt 2007; for my critique, see *The Nation*, April 16, 2007, repeated in Moyn 2014, 1–19.
15. See Edelstein 2018 for the latest try.
16. Barnett and Stein 2012; for the prevalence of Christian forms of humanitarianism today, see Power 2009.
17. Arendt loathed humanitarianism, charging it with fomenting terror; and, for that matter, she was skeptical about human rights whether locally or internationally – though she never conflated the two categories in her own usage. It is still justifiable, in spite of both facts, to cast modern rights for most of their history as part of the citizenship politics that Arendt generally championed in other terms. What I still wonder about is what to say regarding the fact that – long antedating the current theoretical scene – Arendt theorized compassionate humanitarianism in terms of *local* rather than *distant* suffering as well as squarely *within* the revolutionary phenomenon rather than sounding the death knell of revolutionary solidarity.
18. See the chapters by Fabian Klose and especially Alan Lester in this volume. Recent works by Frederick Cooper emphasize that citizenship cuts across both nation-state and imperial forms; both settings feature boundaried stratification, but also "the right to claim rights." But, notwithstanding the potential of imperial citizenship some have perceived, there is no denying the modern ideological affinity between claims to rights *on the basis of humanity* and revolutionary nationalism from the Atlantic revolutions through decolonization. See, for example, Cooper 2018.
19. See Moyn 2010, 33 on general principles and Moyn 2010, 243–444n.17 on Hunt's argument.
20. Green 2014; Green and Viaene 2012; see also my "Human Rights and the Crisis of Liberalism," in Moyn 2017b.
21. The best single account is Rodogno 2012; see also Klose 2016. More broadly, see Klose and Thulin 2016. But compare with Tusan 2014.
22. For a vivid example of post-1865 appeals to "human rights" in the United States, see Stanley 2015, or, in a popular mode, 2017.

23. The sole major counterexample of the propagation of rights beyond borders also concerned Christians under the Ottoman Empire, when instead of humanitarian intervention the non-Christian sovereign was deemed a target for the sort of treaty-based protection of collective rights of religious worship which Christians had once demanded from one another across borders, but dropped in the nineteenth century on the premise that civilized states neither brooked nor required interference. (Jews intelligently piggybacked on such practices, by convincing powerful Western states to lobby for collective Jewish rights in the Ottoman Empire and later semi-civilized new Christian states on the European periphery such as Czechoslovakia and Poland.)

24. See Moyn 2010, 249n.62, 308n.17, and 324.

25. For an especially early and unconvincing dating, see Cabanes 2014.

26. For example, Paulmann 2016a or O'Sullivan, Hilton and Fiori 2016.

27. Moyn 2010, 72, 125.

28. Compare Cohen 2011.

29. Compare Klose 2013. In the law of war, the first sign of attempted merger in our time is the United Nations General Assembly Resolution 2444 (XXIII), "Respect for Human Rights in Armed Conflicts," December 19, 1968 – and in spite of a lot of talk connecting human rights and humanitarian law, this merger has barely progressed to date. See Ohlin 2016.

30. Moyn 2010, 220.

31. I thank Jeffrey Flynn for destabilizing my originally excessive segregation of human rights and humanitarianism in the 1970s; see Barbara Keys, 2014, for details on the gendering of anti-torture politics of the period. As I have argued elsewhere, Elaine Scarry's classic if strange *The Body in Pain*, was born out of Amnesty's anti-torture campaign; see also Moyn, 2013, repeated in Moyn 2017b.

32. Shue 1980; Moyn 2018.

33. Heerten 2017.

34. Moyn 2017b, 103–113.

35. See especially Davey 2015, 212–214, as well as Mohandesi 2017.

36. Moyn 2010, 221.

37. Redfield 2013, 37–68, 98–123, 229–244. See also Givoni 2016 and Malkki 2015.

38. Barnett 2011, 16.

39. See, for example, Marks 2011. Conversely, subsequent research on the history of humanitarianism itself by Keith Watenpaugh has contended that a turn to causal insight into otherwise symptomatic suffering was the central event in its history, taking place in the early twentieth century. See Watenpaugh 2015, 57–90, 124–156.

40. Fassin 2011; Feldman and Ticktin 2010; Bornstein and Redfield 2011; Ticktin 2011a – the main canon and touchstone collections of the contemporary anthropology of humanitarianism. See also Guilhot 2012.

41. Ticktin 2016.

42. Moyn 2018.

43. Feldman 2012; Allen 2013.

44. Compare Toscano 2014.
45. Simmons 2011.
46. For example, see Agier 2010, as well as some aspects of his writings elsewhere in anthropology.
47. Chouliaraki 2013.

2   Suffering and Status

* I am grateful to Nicholas Sooy for assisting with and discussing the research for this chapter, and to all my fellow participants in the workshops organized by Michael Barnett, at George Washington University, for such rich and illuminating discussion of the chapters in this volume.
1. See Halpern 2002 for an excellent genealogy of the modern politics of suffering, and Stuurman 2017 on the history of status equality.
2. Barnett 2011, 49, 133. See also Fassin 2012, 4–5, on two "temporalities."
3. For the former see Hunt 2007; for the latter see Moyn 2010 and Eckel and Moyn 2014. I engage Hunt and Moyn on human rights and humanitarianism in Flynn 2012.
4. I focus on *describing* challenges to status hierarchies rather than the normative question of what makes a status hierarchy unjustifiable. For an account of normative criteria that must be met for any social and political order to be justifiable, see Forst 2011 on the "right to justification."
5. Fiering 1976, 195.
6. Taylor 2007, 23.
7. Fiering 1976.
8. See Hunt 2007, and Wilkinson and Kleinman 2016, ch. 1.
9. Barnett 2011.
10. Feinberg 1973, 88–89.
11. Ibid., 89.
12. Festa 2010, 7. See also Klose this volume.
13. Festa 2010, 5.
14. Ibid., 4. See Klose this volume, on "the cause of humanity" as an ambivalent norm throughout the nineteenth century.
15. Hunt 2007, 39.
16. Hunt 2007, 58.
17. Ibid., 27.
18. Ibid., 29. See also Sliwinski 2011 on the role of eighteenth-century visual culture in the rise of the Rights of Man.
19. Hunt 2007, 213.
20. The later section "Stories of Suffering" aims in part to show that she was overly skeptical in this regard.
21. Arendt 1963b, 85.
22. Ibid., 89.
23. Ibid., 119.
24. Spelman 1997, 65.
25. Spelman 1997, chapter 2 provides a vivid account of how the risks can be mitigated. For a critique of Arendt's distinction between compassion and pity

in relation to humanitarianism, see Fassin 2011, 37. In Nussbaum 1996, Martha Nussbaum argues that "compassion" and "pity" can be used to refer the same basic emotion, and that it was only in the Victorian era that "pity" acquired "nuances of condescension and superiority to the sufferer" (29). I use "politics of pity" to refer to a politics with undertones of those attitudes.

26. Arendt 1963b, 88.
27. Gündogdu 2015, 16. This is one form of "humanitarianization" of "human rights" that predates the periodization in Moyn, this volume. See also Lester this volume for an account of how a "moral economy of suffering" was instrumental within the British Empire in defusing the radical potential of human rights.
28. For a similar argument about contemporary France, see Ticktin 2011a.
29. Habermas 2010.
30. See also Waldron 2012.
31. Marshall 1963, 87.
32. Habermas 2010, 92.
33. See Sangiovanni 2017.
34. Barnett 2011, 82–83. See also Klose this volume, on the early nineteenth-century shift in justifying humanitarian intervention by reference not only to religious affinity but also to a common humanity.
35. Quoted in Slim 2015, 45.
36. Beitz 2009, 1.
37. Buchanan 2013, 69.
38. Ibid., 30.
39. Ibid., 28–30. Buchanan articulates this status egalitarian function in defending his own philosophical position. See Sangiovanni 2017, chs. 5–6 for a similar defense, and Miller 2016 for a critique of Buchanan. My aim here is not to compare philosophical theories; I draw on Buchanan simply to highlight the status-egalitarian elements that are evident in the contemporary human rights system.
40. For the argument that it has not done enough, see Moyn 2018. For a counter-argument, see Sikkink 2018, 235–240.
41. See Flynn 2019, 303–307.
42. Feinberg 1970, 252.
43. Honneth 1996, 107–120.
44. Beitz 2009, 288.
45. Ibid., 289.
46. Merry 2006, 47.
47. Allen 2013, 4.
48. See the contrast between "human rights" and "Human Rights" in Hopgood 2013, viii–ix.
49. See Moyn 2010, and Flynn 2018.
50. Of course, humanitarian practice has not remained untouched by a politics of equal status across that time period either. This is particularly evident in the development of international humanitarian law, with the legal statuses and rights that come with them. See Beitz, this volume and Teitel 2011.

51. On the nineteenth-century discourse of stopping perpetrators, see Klose this volume on the extension of British abolitionism into humanitarian intervention, and Rodogno 2012 on the broader discourse against "massacre" and "atrocity."
52. Boltanski 1999, 48. The long history of a politics of indignation is in part what allows Hunt to look to the eighteenth century for the pre-history of today's human rights activism, but Boltanski views this politics as one of the many strands in the long history of humanitarianism.
53. Ibid., 149.
54. Haskell 1985b, 565.
55. Ibid.
56. Ibid., 566.
57. Hochschild 2006, 6.
58. Barnett 2011, 85.
59. Robbins 2017, 3. See also Flynn 2017.
60. Laqueur 1989.
61. Ibid., 201.
62. Ibid., 178.
63. Ibid. 179. For echoes of this connection in the contemporary work of MSF, see Redfield 2006.
64. Laqueur 1989, 190.
65. Ibid., 191, 192.
66. Ibid., 195, italics added.
67. Laqueur (194) even cites passages in Marx's *Capital* as drawing on this genre when discussing the daily lives of laborers and effects on their health and longevity.
68. Sontag 2003, 102. For insight into the trope of innocence in humanitarian and human rights discourse and practice, see Ticktin this volume.
69. For a philosophical account of emotions as containing judgments, see Nussbaum 2001.
70. See the relative lack of attention to human rights in Fassin 2012 and to humanitarian themes in Moyn 2010. See, however, Moyn 2012b and Moyn this volume, for attempts to theorize them together.
71. Sargent 2014, 142. See also Heerten 2017, esp. 9–10, 339–340.
72. In her memoir, Jeri Laber, one of the founders of Human Rights Watch, vividly depicts being moved to enter human rights work in the first place by reading about Greek torture victims in 1973. See Laber 2002, 8, 229. I discuss this in Flynn 2012.
73. See Moyn 2014 and Moyn this volume, 7.
74. Keys 2012, 201.
75. Ibid., 202.
76. Ibid., 203. See also Keys 2014.
77. Heerten 2015, 263.
78. In Flynn 2017, I situate Peter Singer's classic 1972 essay "Famine, Affluence, and Morality" in this context.
79. Ticktin 2011a, 70.

80. See Davey 2015. On the full scope of how "witnessing" is now conceived by MSF, see Redfield 2013, 104. For a broader treatment of witnessing, see Givoni 2016.
81. Keys 2014, 93.
82. Hopgood 2006, vii.
83. Malkki 1996.
84. Redfield 2005, 346.
85. On mitigating this inequality, see Anderson 1998; on its ineradicable nature see Fassin 2010.
86. Moyn this volume. See also Moyn 2018 on why status equality is not enough.
87. See Gündogdu 2015 and Kennedy 2005.
88. For an approach that does not shy away from the task of clearly articulating these pathologies, while still defending human rights practice, see Beitz 2009, 201–209.
89. Rubenstein 2015. See my review in Flynn 2019.
90. Sontag 2003, 102–103.
91. On the nature of this shared responsibility, see Young 2011. See also Rothberg 2019 on the "implicated subject." On the way the shaming strategies of both human rights and humanitarian organizations can undermine a focus on structural issues, and on possible ways of overcoming this deficit, see Leebaw this volume. On bringing beneficiaries into the picture, see Robbins 2017 on humanitarianism and Marks 2011 on human rights.

3   **Humanitarianism and Human Rights in Morality and Practice**

* For comments and criticisms I am grateful to Michael Barnett and the other contributors to this volume and to audiences at the Florida International University School of Law, the CUNY Center for Global Ethics, and Pompeu Fabra University.
1. These points are related. See Abruzzo 2011, ch. 1.
2. Dunant 1939 [1862].
3. Another body of IHL originated at two conferences held at The Hague in 1899 and 1907 ("Hague law" as distinct from "Geneva law"). For present purposes I leave it aside.
4. Meron 2000, 251–252. See also Hitchcock 2012, 96–97.
5. Barnett 2011, 19.
6. Ibid., 39.
7. Ticktin 2014, 274–277; Fassin 2012, 243–257.
8. Here and in the following two paragraphs I summarize parts of Beitz 2009, ch. 2.
9. For a discussion, see Droege 2008, 520–524, and Oberleitner 2015, ch. 5.
10. Discussed in Beitz 2009, ch. 2.
11. I adopt this formulation from ibid., 42. Michael Barnett surveys the idea of a practice in more detail in the Conclusion to this volume. My notion of the

"distinctive culture" of a practice is meant to embrace what he calls background knowledge as well as the forms of ("moral, technical, and legal") reasoning publicly accepted within the practice. For a review of the literature about international practices taking human rights as a case study, see Karp 2013.

12. Barnett 2011, 8, 13, 16, 19. As Hugo Slim puts it in a guide to humanitarian ethics aimed at practitioners, the "ground of ethics in humanitarian action is a profound feeling of compassion and responsibility towards others who are living and suffering *in extremis*" (Slim 2015, 26). Slim presents an elaboration of this basic "ground" that acknowledges the limited but important appropriation of ideas about human rights in recent humanitarian practice (ibid., 118–121).

13. Elsewhere in the same document he observes: "[T]here are certain principles, such as those of humanity and non-discrimination, which in a sense are common to both [charity and justice]" (Pictet 1979). Compare Miriam Ticktin's observation – meaning to describe a belief found among humanitarian workers – that "humanitarianism is about feelings rather than rights; it is about compassion, not entitlement" (2016, 264).

14. See Barnett this volume.

15. See Dworkin 1986, ch. 2, developing a view he advanced in earlier works. For criticisms with which I largely agree, see Postema 1987.

16. Berman, Felter, and Shapiro 2018, fig. 0.1 and accompanying text.

17. On the interface between IHL and IHRL in these circumstances, see Watkin 2016, ch. 5; also Teitel 2011, 120–133.

18. Then there is the phenomenon of "aerial occupation," for example, by drones, that can impose serious harm on noncombatant populations even in the absence of the use of force. Emery and Brunstetter 2015.

19. Watkin 2016, 312–313.

20. See, for example, Walzer 2006.

21. For a review of the implications of changes in the nature of armed conflict for the legal regulatory frameworks, see Watkin 2016, esp. chs. 1–2.

22. For a detailed account, see Droege 2008, 504–509.

23. For example, Geneva Conventions of August 12, 1949, Protocol Relating to the Protection of Victims of International Armed Conflicts [1977], art. 72.

24. Leebaw's analysis of this contrast is illuminating (2007, 224–227). She notes the association of these organizations' strategic stances with their contrasting conceptions of the relationship of ethics and politics (225). On the shift in AI's orientation in the early 2000s, see Hopgood 2006.

25. Slim describes this as a "role responsibility" of humanitarian workers (2015, 67).

26. There of course need be no inconsistency here: the effort to portray human rights as impartial norms is compatible with regarding them as means of addressing injustice. Leebaw 2007, 227.

27. Ibid., 230–232.

28. Slim 2015, 119.

29. Sphere Project 2018. See also Ferris 2011, 194–196.

30. Cicero 1991 [44 BCE], 1.20. For a discussion of Cicero's distinction, see Nussbaum 2000.

31. On the sources and soundness of the distinction, see Campbell 1975 and Schumaker 1992. J. B. Schneewind traces the career of the distinction (among many other topics) in his masterful 1998.
32. Here I roughly follow Henry Sidgwick's account of what he called the "morality of common sense" in his 1907, bk. 3, chs. 4–5.
33. For example, my colleague, Peter Singer, most famously in Singer 1972.
34. Sidgwick 1907, bk. 3, ch. 4, §3.
35. I say "substantially" because there are some complications. For a discussion, see Pope 1991.
36. I leave aside cases of consensual harm, like the bodily harm done by a surgeon to a patient who has consented to the surgery.
37. Feinberg 1970, 252. See also Flynn 2019.
38. For critical examinations of the traditional view, see Campbell 1975 and Buchanan 1987.
39. For discussion see, for example, Fleischacker 2005.
40. As John Rawls argues, for example (Rawls 1999, sec. 19).
41. International Commission on Intervention and State Sovereignty (ICISS) 2001.
42. Essentially this point was recognized by the authors of the ICISS report, who note that the Commission avoided the phrase "humanitarian intervention" in deference to "the very strong opposition expressed by humanitarian agencies, humanitarian organizations and humanitarian workers towards any militarization of the word 'humanitarian': whatever the motives of those engaging in the intervention, it is anathema for the humanitarian relief and assistance sector to have this word appropriated to describe any kind of military action" (2001, 9).
43. As I argued in Beitz 2009, sec. 21 and ch. 7.
44. This is not an eccentric idea. For a discussion in the context of the welfare state, see Campbell 1974.
45. For such a view, see Forsythe 2013, 59–62.
46. Beitz 2009, sec. 21.

4   For a Fleeting Moment: The Short, Happy Life of Modern Humanism

1. For an alternative, and in some way contrasting, argument, see Moyn this volume.
2. For example, Hannum 2019.
3. Magone, Neuman, and Weissman 2011.
4. There is another alternative – that human rights and humanitarianism evolved because of their contribution to group survival. This structural–functional explanation allows no room for conscious human decision at all, and thus removes agency from the picture entirely.
5. Papal Encyclicals Online 2018.
6. Ibid.
7. Critics (see Hannum 2019) will say: but the ICC is not a human rights court. This is precisely my point. For lots of human rights advocates it is treated as one and, as a result, it becomes one. De jure follows rather than precedes de facto – the law follows the facts.

8. Goodale 2018.
9. Poewe 2005.
10. Mazower 2009.
11. On an "overlapping consensus," see of course Rawls 1993.
12. Hopgood 2013, ch. 2.
13. Ibid.
14. Hopgood 2006.
15. ICRC 2008.
16. ICRC 2016; Amnesty International 2018.
17. ICRC 2016.
18. Amnesty International 2017.
19. UNOCHA 2018.
20. Human Rights Watch 2018.
21. Liu 2016.
22. UNHCR (UK) 2018.
23. ICRC 2008.
24. Freedom House 2018.
25. Pinker 2011.
26. On the humanitarianization of rights, see Moyn this volume.
27. Reuters 2012; Lepora and Goodin 2015. The infibulation story was a personal conversation with an MSF doctor.

5   **Humanitarian Governance and the Circumvention of Revolutionary Human Rights in the British Empire**

1. See Barnett 2013, Hunt 2007, Skinner and Lester 2012. The extent to which these projects had origins in this period has been questioned more recently. Barnett (2013, 379) notes how global humanitarian governance, defined as "the self-conscious effort by the global community to relieve the suffering of distant strangers," was the result of more contemporary "revolutions in international ethics," while Samuel Moyn (2017) argues that the contemporary discourse of human rights is also of a much more recent vintage.
2. Moyn 2017b, xv.
3. My focus thus differs from humanitarian intervention which, as Klose indicates, consists of a more recent entanglement between humanitarianism and human rights. I am concerned with humanitarian practice in the governance of (appropriated) sovereign territory within an imperil world order rather than with intervention in nonsovereign territory within a postimperial state system.
4. Foucault 1979.
5. Fassin 2012, 2.
6. Elden 2007.
7. Reid-Henry 2014, 419.
8. Fassin 2012, x.
9. Quoted Shaw 1980, 197.
10. On the link between terror and a revolution in the sensibility of rights, see Arendt 1963b. As Stefan-Ludwig Hoffman notes, Lynn Hunt's seminal

Inventing Human Rights (2007) "acknowledges the paradoxes of human rights as politics, that rights claims emerged in tandem with revolutionary violence, but insists that their self-evidence ultimately transcends these historical mutations" (Hoffman 2016, 280).

11. Weber 1964, 3; Foucault 1979.
12. Brewer 1989.
13. Shaw 1980 and 2008.
14. Shaw 1980, 15–16.
15. See Maslan 2004.
16. Arthur to Bathurst, November 7, 1816, The National Archives UK (hereafter TNA), CO 123/25.
17. Quoted Shaw 1980, 22.
18. Ibid., 17.
19. Bolland 1977, 70.
20. Ibid., 61–63; Thomson 2004, 58–60.
21. Newson 1976; Brereton 1981.
22. Arthur to Bathurst, June 15, 1820, TNA, CO 123/31.
23. Bolland 1977, 61–63.
24. TNA, CO 123/31.
25. Arthur 1833 and 1835.
26. TNA, CO 280/49, Arthur to Hay September 24, 1834.
27. Reynolds 2004, 143.
28. Ibid., 130.
29. Boyce 2009, 146.
30. Ibid.
31. My emphasis: Plomley 1966, 51. The high death rate among those Aborigines relocated to Bruny Island foreshadowed that which decimated the surviving Aboriginal population as a whole on Flinders Island.
32. Ibid., 576fn.2; Reynolds 2004, 141–143.
33. Quoted Reynolds 2004, 146.
34. Boyce 2009, 268–270.
35. Shaw 1980, 125.
36. Plomley 1966; Edmonds 2014.
37. Shaw 1980, 132. Reynolds 1995 and Boyce 2009 concur that those Aboriginal people who surrendered to Robinson did so only after false promises that their removal to Flinders Island would be a temporary measure until the fighting was over.
38. Plomley 1966, 2.
39. See Ryan 2012.
40. Ryan 1996; Johnston 2004.
41. Buxton 1848, 125.
42. British Parliamentary Papers 1968/1836–7, 75.
43. Laidlaw 2004.
44. Cannon 1983, 365–391; Millis 1992, 375–380.
45. Read 1988; Greer 1993.
46. Quoted Shaw 1980, 197.
47. Rutherford 1961, v.

48. Sinclair 2012, np.
49. Dale 2006.
50. Grey 1840.
51. Salesa 2011, 108.
52. Lawson 2014.
53. Sera-Shriar 2013.
54. Prichard 1839, 1.
55. Grey 1840, np.
56. Ibid.
57. Grey, 1841, 1855; Grant 2005; Stocking 1987; Thornton 1983.
58. Bank 2000; Bleek, 1858–1859; Dubow 1995, 78–79.
59. Stocking 1987, 81. Grey's identification of north-western Aboriginal Australians' ability not only to survive in harsh environments, but also to secure an abundance of resources, was a key inspiration for Marshall Sahlin's famous characterization of poverty as not "just a relation between means and ends," but rather "a relation between people": Sahlins 1974, 37–38.
60. Grant 2005, 36.
61. Peires 1989; Lester 2001.
62. Grant 2005, 36, 46.
63. Marx 1887, 439, 539; Hall 2002, 212–213.
64. Merivale 1861, 499.
65. Ibid., 510–511.
66. Ibid.
67. Agamben 1998.
68. What is missing from the accounts of both Arthur's and Grey's various forms of humanitarian governance here is the agency of those subjected to them: the intended "beneficiaries" among Indigenous peoples. Arguably, this is also what is missing from most scholarly accounts of the forms of humanitarian governance that have succeeded these British colonial ones. Elsewhere I have argued that colonial humanitarian governance, intended to be counter-revolutionary as it was, opened opportunities for colonized peoples to acquire what Tracey Banivanua Mar (2013) called "imperial literacy." This entailed the intended beneficiaries of humanitarian forms of governance gaining some, albeit excessively limited, capacity in their dealings with the colonial state: Lester and Dussart 2014; Laidlaw and Lester 2015. Michael Barnett, too, has critiqued a view of "recipients" only as "victims," for obscuring "the capacity of the affected populations to save themselves and even to act strategically and manipulate outside interventions for their own purposes" (2013, 380).
    For the need to examine contemporary humanitarian camps from the perspective of their residents, see Zaman 2017.
69. In original project outline provided to contributors to this volume.
70. It is no coincidence that a newfound attentiveness to the welfare of enslaved people, rather than simply the fact of their enslavement, took place in the context of the Haitian Revolution. Despite the pioneering work of C. L. R. James, who first pointed out its significance for the creation of the

modern world in 1938, the impact of this successful slave uprising and creation of a republic, in unsettling European notions of entitlement to govern enslaved populations, is only now being reassessed: James 1989 (orig. 1938); May 2008; Trouillot 1995; Geggus 2002; Fischer 2004; Dubois 2005; Bhambra 2016.
71. Merivale 1861, 512.
72. Moyn 2017b, xv.
73. Ibid.
74. Ibid.
75. Johnston 2017, 74. Johnston points out that both projects – humanitarian governance and human rights – can and have been used by Aboriginal people within Australia's legal systems, even if not on the terms in which they were formulated by colonists.

6   **Humanitarian Intervention as an Entangled History of Humanitarianism and Human Rights**

* This chapter is based on the research for my new book, *In the Cause of Humanity. Eine Geschichte der humanitären Intervention im langen 19. Jahrhundert. This chapter profited from the suggestions of many, for which I am grateful. I specifically want to thank Michael Barnett, Marc Lazar, Paul–André Rosental, and the participants of the international doctoral seminar at the Centre d'Histoire at Sciences Po Paris as well as Tobias Grill and Konstantin Rometsch.*
1. Lillich 1969, 216.
2. For instance, new projects such as the Global Humanitarianism Research Academy (GHRA), organized by the Leibniz Institute of European History in Mainz, the University of Exeter, and the University of Cologne in cooperation with the International Committee of the Red Cross in Geneva, connects both fields by bringing together young scholars working on the history of human rights and of humanitarianism. See http://ghra.ieg-mainz.de/ and http://hhr-atlas.ieg-mainz.de/.
3. Geyer 2016.
4. On this, see also Michael Barnett's introduction to this volume.
5. For a clear distinction between humanitarianism and human rights and the risk of conflating both fields, see Moyn 2016.
6. For two important recently published articles emphasizing this fluidity and the close entanglement of both fields, see Thompson 2016b, especially 824–826; Thompson 2018. For further debates about the entanglement of the histories of humanitarianism and human rights, see also Cabanes 2014; Tusan 2014; Watenpaugh 2015, 19–23; and especially the chapters by Stephen Hopgood and Samuel Moyn in this volume.
7. Leebaw 2017.
8. In this chapter, I will follow Jeff L. Holzgrefe, who defines humanitarian intervention as the "threat or use of force across state borders by a state (or group of states) aimed at preventing or ending widespread and grave violations of the fundamental human rights of individuals other than its own citizens" (Holzgrefe 2004, 18). Holzgrefe's definition is closely linked

to the more general conceptual definition proffered by R. J. Vincent, who regards humanitarian intervention as "that activity undertaken by a state, a group within a state, a group of states or an international organization which interferes coercively in the domestic affairs of another state" (Vincent 1974, 13). According to these definitions, humanitarian intervention is also associated with the use of military force, and is explicitly distinguished from other forms of humanitarian action. For more discussion, see Wheeler 2003, 1–2; Welsh 2006, 3; Hehir 2010, 11–21; Weiss 2012, 6–15.

9. While other disciplines such as international law and political science have already focused on the issue of humanitarian intervention for quite a while, this is a rather new topic for historical research. However, in the last couple of years there has been a growing number of publications approaching the topic from a genuine historical perspective. For these approaches, see Bass 2008; Simms and Trim 2011; Rodogno 2012; Klose 2016 and 2019.

10. See for instance Martinez 2012; Simms and Trim 2011, 21–22.

11. On the concept and practices of humanity in historical perspective see: Klose and Thulin 2016.

12. Johnson 1755. As a fourth definition the dictionary referred to "Philology, grammatical studies."

13. Ibid. In Diderot's famous *Encylopédie* the term "humanity" is also closely related to social practice. For the English translation: "Humanity. Is a feeling of good will toward all men. Ordinarily only great and sensitive souls are consumed by it. This noble and sublime enthusiasm is tortured by the sufferings of others and tormented by the need to relieve such suffering; it fills men with the desire to traverse the world in order to do away with slavery, superstition, vice, and misfortune" (Hoyt and Cassirer 2003).

14. Here I refer to the term "humanitarian revolution" in the sense of the revolutionary emergence of humanitarian sensibility and activities rather than as a decline in violence, as it is interpreted by Pinker 2011, 129–188.

15. Laqueur 1989, 176–204; Moyn 2006; Hunt 2007; Wilson and Brown 2009; Festa 2010; Fiering 1976; Halttunen 1995, 304–307; Haskell 1985a and 1985b. On this, see also Samuel Moyn's chapter in this volume.

16. Malik 2014, 189–217. At the end of the nineteenth century, Henry S. Salt, a British social reformer and founder of the association of the Humanitarian League defined the term "humanitarianism" with the words: "by humanitarianism I mean nothing more and nothing less than the study and practice of humane principles – of compassion, love, gentleness, and universal benevolence." Salt 1891, 3; Salt 1907, 178–188. On this, see also Jeffrey Flynn's chapter in this volume.

17. The abolitionists constituted indeed a crucial humanitarian movement in the eighteenth and nineteenth centuries, but were, as Alan Lester's chapter in this volume shows, by far not the only ones.

18. Clarkson 1808, 255–258; Klingberg 1926, 73; Stamatov 2013, 155–174.

19. For this reason most studies explicitly relate the campaign against the slave trade in the course of the eighteenth and nineteenth centuries to the history of

humanitarianism instead of the history of human rights. See Moyn 2012a, 559–561. For two exceptions, see Martinez 2012; Blackburn 2011.

20. Quote by Wilberforce during the debate in the House of Commons on April 18 and 19, 1791 (Great Britain, Parliament, House of Commons 1791, 37).

21. Festa 2010; Stevenson 2017, 414–417. Concerning this idea the abolitionist referred to the older tradition of the Quakers and their campaign against the slave trade. See for instance Benezet 1784.

22. Clarkson 1808, 450; Guyatt 2000; Bourke 2011, 120.

23. Act of the British Parliament for the Abolition of the Slave Trade, March 25, 1807, BFSP 5, 559–568. See also Farrell 2007.

24. Act of the British Parliament, BFSP 5, 567.

25. On this deployment of the Royal Navy, see Lloyd 1968; Ward 1969; Rees 2009.

26. "Déclaration des 8 Cours, relative à l'Abolition Universelle de la Traite des Nègres," February 8, 1815, BFSP 3, 971–972. For a detailed description of these negotiations, see Reich 1968, 137–140; Clark 2007, 37–60.

27. For the beginning of these negotiations from 1816 to 1819, see The National Archives of the UK (TNA), Foreign Office (FO) 84/1 and TNA, FO 84/2; "Note sur le projet d'une ligue maritime pour assurer l'abolition de la traite et la répression de la piraterie des Barbaresques," n.d, Le Ministère des Affaires Étrangères, Archives des Affaires Étrangères (MAE), MD A15; Kielstra 2000, 64–67.

28. For this international treaty regime against the slave trade, see Nadelmann 1990, 491–498; Keene 2007; Mason 2009; Law 2010. For an overview of all treaties concerning the slave trade in the period between 1776 to 1863, see "Slave Trade Suppression Tables; or A Chronologically arranged Statement of the Measures taken by different Nations for the Abolition of the Slave Trade," in Her Majesty's Stationery Office 1865, 131–142.

29. Wheaton 1836, 114–115.

30. "[A] traffic so justly stigmatized by every civilized and Christian powers as a crime against humanity" and "Public opinion stigmatizing the traffic as a crime against humanity," in Wheaton 1842, 4 and 16; Wheaton 1845, 594. The British Navy officer Joseph Denman, who was on duty with the Royal Navy in West Africa, also used the term "crime against humanity" in his publication in 1850: "Public opinion urged on an unwilling government all the efforts against the traffic at the Congress of Vienna; which, in declaring it a crime against humanity and universal morality, spoke the sentiments of the people of England" (Denman 1850, 10).

31. Bassiouni 2011.

32. "Though all but forgotten today, these slave trade courts were the first international human rights courts," in Martinez 2012, 6 and especially 148–157. Also Farida Shaikh speaks in the context of the Mixed Commissions of "one of the earliest attempts to enforce international human rights law." See: Shaikh 2009, 42.

33. Simms and Trim 2011, 22.

34. Bluntschli 1872, 20, 265 and 269.

35. Rolin-Jaequemyns 1876, 675.
36. At this point, I agree with Samuel Moyn's view that transnational anti-slavery and humanitarian intervention were clearly part of the history of humanitarianism. See Moyn 2016, 4. For the importance of the long nineteenth century for a broader perspective, see Hoffmann 2016, 4 and 30–32.
37. For the eventual abolition of slavery, see Drescher 2009, 245–266 and 333–371; Blackburn 2011, 391–454.
38. For the significant entanglement of humanitarianism and European colonialism/imperialism in the nineteenth century, see Paulmann 2016b; Lester and Dussart 2014; Skinner and Lester 2012; Thompson 2016a; Barnett 2011, 29–30 and 47–94. On this issue, see also Alan Lester's chapter in this volume.
39. See, for example, Lingelbach 1900; Rougier 1910.
40. Lingelbach 1900. Not all international legal scholars agreed on the doctrine of humanitarian intervention. For this opposition, see Heraclides and Dialla 2015, 60–61 and 67–69.
41. Lingelbach 1900.
42. Neff 2014, 297.
43. Rougier 1910, 408–525.
44. "Les droits de l'homme seraient les droits antérieurs et supérieurs à toute organisation politique, placés sous la garantie de toutes les nations . . . . Seule la violation de ces droits essentiels serait une juste cause d'intervention." Ibid., 517.
45. Graham 1924, 320–321; Stowell 1932, 148. The historian Bruno Cabanes identifies the interwar period as an important transformative moment, in which an international rights discourse significantly arose. In his opinion debates about "humanitarian rights" emerged during this time, which strongly influenced the further history of human rights. Cabanes 2014.
46. Graham 1924, 320–321.
47. See "There exists now, therefore, not a subjective Law of Nature nor a sentimental Law of Humanity to sanction interventions of a humanitarian character, but a substantive Law of Nations defining the right of humanitarian intervention in a new light" (Ibid., 321–322).
48. Ibid., 326.
49. For a discussion of Mandelstam and his importance, see Burger 2000, 69–82; Aust 2014; Adak 2018.
50. Mandelstam 1931; Aust 2014, 1115–1117. Mandelstam's position on international human rights protection is also described in Mandelstam 1930.
51. Mandelstam 1931, 367–368.
52. Ibid., 375.
53. See Mazower 2006; Pedersen 2014, 107–194; Betts 2016, 53–58.
54. Article 2, Par. 4 and Par. 7 of the UN Charter.
55. Stefan-Ludwig Hoffmann argues that "Between the end of the Second World War and the early 1990s there was not a single humanitarian, political or military intervention that was justified through human rights" (Hoffmann 2016, 285). However, the legal debates about humanitarian intervention to

protect human rights indeed existed in this period and as shown emerged already in the first half of the twentieth century.

56. Koskenniemi 1997, 244.
57. Lauterpacht 1943.
58. Ibid., 27–28. On his repeated references to humanitarian interventions against slavery and on behalf of the protection of minorities in the nineteenth century, see also Lauterpacht 1950, 120–121.
59. Lauterpacht 1943, 28.
60. Lauterpacht 1945, 169–178.
61. Ibid., 194–213.
62. Ibid., 209–210.
63. On this see also Oppenheim 1948, 280–287.
64. See Klose 2013.
65. See The International Law Association 1967, 744–754.
66. Lillich 1969. See also Lillich 1967.
67. Reisman and McDougal 1973, 167–195.
68. Ibid., 194–195. Instead of "Ibos" the correct term is "Igbos."
69. Reisman and McDougal 1973, 179–183.
70. Paxman and Boggs 1973, 103–148; Wiseberg 1974, 61–98; de Schutter 1972; Franck and Rodley 1973; Fonteyne 1973; Murphy 1996, 135–142. For a critical debate, see especially Brownlie 1974; Lillich 1974; Behuniak 1978; Hassan 1981; Bazyler 1987.
71. Bruch 2016; Hehir and Murray 2017; Menon 2016, 22–24; Frei, Stahl, and Weinke 2017; Eckel 2017.
72. On this see also Beitz's chapter in this volume.

7   Mobilizing Emotions: Shame, Victimhood, and Agency

1. Plato 2003, 338c2–3.
2. Pitkin 1993.
3. Barnett 2011; Boltanski 1999; Redfield 2006. See also chapters by Barnett, Beitz, Flynn, Givoni, Ticktin, and Feldman in this volume.
4. Keck and Sikkink 1999.
5. Locke 2016.
6. Lebron 2015.
7. Brysk 1993.
8. Goodman and Jinks 2013; Finnemore and Sikkink 1998; Sikkink 2011.
9. Roth 2004.
10. Foucault 1995; Kahan 2006; Lightfoot 2016; Milgram 1974.
11. Braithwaite 1989; Cohen 2007; Lifton 1973.
12. Dunant 1939, 13.
13. Ibid., 13.
14. Ibid., 13.
15. Arendt 1990; Boltanski 1999.
16. Singer 1972.
17. Pictet 1967.
18. Ibid.

19. Barnett 2011, 23
20. Ibid., 25.
21. Ibid.
22. Dunant 1939, 13.
23. Slim 2015.
24. Berlant 2011.
25. Cohen 2015.
26. Rubenstein 2016, 14.
27. Beltrán 2009.
28. Ibid.; Ticktin 2011a.
29. Anghie 2004; Khalili 2013; Kinsella 2011; Teitel 2011.
30. Arendt 1963.
31. Brauman 1993.
32. Binet 2015.
33. Power 2001, 106.
34. ICISS 2001.
35. See Power 2019.
36. Bali and Rana 2018.
37. Arendt 2007, 269.
38. Pictet 1967.
39. Benenson 1961.
40. Hopgood 2006.
41. Chakravarti 2014; Douglas 2001.
42. Rothberg 2009, 178.
43. Hausner 1977, 341.
44. Segev 1993; Zertal 2006.
45. Keck and Sikkink 1999.
46. Ticktin 2016.
47. Kinsella 2016.
48. Taylor 2001, 100.
49. Ibid., 100.
50. See Teitel 2011.
51. Roth 2004, 68.
52. TRC 1998, 41.
53. Brudholm 2008; Chakravarti 2014; Mihai 2016.
54. Du Bois 1919.
55. Locke 2018, 12.
56. Wells 1900.
57. Ibid.
58. Gooding-Williams 2011.
59. Quoted in Regan 2013, 115.
60. Du Bois 1947.
61. See Bullard 2005; Pellow 2007.
62. COPINH 2019.
63. Montes 2019.
64. Ibid.
65. Aesop 2012.

8   At Odds? Human Rights and Humanitarian Approaches to Violence Against Women During Conflict

1. Swaine 2004.
2. The term "conflict-related sexual violence" (CRSV) is used to refer to forms of sexualized harms that may be directly or indirectly related to a conflict, may be enacted by armed and non-armed/civilian actors and take place in the context of a conflict setting. Swaine 2019.
3. See, for example, UNOHCHR 2018; MONUSCO and UNOHCHR 2013.
4. See Commission of Inquiry report, for example, United Nations Human Rights Council 2017; UNOHCHR 2014.
5. See Justice Rapid Response, JRR Expert Roster, www.justicerapidresponse.org /what-we-do/jrr-roster/.
6. For example, see United Nations Human Rights Council 2013.
7. CEDAW 2013.
8. United Nations General Assembly 2015.
9. United Nations Security Council 2008, 2009, 2010, 2013.
10. IASC 2005 and 2015.
11. See Global Protection Cluster – Gender Based Violence, www.globalprotec tioncluster.org/en/areas-of-responsibility/gender-based-violence.html.
12. UK Foreign and Commonwealth Office 2014.
13. UK Foreign and Commonwealth Office 2013.
14. See, for example, Inter-Agency Standing Committee Gender Marker, www .humanitarianresponse.info/en/topics/gender/page/iasc-gender-marker.
15. Development Initiatives 2014.
16. The term "conflict-related violence against women" (CRVAW) is used here to refer to all forms of physical, sexual, economic, psychological, emotional harms, and abuse that may be directly or indirectly related to a conflict, may be enacted by armed and non-armed/civilian actors and take place in the context of a conflict setting. It is used as an umbrella term to capture all forms of harm women and girls might experience in the conflict, distinctive from CRSV, which only focuses on sexualized harms (see note 2).
17. O'Rourke and Swaine 2018.
18. Teitel 1997, 302–303.
19. Teitel 1997.
20. Leebaw 2007, 224.
21. For example, see UNOHCHR Country Offices, www.ohchr.org/EN/Count ries/Pages/CountryOfficesIndex.aspx. And for an overview of UN system human rights bodies, see Human Rights Bodies, www.ohchr.org/EN/HRBo dies/Pages/HumanRightsBodies.aspx.
22. Leebaw 2007, 224.
23. Barnett 2013, 382.
24. See Inter-Agency Standing Committee on Humanitarian Action, https://int eragencystandingcommittee.org.
25. Barnett 2013, 380.
26. Labbé 2012.
27. Ibid., 6.
28. Nickel 2002; Barnett 2012.

29. Engle 2014; Eriksson Baaz and Stern 2013.
30. Engle 2018.
31. Ní Aoláin 2009.
32. Engle 2018.
33. Alston and Goodman 2013, 166.
34. United Nations General Assembly 1967.
35. United Nations General Assembly 1979.
36. CEDAW 1989 and 1992.
37. United Nations General Assembly 1993.
38. Edwards 2011.
39. CEDAW 1992.
40. IASC 1999.
41. United Nations Economic and Social Council 1997.
42. IASC 1999, Para 2, c.
43. Ibid., Para 4, a.
44. IASC 2008, 3.
45. IASC 2006, 2010, 2017, 2019.
46. UNHCR 1995, 2003.
47. IASC 2015, 5.
48. Sphere 2018.
49. United Nations Security Council 2009, para 12 (1889).
50. United Nations Security Council 2013, para 19 (2106).
51. Charlesworth and Chinkin 2000.
52. Engle 2018; Meger 2016.
53. Engle 2018.
54. See United Nations Security Council 2008, 2009, 2010, 2013.
55. UK Foreign and Commonwealth Office 2013.
56. See, for example, United Nations Development Programme nd; Justice Rapid Response and UN Women 2018.
57. United Nations Security Council 2010.
58. Ibid.
59. See, for example, United Nations Security Council 2018.
60. Engle 2018, 4–5.
61. Médecins Sans Frontières 2014.
62. Freedman 2014, 136.
63. Read-Hamilton 2014.
64. Charlesworth and Chinkin 2000.
65. Ibid.
66. Engle 2018.
67. Anholt 2016, 3.
68. Ticktin 2011b, 251.
69. Freedman 2014.
70. Anholt 2016, 4.
71. Ibid., 3, citing Tiktin 2011b, 260.
72. See Flynn in this volume.
73. Buss 2014; Swaine 2018.
74. Charlesworth and Chinkin 2000; Sideris 2001.

75. Cockburn 2004; Kelly 1998; Moser 2001.
76. Swaine 2018.
77. Ibid.; Urban Walker 2009.
78. Ball 1996, 13.
79. Swaine 2016.
80. Henttonen et al. 2008.
81. IASC 2015.
82. See Flynn in this volume.
83. See Global Protection Cluster, Human Rights in Humanitarian Action, w
ww.globalprotectioncluster.org/en/areas-of-responsibility/human-rights-i
n-humanitarian-action.html.
84. See Barnett's Introduction and Conclusion this volume.
85. Beitz in this volume.
86. Ibid.
87. COFEM 2017.
88. Gouws 1996.
89. Molyneux 1985, 231.
90. Ibid.
91. Ibid., 232.
92. Ibid., 233.
93. IASC 2006
94. Molyneux 1985, 233.
95. Scully 2011, 17.
96. Dobash and Dobash 1983; Swaine 2018.
97. Ticktin 2011b, 250–251.
98. See Ticktin in this volume.
99. IASC 2015; Global Protection Cluster 2019.
100. Fineman 2008, 5.

9   Innocence: Shaping the Concept and Practice of Humanity

1. Le Pape and Salignon 2003, x.
2. *Oxford English Dictionary*, sv "innocence, n.," www.oed.com/view/Entry/96
292?redirectedFrom=Innocence.
3. Ariès 1962.
4. Bernstein 2011.
5. Locke 1975.
6. Malkki 2010.
7. Public lecture at the New School for Social Research, New York, November 5,
2013.
8. Meyerson 2017.
9. Bernstein 2011, 30–35.
10. Fassin 2010.
11. de Torrenté 2004, 4.
12. Redfield 2013, 39.
13. Bouris 2007.

14. Le Pape and Salignon 2003.
15. Redfield 2013; Ross 2002; Vallaeys 2004.
16. Caldwell 2009.
17. MSF, however, grew out of a revolutionary context in which populations in danger, not simply individuals, were also part of its mandate (Redfield 2013).
18. Ticktin 2011a.
19. I am primarily speaking of the type of medical humanitarianism that was shaped by MSF and that includes, for example, Médecins du Monde (Doctors of the World).
20. Brauman 1993, 154.
21. Le Pape and Salignon 2003.
22. Bradol 2003, 11.
23. Ticktin 2011b.
24. Abu-Lughod 2013; Volpp 2015.
25. Fassin 2011, 167.
26. Miller 2004; Rubin 1993.
27. For Joanna Faulkner (2011, 333), carnal knowledge assumes a kind of ignorance that in turn makes way for pleasure.
28. Kincaid 1998, 55.
29. Vance 2012.
30. Ibid., 207.
31. Ibid.
32. Ticktin 2011a.
33. Kelly 2015.
34. Roth 2004, 67; see also Kelly 2014, 323.
35. Kelly 2014.
36. Taken from an interview I conducted with Meryl Schwartz at the Innocence Project in NYC, August 8, 2016.
37. According to the *OED*, Thomas Hobbes invoked this meaning in *Leviathan* (1651) in speaking of a sovereign prince who put to death an innocent subject.
38. Halley 1993.
39. Smith 2010, 321.
40. Ibid., 322.

10   Reckoning with Time: Vexed Temporalities in Human Rights and Humanitarianism

1. UNRWA Archives Box RE 67, RE 500, part 7, Petition from Mukhtar of Balata camp to UNRWA Commissioner General, August 6, 1981. In UNRWA's response to the petition, budget constraints were referenced as the reason no restoration was possible.
2. Käpylä, and Kennedy 2014; Fassin 2005; Ticktin 2011a.
3. Cabanes 2014.
4. Ibid., 6.
5. UNHCR 2010.
6. Final act of the United Nations Conference of Plenipotentiaries on the Status of Refugees and Stateless Persons. July 28, 1951. www.unhcr.org/en-us/3b66c2aa10

7. Kuwali 2013a. See also Kuwali 2013b.
8. Moyn 2018.
9. Rancière 2004, 307.
10. David 2017, 298.
11. Lanegran 2005, 112.
12. Ibid., 112.
13. Huyssen 2011, 611.
14. Ibid., 607.
15. See also Dudai 2012.
16. David 2017, 297.
17. Bosco 2004.
18. Slyomovics 2005.
19. Ibid., 12.
20. Sayigh 2013; Shalhoub-Kevorkian 2014.
21. See also Rashed, Short, and Docker 2014.
22. Butler 2009.
23. Sayigh 2013, 58.
24. Khalidi 1991.
25. Davis 2010.
26. The group Zochrot (memory) is a dissident Israeli organization that insists precisely on a reckoning both with Palestinian presence and Israeli responsibility for Palestinian loss. See http://zochrot.org/.
27. Published as Ashrawi 2002.
28. *Al-Majdal* double issue 39/40 (Autumn 2008/Winter 2009).
29. A reporter in Gaza during this attack recounted that "the paramedic we were with referred to the current displacement of over 46,000 Gazan Palestinians as a continuation of the ongoing Nakba, the dispossession and exile seen through generation after generation enduring massacre after massacre" (Butterly 2009).
30. Hartman 2011.
31. Full official text of President Mahmoud Abbas' speech at the UNGA, *Palestine News & Information Agency (WAFA)*, September 23, 2011.
32. This section includes material from Feldman 2018.
33. Calhoun 2004; Cooper 2015.
34. Eyal Weizman refers to the "humanitarian present" to characterize "our" time. That humanitarianism's time is the present may then also impact this wider experience of time (Weizman 2012).
35. Zetter and Long 2012. This analysis was written before the full unfolding of the Syrian refugee crisis, but there is no reason to think this displacement will be short.
36. Brun 2016.
37. Brun 2015.
38. Redfield 2005.
39. McKay 2012.
40. Norum, Mostafanezhad, and Sebro 2016.
41. Time is also a problem for humanitarian workers, often experienced as boredom. See De Lauri 2014.
42. Chan and Loveridge 1987; Dunn 2014.

43. Roy 1995, 104–106.
44. The editorial argued they would then be "persons who have been resettled into something approaching normal circumstances" (UA OR 60 OR 215 (IS-1) part 3, 25 December 1972). UNRWA's Gaza director commented on the editorial that "it is strictly propaganda in my opinion" (from Director of Operations, Gaza, to Commissioner-General, December 26, 1972).
45. UA OR 60 OR 215 (IS-1) part 3, December 26, 1972, extracts from *Jerusalem Post*.
46. UA, Box OR 60 OR 215, report from UNRWA General Services Officer, Gaza, to director of UNRWA operations, Gaza, July 24, 1971.
47. UA OR 60 OR 215 (IS-1) part 1, letter from President of UNRWA staff association to Commissioner General, July 28, 1971.
48. Ibid.
49. UA OR 60 OR 215 (IS-1) part 1, from UNRWA to Israeli Ministry of Foreign Affairs, August 8, 1971.
50. UA OR 60 OR 215 (IS-1) part 1, UNRWA special report to General Assembly, September 17, 1971.
51. UA OR 60 OR 215 (IS-1) part 1, from Commissioner-General to General Gazit, August 21, 1971.
52. UA OR 60 OR 215 (IS-1) part 1, from teacher in Jabalia elementary school to director of UNRWA operations, Gaza, July 29, 1971.
53. UA OR 60 OR 215 (IS-1) part 2, from Israeli Ministry of Foreign Affairs to Commissioner-General, April 24, 1972.
54. UA OR 60 OR 215 (IS-1) part 3, draft memo from UNRWA to Ministry of Foreign Affairs, October 16, 1972.
55. UA, RE Box 4, RE 200, part 2, memorandum by Department of Relief Services, Cabinet memorandum 7/82.
56. As Arendt puts it: "Privileges in some cases, injustices in most, blessings and doom are meted out to them according to accident and without any relation whatsoever to what they do, did, or may do" (1951, 296).
57. Jelin 1994, 39.
58. Ibid.
59. Nussbaum 2016.
60. Laguardia 2017, 194.
61. Ibid., 212.
62. Babul 2012, 33.
63. Hopgood 2013.
64. Weiss 1990, 200.
65. Hiskes 2005, 1346.
66. Worland 2016.
67. Parker 2017.
68. Hiltermann, cited in Allen 2013, 59–60.
69. Allen 2013, 123–124.
70. Ibid., 104.
71. HRCRT Policy, 6.
72. Bajaj 2011. Human Rights Education Associates is one organization dedicated to advancing this mission (www.hrea.org/).

73. UNRWA reports that there are almost 500,000 students currently in its schools.
74. UNRWA 2013, 8.
75. Oguzertem and McAdams 2015.
76. UNRWA 2013, 7.
77. In detail these are:
    1. Human dignity: all human beings, by virtue of being human, deserve to be respected and treated well.
    2. Universality: human rights are universal. All people everywhere in the world are entitled to them.
    3. Equality and nondiscrimination: all individuals are equal as human beings and by virtue of the inherent dignity of each person. No one should therefore suffer discrimination.
    4. Participation and inclusion: all people have the right to participate in and access information relating to the decision-making processes that affect their lives and wellbeing.
    5. Tolerance: tolerance is respect, acceptance and appreciation of the rich diversity of our world's cultures, our forms of expression and ways of being human. (Toolkit 10)
78. Hamas objected to the program in Gaza in precisely these terms, and it also objected to teaching about the Holocaust (https://prrnblog.wordpress.com/2010/12/20/hamas-unrwa-and-human-rights-education/).
79. Pinto 2014.

11   Between the Border and a Hard Place: Negotiating Protection and Humanitarian Aid after the Genocide in Cambodia, 1979–1999

* I am very grateful to the feedback from colleagues involved in the workshops that took place in GWU and to Michael Barnett for his challenging and attentive reading of drafts of this chapter.
1. Interview with Rob Overtoom, November 10, 2017, Kampot. Cambodia.
2. On paternalism, see Barnett 2016.
3. Arguably the 1990s were a hiatus between two phases of political instrumentalization of the genocide. Since the late 1990s, however, the genocide has become part of the legitimacy of the regime led by Hun Sen. The Prime Minister Hun Sen made considerable use of the genocide in the 2018 electoral campaign, www.phnompenhpost.com/national-politics/analysis-new-propaganda-documentary-hun-sen-attempts-rewrite-history. See www.youtube.com/watch?v=oj3dAlpf7ls released on January 3, 2018 or the re-enactment of Genocidal acts in the National Day or remembrance on May 21, 2018, www.phnompenhpost.com/national/national-day-remembrance-held. Hun Sen's party won all 125 seats in the Cambodian parliamentary election of 2018.
4. The official name of Cambodia was its Khmer shortened name "Kampuchea" between 1975 and 1989 when the transitional "State of Cambodia" was established.
5. On this, see Richmond and Franks 2007.

6. "Operation Plan, Repatriation of Cambodian Refugees and Displaced Persons" January 1992, Archives MSF, Paris, Thailande, Khao I Dang 1990–1992 rapports Kit Medi RP1.
7. www.websitesrcg.com/border/border-camps.html, a website by Richard Rowat.
8. Terry 2002, 131; Mason and Brown 1983.
9. Barber 1997, 8–14; French 2002, 427–470.
10. Locard 2005, 136–137.
11. Roberts 2010.
12. MSF grew from being a small French NGO to becoming a major confederation of operational centers in that era. MSF's logistics also dates from the work done in camps, as did its logistics department
13. Gilles Germain, "Note de synthèse à François Jean," February 3, 1993, Archives MSF, Papiers François Jean, Boite ABILE.
14. Thailand was not a signatory of UN refugee convention and displaced Cambodians had an ambiguous legal status throughout the period.
15. The term and its uses in relation to refugees are object of contention, see Agamben 1998; Owens 2009.
16. Kraus 1944, 5–17. Kraus calls some of the more sophisticated interventions "building community services," beyond and above protection.
17. The concept of nonrefoulement, from the French, was coined it seems by Stéphane Rousseau, protection officer of UNBRO, see Stéphane Rousseau, "Protection Officer's Legal Framework on the Thai-Cambodian Border," 1992, Private archive S. Rousseau, Bangkok. The official archives of UNBRO no longer exist. Many thanks to Stéphane Rousseau for sharing this invaluable private archive.
18. Oesterheld 2014.
19. Shawcross 1984, 52–71.
20. Interview with Philippe The Long, Kampot, November 2017.
21. See the testimonial published on Khmerization.blogspot.co.uk/2010/05/thai-massacre-of-khmer-refugees-at-html or the Cambodia watch attempt at compiling memoirs: http://camwatchblogs.blogspot.co.uk/2011/05/thai-armys-atrocity-at-mount-dangrek.html.
22. https://cwcinternational.wordpress.com/2010/05/17/khmers-in-norway-commemorate-the-deaths-of-khmer-refugees-dumped-in-dangrek-mountains-by-thai-troops/.
23. Jean-Pierre Hiégel who worked originally for the ICRC developed a very original response to the mental health needs of Cambodian patients by integrating Kru Khmer traditional healing. Hiégel was supported by a range of NGOs over the 1980s. See Hiégel-Landrac and Hiégel, 1996.
24. Gyallay-Pap 1989, 261.
25. Ibid., 267.
26. Arguably the 1924 declaration hinted as much but education featured explicitly only in the 1959 UN declaration. Throughout the 1980s preparatory texts leading to the 1989 declaration of the right of children were taking place. www.humanium.org/fr/normes/declaration-1959/texte-integral-declaration-droits-enfant-1959/.
27. Gyallay-Pap, "Reclaiming," 273.

28. Ibid., 273–274.
29. Rithy Panh, "'La Famille Tan' La Sept [Arte], 1995, 31'56," Archives Televisuelles Bophana (Phnom Penh), Collection ITI 20H, fonds Rithy Panh, RIPA VI 871,
30. Boehnlein, Kinzie, Ben, and Fleck 1985.
31. There was considerable divergence of opinion on the validity of PTSD categories. According to my informants working in the camps, humanitarians in the field were skeptical and thought the diagnostic premature. Rob Overtoom interview.
32. Mollica et al. 1993, 581–586; Mollica et al. 2002, 158–166; Sack et al. 1986, 377–383.
33. Sack et al. 1994, 387–395; Nann 2009, 55. Boehnlein 2002, 712.
34. Fassin and Retchman 2007.
35. Blair 2000, 23–30; Carlson and Rosser-Hogan 1994, 43–58.
36. Rechtman 2004, 913–915; also, for a distinct interpretation of the invention of PTSD, see Young 2004, 127–146.
37. Guillou 2012, 212.
38. Bophana, INA VI 1445, Les Dossiers de l'écran, November 27, 1979.
39. Shawcross 1984, 95–111. The famine had been claimed by the Vietnamese and Cambodian authorities but it soon became reinterpreted as a genocidal weapon of war when the Vietnamese proved unwilling to allow food to be delivered. Ultimately there was severe malnutrition but no famine.
40. Davey 2015, 201–209.
41. Follézou was a French communist party and trade unionist leader. See his biographical notice on Maitron, http://maitron-en-ligne.univ-paris1.fr/spip .php?article195255.
42. www.lemonde.fr/archives/article/1980/01/30/la-querelle-des-organisations-humanitaires-une-polemique-sterile-en-marge-du-drame-de-tout-un-peu ple_3070716_1819218.http. Davey 2015, 201; also Shawcross 1984, 207, 253.
43. Brodiez 2006, 151–167.
44. Interview with Jean-Pierre Hocké, High Commissioner 1986–1989. May 2017.
45. Refugee policy group, "Repatriation, Cambodia a Time for Return, Reconci-liation and Reconstruction," unpublished report, Washington and Geneva, October 1991, Archives MSF (Paris), papiers François Jean, ABILE.
46. "Feeding Peace or Feeding War?" Diakonia, Bangkok, News from the Jesuit Refugee Services, November 1989, 1.
47. Minutes of the 6th NGO forum, September 1989, "report from the Border," Archives MSF (Paris), papiers François Jean, Droits de l'homme, 7.
48. Mouvement d'entraide pour le Tiers Monde et la coopération, minutes of the meeting of November 29, 1989, Archives MSF (Paris), papiers François Jean, ABILE.
49. Brown 1992, 88–95.
50. Doyle and Suntharalingam 1994, 118–119.
51. To summarize, the United Nations Advance Mission in Cambodia was subsumed in 1992 within a new larger mission UNTAC (United Nation

Transition Authority in Cambodia) 16,000 soldiers strong and 3,500 policemen strong. See Curtis 1993.

52. Ponchaud 1977.
53. Hall and Getlin 1992.
54. "International Aid Workers in Cambodia on the Thai Cambodian Border demand UN Cambodian Seat to be challenged," August 6, 1990, Archives MSF (Paris), papiers François Jean, Droits de l'Homme.
55. It was occasionally voiced, however: Asian Watch, a US human Right NGO had produced a report in 1988 entitled "Khmer Rouge Abuses along the Thai Cambodian Border," February 1988, Archives MSF (Paris), papiers François Jean, ABILE.
56. Shawcross, Quality of Mercy, 155–156.
57. Walter 2007, 143.
58. Jackson 1987, 2.
59. Ibid., 14–16.
60. Ibid., 21.
61. Walker 2007, 155.
62. The forum's initial budget was 48,000 dollars in 1990, with funding originating from seven large INGOs.
63. Davey 2015.
64. "Au Cambodge Ils reviennent," Opération Cambodge, November 16, 1989, Archives MSF (Paris), papiers François Jean, ABILE; "Les Khmers Rouges Reviennent: Avons-nous le Droit de ne Rien Faire?" Handicap International, 24, 1990, 2–5.
65. Minutes of the 6th meeting of the NGO Forum, Quaker House, Brussels, September 4–6, 1989, Archives MSF (Paris), papiers François Jean, Droits de l'Homme.
66. Memorandum letter from Lucile de la Brabandere to members of the forum, Oxfam Belgium, October 2, 1990. Archives MSF (Paris), papiers François Jean, Droits de l'Homme.
67. Convention entre Lucile de la Brabandere au nom du Forum des ONG et Raoul Jennar, March 29, 1990, Archives MSF (Paris), papiers François Jean, Droits de l'Homme.
68. Jennar 1995.
69. Peschoux 1992.
70. Quaker United Nations Office, "Policies and Procedures Relevant to the Representation of Cambodia in the United Nations," Archives MSF (Paris), papiers François Jean, Droits de l'Homme.
71. Minutes of the 7th meeting of the NGO Forum, Quaker House, Brussels, February 26–27, 1990, Archives MSF (Paris), papiers François Jean, Droits de l'Homme.
72. Fax from Action Nord-Sud and Handicap International to MSF, reporting on the meeting of February 2, 1993, Archives MSF (Paris), papiers François Jean, Droits de l'Homme.
73. "Standard Operating Procedures for Medical Activities during the Repatriation Process," March 18, 1992, Archives MSF (Paris), Thailande, Khao I Dang 1990–1992 rapports Kit Medi RP1.

74. February 4, 1991, Archives MSF (Paris), papiers François Jean, Droits de l'Homme.
75. Hall, John, and Taylor 2003. Lawn et al. 2008.
76. Strangio 2014, 138–139.
77. http://sithi.org/admin/upload/law/Unofficial-Translation-LANGO.pdf.
78. www.cambodiadaily.com/news/two-years-on-ngo-law-remains-ambiguous-132456/.
79. Strangio 2014, 210–213.
80. Taithe 2016, 335–358
81. Jansen 2015.
82. This is rather different from the more commonplace take on the militarization of humanitarianism argued by many in the aftermath of the 1990s military interventions. See, for instance, Chandler 2001.
83. See Guillou 2012, 216–222.
84. See Chandler 2008, 355–369.
85. Rechtman 2006, 1–11; Rechtman 1993, 259–269.
86. Hughes 2007.
87. Far from original hopes: Duffy 1994; Hughes 2007.
88. www.khmertimeskh.com/50517663/people-support-a-multiparty-democracy-hun-sen-says/.

Conclusion: Practices of Humanity

1. www.oed.com/view/Entry/89262?redirectedFrom=human+rights#eid1123373.
2. This is the second entry. The first refers to the belief that Christ was both divine and human. www.oed.com/view/Entry/272189?redirectedFrom=humanitarianism#eid.
3. Hunt 2007, 20. Also see Lauren 1998; Ishay 2008; Beitz 2009; Schmitz and Sikkink 2002.
4. See, for instance, Barnett 2011; Paulmann 2016a; Skinner and Lester 2012.
5. Patten 2014, 41. For the distinction between natural and social kinds, see Hacking 1998.
6. Barnett 2011.
7. This section draws from Barnett 2018.
8. For various statements on practices, see Schatzki, Knorr-Cetina, and von Savigny 2005; Rouse 2007; Nocilini 2012; Ortner 2006; and Adler and Pouliot 2011. For applications to human rights, see Goodale and Merry 2007; Meierhenrich 2013; Schaffer 2014; Beitz 2009; Karp 2013; Lamb 2019; Redhead and Turnbull 2011; Nash 2015; Kurasawa 2007; and Dudai 2019. And for humanitarianism, see Stein 2011; Barnett 2005; Krause 2014; Roth 2015.
9. For discussions of boundaries, see Tilly 2004; Abbott 1995; Helte 2012; Lamont and Molnar 2002; Pachuki, Pendergrass, and Lamont 2007; Wimmer 2008.
10. Wegner 1998.

11. Carruth; Gottlieb, Filc, and Davidovitch 2012.
12. Nussbaum 2001, 306, 314.
13. However, see Ignatieff 2001 on the blurry relationship between rights and needs.
14. Campbell 1974, 9. Also see Willen 2007.
15. For bare life, see Agamben 1988. For regime of life, see Stevenson 2014, 68.
16. Calhoun 2008.
17. Lauren 1998; Hunt 2007; Moyn 2012b; Wilson and Brown 2009; Ishay 2008; Hopgood 2013; Beitz 2009; Karp 2013; Schmitz and Sikkink 2002.
18. Beitz and Goodin 2009; Shue 1980.
19. Zald 1996, 262. Also see Goffman 1974, 21; Snow et al. 1986, 464.
20. Also see Watenpaugh 2015, 57–90; Lidchi 2016; Zacher, Brehm, and Savelsberg 2014; Hoijer 2004; Spelman 2001; Moon 2012.
21. Also see Feldman 2009; and Ticktin 2016.
22. Dudai 2019, 275.
23. Burke 2017; Taithe 2019. Burke, 2019.
24. For an extended discussion, see Ross 2018.
25. See Brown 2006; Keys 2014; and Burke 2017.
26. Sontag 2003.
27. Twomey 2012; Fehrenbach and Rodogno 2015.
28. For discussions of the "victim," complex and otherwise, see Lacerda 2016; Baines. 2009; Govier and Verwoerd 2004; Dean 2010, 1–30; Fassin and Rechtman 2009; and van Wijk 2015.
29. Halttunen 1995.
30. Kennedy 2009; Photographers without Borders, nd.
31. Also see Clark 2016.
32. Ticktin 2016
33. Stein 2011, 89.
34. Wilson and Brown 2009, 7; Wilson 2008, 342, 351; Joas 2013, 186, 195; McManus 2017, 8; Dembour, and Kelly 2017; Bruch 2014, 41; Slim 2015, 17; O'Flaherty and Ulrich 2010, 16; Cody, Wilson, and Rasmussen 2001.
35. Hurwitz 2013, 513; Cody, Wilson, and Rasmussen 2001; Neier 2013.
36. Beitz 2009, 209–210; Goodale 2008, 6.
37. Slim 2015, 17.
38. Moon 2016.
39. Redfield 2015 and 2016.
40. For overviews and assessments of naming and shaming, see Kiznelbach and Lehmann 2015; McEntire, Leiby, and Krain 2015.
41. Slim 2015, 17. Also see Kellenberger 2004; Forsythe 2005a; Magone, Neuman, and Weissman 2011; Pease 2016; Minear and Smith 2007; Slim 2019.
42. Sykes 2012.

43. Schauer 2009.
44. There also is evidence of growing technical reasoning. See Dale and Kyle 2016.
45. Kratochwil 2014, 200.
46. Hurwitz 2003, 510.
47. Niezen 2007. Also see Kurasawa 2007, 194; O'Flaherty and Ulrich 2010; Redhead and Turnbull 2011; Buchanan 2013.
48. Shklar 1964, 1.
49. Fassin 2012, 1.
50. Sphere 2018, 2.
51. Lohne and Sandvik 2017, 14.
52. Willen 2007.
53. Lohne and Sandvik 2017, 16; Rubenstein 2016.
54. Dale and Kyle 2016.
55. Stein 2011; Hopgood 2008; Barnett 2012.
56. Hopgood 2008.
57. Rouse 2007, 503; Adler and Pouliot 2011, 8.
58. Pictet 1979. Also see Weiss 1999.
59. Hilhorst and Jansen 2010.
60. Leebaw 2007; Forsythe 2013.
61. Leebaw 2007; Brown 2004, 453.
62. Leebaw 2007, 226.
63. Ibid., 227.
64. Barnett and Weiss 2013; Cutts 1998; Warner 1999.
65. Although in some religious teachings, it is the sinful behavior of communities that causes God to unleash such destruction. Moreover, often there are parties that are responsible for creating conditions that make some populations more vulnerable to natural disasters, hence, destabilizing the idea of the natural and interjecting the political and social.
66. Schatzki 2005a, 3; Schatzki 2005b 42–55.
67. Wuthnow 1989, 40. Also see Fligstein and McAdam 2002, 43–45.
68. Cladis 2008, xxviii. Also see Joas 2013, 5, 7; Agamben 1998; Levy and Snzaider 2006.
69. Dewey 1934, 19.
70. Taylor 2004, 15–16.
71. Ibid., 456; Casanova 2011.
72. Berger 1967; Frankel 1984.
73. Wydra 2015.
74. Taithe 2004, 156.
75. Arendt 1986, 299.
76. Seligman and Montgomery 2019.
77. Orwell 1949.
78. Sikkink 2018, 10.
79. Alston 2017; Dudai 2017.
80. Hopgood 2019.
81. Bennett 2019.

82. www.icrc.org/en/document/icrc-urge-states-take-action-rules-war-and-cli mate-change.
83. Latour 2018.
84. www.economist.com/open-future/2019/04/25/how-genetic-engineering-will -reshape-humanity. For a past look and justification, see Osborne 1939.

Bibliography

Abbott, Andrew. 1995. "Boundaries of Social Work or Social Work of Boundaries?" *Social Service Review*, 69, 4, 545–562.

Abruzzo, Margaret. 2011. *Polemical Pain: Slavery, Cruelty, and the Rise of Humanitarianism*. Baltimore: Johns Hopkins University Press.

Abu-Lughod, Lila. 2013. *Do Muslim Women Need Saving?* Cambridge, MA: Harvard University Press.

Adak, Hülya. 2018. "The Legacy of André Nikolaievitch Mandelstam (1869–1949) and the Early History of Human Rights," *Zeitschrift für Religions- und Geistesgeschichte*, 70, 2, 117–130.

Adler, Emanuel and Vincent Pouliot. 2011. "Introduction and Framework," in E. Adler and V. Pouliot, eds., *International Practices*, 3–35. New York: Cambridge University Press.

Aesop. 2012. *Aesop's Fables* (Collins Classics). London: HarperCollins UK.

Afshari, Reza. 2007. "On the Historiography of Human Rights: Reflections on Paul Gordon Lauren's *The Evolution of International Human Rights*," *Human Rights Quarterly*, 29, 1, 2007, 1–67.

Agamben, Giorgio. 1998. *Homo Sacer: Sovereign Power and Bare Life*. Stanford: Stanford University Press.

Agier, Michel. 2010. "Humanity as an Identity and Its Political Effects: A Note on Camps and Humanitarian Government," *Humanity*, 1, 1, 29–45.

2011. *Managing the Undesirables: Refugee Camps and Humanitarian Government*. Malden, MA: Polity Press.

Ahmed, S. S. 2014. *The Cultural Politics of Emotion*. Edinburgh: Edinburgh University Press.

Alexander, Jeffrey. 1990. "Between Progress and Apocalypse: Social Theory and the Dream of Reason in the Twentieth Century," in J. Alexander and P. Sztompka, eds., *Rethinking Progress*, 15–38. London: Unwin Hyman.

Allen, Lori. 2013. *The Rise and Fall of Human Rights: Cynicism and Politics in Occupied Palestine*. Stanford, CA: Stanford University Press.

Alston, Philip. 2017. "The Populist Challenge to Human Rights," *Journal of Human Rights Practice*, 9, 1–15.

Alston, Philip and Ryan Goodman. 2013. *International Human Rights*. Oxford: Oxford University Press.

Altwicker, Tillman and Oliver Diggelmann. 2014. "How Is Progress Constructed in International Legal Scholarship?" *European Journal of International Law*, 25, 2, 425–444.

Amnesty International. 2017. Amnesty International Recommendations to the G20 on the Right to health. www.amnesty.org/en/documents/ior30/6580/2017/en/.

2018. Amnesty International's Statute: Core Values. www.amnesty.org/en/ab out-us/how-were-run/amnesty-internationals-statute/.

2020. COVID-19, Surveillance, and the Threat to Your Rights. www.amnesty.org /en/latest/news/2020/04/covid-19-surveillance-threat-to-your-rights/.

Amony, E. 2015. *I Am Evelyn Amony: Reclaiming My Life from the Lord's Resistance Army.* Madison: University of Wisconsin Press.

Anderson, Mary B. 1998. "'You Save My Life Today, but for What Tomorrow?' Some Moral Dilemmas of Humanitarian Aid," in Jonathan Moore, ed., *Hard Choices: Moral Dilemmas in Humanitarian Intervention*, 137–156. Lanham, MD: Rowman & Littlefield.

Anghie, A. 2004. *Colonialism, Sovereignty, and the Making of International Law.* Cambridge, UK: Cambridge University Press.

Anholt, Rosanne Marrit. 2016. "Understanding Sexual Violence in Armed Conflict: Cutting Ourselves with Occam's Razor," *Journal of International Humanitarian Action*, 1, 6–16.

Appiah, Anthony. 2010. *Cosmopolitanism.* New York: Norton.

Arendt, Hannah. 1951. *The Origins of Totalitarianism.* New York: Harcourt Brace Jovanovich.

1963a. *Eichmann in Jerusalem: A Report on the Banality of Evil.* New York: Viking Press.

1963b. *On Revolution.* New York: Penguin Press.

1965. *On Revolution*, new edn. New York: Viking Press.

1986. *The Age of Totalitarianism.* New York: Penguin Press.

1990. *On Revolution.* London: Penguin Press.

2007. *The Jewish Writings.* New York: Penguin.

2013. *The Jewish Writings.* New York: Schocken Books.

Ariès, Philippe. 1962. *Centuries of Childhood: A Social History of Family Life*, trans. Robert Baldick. New York: Vintage Books.

Arthur, George. 1833. *Observations Upon Secondary Punishment.* Hobart: Government Printer.

1835. *Defence of Transportation in Reply to the Remarks of the Archbishop of Durham.* London: George Cowie.

Ashrawi, Hanan. 2002. "Racism, Racial Discrimination, Xenophobia, and Related Intolerances," *Islamic Studies*, 41, 1, 97–104.

Aust, Helmut Philipp. 2014. "From Diplomat to Academic Activist: André Mandelstam and the History of Human Rights," *The European Journal of International Law*, 25, 4, 1105–1121.

Babul, Elif. 2012. "Training Bureaucrats, Practicing for Europe: Negotiating Bureaucratic Authority and Governmental Legitimacy in Turkey," *Political and Legal Anthropology Review*, 35, 1, 30–52.

Baines, Erin. 2009. "Complex Political Perpetrators: Reflections on Dominic Ongwen," *Journal of Modern African Studies*, 47, 2, 163–191.

2011. "Gender, Responsibility, and the Grey Zone: Considerations for Transitional Justice," *Journal of Human Rights*, 10, 4, 477–493.

2017. *Buried in the Heart: Women, Complex Victimhood and the War in Northern Uganda*. New York: Cambridge University Press.

Bajaj, Monisha. 2011. "Human Rights Education: Ideology, Location, and Approaches," *Human Rights Quarterly*, 33, 2, 481–508.

Balaji, Murali. 2011. "Racializing Pity: The Haiti Earthquake and the Plight of 'Others'," *Critical Studies in Media Communication*, 28, 1, March, 50–67.

Bâli, Aslı and Aziz Rana. 2018. "Remember Syria?" *Boston Review*, July. http://bostonreview.net/war-security/asli-bali-aziz-rana-trump-putin-syria.

Ball, Patrick. 1996. *Who Did What to Whom? Planning and Implementing a Large Scale Human Rights Data Project*. Washington, DC: American Association for the Advancement of Science.

Banivanua Mar, Tracey. 2013. "Imperial Literacy and Indigenous Rights: Tracing Transoceanic Circuits of a Modern Discourse," *Aboriginal History*, 37, 1–28.

Bank, A. 2000. "Evolution and Racial Theory: The Hidden Side of Wilhelm Bleek," *South African Historical Journal*, 43, 1, 163–217.

Barber, Ben. 1997. "Feeding Refugees, or War? The Dilemma of Humanitarian Aid," *Foreign Affairs*, 76, 4, 8–14.

Barnett, Michael. 2005. "Humanitarianism Transformed," *Perspectives on Politics*, 3, 4, 723–740.

2011. *Empire of Humanity: A History of Humanitarianism*. Ithaca: Cornell University Press.

2012a. "Faith in the Machine? Humanitarianism in an Age of Bureaucratization," in M. Barnett and J. Stein, eds., *Sacred Aid: Faith and Humanitarianism*, 188–212. New York: Oxford University Press.

2012b. "International Paternalism and Humanitarian Governance," *Global Constitutionalism*, 1, 3, 485–521.

2013. "Humanitarian Governance," *Annual Review of Political Science*, 16, May, 379–398.

ed. 2016. *Paternalism Beyond Borders*. New York: Cambridge University Press.

2018. "Human Rights, Humanitarianism, and the Practices of Humanity," *International Theory*, 10, 3, 314–349.

Barnett, Michael and Raymond Duvall. 2005. "Power in Global Governance," *International Organization*, 59, 1, 1–32.

Barnett, Michael and Janice Stein, eds. 2012. *Sacred Aid: Faith and Humanitarianism*. Oxford: Oxford University Press.

Barnett, Michael and Thomas G. Weiss. 2013. *Humanitarianism Contested: Where Angels Fear to Tread*. New York: Routledge.

Barry, Brian. 1982. "Humanity and Justice in Global Perspective," in Thomas Pogge and Darrel Moellendorf, eds., *Nomos, 24, Ethics, Economics and the Law*, 219–252. New York: New York University Press.

Bass, Gary. 2008. *Freedom's Battle. The Origins of Humanitarian Intervention*. New York: Knopf Doubleday Publishing.

Bassiouni, M. Cherif. 2011. *Crimes Against Humanity. Historical Evolution and Contemporary Application*. Cambridge, UK: Cambridge University Press.

Bayefsky, Rachel. 2013. "Dignity, Honour, and Human Rights: Kant's Perspective," *Political Theory*, 41, 6, 809–837.

Bazyler, Michael J. 1987. "Reexamining the Doctrine of Humanitarian Intervention in the Light of the Atrocities in Kampuchea and Ethiopia," *Stanford Journal of International Law*, 23, 547–619.

Behuniak, Thomas E. 1978. "The Law of Unilateral Humanitarian Intervention by Armed Force: A Legal Survey," *Military Law Review*, 79, 27, 157–191.

Beitz, Charles R. 2009. *The Idea of Human Rights*. Oxford: Oxford University Press.

    2013. "Human Dignity in the Theory of Human Rights: Nothing But a Phrase?" *Philosophy & Public Affairs*, 41, 3, 259–290.

Beitz, Charles and Robert Goodin, eds. 2009. *Global Basic Rights*. New York: Oxford University Press.

Beltrán, C. 2009. "Going Public," *Political Theory*, 37, 5, 595–622.

Benbassa, Esther. 2010. *Suffering as Identity: The Jewish Paradigm*. London: Verso Press.

Bender, Thomas, ed. 1992. *The Antislavery Debate: Capitalism and Abolitionism as a Problem in Historical Interpretation*. Berkeley: University of California Press.

Benenson, Peter. 1961. "The Forgotten Prisoners," *The Observer* (London), May 28.

Bernstein Carlson, Eve and Rhonda Rosser-Hogan. 1994. "Cross-Cultural Response to Trauma: A Study of Traumatic Experiences and Posttraumatic Symptoms in Cambodian Refugees," *Journal of Traumatic Stress*, 7, 1, 43–58.

Benezet, Anthony. 1784. *The Case of Our Fellow-Creatures: The Oppressed Africans, Respectfully Recommended to the Serious Consideration of the Legislature of Great Britain, By the People Called Quakers*. London.

Benison, Audrey. 1999. "War Crimes: A Human Rights Approach to a Humanitarian Law Problem at the International Criminal Court," *Georgetown Law Journal*, 88, 1, 141–175.

Bennett, Christina. 2019. "2019's Biggest Challenge: The Humanitarian Sell-Out," *Overseas Development Institute*, 10, January, www.odi.org/blogs/1072 1–2019s-biggest-challenge-humanitarian-sell-out.

Benton, Lauren. 2011. "Abolition and Imperial Law, 1790–1820," *Journal of Imperial and Commonwealth History*, 39, 3, 355–374.

Benton, Lauren and Lisa Ford. 2018. "Island Despotism: Trinidad, the British Imperial Constitution, and Global Legal Order," *Journal of Imperial and Commonwealth History*, 46, 1, 47–68.

Berger, Peter. 1967. *The Sacred Canopy: Elements of a Sociological Theory of Religion*. New York: Anchor Books.

Berlant, L. 2011. *Cruel Optimism*. Durham, NC: Duke University Press Books.

Berman, Eli, Joseph H. Felter, and Jacob N. Shapiro. 2018. *Small Wars, Big Data: The Information Revolution in Modern Conflict*. Princeton: Princeton University Press.

Bernath, Julie. 2016. "Complex Political Victims' in the Aftermath of Mass Atrocity: Reflections on the Khmer Rouge Tribunal in Cambodia," *International Journal of Transitional Justice*, 10, 1, 46–66.

Bernstein, Robin. 2011. *Racial Innocence: Performing American Childhood from Slavery to Civil Rights.* New York: New York University Press.

Betts, Paul. 2016. "Universalism and Its Discontents. Humanity as a Twentieth-Century Concept," in Fabian Klose and Mirjam Thulin, eds., *Humanity. A History of European Concepts in Practice From the Sixteenth Century to the Present,* 51–70. Goettingen: Vandenhoeck & Ruprecht.

Bhambra, Gurminder K. 2016. "Undoing the Epistemic Disavowal of the Haitian Revolution: A Contribution to Global Social Thought," *Journal of Intercultural* Studies, 37, 1, 1–16.

Binet, Laurence. 2015. *MSF and the War in the Former Yugoslavia 1991–2003.* Médecins Sans Frontières.

Blackburn, Robin. 2011. *The American Crucible. Slavery, Emancipation, and Human Rights.* London: Verso.

Blair, Robert G. 2000. "Risk Factors Associated with PTSD and Major Depression Among Cambodian Refugees in Utah," *Health and Social Work,* 25, 1, 23–30.

Bleek, Willhelm. 1858–1859. *The Library of Sir George Grey Catalogue Vol. I.* London: Trubner.

Bluntschli, Johann Caspar. 1872. Das moderne Voelkerrecht der civilisierten *Staten als Rechtsbuch dargestellt.* Noerdlingen: C.H. Beck'sche Buchhandlung.

Boehnlein, James K. 2002. "La Place de la Culture dans les Études sur le Traumatisme: une Perspective Américaine," *L'Évolution Psychiatrique,* 67, 4, 712–723.

Boehnlein, James K. and J. David Kinzie, Rath Ben, and Jenelle Fleck. 1985. "One-Year Follow-up Study of Posttraumatic Stress Disorder Among Survivors of Cambodian Concentration Camps," *The American Journal of Psychiatry,* 142, 8, 956–959.

Boehnlein, James K. and J. David Kinzie, Utako Sekiya, Crystal Riley, Kanya Pou, and Bethany Rosborough. 2004. "A Ten-year Treatment Outcome Study of Traumatized Cambodian Refugees," *The Journal of Nervous and Mental Disease,* 192, 10, 658–663.

Bolland, O. N. 1977. *The Formation of a Colonial Society: Belize, From Conquest to Crown Colony.* Baltimore: Johns Hopkins University Press.

Boltanski, L. 1999. *Distant Suffering: Morality, Media and Politics.* Cambridge, UK: Cambridge University Press.

Bornstein, Erica and Redfield, Peter, eds. 2011. *Forces of Compassion: Humanitarianism Between Ethics and Politics.* Santa Fe, NM: School for Advanced Research Press.

Bosco, Fernando J. 2004. "Human Rights Politics and Scaled Performances of Memory: Conflicts Among the Madres de Plaza de Mayo in Argentina," *Social & Cultural Geography,* 5, 3, 381–402.

Bouris, Erica. 2007. *Complex Political Victims.* Bloomfield: Kumarian Press.

Bourke, Joanna. 2011. *What It Means to Be Human. Historical Reflections from the 1800s to the Present.* Berkeley: Counterpoint Press.

Boyce, James. 2009. *Van Diemen's Land.* Melbourne: Black Inc.

Bradol, Jean-Hervé. 2003. "How Images of Adversity Affect the Quality of Aid," in Marc Le Pape and Pierre Salignon, eds., *Civilians under Fire:*

Humanitarian Practices in the Congo Republic 1998–2000, 1–26. New York: Médecins sans frontières.

2004. "The Sacrificial International Order and Humanitarian Action," in Fabrice Weissman, ed., *In the Shadow of "Just Wars": Violence, Politics and Humanitarian Action*, 1–22. Ithaca: Cornell University Press.

Braithwaite, J. 1989. *Crime, Shame, and Reintegration.* Cambridge, UK: Cambridge University Press.

Branch, Adam. 2011. *Displacing Human Rights: War and Intervention in Northern Uganda.* New York: Oxford University Press.

Brauman, Rony. 1993. "When Suffering Makes a Good Story," in François Jean, ed., *Life, Death and Aid: The Médecins sans frontières Report on World Crisis Intervention*, 149–158. London: Routledge.

Brereton, Bridget. 1981. *A History of Modern Trinidad 1783–1962.* London: Heinemann.

Brewer, John. 1989. *The Sinews of Power: War, Money and the English State, 1688–1783.* London: Routledge.

British Parliamentary Papers. 1969. *Correspondence Returns and Other Papers Relating to Canada and the Indian Problem Therein 1839*, reprinted. Shannon: Irish University Press.

Brodiez, Axelle. 2004. *Le Secours populaire français 1945–2000: Du communisme à l'humanitaire.* Paris: Sciences Po.

Bromley, Mary Ann. 1987. "New Beginnings for Cambodian Refugees – or Further Disruptions?" *Social Work*, 32, 3, 236–239.

Brown, Christopher L. 1999. "Empire Without Slaves: British Concepts of Emancipation in the Age of Revolution," *William and Mary Quarterly*, 56, 2, 273–306.

2006. *Moral Capital: Foundations of British Abolitionism.* Chapel Hill: University of North Carolina Press.

Brown, Frederick Z. 1992. "Cambodia in 1991: An Uncertain Peace," *Asian Survey*, 32, 1, 88–95.

Brown, Richard D. and Richard Wilson, eds. 2009. *Humanitarianism and Suffering: The Mobilization of Empathy.* Cambridge, UK: Cambridge University Press.

Brown, Wendy. 2004. "'The Most We Can Hope For . . .': Human Rights and the Politics of Fatalism," *South Atlantic Quarterly*, 103, 2/3, 451–463.

Brownlie, Ian. 1974. "Humanitarian Intervention," in John Moore, ed. *Law and Civil War in the Modern World*, 217–228. Baltimore: John Hopkins University Press.

Brudholm, T. 2008. *Resentment's Virtue: Jean Améry and the Refusal to Forgive.* Philadelphia: Temple University Press.

Brudholm, Thomas and Johannes Lang. 2018. "Introduction," in T. Brudholm and J. Lang, eds., *Emotions and Mass Atrocity: Philosophical and Theoretical Explanations*, 1–21. New York: Cambridge University Press.

Bruch, Elizabeth. 2014. "What Do Human Rights Lawyers Do? Examining Practice and Expertise in the Field," *Buffalo Human Rights Law Review*, 20, 37–66.

2016. "Human Rights and Humanitarian Intervention," *Law and Practice in the Field*. New York: Routledge.

Brun, Cathrine. 2015. "Active Waiting and Changing Hopes: Toward a Time Perspective on Protracted Displacement," *Social Analysis*, 59, 1, 19–37.

2016. "There Is No Future in Humanitarianism: Emergency, Temporality and Protracted Displacement," *History and Anthropology*, 27, 4, 393–410.

Brysk, Alison. 1993. "From Above and Below: Social Movements, the International System, and Human Rights in Argentina," *Comparative Political Studies*, 26, 3, 259–285.

2013. *Speaking Rights to Power: Constructing Political Will*. New York: Oxford University Press.

Buchanan, Alan. 1987. "Justice and Charity," *Ethics*, 97, 3, 558–575.

2013. *The Heart of Human Rights*. New York: Oxford University Press.

Bullard, Robert D. 2005. *The Quest for Environmental Justice: Human Rights and the Politics of Pollution*. San Francisco: Sierra Book Club.

Burger, Herman. 2000. "André Mandelstam, Forgotten Pioneer of International Human Rights," in Fons Coomans, Fred Gruenfeld and Ingrid Westendorp, eds., *Rendering Justice to the Vulnerable*, 69–82. Den Haag and London: Kluwer.

Burke, Roland. 2017. "Flat Affect: Revisiting Emotion in the Historiography of Human Rights," *Journal of Human Rights*, 16, 2, 123–141.

Buss, Doris. 2014. "Seeing Sexual Violence in Conflict and Post-Conflict Societies: The Limits of Visibility," in Doris Buss, Joanne Lebert, Blair Rutherford, Donna Sharkey, Obijiofor Aginam, eds., *Sexual Violence in Conflict and Post-Conflict Societies: International Agendas and African Contexts*, 3–27. New York and London: Routledge.

Butler, Judith. 2009. *Frames of War: When Is Life Grievable?* Brooklyn, NY: Verso.

Butterly, Caoimhe. 2009. "Life in Gaza: Still Breathing," *Morning Star*, January 17.

Buxton, Charles, ed. 1848. *Memoirs of Sir Thomas Fowell Buxton, Baronet, with Selections From His Correspondence*. London: John Murray.

Cabanes, Bruno. 2014. *The Great War and the Origins of Humanitarianism, 1918–1924*. Cambridge, UK: Cambridge University Press.

Caldwell, Christopher. 2009. "'Communiste et Rastignac,' Review of Le Monde selon K, by Pierre Péan," *London Review of Books*, July 9.

Calhoun, Craig. 2004. "A World of Emergencies: Fear, Intervention, and the Limits of Cosmopolitan Order," *Canadian Review of Sociology and Anthropology*, 41, 3, 373–395.

2008. "The Imperative to Reduce Suffering: Charity, Progress, and Emergencies in the Field of Humanitarian Action," in M. Barnett and T. Weiss, eds., *Humanitarianism in Question: Politics, Power, Ethics*, 73–97. Ithaca: Cornell University Press.

Campbell, T. D. 1974. "Humanity before Justice," *British Journal of Political Science*, 4, 1, 1–16.

1975. "Perfect and Imperfect Obligations," *The Modern Schoolman*, 52, 3, 285–294

Cannon, Michael. 1983. *Historical Records of Victoria. Vols 2A and 2B*. Melbourne: Melbourne University Press.

Carlson, Eve B. and Rhonda Rosser-Hogan. 1993. "Mental Health Status of Cambodian Refugees Ten Years After Leaving Their Homes," *American Journal of Orthopsychiatry*, 63, 2, 223–231.

Carpenter, R. C. 2006. *Innocent Women and Children: Gender, Norms and the Protection of Civilians*. Aldershot, UK: Ashgate.

Carruth, Lauren. 2020. *Making Aid Work*. Unpublished manuscript

Casanova, Jose. 2011. "The Secular, Secularization, and Secularisms," in C. Calhoun, M. Jurgensmeyer, and J. Vonantwerpen, eds., *Rethinking Secularism*, 54–74. New York: Oxford University Press.

Celermajer, D. 2018. *The Prevention of Torture: An Ecological Approach*. New York: Cambridge University Press.

Chakravarti, S. 2014. *Sing the Rage: Listening to Anger After Mass Violence*. Chicago: University of Chicago Press.

Chan, Kwok B. and David Loveridge. 1987. "Refugees 'in Transit': Vietnamese in a Refugee Camp in Hong Kong," *The International Migration Review*, 21, 3, 745–759.

Chandler, David. 2001. "The Road to Military Humanitarianism: How the Human Rights NGOs Shaped a New Humanitarian Agenda," *Human Rights Quarterly*, 23, 3, 678–700.

  2008. "Cambodia Deals with Its Past: Collective Memory, Demonisation and Induced Amnesia," *Totalitarian Movements and Political Religions*, 9, 2–3, 355–369.

Charlesworth, Hilary and Christine Chinkin. 2000. *The Boundaries of International Law: A Feminist Analysis*. Manchester: Manchester University Press.

Chouliaraki, Lilie. 2010. "Post-Humanitarianism: Humanitarian Communication Beyond a Politics of Pity," *International Journal of Cultural Studies*, 13, 2, 107–126.

  2013. *The Ironic Spectator: Solidarity in the Age of Post-Humanitarianism*. Cambridge, UK: Polity Press.

Cicero. 1991 [44 BCE]. *On Duties*, ed. M. T. Griffin and E. M. Atkins. Cambridge, UK: Cambridge University Press.

Civic Council of Popular and Indigenous Organizations of Honduras (COPINH). 2017. The Berta Cáceres Human Rights Act, H.R. 1299. COPINH English (blog). March. https://copinhenglish.blogspot.com/p/ley-berta-caceres.html.

Cladis, Mark. 2008. "Introduction," *Emile Durkheim, Elementary Forms of Religious Life*. New York: Oxford University Press.

Clark, Anna. 2016. "Humanitarianism, Human Rights, and Biopolitics in the British Empire," *Britain and the World*, 9, 1, 96–115.

Clark, Ian. 2007. *International Legitimacy and World Society*. Oxford: Oxford University Press.

Clarke, K. 2009. *Fictions of Justice: The International Criminal Court and the Challenges of Legal Pluralism in Sub-Saharan Africa*. Cambridge, UK: Cambridge University Press.

Clarkson, Thomas. 1808. *The History of the Rise, Progress, and Accomplishment of the Abolition of the African Slave-Trade by the British Parliament*, Vol. I. London.

Cmeil, Kenneth. 2004. "The Recent History of Human Rights," *American Historical Review*, 109, 1, 117–135.

Coalition of Feminists for Social Change (COFEM). 2017. "Feminist perspectives on addressing violence against women and girls: Reframing the language of 'gender-based violence' away from feminist underpinnings." Feminist Perspectives on Addressing Violence Against Women and Girls Series, Paper No. 2, Coalition of Feminists for Social Change.

Cockburn, Cynthia. 2004. "The Continuum of Violence: A Gender Perspective on War and Peace," in Wenona Giles and Jennifer Hyndman, eds., *Sites of Violence: Gender and Conflict Zones*, 24–44. Berkeley, CA: University of California Press.

Cody, Scott, Richard Wilson, and Jennifer Rasmussen. 2001. *Promoting Justice: A Practical Guide to Strategic Human Rights Lawyering*. Washington, DC: International Human Rights Law Group.

Cohen, Gerald Daniel. 2011. *In War's Wake: European Refugees in the Postwar Order*. New York: Oxford University Press.

Cohen, Stanley. 2001. *States of Denial: Knowing About Atrocities and Suffering*. Waltham, MA: Polity Press.

  2013. *States of Denial: Knowing About Atrocities and Suffering*. Hoboken: John Wiley & Sons.

Cooley, Alex and James Ron. 2002. "The NGO Scramble," *International Security*, 27, 1, 5–39.

Cooper, Frederick. 2018. *Citizenship, Inequality, and Difference: Historical Perspectives*. Princeton: Princeton University Press.

Cooper, Melinda. 2015. "The Theology of Emergency: Welfare Reform, US Foreign Aid, and the Faith-Based Initiative," *Theory Culture & Society*, 32, 2, 53–77.

Coulthard, G. 2014. *Red Skin, White Masks: Rejecting the Colonial Politics of Recognition*. Minneapolis: University of Minnesota Press.

Crane, Ronald Salmon. 1934. "Suggestions towards a Genealogy of the 'Man of Feeling'," *ELH*, 1, 3, 205–230.

Crowe, Jonathan. 1998. "Coherence and Acceptance in International Law: Can Humanitarianism and Human Rights Be Reconciled?" *Adelaide Law Review*, 35,2, 251–267.

Curtis, Grant. 1993. Transition to What? Cambodia, UNTAC and the Peace Process. United Nations Research Institute for Social Development, UNRISD, November.

Cuttitta, Paolo. 2018. "Delocalization, Humanitarianism, and Human Rights: The Mediterranean Border Between Exclusion and Inclusion," *Antipode*, 50, 3, 783–803.

Cutts, Mark. 1998. "Politics and Humanitarianism," *Refugee Survey Quarterly*, 17, 1, 1–15.

Dale, John and David Kyle. 2016. "Smart Humanitarianism: Re-Imagining Human Rights in the Age of Enterprise," *Critical Sociology*, 42, 6, 783–797.

Dale, Leigh. 2006. "George Grey in Ireland: Narrative and Network," in David Lambert and Alan Lester, eds., *Colonial Lives Across the British Empire: Imperial Careering in the Long Nineteenth Century*, 145–175. Cambridge, UK: Cambridge University Press.

Davey, Eleanor. 2015. *Idealism beyond Borders: The French Revolutionary Left and the Rise of Humanitarianism, 1954–1988.* Cambridge, UK: Cambridge University Press.

David, Lea. 2017. "Against Standardization of Memory," *Human Rights Quarterly*, 39, 2, 296–318.

Davis, David Brion. 1966. *The Problem of Slavery in Western Culture.* Ithaca: Cornell University Press.

1975. *The Problem of Slavery in the Age of Revolution, 1770–1823.* Ithaca: Cornell University Press.

Davis, Rochelle. 2010. *Palestinian Village Histories: Geographies of the Displaced.* Stanford: Stanford University Press.

Dawes, James. 2007. *That the World May Know: Bearing Witness to Atrocity.* Cambridge, MA: Harvard University Press.

Dawes, James, Samantha Gupta, and C. Jayasinghe. 2014. "Narratives and Human Rights," *Humanity*, June 5.

Dean, Carolyn. 2010. *Aversion and Erasure: The Fate of the Victim after the Holocaust.* Ithaca: Cornell University Press.

De Lauri, Antonio. 2014. "Boredom and Crisis in the Humanitarian Realm," *Anthropology Today*, 30, 23–25.

Dembour, Marie-Benedict and Tobias Kelly, eds. 2017. *Paths to International Justice: Social and Legal Perspectives.* New York: Cambridge University Press.

Deneen, Patrick. 1999. "The Politics of Hope and Optimism: Rorty, Havel, and the Democratic Faith of John Dewey," *Social Research*, 66, 2, 578–598.

Denman, Joseph. 1850. *The Slave Trade, the African Squadron, and Mr. Hutt's Committee.* London: J. Mortimer.

De Torrenté, Nicolas. 2004. "Humanitarian Action under Attack: Reflections on the Iraq War," *Harvard Human Rights Journal 17*, 1–29.

Development Initiatives. 2014. "Trends in Donor Spending on Sexual and Gender-Based Violence (SGBV)," *Development Initiatives.*

De Waal, Alex. 2010. "The Humanitarians' Tragedy: Escapable and Inescapable Cruelties," *Disasters*, 34, S2, S130–S137.

Dewey, John. 1934. *A Common Faith.* New Haven: Yale University Press.

Dixon, Paul. 2019. "'Endless Wars of Altruism': Human Rights, Humanitarianism, and the Syrian War," *The International Journal of Human Rights*, 23, 5, 819–842.

Dobash, Russell P. and Emerson R. Dobash. 1983. "Context Specific Approach," in David Finkelhor et al., *The Dark Side of Families: Current Family Violence Research*, 261–276. Beverly Hills: Sage.

Donini, Antonio. 2010. "The Far Side: The Meta Functions of Humanitarianism in a Globalised World," *Disasters*, 34, S220–237.

ed. 2012. *The Golden Fleece: Manipulation and Independence in Humanitarian Action.* Bloomfield, CT: Kumarian Press.

Douglas, Lawrence. 2001. *The Memory of Judgment: Making Law and History in the Trials of the Holocaust.* New Haven: Yale University Press.

Doyle, Michael W. and Nishkala Suntharalingam. 1994. "The UN in Cambodia: Lessons for Complex Peacekeeping," *International Peacekeeping*, 1, 2, 117–147.

Drescher, Seymour. 2009. *Abolition: A History of Slavery and Antislavery*. Cambridge, UK: Cambridge University Press.

Droege, Cordula. 2007. "The Interplay Between International Humanitarian Law and International Human Rights Law in Situations of Armed Conflict," *Israel Law Review*, 40, 2, 310–355.

2008. "Elective Affinities? Human Rights and Humanitarian Law," *International Review of the Red Cross*, 90, 871, 501–548.

Dubois, Laurent. 2005. *Avengers of the New World: The Story of the Haitian Revolution*. Cambridge, MA: Harvard University Press.

Dubois, Marc. 2009. "Protection: The New Humanitarian Fig Leaf," https://urd .org/IMG/pdf/Protection_Fig-Leaf_DuBois.pdf.

2018. "The New Humanitarian Basics," HPG Working Paper. London: Overseas Development Institute, May.

Du Bois, W. 1868–1963. Introduction to An Appeal to the World, ca. 1946. W. E. B. Du Bois Papers (MS 312). Special Collections and University Archives, University of Massachusetts Amherst Libraries.

1919. "Returning Soldiers," *The Crisis*, May 18.

1970. *W.E.B. Du Bois Speaks: Speeches and Addresses*. New York: Pathfinder Press.

Du Bois, W., Gates, H., and Oliver, T. 1999. *The Souls of Black Folk: Authoritative Text, Contexts, Criticism*. New York: W. W. Norton.

Dubow, Saul. 1995. *Scientific Racism in Modern South Africa*. Cambridge, UK: Cambridge University Press.

Dudai, Ron. 2012. "'Rescues for Humanity': Rescuers, Mass Atrocities, and Transitional Justice," *Human Rights Quarterly*, 34, 1, 1–38.

2017. "Human Rights in the Populist Era: Mourn then (Re)Organize," *Journal of Human Rights Practice*, 9, 16–21.

2019. "The Study of the Art of Human Rights Practice: State of the Art," *Journal of Human Rights Practice*, 11, 273–295.

Duffield, Mark. 2019. "Post-Humanitarianism: Governing Precarity Through Adaptive Design," *Journal of Humanitarian Affairs*, 1, 1, 15–27.

Duffy, Terence. 1994. "Toward a Culture of Human Rights in Cambodia," *Human Rights Quarterly*, 16, 1, 82–104.

Dunant, Henry. 1939 [1862]. *A Memory of Solferino*. Washington, DC: American National Red Cross.

Dunn, Elizabeth Cullen. 2014. "Humanitarianism, Displacement, and the Politics of Nothing in Postwar Georgia," *Slavic Review*, 73, 2, 287–306.

Dutton, Alistair. 2001. "Comment: The Moral Legitimacy of 'Conditionality' in Humanitarian Relief," *Journal of Humanitarian Assistance*, August.

Dworkin, Ronald. 1986. *Law's Empire*. Cambridge, MA: Harvard University Press.

Eagleton, Terry. 2015. *Hope Without Optimism*. Charlottesville: University of Virginia Press.

Eckel, Jan. 2017. "Humanitarian Intervention as Global Governance: Western Governments and Suffering 'Others' before and after 1990," in Nobert Frei,

Daniel Stahl and Annette Weinke, eds., *Human Rights and Humanitarian Intervention. Legitimizing the Use of Force Since the 1970s*, 64–85. Göttingen: Wallstein.

Eckel, Jan and Samuel Moyn. 2014. *The Breakthrough: Human Rights in the 1970s.* Philadelphia: University of Pennsylvania Press.

Edelstein, Dan. 2018. *On the Spirit of Rights.* Chicago: University of Chicago Press.

Edmonds, Penelope. 2014. "Collecting Looerryminer's 'Testimony': Aboriginal Women, Sealers, and Quaker Humanitarian Anti-Slavery Thought and Action in the Bass Strait Islands," *Australian Historical Studies*, 45, 1, 13–33.

Edwards, Alice. 2011. *Violence Against Women Under International Human Rights Law.* New York: Cambridge University Press.

Elden, Stuart. 2007. "Governmentality, Calculation, Territory," *Environment and Planning D: Society and Space*, 25, 562–580

Emery, John. 2016. "The Possibilities and Pitfalls of Humanitarian Drones," *Ethics and International Affairs*, 30, 2, 153–165.

Emery, John and Daniel Brunstetter. 2015. "Drones as Aerial Occupation," *Peace Review*, 27, 4, 424–431.

Engle, Karen. 2014. "The Grip of Sexual Violence: Reading UN Security Council Resolutions on Human Security," in Dianne Otto and Gina Heathcote, eds., *Rethinking Peacekeeping, Gender Equality and Collective Security*, 23–47. Basingstoke: Palgrave Macmillan.

2018. "Feminist Governance and International Law: From Liberal to Carceral Feminism," in Janet Halley, Prabha Kotiswaran, Rachel Rebouché, and Hila Shamir, eds., *Governance Feminism: Notes from the Field*. Minneapolis, London: University of Minnesota Press.

Eriksson Baaz, Maria and Maria Stern. 2013. *Sexual Violence as a Weapon of War: Perceptions, Prescriptions, Problems in the Congo and Beyond*. London and New York: Zed Books.

Etinson, Adam, ed. 2018. *Human Rights: Moral or Political?* New York: Oxford University Press.

Fanon, F. 1966. *The Wretched of the Earth*. New York: Grove Press.

Farrell, Stephen. 2007. "'Contrary to the Principle of Justice, Humanity and Sound Policy': The Slave Trade, Parliamentary Politics and the Abolition Act, 1807," in Stephen Farrell, et al., *The British Slave Trade: Abolition, Parliament and People*, 141–171. Edinburgh: Edinburgh University Press.

Fassin, Didier. 2005. "Compassion and Repression: The Moral Economy of Immigration Policies in France," *Cultural Anthropology*, 20, 3, 362–387.

2007. "Humanitarianism: A Nongovernment Government," in M. Feher., ed., *Nongovernmental Politics*, 149–160. New York: Zone Books.

2010. "Inequality of Lives, Hierarchies of Humanity: Moral Commitments and Ethical Dilemmas of Humanitarianism," in Ilana Feldman and Miriam Ticktin, eds., *In the Name of Humanity: The Government of Threat and Care*, 238–255. Durham, NC: Duke University Press.

2011. "Noli Me Tangere: The Moral Untouchability of Humanitarianism," in Erica Bornstein and Peter Redfield, eds., *Forces of Compassion: Humanitarianism*

Between Ethics and Politics, 35–53. Sante Fe: School for Advanced Research Press.

2012. *Humanitarian Reason: A Moral History of the Present*. Berkeley: University of California.

Fassin, Didier and Richard Rechtman.2009. *The Empire of Trauma: An Inquiry into the Conditions of Victimhood*. Princeton University Press.

Faulkner, Joanna. 2011. "Innocents and Oracles: The Child as a Figure of Knowledge and Critique in the Middle-Class Philosophical Imagination," *Critical Horizons*, 12, 3, 323–346.

Fehrenbach, Heide and Davide Rodogno, eds. 2015. *Humanitarian Photography: A History*. Cambridge, UK: Cambridge University Press.

Feinberg, Joel. 1970. "The Nature and Value of Rights," *Journal of Value Inquiry*, 4, 4, 243–260.

1973. *Social Philosophy*. Englewood Cliffs, NJ: Prentice Hall.

Feldman, Ilana. 2009. "Gaza's Humanitarian Problem," *Journal of Palestine Studies*, 38, 3, 22–37.

2012. "The Humanitarian Condition: Palestinian Refugees and the Politics of Living," *Humanity*, 3, 2, 155–172.

2017. "Humanitarian Care and the Ends of Life: The Politics of Aging and Dying in a Palestinian Refugee Camp," *Cultural Anthropology*, 32, 1, 42–67.

2018. *Life Lived in Relief: Humanitarian Predicaments and Palestinian Refugee Politics*. Berkeley: University of California Press.

Feldman, Ilana and Miriam Ticktin, eds. 2010. *In the Name of Humanity*. Durham: Duke University Press.

Ferris, Elizabeth G. 2011. *The Politics of Protection: The Limits of Humanitarian Action*. Washington, DC: Brookings Institution Press.

Festa, Lynn M. 2006. *Sentimental Figures of Empire in Eighteenth-Century Britain and France*. Baltimore, MD: Johns Hopkins University Press.

2010. "Humanity Without Feathers," *Humanity: An International Journal of Human Rights, Humanitarianism, and Development*, 1, 1, 3–27.

Fiering, Norman. 1976. "Irresistible Compassion: An Aspect of Eighteenth Century and Humanitarianism," *Journal of the History of Ideas*, 37, 2, 195–218.

Fineman, Martha Albertson. 2008. "The Vulnerable Subject: Anchoring Equality in the Human Condition," *Yale Journal of Law and Feminism*, 1, 1–23.

Finkielkraut, Alain. 2001. *In the Name of Humanity*. Lincoln, NE: University of Nebraska Press.

Finnemore, Martha and Kathryn Sikkink. 1998. "International Norm Dynamics and Political Change," *International Organization*, 52, 4, 887–917.

Fischer, Sibylle. 2004. *Modernity Disavowed: Haiti and the Cultures of Slavery in the Age of Revolution*. Durham, NC: Duke University Press.

Fleischacker, Samuel. 2005. *A Short History of Distributive Justice*. Cambridge, MA: Harvard University Press.

Fligstein, Neil and Douglas McAdam. 2012. *A Theory of Fields*. New York: Oxford University Press.

Flynn, Jeffrey. 2003. "Habermas on Human Rights: Law, Morality, and Intercultural Dialogue," *Social Theory and Practice*, 29, 3, 431–457.

2012. "Human Rights in History and Contemporary Practice: Source Materials for Philosophy," in Claudio Corradetti, ed., *Philosophical Dimensions of Human Rights*, 3–22. Berlin: Springer.

2017. "Philosophers, Historians, and Suffering Strangers," *Moving the Social: Journal of Social History and the History of Social Movements*, 37, 137–158.

2018. "Genealogies of Human Rights: What's at Stake?" in Adam Etinson, ed., *Human Rights: Moral or Political?*, 103–113. Oxford: Oxford University Press.

2019. "Do-Gooders," *Humanity*, 10, 2, 299–319.

Fonteyne, Jean-Pierre L. 1973. "The Customary International Law Doctrine of Humanitarian Intervention: Its Current Validity Under the U.N. Charter," *California Western International Law Journal*, 4, 203–270.

Foreign Office, ed. 1837. *British and Foreign State Papers, Vol. 5 (1817–1818)*. London.

1838. *British and Foreign State Papers, Vol. 3 (1815–1816)*. London.

Forst, Rainer. 2011. *The Right to Justification: Elements of a Constructivist Theory of Justice*. New York: Columbia University Press.

Forsythe, D. 2005a. *The Humanitarians: The International Committee of the Red Cross*. Cambridge, UK: Cambridge University Press.

2005b. "Naming and Shaming: The Ethics of ICRC Discretion," *Millennium*, 34, 461–474.

2013. "On Contested Concepts: Humanitarianism, Human Rights, and the Notion of Neutrality," *Journal of Human Rights*, 12, 1, 59–68.

Fortin, Katharine. 2012. "Complementarity Between the ICRC and the United Nations and International Humanitarian Law and International Human Rights Law, 1948–1968," *International Review of the Red Cross*, 94, 888, 1433–1454.

Fortrun, Kim. 2012. "Ethnography in Late Industrialism," *Cultural Anthropology*, 27, 3, 446–464.

Foucault, Michel. 1979. "Omnes et Singulatim: Towards a Criticism of Political Reason," presented at *The Tanner Lectures on Human Values*, Stanford University, October 10 and 16, 1979. http://foucault.info/documents/foucault.omnesEtSingulatim.en.html.

1994. *Dits et écrits*. Paris: Gallimard.

1995. *Discipline and Punish: The Birth of the Prison*. New York: Vintage.

Fox, Fiona. 2002. "Conditioning the Right to Humanitarian Aid? Human Rights and the 'New Humanitarian,'" in David Chandler, ed., *Rethinking Human Rights: Critical Approaches to International Rights*, 19–37. New York: Palgrave.

Frankel, Victor. 1984. *Man's Search for Meaning*. New York: Pocket Books.

Franck, Thomas M. and Nigel S. Rodley. 1973. "After Bangladesh: The Law of Humanitarian Intervention by Military Force," *American Journal of International Law*, 67, 2, 275–305.

Frazer, Michael. 2010. *The Enlightenment of Sympathy: Justice and the Moral Sentiments in the Eighteenth Century and Today*. New York: Oxford University Press.

Freedman, Jane. 2014. "Treating Sexual Violence as a 'Business': Reflections on National and International Responses to Sexual and Gender-Based Violence in the Democratic Republic of Congo," *Gendered Perspectives on Conflict and Violence: Part B*, 125–143.

Freedom House. 2018. *Democracy in Crisis*. https://freedomhouse.org/report/free dom-world/freedom-world-2018.

Frei, Norbert, Daniel Stahl, and Annette Weinke, eds. 2017. *Human Rights and Humanitarian Intervention: Legitimizing the Use of Force Since the 1970s*. Göttingen: Wallstein.

French, Lindsay. 2002. "From Politics to Economics at the Thai–Cambodian Border: Plus Ça Change," *International Journal of Politics, Culture, and Society*, 15, 3, 427–470.

Fulton, Rachel. 2002. *From Judgment to Passion: Devotion to Christ and the Virgin Mary, 800–1200*. New York: Columbia University Press.

Gaggioli, Gloria. 2013. "'Humanitarian Rights': How to Ensure Respect for Human Rights and Humanitarian Law in Armed Conflicts," in Robert Kolb and Gloria Gaggioli, eds., *Research Handbook on Human Rights and Humanitarian Law*, 343–370. Northampton: Edward Elgar.

Geggus, David P. 2002. *Haitian Revolutionary Studies*. Bloomington: Indiana University Press.

Geneva Conventions. August 12, 1949. *Protocol Relating to the Protection of Victims of International Armed Conflicts* (Protocol I), June 8, 1977. www.icrc.org/ihl .nsf/INTRO/470?OpenDocument.

Geyer, Michael. 2016. "Humanitarianism and Human Rights: A Troubled Rapport," in Fabian Klose, ed., *Humanitarian Intervention: Ideas and Practice from the Nineteenth Century to the Present*, 31–55. New York: Cambridge University Press.

Gillard, Emanuela-Chiara. 2005. ICRC Legal Adviser, "Statement Delivered to the International Association of Refugee Law Judges," Netherlands, April 23.

Giridharadas, Anand. 2018. *Winner Take All: The Elite Charade of Changing the World*. New York: Alfred Knopf.

Givoni, Michal. 2011. *Humanitarian Governance and Ethical Cultivation: Médecins sans Frontières and the Advent of the Expert-Witness*, 40, 1, 43–63.

  2016. *The Care of the Witness: A Contemporary History of Testimony in Crises*. Cambridge, UK: Cambridge University Press.

Glendon, Mary Ann. 2002. *A World Made New: Eleanor Roosevelt and the Universal Declaration of Human Rights*. New York: Random House.

Global Protection Cluster. 2019. *Handbook for Coordinating Gender-Based Violence Interventions in Emergencies*. GBV Area of Responsibility. https://gb vaor.net/sites/default/files/2019-07/Handbook%20for%20Coordinating%2 0GBV%20in%20Emergencies_fin.pdf.

Goffman, Erving. 1974. *Frame Analysis*. Cambridge, MA: Harvard University Press.

Goodale, Mark. 2008. "Introduction: Locating Rights, Envisioning Law Between the Global and Local," in Mark Goodale and Sally Engle Merry, eds., *The Practice of Human Rights: Tracking Law Between the Global and the Local*, 1–38. New York: Cambridge University Press.

ed. 2018. *Letters to the Contrary: A Curated History of the UNESCO Human Rights Survey*. Stanford, CA: Stanford University Press.

Goodale, Mark and Sally Engle Merry, eds. 2007. *The Practice of Human Rights*. New York: Cambridge University Press.

Gooding-Williams, Robert. 2010. *In the Shadow of Du Bois*. Cambridge, MA: Harvard University Press.

Goodman, R. and D. Jinks. 2013. *Socializing States: Promoting Human Rights Through International Law*. Oxford: Oxford University Press.

Gordon, Diane. 2007. "From Humanitarianism to Human Rights and Justice: A Way to Go," *Australian Journal of Human Rights*, 13, 1, 149–176.

Gottlieb, Nora, Dani Filc, and Nadav Davidovitch. 2012. "Medical Humanitarianism, Human Rights and Political Advocacy: The Case of the Israeli Open Clinic," *Social Science & Medicine*, 74, 6, 839–845.

Gouws, Amanda. 1996. "The Rise of the Femocrat?" *Agenda: Empowering Women for Gender Equity*, 30, 31–43.

Govier, Trudy and Wilhelm Verwoerd. 2004. "Transcending Victims and Perpetrators," *International Journal of Humanities and Peace*, 20, 1, 84–90.

Graham, Malbone W. 1924. "Humanitarian Intervention in International Law as Related to the Practice of the United States," *Michigan Law Review*, 22, 4, 312–328.

Grant, S. 2005. *God's Governor: George Grey and Racial Amalgamation in New Zealand, 1845–1853*. PhD thesis, Department of History, University of Otago.

Great Britain, Parliament, House of Commons, ed. 1791. *The Debate on a Motion for the Abolition of the Slave-Trade, in the House of Commons on Monday and Tuesday, April 18th and 19th 1791*. London.

Green, Abigail. 2014. "Humanitarianism in Nineteenth-Century Context: Gendered, Religious, National," *Historical Journal*, 57, 4, 1157–1175.

Green Abigail and Viaene, Vincent, eds. 2012. *Religious Internationals in the Modern World: Globalization and Faith Communities Since 1750*. New York: Palgrave MacMillan.

Greer, A. 1993. *The Patriots and the People: The Rebellion of 1837 in Rural Lower Canada*. Toronto: University of Toronto Press.

Grey, G. 1840. Report on the Best Means of Promoting the Civilization of the Aboriginal Inhabitants of Australia. Reproduced in State Library of New South Wales, NSW Legislative Council Votes and Proceedings 1839–42, 1/MAV/FN4/0867, Russell to Gipps, August 25.

1841. *Journals of Two Expeditions of Discovery in North-West and Western Australia During the Years 1837, 38, and 39, vols. 1 and 2*. London: T. and W. Boone.

1855. *Polynesian Mythology and Ancient Traditional History of the New Zealand Race as Furnished by Their Priests and Chiefs*. London: John Murray.

Guilhot, Nicolas. 2012. "The Anthropologist as Witness: Humanitarianism Between Ethnography and Critique," *Humanity*, 3, 1, 81–101.

Guillou, Anne Yvonne. 2012. "An Alternative Memory of the Khmer Rouge Genocide: The Dead of the Mass Graves and the Land Guardian Spirits [neak ta]," *South East Asia Research*, 20, 2, 207–226.

Gündogdu, Ayten. 2015. *Rightlessness in an Age of Rights: Hannah Arendt and the Contemporary Struggles of Migrants*. Oxford: Oxford University Press.

Guyatt, Mary. 2000. "The Wedgwood Slave Medallion. Values in Eighteenth-Century Design," *Journal of Design History*, 13, 2, 93–105.

Gyallay-Pap, Peter. 1989. "Reclaiming a Shattered Past: Education for the Displaced Khmer in Thailand," *Journal of Refugee Studies*, 2, 2, 257–275.

Habermas, Jürgen. 2010. "The Concept of Human Dignity and the Realistic Utopia of Human Rights," *Metaphilosophy*, 41, 4, 464–480.

Hacking, Ian. 1998. "Kinds of People, Moving Targets," *Social Research*, 65, 2, 291–314.

Hall, Catherine. 2002. *Civilizing Subjects: Metropole and Colony in the English Imagination 1830–1867*. Cambridge, UK: Polity.

Hall, John and Richard Taylor. 2003. "Health for all Beyond 2000: The Demise of the Alma-Ata Declaration and Primary Health Care in Developing Countries," *The Medical Journal of Australia*, 178, 1, 17–20.

Hall, Kari Rene and Josh Getlin. 1992. *Beyond the Killing Fields*. Reading, PA: Aperture.

Halley, Janet. 1993. "Reasoning About Sodomy: Act and Identity in and after Bowers v. Hardwick," *Virginia Law Review*, 79, 7, 1721–1780.

Halpern, Cynthia. 2002. *Suffering, Politics, and Power: A Genealogy in Modern Political Theory*. Albany: SUNY Press.

Halttunen, Karen. 1995. "Humanitarianism and the Pornography of Pain in Anglo-American Culture," *American Historical Review*, 100, 2, 303–334.

Hammond, John L. 1993. "War-Uprooting and the Political Mobilization of Central American Refugees," *Journal of Refugee Studies*, 6, 2, 105–122.

Hampson, Francoise. 2008. "The Relationship Between International Humanitarian Law and Human Rights Law from the Perspective of a Human Rights Treaty Body," *International Review of the Red Cross*, 50, 871, 549–572.

Hannum, Hurst. 2019. *Rescuing Human Rights: A Radically Moderate Approach*. Cambridge, UK: Cambridge University Press.

Hans-Joachim, Heintze. 2004. "On the Relationship Between Human Rights Law Protection and International Humanitarian Law," *International Review of the Red Cross*, 86, 856, 789–813.

Hartman, Ben. 2011. "Lod Protesters Vow to Stay in Tents at City Hall until Housing Dispute Is Resolved," *Jerusalem Post*, March 4.

Haskell, Thomas. 1985a. "Capitalism and the Origins of the Humanitarian Sensibility, Part 1," *American Historical Review*, 90, 2, 339–361.

1985b. "Capitalism and the Origins of Humanitarian Sensibility, Part 2," *American Historical Review* 90, 3, 547–566.

Hassan, Farooq. 1981. "Realpolitik in International Law: After Tanzanian-Ugandan Conflict: 'Humanitarian Intervention' Reexamined," *Willamette Law Review*, 17, 859–912.

Hausner, G. 1977. *Justice in Jerusalem*. New York: Holocaust Library.

Heerten, Lasse. 2015. "'A' as in Auschwitz, 'B' as in Biafra," in Heide Fehrenbach and Davide Rodogno, eds., *Humanitarian Photography: A History*, 249–274. New York: Cambridge University Press.

2017. *The Biafran War and Postcolonial Humanitarianism: Spectacles of Suffering*. Cambridge, UK: Cambridge University Press.

Hehir, Aidan. 2010. *Humanitarian Intervention: An Introduction*. Basingstoke: Palgrave Macmillan.

Hehir, Aidan and Robert W. Murray, eds. 2017. *Protecting Human Rights in the 21st Century*. New York: Routledge.

Hein, Jeremy. 2006. *Ethnic Origins: The Adaptation of Cambodian and Hmong Refugees in Four American Cities*. New York: Russell Sage Foundation.

Helte, Catrin. 2012. "Setting and Crossing Boundaries: Professionalization of Social Work and Social Work Professionalism," *Social Work and Society*, 10, 2.

Henttonen, M, C. Watts, B. Roberts, F. Kaducu, and M. Borchert. 2008. "Health Services for Survivors of Gender-Based Violence in Northern Uganda: A Qualitative study. *Reproductive Health Matters*, 16, 31, 122–131.

Heraclides, Alexis and Ada Dialla. 2015. *Humanitarian Intervention in the Long Nineteenth Century. Setting Precedent*. Manchester: Manchester University Press.

Her Majesty's Stationery Office, ed. 1865. *Slave Trade Instructions, being Instructions for the Guidance of the Commanders of Her Majesty's Ships of War employed in The Suppression of the Slave Trade*. London.

Hiégel-Landrac, Colette and Jean-Pierre Hiégel. 1996. *Vivre et revivre au camp de Khao I Dang*. Paris: Fayard.

Hilhorst, Dorothea and Bram Jansen. 2010. "Humanitarian Space as Arena: A Perspective on the Everyday Politics of Aid," *Development and Change*, 41, 6, 1117–1139.

2012. "Constructing Rights and Wrongs in Humanitarian Action: Contributions from the Sociology of Praxis," *Sociology*, 46, 5, 891–905.

Hilton, Matthew, Emily Baughan, Eleanor Davey, Bronwen Everill, Kevin O'Sullivan, and Tehila Sasson. 2018. "History and Humanitarianism: A Conversation," *Past & Present*, 241, 1, e1–e38.

Hiskes, Richard P. 2005. "The Right to a Green Future: Human Rights, Environmentalism, and Intergenerational Justice," *Human Rights Quarterly*, 27, 4, 1346–1364.

Hitchcock, William. 2012. "Human Rights and the Laws of War: The Geneva Conventions of 1949," in Akira Iriye, Petra Goedde, and William I. Hitchcock, eds., *The Human Rights Revolution: An International History*, 93–112. Oxford: Oxford University Press.

Hochschild, Adam. 2006. *Bury the Chains: Prophets and Rebels in the Fight to Free an Empire's Slaves*. New York: Mariner Books.

Hoffmann, Stefan Ludwig. 2016. "Human Rights and History," *Past and Present*, 232, 1, 279–310.

Hoijer, Birgitta. 2004. "The Discourse of Global Compassion: The Audience and Media Reporting of Human Suffering," *Media, Culture, and Society*, 26, 4, 513–531.

Hollinger, David. 1985. *American Province: Studies in the History and Historiography of Ideas*. Baltimore: Johns Hopkins University Press.

Holzgrefe, Jeff L. 2004. "The Humanitarian Intervention Debate," in Jeff L. Holzgrefe and Robert O. Keohane, eds., *Humanitarian Intervention: Ethical, Legal, and Political Dilemmas*, 15–52. Cambridge, UK: Cambridge University Press.

Honneth, Axel. 1996. *The Struggle for Recognition: The Moral Grammar of Social Conflicts*, trans. Joel Anderson. Cambridge, MA: MIT Press.

Hopgood, Stephen. 2006. *Keepers of the Flame: Understanding Amnesty International*. Ithaca: Cornell University Press.

2008. "Saying 'No' to Walmart? Money and Morality in Professional Humanitarianism," in Michael Barnett and Tom Weiss, eds., *Humanitarianism in Question*, 98–123. Ithaca: Cornell University Press.

2013. *The Endtimes of Human Rights*. Ithaca: Cornell University Press.

2019. "When the Music Stops: Humanitarianism in a Post-Liberal World Order," *Journal of Humanitarian Affairs*, 1, 1, 1–14.

Hopgood, Stephen, Jack Snyder, and Leslie Vinjamuri, eds. 2017. *Human Rights Futures*. New York: Cambridge University Press.

Hopkins, MaryCarol. 1996. *Braving a New World: Cambodian (Khmer) Refugees in an American City*. New York: Greenwood.

Hoyt, Nelly S. and Thomas Cassirer, trans. 2003. "Humanity," *The Encyclopedia of Diderot & d'Alembert Collaborative Translation Project*. http://hdl.handle.net/2027/spo.did2222.0000.172.

Hughes, Caroline. 2007. "Transnational Networks, International Organizations and Political Participation in Cambodia: Human Rights, Labour Rights and Common Rights," *Democratization*, 14, 5, 834–852.

Human Rights Watch. 2018. Syria: Events of 2017. www.hrw.org/world-report/2018/country-chapters/syria.

Hunt, Lynn. 2007. *Inventing Human Rights: A History*. New York: W. W. Norton.

Hunt, Matthew et al. 2018. "Moral Experiences of Humanitarian Health Professionals Caring for Patients Who Are Dying or Likely to Die in a Humanitarian Crisis," *Journal of International Humanitarian Action*, 3, 1, https://doi.org/10.1186/s41018-018-0040-9.

Hurwitz, Deana. 2003. "Lawyering for Justice and the Inevitability of International Human Rights Clinics," *Yale Journal of International Law*, 28, 505–561.

Hutchinson, John. 1997. *Champions of Charity*. New York: Routledge.

2014. "A Global Politics of Pity? Disaster Imagery and the Emotional Construction of Solidarity after the 2004 Asian Tsunami," *International Political Sociology*, 8, 1, 1–19.

Huyssen, Andreas. 2011. "International Human Rights and the Politics of Memory: Limits and Challenges," *Criticism*, 53, 4, 607–624.

Hyndman, Jennifer. 1998. "Managing Difference: Gender and Culture in Humanitarian Emergencies," *Gender, Place & Culture: A Journal of Feminist Geography*, 5, 3, 241–260.

Ignatieff, Michael. 2001. *The Needs of Strangers*. New York: Picador.

Inter-Agency Standing Committee on Humanitarian Action (IASC). 1999. *Policy Statement for the Integration of a Gender Perspective in Humanitarian Assistance.* New York: United Nations.

2005. *Guidelines for Gender-Based Violence Interventions in Humanitarian Settings.* Geneva: Inter-Agency Standing Committee.

2006. *Gender Handbook in Humanitarian Action, Women, Girls, Boys and Men: Different Needs – Equal Opportunities.* New York: United Nations.

2008. *Gender Equality in Humanitarian Action: Gender Equality Policy Statement.* New York: United Nations.

2015. *Guidelines for Gender-Based Violence Interventions in Humanitarian Settings: Reducing Risk, Promoting Resilience and Aiding Recovery.* Geneva: Inter-Agency Standing Committee.

2017. *The Gender Handbook for Humanitarian Action.* New York: United Nations.

International Commission on Intervention and State Sovereignty (ICISS). 2001. *The Responsibility to Protect.* Ottawa: International Development Research Center.

International Committee of the Red Cross. 2008. "ICRC Protection Policy: Institutional Policy," *International Review of the Red Cross*, 90, 871, 751–775.

2010. "IHL and Human Rights Law," October 29. www.icrc.org/en/docu ment/ihl-human-rights-law.

2016. Fundamental Principles of the Red Cross and Red Crescent Movement. www.icrc.org/en/document/fundamental-principles-red-cross-and-red-crescent.

International Federation of Red Cross and Red Crescent Societies. 2016. Humanity. www.ifrc.org/en/who-we-are/vision-and-mission/the-seven-fundamental-principles/humanity/.

The International Law Association. 1967. *Report of the Fifty-Second Conference Held at Helsinki, August 14th to August 20th, 1966.* London: Cambrian News.

Iriye, Akira, Petra Goedde and William Hitchcock, eds. 2012. *The Human Rights Revolution.* New York: Oxford University Press.

Ishay, Micheline. 2008. *The History of Human Rights.* Berkeley: University of California Press.

Jackson, Tony. 1987. *Just Waiting to Die.* Oxfam Research and Evaluation Unit.

Jansen, Annette. 2015. *Don't Let Us Be Bystanders! Anti-Genocide Activists and the Sacralization of Humanity.* PhD diss. University of Amsterdam.

James, C.L.R. 1989 [1963, 1938]. *The Black Jacobins: toussaint L'Ouverture and the San Domingo Revolution.* New York: Vintage Books

Jelin, Elizabeth. 1994. "The Politics of Memory: The Human Rights Movement and the Construction of Democracy in Argentina," *Latin American Perspectives*, 21, 2, 38–58.

Jennar, Raoul Marc. 1995. *Chroniques Cambodgiennes, 1990–1994: Rapports au Forum International des ONG au Cambodge.* Paris: L'Harmattan.

Jensen, Steven L. B. 2016. *The Making of International Human Rights: The 1960s, Decolonization, and the Reconstruction of Global Values.* Cambridge, UK: Cambridge University Press, 2016.

Joas, Hans. 2013. *The Sacredness of the Person: A New Genealogy of Human Rights*. Washington, DC: Georgetown University Press.

Johnson, Samuel. 1755. "Humanity," *A Dictionary of the English Language: in Which the Words are Deduced from Their Originals, and Illustrated in Their Different Significations by Examples Form the Best Writers* Vol. 1. London.

Johnston, Anna. 2004. "The 'Little Empire of Wybalenna': Becoming Colonial in Australia," *Journal of Australian Studies*, 28, 17–31.

2017. "The Language of Colonial Violence: Lancelot Threlkeld, Humanitarian Narratives and the New South Wales Law Courts," *Law & History*, 4, 2, 72–102.

Justice Rapid Response and UN Women. 2018. In Brief: Securing Accountability for Sexual and Gender-Based Violence as an International Crime. www.justicerapi dresponse.org/wp-content/uploads/2018/04/In-Brief-Securing-Accountability-f or-SGBV-as-International-Crimes-April-2018-Reduced-Size.pdf.

Kahan, D. 2006. "What's Really Wrong with Shaming Sanctions," *Texas Law Review*, 84, 2075.

Käpylä, Juha and David Kennedy. 2014. "Cruel to Care? Investigating the Governance of Compassion in the Humanitarian Imaginary," *International Theory*, 6, 2, 255–292.

Karp, David Jason. 2013. "The Location of International Practices: What Is Human Rights Practice?" *Review of International Studies*, 39, 4, 969–992.

Keck, Margaret and Kathryn Sikkink. 1998. *Activists beyond Borders: Advocacy Networks in International Politics*. Ithaca: Cornell University Press.

2014. *Activists beyond Borders*. Ithaca: Cornell University Press.

Keene, Edward. 2007. "A Case Study of the Construction of International Hierarchy: British Treaty-Making Against the Slave-Trade in the Early Nineteenth Century," *International Organization*, 61, 311–339.

Kellenberger, J. 2004. "Speaking Out or Remaining Silent in Humanitarian Work," *International Review of the Red Cross*, 86, 855, 593–609.

Kelly, Liz. 1998. *Surviving Sexual Violence*. Minneapolis: University of Minnesota.

Kelly, Lisa M. 2014. "Reckoning with Narratives of Innocent Suffering in Transnational Abortion Litigation," in Rebecca Cook, Joanna N. Erdman and Bernard M. Dickens, eds., *Abortion Law in Transnational Perspective*, 303–326. Philadelphia: University of Pennsylvania Press.

Kelsall, Michelle Staggs and Shanee Stepakoff. 2007. "'When We Wanted to Talk About Rape': Silencing Sexual Violence at the Special Court for Sierra Leone," *The International Journal of Transitional Justice*, 1, 3, 355–374.

Kendall, Sara. 2015. "Beyond the Restorative Turn: The Limits of Legal Humanitarianism," in Christian De Vos, Sara Kendall, and Carsten Stahn, eds., *Contested Justice: The Politics and Practice of International Criminal Court Investigations*, 352–376. New York: Cambridge University Press.

Kendall, Sara and Sara Nouween. 2018. "International Criminal Justice and Humanitarianism," Legal Studies Research Paper Series, No. 69/2018. University of Cambridge Faculty of Law Legal Studies.

Kennedy, Denis. 2009. "Selling the Distant Other – Ethical Dilemmas of Humanitarian Action," *Journal of Humanitarian Assistance*, 29, 1–25.

Kennedy, David. 2005. *The Dark Sides of Virtue: Reassessing International Humanitarianism*. Princeton: Princeton University Press.

Keohane, Nannerl. 1982. "The Enlightenment Idea of Progress Revisited," in G. Almond M. Chodorow, and R. H. Pierce, eds. *Progress and its Discontents*, 21–40. Berkeley: University of California Press.

Keys, Barbara. 2012. "Anti-Torture Politics: Amnesty International, the Greek Junta, and the Origins of the Human Rights 'Boom' in the United States," in A. Iriye et al., eds., *The Human Rights Revolution: An International History*, 201–222. Oxford: Oxford University Press.

2014. *Reclaiming American Virtue: The Human Rights Revolution of the 1970s*. Cambridge, MA: Harvard University Press.

Khalidi, Walid. 1991. *Before Their Diaspora: A Photographic History of the Palestinians, 1876–1948*. Washington, DC: Institute for Palestine Studies.

Khalili, L. 2013. *Time in the Shadows Confinement in Counterinsurgencies*. Stanford, CA: Stanford University Press.

Kielstra, Paul M. 2000. *The Politics of Slave Trade Suppression in Britain and France 1814–1848. Diplomacy, Morality and Economics*. Basingstoke: MacMillan Press.

Kincaid, James. 1998. *Erotic Innocence: The Culture of Child Molesting*. Durham, NC: Duke University Press.

Kinsella, H. 2011. *The Image Before the Weapon: A Critical History of the Distinction Between Combatant and Civilian*. New York: Cornell University Press.

2016. *The Image Before the Weapon: A Critical History of the Distinction Between Combatant and Civilian*. New York: Cornell University Press.

Kiznelbach, Katrin and Julian Lehmann. 2015. Can Shaming Promote Human Rights? Publicity in Human Rights Foreign Policy, A Review and Discussion Paper, European Liberal Forum. www.gppi.net/fileadmin/user_upload/media/pub/2015/Kinzelbach_Lehmann_2015_Can_Shaming_Promote_Human_Rights.pdf.

Klingberg, Frank Joseph. 1926. *The Anti-Slavery Movement in England: A Study in English Humanitarianism*. New Haven: Yale University Press.

Klose, Fabian. 2013. *Human Rights in the Shadow of Colonial Violence: The Wars of Independence in Kenya and Algeria*, trans. Dona Geyer. Philadelphia, PA: University of Pennsylvania Press.

ed. 2016. *The Emergence of Humanitarian Intervention: Ideas and Practice from the Nineteenth Century to the Present*. Cambridge, UK: Cambridge University Press.

2019. *In the Cause of Humanity: Eine Geschichte der humanitären Intervention im langen 19. Jahrhundert*. Gottingen: Vandenhoeck & Ruprecht.

Klose, Fabian and Mirjam Thulin, eds. 2016. *Humanity: A History of European Concepts in Practice from the Sixteenth Century to the Present*. Gottinghem, Germany: Vandenhoeck & Ruprecht.

Koh, Harold. 1998. "Is International Law Really State Law?" *Harvard Law Review*, 11, 7, 1824–1862.

Koskenniemi, Martti. 1997. "Lauterpacht: The Victorian Tradition in International Law," *European Journal of International Law*, 8, 2, 215–263.

Kratochwil, Fredrech. 2014. *The Status of Law in World Society.* New York: Cambridge University Press.

Kraus, Hertha. 1944. *International Relief in Action, 1914–1943.* Philadelphia: Research Centre.

Krause, Monika. 2014. *The Good Project: Humanitarian Relief NGOs and the Fragmentation of Reason.* Chicago: University of Chicago Press.

Kurasawa, Fuyuki. 2007. *The Work of Global Justice: Human Rights as Practices.* New York: Cambridge University Press.

Kuwali, Dan. 2013a. "'Humanitarian Rights': Bridging the Doctrinal Gap Between the Protection of Civilians and the Responsibility to Protect," *Journal of International Humanitarian Legal Studies,* 4, 5–46.

2013b. "'Humanitarian Rights': How to Ensure Respect for Human Rights and Humanitarian Law in Armed Conflicts," in Robert Kolb and Gloria Gaggioli, eds., *Research Handbook on Human Rights and Humanitarian Law,* 343–370. Northampton: Edward Elgar.

Labbé, Jérémie. 2012. *Rethinking Humanitarianism: Adapting to 21st Century Challenges.* New York: International Peace Institute.

Laber, Jeri. 2002. *The Courage of Strangers: Coming of Age with the Human Rights Movement.* New York: Public Affairs.

Lacerda, Tessa. 2016. "'Victim': What Is Hidden Behind This Word?" *International Journal of Transitional Justice,* 10, 179–188.

Lacroix, Justine and Jean-Yves Prachére, eds. 2018. *Human Rights on Trial: A Genealogy of the Critique of Human Rights.* New York: Cambridge University Press.

Laguardia, Francesca. 2017. "Deterring Torture: The Preventive Power of Criminal Law and Its Promise for Inhibiting State Abuses," *Human Rights Quarterly,* 39, 1, 189–212.

Laidlaw, Zoë. 2004. "'Aunt Anna's Report': The Buxton Women and the Aborigines Select Committee, 1835–37," *The Journal of Imperial and Commonwealth History,* 32, 2, 1–28.

2007. "Heathens, Slaves and Aborigines: Thomas Hodgkin's Critique of Missions and Antislavery," *History Workshop Journal,* 64, 1, 133–161.

Laidlaw, Zoe and Alan Lester. 2015. *Indigenous Communities and Settler Colonialism: Land Holding, Loss and Survival in an Interconnected World.* Basingstoke: Palgrave Macmillan.

Lamb, Robert. 2019. "Pragmatism, Practices, and Human Rights," *Review of International Studies,* 45, 4, 550–568.

Lamont, Michelle and Vigar Molnar. 2002. "The Study of Boundaries in the Social Sciences," *Annual Review of Sociology,* 28, 167–195.

Lanegran, Kimberley Rae. 2005. "Truth Commissions, Human Rights Trials, and the Politics of Memory," *Comparative Studies of South Asia, Africa and the Middle East,* 25, 1, 111–121.

Langer, L. 1991. *Holocaust Testimonies: The Ruins of Memory.* New Haven: Yale University Press.

Latonero, Mark. 2019. "Stop Surveillance Humanitarianism," *New York Times,* July 11. www.nytimes.com/2019/07/11/opinion/data-humanitarian-aid.html.

Latour, Bruno. 2018. "For a Terrestrial Politics: An Interview with Bruno Latour," *Eurozine*, February 6. www.eurozine.com/terrestrial-politics-interview-bruno-latour/.

Laqua, Daniel. 2014. "Inside the Humanitarian Cloud: Causes and Motivations to Help Friends and Strangers," *Journal of Modern European History*, 12, 2, 175–185.

Laqueur, Thomas W. 1989. "Bodies, Details, and the Humanitarian Narrative," in Lynn Hunt, ed., *The New Cultural History*, 176–204. Berkeley, CA: University of California Press.

2009. "Mourning, Pity, and the Work of Narrative in the Making of 'Humanity'," in R. Wilson and R. Brown, eds., *Humanitarianism and Suffering: The Mobilization of Empathy*, 31–57. New York: Cambridge University Press.

Lauren, Paul. 1998. *The Evolution of International Human Rights*. Philadelphia: University of Pennsylvania Press.

Lauterpacht, Hersch. 1943. "The Law of Nations, the Law of Nature and the Rights of Man," *Transactions of the Grotius Society*, 29, 1–33.

1945. *An International Bill of the Rights of Man*. New York and London: Columbia University Press.

1950. *International Law and Human Rights*. London: Praeger.

Law, Robin. 2010. "Abolition and Imperialism. International Law and the British Suppression of the Atlantic Slave Trade," in Derek Peterson, ed., *Abolitionism and Imperialism in Britain, Africa, and the Atlantic*, 150–174. Athens, OH: Ohio University Press.

Lawn, J. E., J. Rohde, S. Rifkin, M. Were, V. K. Paul, and M. Chopra. 2008. "Alma-Ata 30 Years on: Revolutionary, Relevant, and Time to Revitalise," *The Lancet*, 372, 9642, 917–927.

Lawson, Tom. 2014. *The Last Man: A British Genocide in Tasmania*. London: I. B. Tauris.

Le Pape, Marc and Pierre Salignon, eds. 2003. *Civilians under Fire: Humanitarian Practices in the Congo Republic 1998–2000*. London: Médecins sans Frontières.

Lebron, C. 2015. *The Color of Our Shame: Race and Justice in Our Time*. Oxford: Oxford University Press.

Leebaw, Bronwyn. 2007. "The Politics of Impartial Activism: Humanitarianism and Human Rights," *Perspectives on Politics*, 5, 2, 223–239.

2017. "Legitimating Interventions: Humanitarianism and Human Rights," in N. Frei, D. Stahl, and A. Weinke, eds., *Human Rights and Humanitarian Intervention: Legitimizing the Use of Force Since the 1970s*, 27–45. Gottingen: Wallstein.

Lepora, Chiara and Robert E Goodin. 2015. *On Complicity and Compromise*. Oxford: Oxford University Press.

Lester, Alan. 2001. *Imperial Networks: Creating Identities in Nineteenth Century South Africa and Britain*. London: Routledge.

Lester, Alan and Dussart, Fae. 2014. *Colonization and the Origins of Humanitarian Governance: Protecting Aborigines across the Nineteenth-Century British Empire*. Cambridge, UK: Cambridge University Press.

Levy, Daniel and Natan Snzaider. 2006. "Sovereignty Transformed: A Sociology of Human Rights," *British Journal of Sociology*, 57, 4, 657–676.

Lidchi, Henrietta. 2016. "Finding the Right Image: British Development NGOs and the Regulation of Imagery," in Heidi Fehrenbach and Davide Rodogno, eds., *Humanitarian Photography: A History*, 275–296. New York: Cambridge University Press.

Lifton, R. J. 1973. *Home from the War: Vietnam Veterans: Neither Victims nor Executioners*. New York: Simon & Schuster.

Lightfoot, S. 2016. *Global Indigenous Politics: A Subtle Revolution*. New York: Routledge.

Lillich, Richard B. 1967. "Forcible Self-Help by States to Protect Human Rights," *Iowa Law Review*, 53, 325–351.

   1969. "Intervention to Protect Human Rights," *McGill Law Journal*, 15, 205–219.

   1974. "Humanitarian Intervention: A Reply to Ian Brownlie and a Plea for Constructive Alternatives," in John Moore, ed., *Law and Civil War in the Modern World*, 229–251. Baltimore: John Hopkins University Press.

Lingelbach, William E. 1900. "The Doctrine and Practice of Intervention in Europe," *Annals of the American Academy of Political and Social Science*, 16, 1–32.

Linklater, Andrew. 2007. "Towards a Sociology of Global Morals with an 'Emancipatory Intent'," *Review of International Studies*, 33, April, 135–150.

Liu, Joanne. 2016. MSF President to UN Security Council: "Stop these Attacks." www.msf.org/msf-president-un-security-council-stop-these-attacks.

Liu, Joanne and Pierre Salignon. 2003. "Health Services for Rape Victims: Humanitarian Practices in the Congo Republic, 1998–2000," *Civilians Under Fire*. Paris: MSF.

Lloyd, Christopher. 1968. *The Navy and the Slave Trade. The Suppression of the African Slave Trade in the Nineteenth Century*. London: Routledge.

Locard, Henri. 2005. "State Violence in Democratic Kampuchea (1975–1979) and Retribution (1979–2004)," *European Review of History – Revue européenne d'Histoire*, 12, 1, 121–143.

Locke, Jill. 2016. *Democracy and the Death of Shame*. Cambridge, UK: Cambridge University Press.

Locke, John. 1975 [1689]. *An Essay Concerning Human Understanding*, ed. Peter H. Nidditch. New York: Oxford University Press.

Lohne Kejrsti and Kirstin Bergtora Sandvick. 2017. "Bringing Law into the Political Sociology of Humanitarianism," *Oslo Law Review*, 4, 1, 4–27.

Lubell, Noam. 2005. "Challenges Applying Human Rights Law to Armed Conflict," *International Review of the Red Cross*, 87, 860, 737–754.

Magone, Claire, Michael Neuman, and Fabrice Weissman, eds. 2011. *Humanitarian Negotiations Revealed: The MSF Experience*. London: Hurst Publishers.

Malik, Kenan. 2014. "The Quest for a Moral Compass," *A Global History of Ethics*. London: Atlantic Books.

Malkki, Lisa H. 1996. "Speechless Emissaries: Refugees, Humanitarianism, and Dehistoricization," *Cultural Anthropology*, 11, 3, 377–404.

2010. "Children, Humanity and the Infantilization of Peace," in Ilana Feldman and Miriam Ticktin, eds., *In the Name of Humanity: The Government of Threat and Care*, 58–85. Durham, NC: Duke University Press.

2015. *The Need to Help: The Domestic Arts of International Humanitarianism*. Durham, NC: Duke University Press.

Mandelstam, André N. 1930. "La généralisation de la protection internationale des droits de l'homme," *Revue de droit international et de législation comparée*, Series 3, XI, 297–325 and 699–713.

1931. "Der internationale Schutz der Menschenrechte und die New-Yorker Erklaerung des Instituts fuer Voelkerrecht. Zeitschrift fuer auslaendisches oeffentliches," *Recht und Voelkerrecht*, 2, 335–377.

Macrolas, Geneva. 2020. COVID-19: Privacy Versus Health, April 29. http://er bguth.ch/COVID-19_tracing_privacy.mp4.

Marks, Susan. 2011. "Human Rights and Root Causes," *Modern Law Review*, 74, 1, 57–78.

Marshall, Thomas H. 1963. "Citizenship and Social Class," *Sociology at the Crossroads*. London: Heinemann.

Martinez, Jenny. 2012. *The Slave Trade and the Origins of International Human Rights Law*. Oxford: Oxford University Press.

Marx, Karl. 1887. *Capital: A Critique of Political Economy, Volume I, Book One: The Process of Production of Capital*. Moscow: Progress.

Marx, Karl and Fredrich Engels. 1848. *The Communist Manifesto*.

Maslan, Susan. 2004. "The Anti-Human: Man and Citizen before the Declaration of the Rights of Man and of the Citizen," *The South Atlantic Quarterly*, 103, 2/3, 357–374.

Mason, Linda and Roger Brown. 1983. *Rice, Rivalry and Politics: Managing Cambodian Relief*. South Bend: University of Notre Dame Press.

Mason, Matthew. 2009. "Keeping Up Appearances. The International Politics of Slave Trade Abolition in the Nineteenth-Century Atlantic World," *The William and Mary Quarterly*, 66, 1, 809–832.

May, Vivian M. 2008. "'It Is Never a Question of the Slaves': Anna Julia Cooper's Challenge to History's Silences in Her 1925 Sorbonne Thesis," *Callaloo*, 31, 3, 903–918.

Mazower, Mark. 2006. "An International Civilization? Empire, Internationalism and the Crisis of the Mid-Twentieth Century," *International Affairs*, 82, 3, 559–563.

2009. *No Enchanted Palace: The End of Empire and the Ideological Origins of the United Nations*. Princeton, NJ: Princeton University Press.

McEntire, K., M. Leiby, and M. Krain. 2015. "How to Ask People for Change: Examining Peoples' Willingness to Donate to Human Rights Campaigns," in Joel Pruce, ed., *The Social Practice of Human Rights*, 43–62. New York: Palgrave McMillan.

2015. "Human Rights Organizations as Agents of Change: An Experimental Examination of Framing and Micromobilization," *American Political Science Review*, 109, 3, 407–426.

McKay, Ramah. 2012. "Afterlives: Humanitarian Histories and Critical Subjects in Mozambique," *Cultural Anthropology*, 27, 2, 286–309.

McManus, Shea. 2017. "The Right to Know: Suffering, Human Rights, and Perplexities in Politics in Lebanon," *American Ethnologist*, 44, 1, 1–14.

Médecins Sans Frontières. 2014. *Where is Everyone? Responding to Emergencies in the Most Difficult Places*. London: MSF.

Meger, Sara. 2016. "The Fetishization of Sexual Violence in International Security," *International Studies Quarterly*, 60, 149–159.

Meierhenrich, Jens. 2013. "The Practice of International Law: A Theoretical Analysis," *Law and Contemporary Problems*, 76, 1, 1–83.

Meister, R. 2011. *After Evil: A Politics of Human Rights*. New York: Columbia University Press.

Merivale, Herman. 1841, rept. 1861. *Lectures on Colonisation and the Colonies at the University of Oxford*, Vol. I. London: Longman.

Menon, Rajan. 2016. *The Conceit of Humanitarian Intervention*. New York: Oxford University Press.

Meron, Theodor. 2000. "The Humanization of Humanitarian Law," *American Journal of International Law*, 94, 2, 239–278.

Merry, Sally Engle. 2006. "Transnational Human Rights and Local Activism: Mapping the Middle," *American Anthropologist*, 108, 1, 38–51.

Meyerson, Collier. 2017. "Adults Think Black Girls Are Older Than They Are – and It Matters," *Nation*, July 6.

Mihai, M. 2016. *Negative Emotions and Transitional Justice*. New York: Columbia University Press.

Milgram, S. 2017. *Obedience to Authority: An Experimental View*. New York: Harper & Row.

Miller, Alice M. 2004. "Sexuality, Violence against Women and Human Rights: Women Make Demands and Ladies Get Protection," *Health and Human Rights*, 7, 2, 17–47.

Miller, David. 2016. "Human Rights and Status Egalitarianism," *Ethics & International Affairs*, 30, 4, 461–469.

Millis, Roger. 1992. *Waterloo Creek: The Australia Day Massacre of 1838*. Sydney: University of New South Wales Press.

Minear, Larry and Hazel Smith, eds. 2007. *Humanitarian Diplomacy: Practitioners and Their Craft*. New York: United Nations University Press.

Le Ministère des Affaires Étrangères, Archives des Affaires Étragères (MAE), *Série Mémoires et Documents, Afrique* (MAE MD A).

Mohandesi, Salar. 2017. *From Anti-Imperialism to Human Rights: The Vietnam War, Internationalism, and the Radical Left in the Long 1960s*. PhD diss., University of Pennsylvania.

Moinar, Petra. 2020. "COVID-19: Can Technology Become a Tool of Oppression and Surveillance?" *OpenDemocracy*, May 1. www.opendemocracy.net/en/pandemic-border/covid-19-can-technology-become-tool-oppression-and-surveillance/.

Mollica, Richard F., Karen Donelan, Svang Tor, James Lavelle, Christopher Elias, Martin Frankel, and Robert J. Blendon. 1993. "The Effect of Trauma and Confinement on Functional Health and Mental Health Status of Cambodians Living in Thailand-Cambodia Border Camps," *Jama*, 270, 5, 581–586.

Mollica, Richard F., Xingjia Cui, Keith McInnes, and Michael Massagli. 2002. "Science-Based Policy for Psychosocial Interventions in Refugee Camps: A Cambodian Example," *The Journal of Nervous and Mental Disease*, 190, 3, 158–166.

Molyneux, Maxine. 1985. "Mobilisation Without Emancipation? Women's Interests, the State and Revolution in Nicaragua," *Feminist Studies*, 11, 2, 227–254.

Moniz, Amanda B. 2016. *From Empire to Humanity: The American Revolution and the Origins of Humanitarianism*. Oxford: Oxford University Press.

Moon, Claire. 2012. "What One Sees and How One Files Seeing: Human Rights Reporting, Representation, and Action," *Sociology*, 46, 5, 876–890.

2016. "Human Rights, Human Remains: Forensic Humanitarianism and the Human Rights of the Dead," *International Political Science Review*, 65, 49–63.

Montes, N. 2019. *Noe Montes – Farm Workers in the Coachella Valley*. Retrieved from www.lensculture.com/projects/373342-farm-workers-in-the-coachella

Morgan, David and Iain Wilkinson. 2001. "The Problem of Suffering and the Sociological Task of Theodicy," *European Journal of Social Theory*, 4, 2, 199–214.

Moser, Caroline O. 2001. "The Gendered Continuum of Violence and Conflict: An Operational Framework," in Caroline O. Moser and Fiona Clark, eds., *Victims, Perpetrators or Actors? Gender, Armed Conflict and Political Violence*, 30–52. New York: Zed Books.

Moyn, Samuel. 2006. "Empathy in History: Empathizing with Humanity," *History and Theory*, 45, 397–415.

2010. *The Last Utopia: Human Rights in History*. Cambridge, MA: Harvard University Press.

2012a. "Die neue Historiographie der Menschenrechte," *Geschichte und Gesellschaft*, 38, 545–572.

2012b. "Substance, Scale, and Salience: The Recent Historiography of Human Rights," *Annual Review of Law and Social Science*, 8, 123–140.

2013. Torture and Taboo. *The Nation February 25*.

2014. *Human Rights and the Uses of History*. London and New York: Verso.

2016. *Theses on Humanitarianism and Human Rights*. http://humanityjournal.org/blog/theses-on-humanitarianism-and-human-rights/.

2017a. "Human Rights and the Crisis of Liberalism," in S. Hopgood, L. Vinjamuri, and J. Snyder, eds., *Human Rights Futures*, 261–282. New York: Cambridge University Press.

2017b. *Human Rights and the Uses of History*, rev. edn. New York: Verso.

2018. *Not Enough: Human Rights in an Unequal World*. Cambridge, MA: Harvard University Press.

2019. "The Doctor's Plot: The Origins of the Philosophy of Human Rights," in Duncan Bell, ed., *Race, Empire, and Global Justice*, 52–73. Cambridge, UK: Cambridge University Press.

Murphy, Sean D. 1996. *Humanitarian Intervention: The United Nations in an Evolving World Order*. Philadelphia: University of Pennsylvania Press.

Nadelmann, Ethan A. 1990. "Global Prohibition Regime: The Evolution of Norms in International Society," *International Organization*, 44, 479–526.

Nann, Stéphanie. 2009. "Les Familles Cambodgiennes en France: Histoires de Vie et Reconstruction," *Dialogue*, 185, 3, 55–66.

Nascimento, Daniela Santos. 2004. "The Inclusion of Human Rights in Humanitarian Assistance," *Yearbook of Humanitarian Action and Human Rights*, Universidad de Deusto.

Nash, Kate. 2015. *The Political Sociology of Human Rights*. New York: Cambridge University Press.

Neff, Stephen C. 2014. *Justice Among Nations. A History of International Law*. Cambridge, MA: Harvard University Press.

Neier, Aryeh. 2013. *The International Human Rights Movement: A History*. Princeton: Princeton University Press.

Neiman, Susan. 2015. *Evil in Modern Thought*. Princeton: Princeton University Press.

Nelson, Paul J. and Ellen Dorsey. 2018. "Who Practices Rights-Based Development? A Progress Report on Work at the Nexus of Human Rights and Development," *World Development*, 104, 97–107.

Newson, Linda. 1976. *Aboriginal and Spanish Colonial Trinidad: A Study in Cultural Contact*. New York: Academic Press.

Nguyen, Vinh-Kim. 2010. *The Republic of Therapy: Triage and Sovereignty in West Africa's Time of AIDS*. Durham, NC: Duke University Press.

Ní Aoláin, Fionnuala. 2009. "Gendering the Declaration," *Maryland Journal of International Law*, 24, 1, 335–345.

Nickel, James W. 2002. "Is Today's International Human Rights System a Global Governance Regime?" *The Journal of Ethics*, 6, 4, 353–371.

Niezen, Ronald. 2007. "The Law's Legal Anthropology," in Mark Goodale, ed., *Human Rights at the Crossroads*, 186–195. New York: Oxford University Press.

Nocilini, Davide. 2012. *Practice Theory, Work, and Organization: An Introduction*. New York: Oxford University Press.

Norum, Roger, Mary Mostafanezhad, and Tani Sebro. 2016. "The Chronopolitics of Exile: Hope, Heterotemporality, and NGO Economics along the Thai–Burma Border," *Critique of Anthropology*, 36, 1, 61–83.

Nussbaum, Martha. 1996. "Compassion: The Basic Social Emotion," *Social Philosophy and Policy*, 13, 1, 27–58.

  2000. "Duties of Justice, Duties of Material Aid: Cicero's Problematic Legacy," *Journal of Political Philosophy*, 8, 2, 176–206.

  2001. *Upheavals of Thought: The Intelligence of Emotions*. Cambridge, UK: Cambridge University Press.

  2016. "Women's Progress and Women's Human Rights," *Human Rights Quarterly*, 38, 3, 589–622.

Oberleitner, Gerd. 2015. *Human Rights in Armed Conflict: Law, Practice, Policy*. Cambridge, UK: Cambridge University Press.

Oesterheld, Christian. 2014. "Cambodian Thai Relations during the Khmer Rouge Regime: Evidence from the East German Diplomatic Archives," *Silpakorn University Journal of Social Sciences, Humanities, and Arts*, 14, 2, 161–182.

O'Flaherty, Michael and George Ulrich. 2010. "The Professionalization of Human Rights Field Work," *Journal of Human Rights Practice*, 2, 1, 1–27.

Ogata, Sadako. 1997. "Humanitarianism, Human Rights Law, and Refugee Protection," in Daniel Warner, ed., *Human Rights and Humanitarian Law*, 43–78. The Hague: Martinus Nijhoff.

Oguzertem, Ozlem Eskiocak and Paul McAdams. 2015. "Human Rights, Conflict Resolution, and Tolerance Education: UNRWA Experience from the Field," *Human Rights Education in Asia-Pacific*, 6, 59–86. www.hurights.or.jp/archiv es/asia-pacific/section1/7%20UNRWA%20Experience.pdf.

Ohlin, Jens David, ed. 2016. *Theoretical Boundaries of Armed Conflict and Human Rights*. Cambridge, UK: Cambridge University Press.

Ong, Aihwa. 2003. *Buddha Is Hiding: Refugees, Citizenship, the New America*. Berkeley: University of California Press.

Oppenheim, Lassa. 1948. *International Law. A Treatise, Vol. I, Peace*, ed. Hersch Lauterpacht. London and New York: Longmans.

O'Rourke, Catherine and Swaine, Aisling. 2018. "CEDAW and the Security Council: Enhancing Women's Rights in Conflict," *International and Comparative Law Quarterly*, 67, 1, 167–199.

Ortner, Sherry. 2006. *Anthropology and Social Theory: Culture, Power, and the Acting Subject*. Durham: Duke University Press.

Orwell, George. 1949. "Reflections on Gandhi," *Partisan Review*, May. www.or wellfoundation.com/the-orwell-foundation/orwell/essays-and-other-works/r eflections-on-gandhi/

Osborne, Frederick. 1939. "The Comprehensive Program of Eugenics and Its Social Implications," *Living*, 1, 2/3, 33–38.

O'Sullivan, Kevin, Matthew Hilton, and Juliano Fiori. 2016. "Humanitarianisms in Context: Histories of Non-State Actors, from the Local to the Global," *European Review of History*, 23, 1–2, 1–15.

Owens, Patricia. 2009. "Reclaiming 'Bare Life'? Against Agamben on Refugees," *International Relations*, 23, 4, 567–582.

Oxfam. 2019. *The Humanitarian-Development-Peace Nexus*. June. https://reliefweb.in t/sites/reliefweb.int/files/resources/dp-humanitarian-development-peace-nexus-260619-en_0.pdf

Pachucki, Mark A., Sabrina Pendergrass, and Michele Lamont. 2007. "Boundary Processes: Recent Theoretical Developments and New Contributions," *Poetics*, 35, 6, 331–351.

Panh, Rithy. 1995. "La Famille Tan," La Sept (documentary).

Papal Encyclicals Online. nd. www.papalencyclicals.net/pius09/p9ineff.htm.

Parker, Laura. 2017. "'Biggest Case on the Planet' Pits Kids vs. Climate Change," *National Geographic*, March 17. http://news.nationalgeographic.com/2017/0 3/kids-sue-us-government-climate-change/.

Patten, Allen. 2014. *Equal Recognition: The Moral Foundation of Minority Rights*. Princeton: Princeton University Press.

Paulmann, Johannes. ed. 2016a. *Dilemmas of Humanitarian Aid in the Twentieth Century*. Oxford: Oxford University Press.

2016b. "Humanitarianism and Empire," in John M. MacKenzie et al., eds., *Encylopedia of Empire, Volume II, D-J*, 1112–1123. Chichester, UK: John Wiley & Sons.

Paxman, John M. and George T. Boggs, eds. 1973. *The United Nations: A Reassessment. Sanctions, Peacekeeping, and Humanitarian Assistance.* Charlottesville: University Press of Virginia.

Pease, Kelly. 2016. *Human Rights and Humanitarian Diplomacy: Negotiating for Human Rights Protection and Humanitarian Access.* Manchester: University of Manchester Press.

Pedersen, Susan. 2014. *The Guardians: The League of Nations and Crisis of Empire.* Oxford: Oxford University Press.

Pellow, David N. 2007. *Resisting Global Toxics: Transnational Movements for Environmental Justice.* Cambridge, MA: MIT Press.

Peires, Jeff B. 1989. *The Dead Will Arise: Nongqawuse and the Great Xhosa Cattle Killing Movement of 1856–7.* Johannesburg: Ravan Press.

Perkowski, Nina. 2016. "Deaths, Interventions, Humanitarianism and Human Rights in the Mediterranean Migration Crisis," *Mediterranean Politics*, 21, 2, 331–335.

Perugini, Nicola and Neve Gordon. 2015. *The Human Right to Dominate.* New York: Oxford University Press.

Peschoux, Christophe. 1992. *Les "Nouveaux" Khmers Rouges: Enquête (1979–1990) Reconstruction du Mouvement et Reconquête des villages.* Paris: L'Harmattan.

Pflanz, Mike. 2009. "Sudan Expels Oxfam and Medicines Sans Frontieres from Darfur Over War Crimes Threat to Omar al-Bashir," *The Telegraph*, March 4. www.telegraph.co.uk/news/worldnews/africaandindianocean/sud an/4940315/Sudan-expels-Oxfam-and-Mdecins-Sans-Frontires-from-Darf ur-over-war-crimes-threat-to-Omar-al-Bashir.html.

Photographers without Borders. nd. *Code of Ethics.* www.photographerswithout borders.org/code-of-ethics.

Pictet, Jean. 1967. *The Principles of International Humanitarian Law [by] Jean Pictet.* Geneva: International Committee of the Red Cross.

1979. *The Fundamental Principles of the Red Cross: Commentary (1 January 1979).* www.icrc.org/eng/resources/documents/misc/fundamental-principles-com mentary-010179.htm.

Pinker, Steven. 2011. *The Better Angels of Our Nature: Why Violence Has Declined.* New York: Viking.

Pinto, Gabriella. 2014. "'A Cultural Occupation?' UNRWA's Human Rights, Conflict Resolution and Tolerance Programme: Perspectives from Balata Camp," *Educate~*, 14, 2, 57–74.

Pitkin, H. F. 1993. *Wittgenstein and Justice: On the Significance of Ludwig Wittgenstein for Social and Political Thought.* Oakland, CA: University of California Press.

Plato and Sir H. Lee. 2003. *The Republic.* London: Penguin.

Plato, Ferrari, G. R. and Griffith, T. 2000. *Plato: "The Republic."* Cambridge, UK: Cambridge University Press.

Plomley, N. J. B. 1966. *Friendly Mission. The Tasmanian Journals and Papers of George Augustus Robinson, 1829–1834.* Hobart: Tasmanian Historical Research Association.

Poewe, Karla. 2005. *New Religions and the Nazis.* New York: Routledge.

Ponchaud. François. 1977. *Cambodge Année Zéro*. Paris: Julliard.
Pope, Stephen J. 1991. "Aquinas on Almsgiving, Justice and Charity: An Interpretation and Reassessment," *The Heythrop Journal*, 32, 2, 167–191.
Postema, Gerald. 1987. "'Protestant' Interpretation and Social Practices," *Law and Philosophy*, 6, 3, 283–319.
Power, Samantha. 2001. "Bystanders to Genocide," *Atlantic Monthly*, September 1.
  2002. *A Problem from Hell: America and the Age of Genocide*. New York: Basic Books.
  2009. "The Enforcer: A Christian Lawyer's Global Crusade," *The New Yorker*, January 19.
  2019. *The Education of an Idealist: A Memoir*. New York: HarperCollins.
Prichard, James Cowles. 1839. "On the Extinction of Human Races," *Edinburgh New Philosophical Journal*, 28, 166.
Prosecutor v. Furundzija, Judgment, Case No. IT-95–17/1-T, T.Ch. II, December10, section 183.
Rainger, R. 1980. "Philanthropy and Science in the 1830's: The British and Foreign Aborigines' Protection Society," *Man*, 15, 4, 702–717.
Rancière, Jacques. 2004. "Who Is the Subject of the Rights of Man?" *South Atlantic Quarterly*, 103, 2/3, 297–310.
Rashed, Haifa, Damien Short, and John Docker. 2014. "Nakba Memoricide: Genocide Studies and the Zionist/Israeli Genocide of Palestine," *Holy Land Studies*, 13, 1, 1–23.
Rawls, John. 1993. *Political Liberalism*. Columbia, NY: Columbia University Press.
  1999. *A Theory of Justice*, rev. edn. Cambridge, MA: Harvard University Press.
Read, Colin. 1988. *The Rebellion of 1837 in Upper Canada*. Ottawa: The Canadian Historical Association.
Read-Hamilton, Sophie. 2014. "Gender-based Violence: A Confused and Contested Term," *Humanitarian Exchange*, 60. https://odihpn.org/maga zine/gender-based-violence-a-confused-and-contested-term/.
Rechtman, Richard. 1993. "Rêve, réalité, et expériences traumatiques chez les réfugiés Cambodgiens," *Cahiers d'anthropologie et biométrie humaine*, 11, 3–4, 259–279.
  2004. "The Rebirth of PTSD: The Rise of a New Paradigm in Psychiatry," *Social Psychiatry and Psychiatric Epidemiology*, 39, 11, 913–915.
  2006. "The Survivor's Paradox: Psychological Consequences of the Khmer Rouge Rhetoric of Extermination," *Anthropology & Medicine*, 13, 1, 1–11.
Redfield, Peter. 2005. "Doctors, Borders, and Life in Crisis," *Cultural Anthropology*, 20, 3, 328–361.
  2006. "A Less Modest Witness: Collective Advocacy and Motivated Truth in a Medical Humanitarian Movement," *American Ethnologist*, 33, 1, 3–26.
  2013. *Life in Crisis: The Ethical Journey of Doctors Without Borders*. Berkeley: University of California Press.
  2015. "A Measured Good," in S. Abramowitz and C. Panter-Brick, eds., *Medical Humanitarianism: Ethnographies of Practice*, 242–251. Philadelphia: University of Pennsylvania Press.
  2016. "Fluid Technologies: The Bush Pump, the LifeStraw® and Microworlds of Humanitarian Design," *Social Studies of Science*, 46, 2, 159–183.

Redhead, Robin and Nick Turnbull. 2011. "Towards a Study of Human Rights Practitioners," *Human Rights Review*, 12, 2, 173–189.

Rees, Siân. 2009. *Sweet Water and Bitter: The Ships that Stopped the Slave Trade.* London: Chatto & Windus.

Regan, Paulette. 2010. *Unsettling the Settler Within: Indian Residential Schools, Truth Telling, and Reconciliation in Canada.* Vancouver: UBC Press.

Reich, Jerome. 1968. "The Slave Trade at the Congress of Vienna. A Study in English Public Opinion," *Journal of Negro History*, 53, 2, 129–163.

Reid-Henry, Simon. 2014. "Humanitarianism as Liberal Diagnostic: Humanitarian Reason and the Political Rationalities of the Liberal Will-to-Care," *Transactions of the Institute of British Geographers*, 39, 3, 418–431.

Reidy, A. 1998. "The Approach of the European Commission and Court of Human Rights to International Humanitarian Law," *International Review of the Red Cross*, 324, 513–529.

Reisman, Michael with the collaboration of Myers S. McDougal. 1973. "Humanitarian Intervention to Protect the Ibos," in Richard B. Lillich, ed., *Humanitarian Intervention and the United Nations*, 167–195. Charlottesville: University Press of Virginia.

Reuters. 2012. MSF quits prison in Libya city over torture. www.reuters.com/article/us-libya-torture/msf-quits-prisons-in-libya-city-over-torture-idUSTRE80P1K N20120126.

Reynolds, Henry. 1995. *Fate of a Free People.* London: Penguin.

2004. *Fate of a Free People: The Classic Account of the Tasmanian Wars*, rev. edn. Camberwell: Penguin.

Richmond, Oliver P. and Jason Frank. 2007. "Liberal Hubris? Virtual Peace in Cambodia," *Security Dialogue*, 38, 1, 27–48.

Robbins, Bruce. 2017. *The Beneficiary.* Durham, NC: Duke University Press.

Roberts, D. 2010. "Political Transition and Elite Discourse in Cambodia, 1991–99," *Journal of Communist Studies and Transition Politics*, 18, 4, 101–118.

Rodogno, Davide. 2012. *Against Massacre. Humanitarian Interventions in the Ottoman Empire 1815–1914.* Princeton: Princeton University Press.

Rolin-Jaequemyns, Gustave. 1876. "Note sur la Théorie du Droit d'Intervention:- À propos d'une lettre de M. le professeur Arntz," *Revue de Droit International et de Législation Comparée*, 8, 673–682.

Rome Statute of the International Criminal Court. nd. http://legal.un.org/icc/sta tute/romefra.htm.

Rorty, Richard. 1993. "Human Rights, Rationality, and Sentimentality," in Stephen Shute, ed., *On Human Rights*, 111–134. New York: Basic Books.

1996. "Who Are We? Moral Universalism and Economic Triage," *Diogenes*, 173, 44, 1.

Ross, Andrew. 2018. "Beyond Empathy and Compassion: Genocide and the Emotional Complexities of Humanitarian Politics," in Thomas Brudholm and Johannes Lange, eds., *Emotions and Mass Atrocity*, 185–208. New York: Cambridge University Press.

Ross, Kristin. 2002. *May '68 and Its Afterlives.* Chicago: University of Chicago Press.

Roth, Kenneth. 2004. "Defending Economic, Social and Cultural Rights: Practical Issues Faced by an International Human Rights Organization," *Human Rights Quarterly*, 26, 1, 63–73.

Roth, Silke. 2015. *The Paradoxes of Aid Work: Passionate Professionals*. New York: Routledge.

Rothberg, Michael. 2009. *Multidirectional Memory: Remembering the Holocaust in the Age of Decolonization*. Stanford: Stanford University Press.

2019. *The Implicated Subject: Beyond Victims and Perpetrators*. Stanford: Stanford University Press.

Rougier, Antoine. 1910. "La théorie de l'intervention d'humanité," *Revue générale de droit internationale public*, XVII, 468–526.

Rouse, Joseph. 2007. Practice Theory. http://wesscholar.wesleyan.edu/div1fac pubs/43.

Rousseau, Jean-Jacques. 1987 [1794]. "Discourse on the Origin and Foundations of Inequality Among Men," in *The Basic Political Writings*, trans. Donald Cress, 27–92. Indianapolis: Hackett.

Rousseau, Stéphane. 2020. *Tranches de Vie d'un expat' de l'humanitaire*. Paris: L'Harmattan.

Roy, Sara. 1995. *The Gaza Strip: The Political Economy of De-Development*. Washington, DC: Institute for Palestine Studies.

Rozée, Patricia D. and Gretchen Van Boemel. 1990. "The Psychological Effects of War Trauma and Abuse on Older Cambodian Refugee Women," *Women and Therapy*, 8, 4, 23–50.

Rubenstein, J. C. 2015. *Between Samaritans and States: The Political Ethics of Humanitarian INGOs*. Oxford: Oxford University Press.

Rubin, Gayle. 1995 [1986]. "Thinking Sex: Notes for a Radical Theory of the Politics of Sexuality," in Henry Abelove, Michèle Aina Barale, and David M. Halpern, eds., *The Lesbian and Gay Studies Reader*, 3–44. New York: Routledge.

Rutazibwa, Olivia Umurerwa. 2019. "What's There to Mourn? Decolonial Reflections on (the End of) Liberal Humanitarianism," *Journal of Humanitarian Affairs*, 1, 1, 65–67.

Rutherford J. 1961. *Sir George Grey K.C.B.: A Study in Colonial Government*. London: Cassell.

Ryan, Lyndall. 1996. *The Aboriginal Tasmanians*, 2nd edn. Crows Nest: Allen and Unwin.

2012. *Tasmanian Aborigines: A History Since 1803*. Crows Nest: Allen and Unwin.

Sack, William H., Richard H. Angell, J. David Kinzie, and Ben Rath. 1986. "The Psychiatric Effects of Massive Trauma on Cambodian Children: II. The Family, the Home, and the School," *Journal of the American Academy of Child Psychiatry*, 25, 3, 377–383.

Sack, William H., Shirley McSharry, Gregory N. Clarke, Ronald Kinney, John Seeley, and Peter Lewinsohn. 1994. "The Khmer Adolescent Project: I. Epidemiologic Findings in Two Generations of Cambodian Refugees," *The Journal of Nervous and Mental Disease*, 182, 7, 387–395.

Salesa, Damon Ieremia. 2011. *Racial Crossings: Race, Intermarriage, and the Victorian British Empire*. Oxford: Oxford University Press.

Salt, Henry S. 1891. *Humanitarianism: Its General Principles and Progress*. London. 1907. "What Is Humanitarianism?" *The Humane Review*, 8, 178–188.

Sangiovanni, Andrea. 2017. *Humanity Without Dignity*. Cambridge, MA: Harvard University Press.

Sargent, Daniel. 2014. "Oasis in the Desert? America's Human Rights Rediscovery," in Jan Eckel and Samuel Moyn, eds., *The Breakthrough: Human Rights in the 1970s*, 125–145. Philadelphia: University of Pennsylvania Press.

Sayigh, Rosemary. 2013. "On the Exclusion of the Palestinian Nakba from the 'Trauma Genre'," *Journal of Palestine Studies*, 43, 1, 51–60.

Scarry, Elaine. 1985. *The Body in Pain: The Making and Unmaking of the World*. NY: Oxford University Press.

Schaffer, Karlsson Johan. 2014. A Pluralist Approach to the Practice of Human Rights, June 4. http://ssrn.com/abstract=2490964.

Schauer, Frederick. 2009. *Thinking Like a Lawyer*. Cambridge, MA: Harvard University Press.

Schatzki, T. R. 2005a. "Introduction: Practice Theory," in T. R. Schatzki, K. Knorr-Cetina, and E. von Savigny, eds., *The Practice Turn in Contemporary Theory*, 1–14. New York: Routledge.

2005b. "Practice Mind-ed Orders," in T. R. Schatzki, K. Knorr-Cetina, and E. von Savigny, eds., *The Practice Turn in Contemporary Theory*, 42–55. New York: Routledge Press.

Schatzki T. R., K. Knorr-Cetina, and E. von Savigny, eds. 2005. *The Practice Turn in Contemporary Theory*. New York: Routledge.

Schmitz, Peter Hans and Kathryn Sikkink. 2002. "International Human Rights," in W. Carlsnaes, T. Risse, and B. Simmons, eds., *Handbook of International Relations*, 517–537. Beverley Hills: Sage.

Schneewind, J. B. 1998. *The Invention of Autonomy*. Cambridge, UK: Cambridge University Press.

Schopper, Doris. 2014. "Responding to the Needs of Survivors of Sexual Violence: Do We Know What Works?" *International Review of the Red Cross*, 96, 585–560.

Schumaker, Millard. 1992. *Sharing Without Reckoning: Imperfect Right and the Norms of Reciprocity*. Waterloo, Canada: Wilfrid Laurier University Press.

Schutter, B. de. 1972. "Humanitarian Intervention: A United Nations Task," *California Western International Law Journal*, 21, 3, 21–36.

Sciurba, Alessandra and Fililpo Furri. 2018. "Human Rights Beyond Humanitarianism: The Radical Challenge to the Right to Asylum in the Mediterranean Zone," *Antipode*, 50, 3, 763–782.

Scully, Pamela. 2011. "Gender, History and Human Rights," in Dorothy Hodgson, ed., *Gender and Culture at the Limit of Rights*, 17–31. Philadelphia: University of Pennsylvania Press.

Segev, Tom. 1993. *The Seventh Million: The Israelis and the Holocaust*. New York: Hill and Wang.

Seligman, Adam and David Montgomery. 2019. "The Tragedy of Human Rights: Liberalism and the Loss of Belonging," Society, 24 June, 203–209.

Sera-Shriar, Efram. 2013. *The Making of British Anthropology, 1813–1871*. London: Pickering and Chatto.

Shaikh, Farida. 2009. "Judicial Diplomacy. British Officials and the Mixed Commission Courts," in Keith Hamilton and Patrick Salmon, eds., *Slavery, Diplomacy and Empire: Britain and the Suppression of the Slave Trade, 1807–1975*, 42–64. Brighton: Sussex Academic Press.

Shalhoub-Kevorkian, Nadera. 2014. "Human Suffering in Colonial Contexts: Reflections from Palestine," *Settler Colonial Studies*, 4, 3, 277–290.

Shapcott, Richard. 2008. "Anti-Cosmopolitanism, Pluralism, and the Cosmopolitan Harm Principle," *Review of International Studies*, 34, 2, 185–205.

2010. *International Ethics: An Introduction*. Malden, MA: Polity Press.

Sharpe, C. 2016. *In the Wake: On Blackness and Being*. Durham, NC: Duke University Press.

Shaw, A. G. L. 1980. *Sir George Arthur, Bart, 1784–1854*. Melbourne: University of Melbourne Press.

2008. Arthur, Sir George, first baronet (1784–1854). *Oxford Dictionary of National Biography*. Oxford: Oxford University Press. www.oxforddnb.com/vi ew/article/707.

Shawcross, William. 1984. *The Quality of Mercy: Cambodia, Holocaust and Modern Conscience*. New York: Simon & Schuster.

Sahlins, Marshall. 1974. *Stone Age Economics*. London: Tavistock Publications.

Shklar, J. N. 1964. *Legalism*. Cambridge, MA: Harvard University Press.

Shue, Henry. 1980. *Basic Rights: Subsistence, Affluence, and U.S. Foreign Policy*. Princeton, NJ: Princeton University Press.

Sideris, Tina. 2001. "Rape in War and Peace: Social Context, Gender, Power and Identity," in Shiela Meintjes, Anu Pillay, and Meredeth Turshen, eds., *The Aftermath: Women in Post-Conflict Transformation*, 142–158. London and New York: Zed Books.

Sidgwick, Henry. 1907. *The Methods of Ethics*, 7th edn. London: Macmillan.

Sikkink, Kathryn. 2011. *The Justice Cascade: How Human Rights Prosecutions Are Changing World Politics*. New York: W. W. Norton.

2017. *Evidence for Hope: Making Human Rights Work in the 21st Century*. Princeton: Princeton University Press.

2018. "Human Rights: Advancing the Frontier of Emancipation," *Great Transformation Initiative*, April. https://greattransition.org/contributor/kathr yn-sikkink

Simms, B. and D. J. B. Trim, eds. 2011. *Humanitarian Intervention: A History*. Cambridge, UK: Cambridge University Press.

Simmons, Beth A. 2011. *Mobilizing for Human Rights: International Law in Domestic Politics*. Cambridge, UK: Cambridge University Press.

Simmons, Beth and A. Strezhnev. 2017. "Human Rights and Human Welfare: Looking for a 'Dark Side' to International Human Rights Law," in S. Hopgood, L. Vinjamuri, and J. Snyder, eds., *Human Rights Futures*, 60–87. New York: Cambridge University Press.

Sinclair, K. 2012. "Grey, George. Dictionary of New Zealand Biography," *Te Ara – the Encyclopedia of New Zealand*. www.TeAra.govt.nz/en/biographies/ 1g21/grey-george.

Singer, Peter. 1972. "Famine, Affluence, and Morality," *Philosophy & Public Affairs*, 1, 3, 229–243.

2010. *The Life You Save: How to Do Your Part to End World Poverty.* New York: Random House.

Skinner, Robert and Alan Lester. 2012. "Humanitarianism and Empire: Introduction," *Journal of Imperial and Commonwealth History*, 40, 5, 729–747.

Slaughter, Joseph. 2014 "The Enchantment of Human Rights; or, What Difference Does Humanitarian Indifference Make?" *Critical Inquiry*, December, 46–66.

2018. "Hijacking Human Rights: Neoliberalism, the New Historiography, and the End of the Third World," *Human Rights Quarterly*, 40, 4, 735–775.

Slim, Hugo. 1997. *Doing the Right Thing: Relief Agencies, Moral Dilemmas, and Moral Responsibility in Political Emergencies and War.* Uppsala: Nordiska Afrikainstitutet.

2001. "Military Intervention to Protect Human Rights: The Humanitarian Agency Perspective," *International Council for Human Rights Policy*, March.

2004. "Protecting Civilians: Putting the Individual at the Humanitarian Centre," in *Office of the Coordinator of Humanitarian Affairs, The Humanitarian Decade: Challenges for Humanitarian Assistance in the Last Decade and into the Future*, vol. 2, 154–170. New York: United Nations.

2015. *Humanitarian Ethics: A Guide to the Morality of Aid in War and Disaster.* Oxford: Oxford University Press.

2019. "Humanitarian Diplomacy: The ICRC's Neutral and Impartial Advocacy in Armed Conflict," *Ethics and International Affairs*, 33, 1, 67–77.

Sliwinski, Sharon. 2011. *Human Rights in Camera.* Chicago: University of Chicago Press.

Sluga, Glenda. 2013. *Internationalism in an Age of Nationalism.* Philadelphia: University of Pennsylvania Press.

Slyomovics, Susan. 2005. *The Performance of Human Rights in Morocco.* Philadelphia: University of Pennsylvania Press.

Smith, Abbe. 2010. "In Praise of the Guilty Project: A Criminal Defense Lawyer's Growing Anxiety About Innocence Projects," *University of Pennsylvania Journal of Law and Social Change*, 13, 315–329.

Smith, Nicholas. 2005. "Rorty on Religion and Hope," *Inquiry*, 48, 1, 94.

Snow, David E., B. Rochford, S. Worden, and R. Benford. 1986. "Frame Alignment Processes, Micromobilization, and Movement Participation," *American Sociological Review*, 51, August, 464–481.

Spelman, Elizabeth. 1997. *Fruits of Sorrow: Framing Our Attention to Suffering.* Boston: Beacon.

2001. *Fruits of Sorrow: Framing Our Attention to Suffering*, 2nd edn. Boston: Beacon Press.

Sphere. 2018. *The Humanitarian Charter.* Geneva. www.spherestandards.org/wp-content/uploads/2018/07/the-humanitarian-charter.pdf.

Spivak, Chakrovorty Gayatri. 2004. "Righting Wrongs," *South Atlantic Quarterly*, 103, 2/3, 523–524.

Sontag, Susan. 2003. *Regarding the Pain of Others.* New York: Picador Press.

Sriram, C. L. 2013. *Globalizing Justice for Mass Atrocities.* NY: Routledge.

Stamatov, Peter. 2013. *Global Humanitarianism: Religion, Empires, and Advocacy.* New York: Cambridge University Press.

Stanley, Amy Dru. 2015. "Slave Emancipation and the Revolutionizing of Human Rights," in Gregory P. Downs and Kate Masur, eds., *The World the Civil War Made*, 269–303. Chapel Hill, NC: University of North Carolina Press.

2017. "A Radical Right to Happiness," *Slate* 21 December.

Stein, Janice. 2011. "Background Knowledge in the Foreground: Conversations About Competent Practice in Shared Space," in E. Adler and V. Pouliot, eds., *International Practices*, 87–108. New York: Cambridge University Press.

Stevens, Dallal. 2016. "Rights, Needs or Assistance? The Role of the UNHCR in Refugee Protection in the Middle East," *The International Journal of Human Rights*, 20, 2, 264–283.

Stevenson, Ana. 2017. "The 'Great Doctrine of Human Rights': Articulation and Authentication in the Nineteenth-Century U.S. Antislavery and Women's Rights Movements," *Humanity*, 8, 3, 413–439.

Stevenson, Lisa. 2014. *Life Beside Itself: Imagining Care in the Canadian Arctic.* Berkeley: University of California Press.

Stocking George W. Jr. 1987. *Victorian Anthropology.* New York: Free Press.

Stowell, Ellery C. 1932. "La théorie et la pratique de l'intervention," *Recueil des cours de l'Académie de droit international*, 40, 91–148.

Strangio, Sebastian. 2014. *Hun Sen's Cambodia.* New Haven, CT: Yale University Press.

Stuurman, Siep. 2017. *The Invention of Humanity: Equality and Cultural Difference in World History.* Cambridge, MA: Harvard University Press.

Swaine, Aisling. 2004. "A Neglected Perspective: Adolescent Girls Experiences of the Kosovo Conflict," in Jo Boyden and Joanna de Berry, eds., *Children and Youth on the Frontline*, 63–86. New York: Berghan Books.

2016. "Enabling or Disabling Paternalism: (In)attention to Gender and Women's Knowledge, Capacity and Authority in Humanitarian Contexts," in Michael Barnett, ed., *Paternalism Beyond Borders*, 185–223. New York: Cambridge University Press.

2018. *Conflict-Related Violence Against Women: Transforming Transition.* New York: Cambridge University Press.

2019. "Reshaping How Political Settlements Engage with Conflict-Related Violence Against Women," *feminists@law*, 9, 1.

Swamy, Raja. 2017. "Humanitarianism and Unequal Exchange," *Journal of World-Systems Research*, 23, 2, 353–371.

Sykes, Karen. 2012. "Moral Reasoning," in Didier Fassin, ed., *A Companion to Moral Anthropology*, 169–185. New York: Wiley and Sons.

Taithe, Bertrand. 2004. "Reinventing (French) Universalism: Religion, Humanitarianism, and the 'French Doctors'," *Modern and Contemporary France*, 12, 2, 147–158.

2016. "The Cradle of the New Humanitarian System? International Work and European Volunteers at the Cambodian Border Camps, 1979–1993," *Contemporary European History*, 25, 2, 335–358.

2019. "Compassion Fatigue and the Changing Nature of Humanitarian Emotions," in Delores Martin-Moruno and Beatriz Pichel, eds., *Emotional Bodies: The Historical Performativity of Emotions: Urbana: University of Illinois Press.*

Taylor, Charles. 2007. *Modern Social Imaginaries.* Durham, NC: Duke University Press.

Taylor, Diane. 2002. *Revolutionizing Motherhood: The Mothers of the Plaza de Mayo (Latin American Silhouettes).* Lanham, MD: Rowman & Littlefield.

Teitel, Ruti. 1997. "Human Rights Genealogy," *Fordham Law Review,* 66, 301–317.

2001. *Transitional Justice.* New York: Oxford University Press.

2011. *Humanity's Law.* New York: Oxford University Press.

Terry, Fiona. 2002. *Condemned to Repeat: The Paradox of Humanitarian Action.* Ithaca: Cornell University Press.

Thompson, Andrew. 2016a. "Humanitarian Interventions, Past and Present," in Fabian Klose, ed., *The Emergence of Humanitarian Intervention. Ideas and Practice from the Nineteenth Century to the Present,* 331–356. New York: Cambridge University Press.

2016b. "'Restoring Hope Where All Hope Was Lost': Nelson Mandela, the ICRC and the Protection of Political Detainees in Apartheid South Africa," *International Review of the Red Cross,* 98, 3, 799–829.

2018. "Unraveling the Relations Between Humanitarianism, Human Rights, and Decolonization: Time for a Radical Rethink?" in Martin Thomas and Andrew Thompson, eds., *The Oxford Handbook of the End of Empires,* 453–476. New York: Oxford University Press.

Thomson, P. A. B. 2004. *Belize: A Concise History.* Oxford: Macmillan Caribbean.

Thornton, R. J. 1983. "'This Dying Out Race': W.H.I. Bleek's Approach to the Languages of Southern Africa," *Social Dynamics: A Journal of African Studies,* 9, 2, 1–10.

Ticktin, Miriam Iris. 2011a. *Casualties of Care: Immigration and the Politics of Humanitarianism in France.* Berkeley, CA: University of California Press.

2011b. "The Gendered Human of Humanitarianism: Medicalizing and Politicizing Sexual Violence," *Gender and History,* 23, 2, 250–265.

2014. "Transnational Humanitarianism," *Annual Review of Anthropology,* 43, 273–289.

2016. "Thinking Beyond Humanitarian Borders," *Social Research,* 83, 2, 255–271.

Tilly, Charles. 2004. "Social Boundary Mechanisms," *Philosophy of Social Sciences,* 34, 2, 211–236.

Topak, Özgün, 2019. "Humanitarianism and Human Rights Surveillance: The Challenge to Border Surveillance and Invisibility?" *Surveillance and Society,* 17, 3/4, 382–404.

Toscano, Alberto. 2014. "The Tactics and Ethics of Humanitarianism," *Humanity,* 5, 1, 123–147.

Trouillot, Michel-Rolph. 1995. *Silencing the Past: Power and the Production of History.* Boston, MA: Beacon Press.

Truth and Reconciliation Commission of Canada. 2015. Canada's Residential Schools: The Final Report of the Truth and Reconciliation Commission of Canada.

Truth and Reconciliation Commission of South Africa (TRC). 1998. *Truth and Reconciliation Commission of South Africa Report: Volume I.* Cape Town: The Commission.

Tusan, Michelle. 2014. "'Crimes against Humanity': Human Rights, the British Empire, and the Origins of the Response to the Armenian Genocide," *American Historical Review*, 119, 1, 47–77.

Twomey, Christina. 2012. "Framing Atrocity: Photography and Humanitarianism," *History of Photography*, 36, 3, 255–264.

UK Foreign and Commonwealth Office G8. 2013. Declaration on Preventing Sexual Violence in Conflict.

UK Foreign and Commonwealth Office. 2014. *Summit Report: The Global Summit to End Sexual Violence in Conflict*. London: UK Foreign and Commonwealth Office.

United Nations. 1945. Charter of the United Nations, Article 2, Par. 4 and Par. 7. www.un.org/en/sections/un-charter/chapter-i/index.html.

1993. *Interim Report of the Commission of Experts Established Pursuant to Security Council Resolution* 780, (1992), S/25274, February 10. New York: United Nations.

United Nations Committee on the Elimination of Discrimination Against Women (CEDAW). 1989. General Recommendation No. 12, Violence Against Women.

1992. General Recommendation No. 19, Violence Against Women.

2013. General Recommendation No. 30 on Women in Conflict Prevention, Conflict and Post-Conflict Situations, CEDAW/C/GC/30.

United Nations Development Programme (UNDP). nd. Addressing Sexual and Gender Based Violence. www.undp.org/content/undp/en/home/ourwork/democratic-governance-and-peacebuilding/rule-of-law–justice-and-security/sexual-and-gender-based-violence/.

United Nations Economic and Social Council. 1997. Agreed Conclusions, E/1997/66.

United Nations General Assembly. 1967. Declaration on the Elimination of Discrimination Against Women, A/RES/22/2263. November 7.

1979. The Convention on the Elimination of Discrimination Against Women (CEDAW). December 18.

1993. *Declaration on the Elimination of Violence Against Women (DEVAW)*. A/RES/48/104, February, 23. New York: United Nations.

2015. *Resolution Adopted by the General Assembly on 19 June 2015: International Day for the Elimination of Sexual Violence in Conflict*. A/Res/69/293, July 13. New York: United Nations.

United Nations High Commission for Refugees (UNHCR). 1995. *Sexual Violence Against Refugees: Guidelines for Prevention and Response*. New York: United Nations.

2003. *Sexual and Gender-Based Violence against Refugees, Returnees and Internally Displaced Persons: Guidelines for Prevention and Response*. New York: United Nations.

2010. Introductory Note to the 1951 Convention Relating to the Status of Refugees. www.unhcr.org/en-us/3b66c2aa10.

United Nations High Commission for Refugees, UK. 2018. Protection. www.unhcr.org/uk/protection.html.

United Nations Human Rights Council. 2013. *Accelerating Efforts to Eliminate all Forms of Violence Against Women: Preventing and Responding to Rape and Other*

Forms of Sexual Violence. A/HRC/23/L.28, June, 11. New York: United Nations General Assembly.

2017. *Report of the Commission of Inquiry on Burundi.* A/HRC/36/54, August, 11. New York: United Nations General Assembly.

United Nations Office of the High Commission for Human Rights (UNOHCHR). 2014. *Investigating Sexual Violence in Conflict: Lessons Learned and Future Strategies.* New York: UN.

2015. *Commissions of Inquiry and Fact-Finding Missions on International Human Rights and Humanitarian Law: Guidance and Practice.* New York and Geneva: United Nations. www.ohchr.org/EN/NewsEvents/Pages/DisplayNews.aspx? NewsID=14684&LangID=E

United Nations Organization for the Coordination of Humanitarian Assistance. 2018. Strategic Plan, 2018–2021. www.unocha.org/sites/unocha/files/OCH A%202018–21%20Strategic%20Plan.pdf.

United Nations Organisation Stabilisation Mission in the Democratic Republic of Congo (MONUSCO) and United Nations Office of the High Commissioner for Human Rights (UNOHCHR). 2013. *Report of the United Nations Joint Human Rights Office on Human Rights Violations Perpetrated by Soldiers of the Congolese Armed Forces and Combatants of the M23 in Goma and Sake, North Kivu Province, and in and around Minova, South Kivu Province, from 15 November to 2 December, 2012.* Democratic Republic of Congo: MONUSCO and UNOHCHR.

United Nations Relief and Works Agency (UNRWA). 2013. *Human Rights, Conflict Resolution, and Tolerance Education: Teacher Toolkit.* www.unrwa.org/sites/defa ult/files/hrcrt_teacher_toolkit.pdf.

United Nations Security Council. 2008. Resolution 1820, S/RES/1820. New York: United Nations.

2009. Resolution 1888, S/RES/1888. New York: United Nations.

2010. Resolution 1960, S/RES/1960. New York: United Nations.

2013. Resolution 2106, S/RES/2106. New York: United Nations.

2018. Report of the Secretary-General on Conflict-Related Sexual Violence. S/ 2018/250, 23 March. New York: United Nations.

Urban Walker, Margaret. 2009. "Gender and Violence in Focus: A Background for Gender Justice in Reparations," in Ruth Rubio-Marín, ed., *The Gender of Reparations: Unsettling Sexual Hierarchies While Redressing Human Rights Violations,* 18–62. New York: Cambridge University Press.

Valenti, Laura. 2015. "Social Samaritan Justice: When and Why Needy Fellow Citizens Have a Right to Assistance," *American Political Science Review,* 109, 4, 735–749.

Vallaeys, Anne. 2004. *Médecins sans Frontières: La Biographie.* Paris: Fayard.

Van Beers, Britta, Luigi Corrias, and Wouter Werner, eds. 2014. *Humanity Across International Law and Biolaw.* New York: Cambridge University Press.

Vance, Carole. 2012. "Innocence and Experience: Melodramatic Narratives of Sex Trafficking and Their Consequences for Law and Policy," *History of the Present,* 2, 2, 200–218.

van Wijk, Joris. 2015 "Who Is the 'Little Old Lady' of International Crimes? Nils Christie's Concept of Ideal Victim Reinterpreted," *International Review of Victimology,* 19, 2, 159–179.

Viera de Mello, Sergio. 2004. "Protection, Humanitarianism, and Human Rights," in *Office of the Coordinator of Humanitarian Affairs, The Humanitarian Decade: Challenges for Humanitarian Assistance in the Last Decade and into the Future*, vol. 2. 170–173. New York: United Nations.

Vincent, R. J. 1974. *Nonintervention and International Order*. Princeton: Princeton University Press.

Volpp, Leti. 2015. "Saving Muslim Women," *Public Books*. August 1. www .publicbooks.org/saving-muslim-women/.

Waldron, Jeremy. 2012. *Dignity, Rank, and Rights*. Oxford: Oxford University Press.

Walker, Brian. 2007. "NGOs Break the Cold War Impasse in Cambodia," in Larry Minear and Hazel Smith, eds., *Humanitarian Diplomacy: Practitioners and Their Craft*, 133–146. Paris: United Nations University Press.

Walzer, Michael. 2006. "Terrorism and Just War," *Philosophia*, 34, 1, 3–12.

Ward, William Ernest Frank. 1969. "The Royal Navy and the Slavers," in *The Suppression of the Atlantic Slave Trade*. London: Allen & Unwin.

Warner, Daniel. 1999. "The Politics of the Political/Humanitarian Divide," *International Review of the Red Cross*, 81, 833, 109–118.

Watenpaugh, Keith David. 2015. *Bread from Stones: The Middle East and the Making of Modern Humanitarianism*. Berkeley: University of California Press.

Watkin, Kenneth. 2016. *Fighting at the Legal Boundaries: Controlling the Use of Force in Contemporary Conflict*. New York: Oxford University Press.

Weber, Max. 1946. "Religious Rejections of the World and Their Directions," and "The Social Psychology of the World's Religions," in H.H. Gerth and C. Wright Mills, eds., *From Max Weber*, 267–362. New York: Oxford University Press.

   1964. *The Theory of Social and Economic Organization*. New York: Free Press of Glencoe.

Wegner, Etienne. 1998. *Communities of Practice: Learning, Meaning, and Identity*. New York: Cambridge University Press.

Weinert, Matthew. 2015. *Making Human: World Order and the Global Governance of Dignity*. Ann Arbor: University of Michigan Press.

Weiss, Edith Brown. 1990. "Our Rights and Obligations to Future Generations for the Environment," *American Journal of International* Law, 84, 1, 198–207.

Weiss, Thomas. 1999. "Principles, Politics, and Humanitarian Action," *Ethics and International Affairs*, 13, 1–22.

   2012. *Humanitarian Intervention: Ideas in Action*. Malden, MA: Polity.

   2013. *Humanitarian Business*. Boston: Polity Press.

Weizman, Eyal. 2012. *The Least of All Possible Evils: Humanitarian Violence from Arendt to Gaza*. New York: Verso Press.

Wells Barnett, Ida B. 1900. "Lynch Law in America," *The Arena*, June 15–24.

Welsh, Jennifer M., ed. 2006. *Humanitarian Intervention and International Relations*. Oxford: Oxford University Press.

We Robotics. 2018. Humanitarian Drones Experts Meeting: Insights and Next Steps, May 22. https://blog.werobotics.org/2018/05/22/humanitarian-drones-experts-meeting.

Wheaton, Henry. 1836. *Elements of International Law with a Sketch of the History of the Science*. Philadelphia: Carey, Lea & Blanchard.

1842. *Enquiry into the Validity of the British Claim to a Right of Visitation and Search of American Vessel Suspected to be Engaged in the African Slave Trade*. Philadelphia: Lea & Blanchard.

1845. *History of the Law of Nations in Europe and America from the Earliest Times to the Treaty of Washington, 1842*. New York: Gould, Banks & Co.

Wheeler, Nicolas J. 2003. *Saving Strangers: Humanitarian Intervention in International Society*. Oxford: Oxford University Press.

Whyte, Jessica. 2019. *The Morals of the Market: Human Rights and the Rise of Neoliberalism*. London: Verso Press.

Wichmann, Soren. 2019. "Why Languages and Dialects Really Are Different Animals," *Aeon*. https://aeon.co/ideas/why-languages-and-dialects-really-are-different-animals.

Willen, Sarah. 2007. "Darfur Through a Shoah Lens: Sudanese Asylum Seekers, Unruly Biopolitical Dramas, and the Politics of Humanitarian Compassion in Israel," in Byron Good et al., eds., *A Reader in Medical Anthropology: Theoretical Trajectories and Emergent Realities*, 505–521. Chichester, UK: Wiley and Blackwell.

Wilkinson, Iain. 2013. "The Problem of Suffering as a Driving Force of Rationalization and Social Change," *British Journal of Political Sociology*, 64, 1, 123–141.

2014. "The New Social Politics of Pity," in Michael Ure and Mervyn Frost, eds., *The Politics of Compassion*, 121–136. New York: Routledge.

Wilkinson, Iain and Arthur Kleinman. 2016. *A Passion for Society: How We Think About Human Suffering*. Berkeley: University of California Press.

Wilson, Richard Ashby. 2008. "Tyrannosaurus Lex: The Anthropology of Human Rights and Transnational Law," in Sally Engle Merry and Richard Goodale, eds., *The Practice of Human Rights: Tracking Law Between the Global and the Local*, 342–369. New York: Cambridge University Press.

Wilson, Richard Ashby and Richard Brown, eds. 2009. *Humanitarianism and Suffering: The Mobilization of Empathy*. New York: Cambridge University Press.

Wilson, Richard Ashby, and Richard Brown 2009. "Introduction," in Wilson and Brown, eds., 1–13. NY: Cambridge University Press.

Wimmer, Andreas. 2008. "The Making and Unmaking of Ethnic Boundaries: A Multilevel Process," *American Journal of Sociology*, 113, 4, 970–1022.

Wiseberg, Laurie S. 1974. "Humanitarian Intervention: Lessons from the Nigerian Civil War," *Revue des droits de l'homme*, 70, 1, 61–98.

Worland, Justin. 2016. "These Kids Are Suing the Federal Government to Demand Climate Action. They Just Won an Important Victory," *Time*, November 10. http://time.com/4567012/federal-government-lawsuit-climate-change/.

Wuthnow, Robert. 1989. *Meaning and Moral Order: Explorations in Cultural Analysis*. Berkeley: University of California Press.

Wydra, Harald. 2015. "Spells of the Sacred in a Global Age," *Journal of International Political Theory*, 11, 1, 95–110.

Young, Allan. 2004. "When Traumatic Memory Was a Problem: On the Historical Antecedents of PTSD," in Gerald M. Rosen, ed., *Posttraumatic Stress Disorders: Issues and Controversies*, 127–146. Chichester: John Wiley.

Young, Iris Marion. 2006. "Responsibility and Global Justice: A Social Connection Model," *Social Philosophy and Policy*, 23, 1, 102–130.

   2011. *Responsibility for Justice*. Oxford: Oxford University Press.

Zacher, Meghan, Hollie Nyseth Brehm, and Joachim Savelsberg. 2014. "NGOs, IOs and the ICC: Diagnosing and Framing Darfur," *Sociological Forum*, 29, 1, 29–51.

Zald, Mayer. 1996. "Culture, Ideology, and Strategic Framing," in D. Mcadam, J. McCarthy, and M. Zald, eds., *Comparative Perspective on Social Movements: Political Opportunities, Mobilizing Structures, and Cultural Framing*, 261–274. New York: Cambridge University Press.

Zaman, S., Whitelaw, A., Richards, N., Inbadas, H., and Clark, D. 2018. "A Moment for Compassion: Emerging Rhetorics in End-of-Life Care," *Medical Humanities*, 44, 2, 140–143.

Zaman, Tahir. 2017. *Traditions of Refuge in the Crises of Iraq and Syria*. Basingstoke: Palgrave Macmillan.

Zertal, Idith. 2005. *Israel's Holocaust and the Politics of Nationhood*. Cambridge, UK: Cambridge University Press.

Zetter, Roger and Katy Long. 2012. "Unlocking Protracted Displacement," *Forced Migration Review*, 40, 34–37.

Index

abolition, 123, 130, 131, 132–134
  as humanitarian intervention in
    nineteenth vs. twentieth centuries,
    128, 134
  legitimization of colonialism and
    imperialism, 133
  Slave Trade Act (1807), 131
  Slavery Abolition Act (1833), 133
abolitionism
  British, 9, 63, 130, 240
abolitionists, 62, 130, 131, 133
  as advocates for colonialists and
    missionaries, 20
  "Am I not a man and a brother?" as
    emblem for, 131
  humanity as moral category for argument
    of, 131
  sentimental appeals by, 53
Aboriginal languages, vocabulary of, 118
Aboriginal people, 113
  of Australia, 113, 118, 119, 120, *266n75*
  of Bruny Island, 113, *264n31*
  "extermination" of, 114, 119
  of Flinders Island, 115, *264n31*
  of Van Diemen's Land, 113
abortion, 196–197, 198
accountability, 141, 142–143, 152, 154,
    165–166
  legal accountability, 26, 147, 162, 169,
    171, 176
  of states, 174, 178, 180
activism, 44 *see* humanitarianism, activism
  of; human rights, activism of
Africa
  "Scramble for Africa," 40
  slave trade with, 121, 131, 132, 133
  see also entries for various African countries
Africans
  paternalistic treatment of, 133
Agamben, Giorgio, 5, 223
Age of Reason, 1 *see* Enlightenment
AI, 66 *see* Amnesty International

aid, 1, 21, 148, 159, 160, 190, 191
  conditionality of, 1
  humanitarian aid, 98, 194, 223, 225
  organizations, 1, 2, 4–5, 28,
    244–245, 246
  workers, 3, 12, 18, 28, 194, 244
  see also recipients of aid
amalgamation, as "humane" alternative to
    extermination, 109, 117, 121, 122,
    124–125
amelioration, 107, 110, 112–114,
    123–124
  ameliorative codes, 112, 123
  of slavery, 24, 109, 110
Amnesty International (AI), 66, 68, 78–79,
    96, 97–98, 150
  Campaign against Torture, 44
anti-Palestinianism, 207 *see also* racism
anti-slavery, 35, 36, 41, 116, 120, 123 *see
    also* slavery
"Appeal to the World, An" (Du Bois),
    155–156
Arendt, Hannah, 9, 15, 35, 43, 54–55, 57,
    61, 144, 146, 148, 159, 213, 249,
    255n17, 277n56
Argentina, 150–151, 206
Arish, El, 211, 212–213
Arthur, George, 24, 109–117, 119, 122,
    123–124, 125, *265n68*
Atlantic Revolutions, 38, *255n18*
atrocities, 40, 44, 45, 100, 103, 206
  international tribunals for, 205
  lynching as institutionalized atrocity, 155
  in refugee camps, 224
  in Van Diemen's Land, 2, 116
  see also genocide; massacres

BAAS (British Association for the
    Advancement of Science), 119
background knowledge, 237, 245, *261n11*
  human rights vs. humanitarianism,
    29, 245

332   Index